I0003568

CYBER WARFARE AND NAVIES

CYBER WARFARE AND NAVIES

DIGITAL CONFLICT IN THE MARITIME DOMAIN

EDITED BY

CHRIS C. DEMCHAK AND
SAM J. TANGREDI

Naval Institute Press
Annapolis, Maryland

Naval Institute Press
291 Wood Road
Annapolis, MD 21402

© 2025 by Chris C. Demchak and Sam J. Tangredi
All rights reserved. No part of this book may be reproduced or utilized in any form or by any means, electronic or mechanical, including photocopying and recording, or by any information storage and retrieval system, without permission in writing from the publisher.

Library of Congress Cataloging-in-Publication Data
Names: Demchak, Chris C. editor | Tangredi, Sam J. editor
Title: Cyber warfare and navies : high-tech conflict in the maritime domain
    / edited by Chris C. Demchak and Sam J. Tangredi.
Other titles: Cyberwarfare and navies
Description: Annapolis, Maryland : Naval Institute Press, [2025] |
    Collection of essays by Camino Kavanaugh and 41 others. | Includes
    bibliographical references and index.
Identifiers: LCCN 2025012138 (print) | LCCN 2025012139 (ebook) | ISBN
    9781682475850 hardback | ISBN 9781682476079 ebook
Subjects: LCSH: Cyberspace operations (Military science) | Naval art and
    science—Technological innovations | Maritime terrorism—Prevention |
    Cyberspace—Security measures | Sea control | Naval strategy
Classification: LCC U167.5.C92 C93435 2025 (print) | LCC U167.5.C92
    (ebook) | DDC 359.4—dc23/eng/20250626
LC record available at https://lccn.loc.gov/2025012138
LC ebook record available at https://lccn.loc.gov/2025012139

∞ Print editions meet the requirements of ANSI/NISO z39.48–1992 (Permanence of Paper).
Printed in the United States of America.

9 8 7 6 5 4 3 2 1

CONTENTS

ILLUSTRATIONS

TABLES

FIGURES

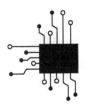

Introduction

Navies, Cyber, and Warfare Gap

CHRIS C. DEMCHAK and SAM J. TANGREDI

igital circuitry does not work well when it encounters water. But the study of cyber operations and cyber security needs to get "wet."

The maritime environment's dependence on digital information and operational technologies is underexamined. Only a modest number of public articles and reports have been written (many of them by the contributors to this volume) and just three books published so far that are on cyber operations in the maritime environment.[1] Few articles focus on the cyber elements of specifically naval operations.[2] Considering the many publications describing cyber warfare in general, this apparent lack of interest in the combination of maritime, cyber, and naval affairs from peace to war is striking and, ultimately, perilous.

This gap is dangerous for the democratic societies whose economies and security depend on maritime trade and protection. To safeguard national and international security, the study of cyber operations and cyber security does indeed need to get wet and in touch with its naval and maritime aspects. That is the purpose of this book.

⊢• BRIDGING SEA-BLINDNESS, CYBER NEGLECT, AND MILITARY SEA VERSUS LAND BIAS

Even before 2006 when the U.S. Department of Defense (DoD) declared cyberspace its own warfighting "domain," there were strong attentional differences among cyber, maritime, and specifically naval practitioners.[3] Nearly all cyber professionals live on land and are "sea-blind" to the cyber aspects of the maritime environment. In general, what happens on the oceans, among navies, or within the maritime transportation infrastructure does not make headlines like cyber attacks on medical centers, banking systems, and government agencies. Actors key to the global maritime system such as shipping or port operators are similarly prone to "cyber neglect" of their own rising digitization, especially how the land-based cyber risks threatening their operations may be intensified by the sea's realities. (See deWitte and Lehto in this volume.)

Similarly, naval leaders and practitioners with their culturally embedded sea versus land bias have difficulties accepting and integrating for a cyber threat largely viewed as mainly a land problem. Effectively and systemically integrating cyber operations into its naval warfighting planning and concepts has accordingly proven challenging for not only the U.S. Navy but allied and adversary navies as well.[4] (See discussions by Dombrowski, Tiirmaa-Klaar, Kim, Kania, and Work in this volume.) The U.S. Navy created Fleet Cyber Command, with the U.S. Navy's Tenth Fleet as its cyber operational arm and the Navy's component contributing to U.S. Cyber Command.[5] The Fleet Cyber Command commander, however, has multiple responsibilities, being quadruple-hatted with not only cyber, but also space, network security, and cryptologic services missions.[6] (See White and Bebber in this volume.)

Thus far, these efforts appear not to have served the Navy or U.S. Cyber Command particularly well. The U.S. Congress in 2022 publicly issued highly unusual and explicit demands on the Navy to remove cyber from its cryptology community by establishing separate cyber operations officer and enlisted specialties, while the Secretary of the Navy was to provide an inventory and position description for all Navy cyber billets including cyber resource, manning, and training managers.[7] The secretary of defense was told to report to Congress by December 2024 on whether the Navy should even continue contributing forces to U.S. Cyber Command given the service's difficulty with cyber in particular.[8] In contrast, the other sea services—the U.S. Marine Corps and U.S. Coast Guard—appear to have had more conceptual and organizational success in employing their cyber forces.[9] (See, respectively, Morse and Koch in this volume.)

Compounding the Navy Department's cyber integration difficulties are unintended one-size-fits-all effects of jointness. This approach downplays the importance of any unique requirements of the services and biases organizational decisions toward centralized operations providing nearly identical support to all services.[10] Furthermore, if cyberspace is conceived of as a distinct and separate domain, it is easier to argue that cyber warfare support to any individual service is best provided by a centralized and dedicated U.S. Cyber Command from its operations *within* cyberspace rather than through combat operational support from within the service itself.

The result is a dangerous disconnect between the realities of future war and the organizational preferences emerging from this combination of sea-blindness within the cyber professional community, cyber neglect in the maritime infrastructure, and the land-sea-cyber separate domains bias in the military enhanced by standardization preferences of jointness. To bridge the straits and help mitigate the disconnect, this volume, *Cyber Warfare and Navies*, seeks to refocus cyber professionals (both civilian and military) on wider systemic realities shaping and possibly distorting the maritime environment and naval operations in peace and war, and to enhance the full integration of cyber operations into the strategic and organizational thinking of both naval professionals and national security professionals in general.[11]

⊢• GUIDING INSIGHTS

This book is guided by a series of insights drawn from the collective wisdom of over one hundred cyber professionals, military officers, defense analysts, and scholars and was developed over several years of briefings, workshops, and conferences. These insights guided the volume's choices of topics and sections in order to address key underlying questions. What do cyber, maritime, naval, sea service, and other military professionals most need to know about cyber warfare and navies? What are the most critical issues—both vulnerabilities and advantages? What are the viable solutions to these issues?

Of all the insights guiding the development of this book, four themes in particular were formative, and the volume has been organized into four sections reflecting these insights. They steer the reader along a voyage from concerns in the present to proposals for the future: fundamentals, operations, technologies, and futures for the navies of democracies.

The chapters of each section add interweaving elements, building from keel to mast. It is important to note that not every chapter focuses solely on navies themselves, but all analyze critical systemic elements affecting the combination of cyber operations, the maritime environment, and navies. Each chapter author therefore addresses one or more of the key background questions, contributes to the insights, and provides potential solutions in their own manner.

⊢—o Section One Fundamentals Insight:
There Is Limited Awareness of Cyber's Strategic Impacts and Extensive Reach, and Just Sailing Away Is Not an Option

Awareness of the full reach of cyber effects on maritime operations and the ripple effects of the maritime environment on the nation's functions is limited among national security and maritime professionals and the public. Almost every aspect of commercial maritime activities has become digitized and interconnected, and thereby vulnerable to cyber insecurities. (See deWitte and Lehto in this volume.) Cyber effects reach out from, and intrude into, the maritime environment far beyond sea and shores, imposing tremendous effects deep into the socio-technical-economic systems and security of nations outside of solely the maritime industry.

When 85 percent of global trade (measured in volume) and 70 percent of all liquid fuels travel by sea, cyber effects on ships, port handling equipment, shipping companies, maritime suppliers, and other maritime industries can cripple manufacturing industries and retail businesses on a global basis. The majority of global economic transactions and information travels by undersea cables, with less than twenty ships available globally for accidentally or deliberately cut cable repairs. (See discussions by Jones, and Kavanagh and Leconte in this volume.) Cutting undersea cables or cyber disrupting ports could be the modern equivalent of warfare to destroy an enemy's economic supply lines.

Navies or commercial shipping cannot "sail away" from cyber threats. Distance at sea does not mean distance from adversary cyber campaigns that can be long in the making and present in the informational technology and digital-mechanical operational technology systems on board.

As an example, commercial port operations have become particularly vulnerable when over 80 percent of ship container offloading and on-loading cranes in global ports are currently built by ZPMC, a Chinese company subject by Chinese law to government demands and whose digital control systems are delivered to foreign ports completely sealed.[12] These are suspected of transmitting information directly or indirectly to the Chinese government, providing a potential wealth of economic and naval data useful for ransoms, coercion, or even covert advantage in wartime.[13]

All engineering systems are vulnerable if connected to a network or program logic controller software or hardware through digitized on-shore or underway maintenance systems or even original manufacturing. (See Hilger in this volume.) Furthermore, autonomous naval vessels may have even greater vulnerabilities since the digital long-distance command and control required can be compromised by an especially skilled and persistent opponent. (See Falcone and Panter in this volume.)

Importantly, commercial maritime realities and naval peace-to-wartime operations are risk-interdependent. Even the shore power cables used to save load on a ship's systems while docked can be a source of infection from cyber-compromised port operations. Who owns and operates a key port and how transparently—even legally—they run and secure their activities in peace through wartime matters critically for the Navy's future operations. (See discussions by Klimburg and Wells, Higson and Passerello, and Poznansky in this volume.) The strategic, maritime, economic, and naval reality is that, as identified by Chris Demchak in this volume, "there is no separation of cyber space from real space."

⊢○ **Section Two Operations Insight:**
Operational Demands Bind Cyber, Navies, and Warfare Immutably

Navies cannot "offload" cyber without affecting their abilities to conduct maritime operations.[14] The sea services have long needed digitization to support the entire range of their missions, and they now need to similarly retain and expand their cyber warfare capability. (See Freedman, and Bebber and White in this volume.) A number of navies do not appear publicly to have embedded cyber-competent units, as argued in chapters by Tiirmaa-Klaar, Kania, and Work, and so the sister sea services have begun to fill the gap. As discussed by Morse in his chapter, the U.S. Marine Corps is developing cyber capabilities that can be transferred in deployed units and could offer a form of "cyber special operations force" conducting "cyber amphibious operations" for naval commanders, especially in the context of amphibious ships with large Marine Corps contingents.

As described by Koch and by Kim, respectively, in this volume, the U.S. and Korean coast guards are already advancing in cyber competence as well. Their peacetime authorities present opportunities for naval planners and strategists to incorporate cyber in their operational recommendations and implementation. Since the Coast Guard holds law enforcement authority, this service is in effect the bridge between the sea services and the commercial maritime world.

⊢—○ Section Three Technologies Insight:
Cyber Command Is Naval Command with Emerging Technologies

For command of digitized naval forces, cyber "sea legs" for cyber command are also required. Commanders are reluctant to rely on cyber fires as a primary method of combat because they have not been educated as to what happens "underneath the hood." (See Kuo and Lindsay in this volume.) Currently cyber experts are generally not embedded into the U.S. Navy's acquisition and maintenance process. Fleets are forced to rely on shore-based commercial firms' cyber expertise and willingness to spend resources mitigating vulnerabilities, as well as on their dedication to national security, with mixed results at best. In contrast, the training for electronic warfare and undersea operations—both long accepted as essential elements of naval combat—has been extensive and well applied. (See discussions by Pugh, and McGunnigle and Breuer in this volume.)

This expertise gap in command problem will worsen with newer emerging technologies unless effective means of education and training that can create trust are developed. Compartmentalized cyber, space, artificial intelligence, and autonomous systems operations may be initially efficient, but the silos do not create solid trust foundations with kinetic warfighting sea service commanders. (See discussions by Long and Vaughan, Smith, Sandhoo, and Falcone and Panter in this volume.) Otherwise, cyber and other emerging technology operations will remain perceived as isolated aspects of warfare, resulting in the underutilization of potentially game-changing cyber or other advanced capabilities.

├─○ Section Four Futures Insight:
Future Cyber and Naval Warfares Are Conceptual Cousins Whose Success Is Intensely Dependent on Underlying Systemic Resilience

Conceptual similarities make naval doctrine and operations seem an older cousin to the effective cyber warfighting operations. For example, peacetime cyber operations have evolved into "defend forward" and "persistent engagement" approaches, which bear a striking resemblance to well-established naval concepts.[15] (See Tangredi in this volume.) U.S. Cyber Command is now focused on bringing "concurrent campaigning" to "set favorable conditions"—in effect, the naval concept of "forward presence/forward deployment"—into the whole-of-government approach to cyber operations.[16] The similarities are strained, however, if one assumes that non-naval, shore-based, centralized, cyber warfighting commands (that is, U.S. Cyber Command) can solely mitigate naval cyber threats embedded across the maritime system. Embedded supply chains, support activities, and maintenance concepts and processes are derived systemically from land-biased and sea-blind commercial sources, meaning the first line of defense must be naval forces (and maritime companies) themselves. (See Vogt and Kollars this volume.) Deploying small teams—including cyber targeteers and developers as detachments (or permanent crew members)—along with cyber warfare "kits" to forward-deployed forces is likely to be a more effective and operationally congruent, as well as more resilient, method for navalizing cyber. (See Myers and Warner in this volume.) Required for resilience are the capabilities to conduct operations when and where they are needed whether or not one's networks are fully functional, and for this, one needs not only proper strategy and doctrine, but also the funding. (See discussions by Arquilla, Dombrowski, and Cleary in this volume.) The Naval Postgraduate School, for example, refers to this as network-optional warfare, as detailed in the chapter by Brutzman and Kline. Furthermore, new, non-centralized approaches are critical to bringing cyber offense and defense capabilities to sea.[17] The last section addresses this insight in depth.

⊢• INDIVIDUAL EFFORTS, COLLECTIVE BENEFITS, CONTINUING PROCESS

This book is aided by the ongoing efforts of the team of scholars at the Cyber and Innovation Policy Institute (CIPI) of the U.S. Naval War College who provide research to support the strategies and policies of sea services—and DoD overall—concerning all elements of cyberspace, as well as on the wider strategic environment and other emerging technologies. Part of these efforts is meant to invite cooperation with other institutions studying cyber security, infrastructure protection, and offensive and defensive cybered operations, as well as with individual members of the armed services who are willing—on their own time and often with little official encouragement—to examine cyberspace issues from alternate perspectives. The objective for all this effort is to contribute to the overall security of the nation in an increasingly hostile cybered world as well as to improve current maritime and military postures and practices in preparation for the technical, political, and military environments of the future.

We have attempted to include the widest range of perspectives of those involved in maritime and naval cyber. Chapter authors and other participants contributing to background studies include active-duty and reserve sea services officers involved in cyber operations, retired naval and diplomatic personnel with cyber operations experience at various levels of command, Department of the Navy civilians involved in technology management, scholars at professional military education institutions, scholars at public universities including those outside the United States, citizens of allied nations, members of public policy think tanks, and cyber professionals in maritime industry and other commercial enterprises.

No matter the affiliation, all the authors worked exclusively on their own account and from their own perspective. Only unclassified information was utilized in the research. Inevitable gaps between classified sources and unclassified information may exist, but that in no way invalidates the basic premises and underlying principles of any of the chapters. This is true for changes in policy and technology. Although current U.S. government policies are discussed, this book is decidedly not an official publication of the U.S. government or of any of the affiliated departments, agencies, or organization. As the standard disclaimer reads: The views expressed in these chapters are those of the authors and do not necessarily reflect the official policy or position of the U.S. Navy, U.S. Department of Defense, or the U.S. government. Discussions of the cyber postures of the European Union, Republic of Korea, and other nations are likewise expressing their authors' own individual findings.

In addition to the resolute efforts of the chapter authors, we would like to recognize the assistance of Dan J. Grobarcik of CIPI in helping to shape this volume.

In providing the collective analyses, we hope to contribute to what should be a continuing and critical discussion of the effect of cyber operations in the maritime and naval environments and their effects in cyberspace and beyond. Parts of the analyses also apply to other armed services and operations in other environments. We invite all readers to join in this discussion.

NOTES

1. Joseph Direnzo III, Nicole K. Drumhiller, and Fred S. Roberts, eds., *Issues in Maritime Cyber Security* (Washington, DC: Westphalia Press, 2017); Gary C. Kessler and Stephen D. Shepard, *Maritime Cybersecurity: A Guide for Leaders and Managers*, 2nd ed. (independently published, 2022); M. Konstantinos, *The Cyber Threat Below Deck: Protecting Maritime Assets* (Kindle, 2023).

2. The majority of open discussions of the impact of cyber on naval operations have appeared in the U.S. Naval Institute *Proceedings*, CIMSEC.org, and *War on the Rocks*. A particularly prescient article is Don Walsh, "Oceans—Maritime Cyber Security: Shoal Water Ahead?" U.S. Naval Institute *Proceedings* 141, no. 7 (July 2015), https://www.usni.org/magazines/proceedings/2015/july/oceans-maritime-cyber-security-shoal-water-ahead.

3. Cyberspace as a separate domain was first codified in *The National Military Strategy for Cyberspace Operations* (Washington, DC: Chairman of the Joint Chiefs of Staff, December 2006), https://nsarchive2.gwu.edu/NSAEBB/NSAEBB424/docs/Cyber-023.pdf. It was distributed with an endorsing cover letter by

Secretary of Defense Donald Rumsfeld dated 11 December 2005. Up to that time, the dominant public expression of U.S. military planning objectives, *Joint Vision 2020*, referred only to the "information environment." Chairman of the Joint Chiefs of Staff, *Joint Vision 2020* (Washington, DC: Government Printing Office, June 2000), https://apps.dtic.mil/sti/pdfs/ADA377926.pdf. Once U.S. Cyber Command was established in 2010, the concept of cyber as a separate domain was bureaucratically entrenched, although there has been continuing disagreement from some defense analysts. See, for example, Michael P. Kreuzer, "Cyberspace Is an Analogy, Not a Domain: Rethinking Domains and Levels of Warfare for the Information Age," *The Strategy Bridge*, 8 July 2012, https://thestrategybridge .org/the-bridge/2021/7/8/cyberspace-is-an-analogy-not-a-domain-rethinking -domains-and-layers-of-warfare-for-the-information-age.

4. T. J. White, Danelle Barrett, and Jake Bebber, "The Navy Is Not Ready for the Information War of 2026," U.S. Naval Institute *Proceedings* 150, no. 2 (February 2024): 22–29, https://www.usni.org/magazines/proceedings/2024/february navy-not-ready-information-war-2026; Eric Seligman, "Changing the Cyber Warfare Leadership Paradigm," U.S. Naval Institute *Proceedings* 149, no. 6 (June 2023), https://www.usni.org/magazines/proceedings/2023/june/changing -cyber-warfare-leadership-paradigm; Jessica A. Burrell, "The Navy Still Suffers from Cybersecurity Complacency," U.S. Naval Institute *Proceedings* 149, no. 3 (March 2023), https://www.usni.org/magazines/proceedings/2023/march /navy-still-suffers-cybersecurity-complacency; Tyson B. Meadors, "Cyber Warfare Is a Navy Mission," U.S. Naval Institute *Proceedings* 148, no. 9 (September 2022): 68–73, https://www.usni.org/magazines/proceedings/2022/september /cyber-warfare-navy-mission; Derek Bernsen, "The Navy Needs a Cyber Course Correction," U.S. Naval Institute *Proceedings* 148, no. 8 (August 2022), https:// www.usni.org/magazines/proceedings/2022/august/navy-needs-cyber-course -correction; Dusty McKinney, "Navy Cyber Needs a Refit," U.S. Naval Institute *Proceedings* 148, no. 2 (February 2022): 20–25, https://www.usni.org/magazines /proceedings/2022/february/navy-cyber-needs-refit; Derek Bernsen, "Navy Cryptologic Officers Cannot Do Cyber," U.S. Naval Institute *Proceedings* 148, no. 1 (January 2022), https://www.usni.org/magazines/proceedings/2022/january navy-cryptologic-warfare-officers-cannot-do-cyber; Patrick Casey, "The Navy Needs a Real Cyber Warfare Community," U.S. Naval Institute *Proceedings* 147, no. 4 (April 2021), https://www.usni.org/magazines/proceedings/2021/april /navy-needs-real-cyber-warfare-community; Brian Evans, "Take Cyber Tactical," U.S. Naval Institute *Proceedings* 145, no. 2 (February 2019), https://www .usni.org/magazines/proceedings/2019/february/take-cyber-tactical; William J. Toti, "Nobody Asked Me, but . . . Where Are the Cyber Warriors," U.S. Naval

Institute *Proceedings* 143, no. 7 (July 2017): 13, https://www.usni.org/magazines /proceedings/2017/july/nobody-asked-me-where-are-cyber-warriors.

5. "Command Description," U.S. Fleet Cyber Command/U.S. TENTH Fleet official website, https://www.fcc.navy.mil/.

6. Commander, Naval Information Forces, "CWG-6/Cryptologic Warfare Group 6," official website, https://www.navifor.usff.navy.mil/cwg6/.

7. U.S. 117th Congress (2021–22), H.R.7776—James M. Inhofe National Defense Authorization Act for Fiscal Year 2023 (Public Law 117–263), Section 1532(a) (1&2), 136 STAT. 2905, 23 December 2022.

8. Inhofe National Defense Authorization Act for Fiscal Year 2023, Section 1533(c) (2)(A), 136 STAT 2901, 23 December 2022. See discussion in Chris C. Demchak, Michael Poznansky, and Sam Tangredi, "A Divorce between the Navy and Cyber Command Would Be Dangerous," *War on the Rocks*, 23 August 2023, https:// warontherocks.com/2023/08/a-divorce-between-the-navy-and-cyber-command -would-be-dangerous/.

9. As traditionally used, the term "naval services" apply to the U.S. Navy and U.S. Marine Corps, whereas the term "sea services" apply to the U.S. Navy, U.S. Marine Corps, and U.S. Coast Guard. The distinction is made because the U.S. Coast Guard is not part of the Department of Defense (except in times of a declared war).

10. Sam J. Tangredi, "Jointness versus Strategy: How Joint Ideology Distorts U.S. National Security," *Proceedings This Week*, 1 June 2022, https://www.usni .org/magazines/proceedings/2022/june/jointness-versus-strategy-how-joint -ideology-distorts-us-national.

11. Credit for the term "bridging the strait" to refer to closing a gap between civilian analysts and scholars and naval professionals belongs to U.S. Naval War College professors Jon Caverley and Peter Dombrowski.

12. Lori Ann La Rocco, "A Look Inside the Chinese Cyber Threat at the Biggest Ports in U.S.," *CNBC*, 13 March 2024, https://www.cnbc.com/2024/03/13/a-look -inside-the-true-nature-of-chinese-cyber-threat-at-us-ports.html.

13. U.S. House of Representatives, Letter to Mr. Richard Pope and Mr. Liu Chengyun, 29 February 2024, https://fm.cnbc.com/applications/cnbc.com/resources /editorialfiles/2024/03/12/China-Select-to-ZPMC-re-PRC-Security-Threats89 .pdf. ZPMC has denied that charge, but as sources note, "ZPMC's statement[s] did not directly address the claims about the installation of [unnecessary] modems." Robert Wright, "China's ZPMC Insists Its U.S. Cranes Present 'No Cyber Security Risk'," *Financial Times*, 11 March 2024, https://www.ft.com /content/8505e35d-bf58–4531-a10b-ab45d59977b6.

14. Meadors.

15. Michael P. Fischerkeller, Emily O. Goldman, and Richard J. Harknett, *Cyber Persistence Theory: Redefining National Security in Cyberspace* (Oxford: Oxford University Press, 2022).

16. Jeffrey Mankoff, *Lessons and Legacies of the War in Ukraine: Conference Report*, Strategic Perspectives 43 (Washington, DC: National Defense University Press, 2024).

17. Phillip Null, "Enable Cyber Action at Sea," U.S. Naval Institute *Proceedings* 149, no. 1 (November 2018), https://www.usni.org/magazines/proceedings/2018/november/enable-cyber-action-sea; Andre Thaeler, "Tactical Units Need Better Cyber Support," U.S. Naval Institute *Proceedings* 144, no. 11 (November 2018), https://www.usni.org/magazines/proceedings/2018/november/tactical-units-need-better-cyber-support.

SECTION 1

FUNDAMENTALS

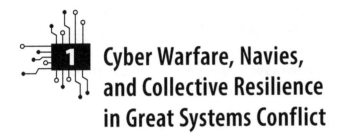

Cyber Warfare, Navies, and Collective Resilience in Great Systems Conflict

CHRIS C. DEMCHAK

yberspace and its "offspring" in artificial intelligence and advanced electronics are systemically changing societies as radio once did in the early twentieth century. From the electromagnetic wave sciences behind the radio came radar, signals intelligence, television broadcasts, satellites, and a host of over-the-air and undersea innovations. From the electrons organized by software code in computer science and statistics have come fiber-optic networks, geolocation tools like the global positioning system, cell phones, social media, autonomous cars, brain image–driven prosthetic arms, and drone swarms. But radio also facilitated negative societal alterations—for example, supporting Nazi and Soviet propaganda that mobilized whole populations for war or paralyzed them for oppression. In this century, cyberspace enables a global reach for malicious and adversarial manipulations, extractions, and threats encouraging cybered conflict and warfare among peoples. Navies and their parent democracies must now learn to fight differently to survive over time.

Understanding how cyber warfare appeared is critical to knowing how to fight competently in this new era. This chapter explains the fundamentals by tracing how cyberspace became a complex, global driver of conflict forcing new responses for survival. It is now a critical substrate underlying all societies and altering global systems and forms of conflict among major nations. Navies must understand the drivers changing their operational environment and threats. As geoeconomic actors and deployed but connected defenders of their homelands, they cannot sail away from cyber warfare or their role in ensuring the collective cyber resilience across allied democracies. That competence begins with command of these basics.

⊢• INSECURABLE GLOBAL SUBSTRATE—IMMENSELY PROFITABLE TO ABUSE

Cyber warfare was born in the utopian vision of universal connectivity that established the internet in the 1990s. Cyberspace grew up around the internet's complexifying system of networks as promoters, free-floating coders, and information technology (IT) capital goods entrepreneurs breathlessly promised a new age of shared information freely available, transparent, and automatically democratizing.[1] But, due to convenience, greed, naivete, and hubris, this promised universal digitized democratic nirvana was never built.[2]

Security was never key to the new information age sales pitch of the 1990s.[3] Rather, the emerging IT industries early on abandoned the established, more securable, rigorous, time-consuming, and fault-intolerant academic languages in favor of fault-tolerant, user-friendly, and cheap-to-program newer computer languages.[4] Errors in this more insecure code could be ignored if the overall program mostly did what was expected. And companies rushed products out for the convenience of customers, ignored errors out of greed, and complacently transferred any buried security problems to customers and the wider underlying social system.

At the same time, the burgeoning open source community of the 1990s and beyond also adopted these hackable languages. Naive and complacent in their assumptions about the benign, universally beneficial character of a digitized government-free world, these coders offered intentionally open and hackable software for free all over the world. To save even more time and money, IT commercial firms adopted the free online but unchecked software and embedded it deeply and obscurely into their commercial products.[5] Over time, the internet's own parents made the foundations of today's global cyberspace fundamentally insecurable.[6]

Today, this shoddily constructed cyber substrate offers five offense advantages that were historically reserved for superpowers nearly for free to attackers living anywhere with internet access. Malicious individual or grouped bad actors with limited resources can now operate a large-*scale* organization via hordes of infected computers, and can attack from any *proximity* to victims via global underground or undersea cables. They can attack with massive *precision* in attack choices of tools, techniques, or targets via the global underground cyber crime market's information, code, and services offerings while maintaining operationally essential *deception* in the tools and self-protection in the *opaqueness* hiding originators across the open global networks. (See related discussion by Hilger in this volume.) And they do it largely "because they can."[7] According to the theory of action, the insecure foundations of today's cyberspace encouraged the exploitation to follow. Once actors' internalized thresholds of legitimacy, need, and confidence requirements are exceeded, individuals will indeed allow themselves to use new and old technologies against others.[8] Cyberspace's five offense advantages made it profitable and easy to act maliciously without moral hesitation. The result has been a global tsunami of cyber attacks, with bad actors free to roam digitally anywhere to find the buried bad code and poor architectures.

⊢• UNPLANNED ECONOMIC ATTRITION

Industrialized democracies today are economically paying for their hubris, greed, complacency, and naivete in embracing the utopian vision without question. For more than a generation, massive wealth has been extracted from the forty-odd consolidated democracies now facing cyber-competent adversaries as well as a huge, increasingly sophisticated underground global cyber crime market. This global thieves' quarter—otherwise known as the dark web—offers malicious, often innovative software tools, bragging rights, criminal IT services, and massive amounts of stolen and damaging data.[9] Annual losses through cyber insecurity to consolidated democratic civil society are estimated to be an unsustainable 2 percent or more of their individual national gross domestic product per year.[10]

Until the mid-2010s, the systemic costs of this unfettered generation-long cyber offense development went unrecognized by often politely fractious democracies.

Their political, corporate, and academic leaders—and international allies—presented a remarkably stubborn strategic blindness in not recognizing the consequences of the cyber substrate's insecurity.[11] They and their IT capital goods (software and hardware) corporations still embraced the internet nirvana myth, only episodically focusing on cyber crime. National elites assumed their form of governance had won the Cold War and their international economic and rule of law regime was permanent.[12] Meanwhile, a huge cyber security industry arose to profit from the losses clients faced with limited to no wider systemic government support or mitigating regulation.[13] Only the military and intelligence agencies looked systemically beyond crime, but they were generally constrained to defending only their own operations and networks.

Conversely, adversaries were not so blind to the opportunities in this globally systemic change. They spent the same decades participating in multiyear unlimited campaigns to produce the "greatest transfer of wealth in human history" from industrialized states to non-industrialized authoritarian states.[14] Serendipitously, both Russia and the People's Republic of China emerged from years of isolation in the early 1990s. Democratic leaders smugly assumed all states, including Russia and China, would automatically accept the existing liberal international system's rules and intoned dire warnings of economic disaster if any state controlled its internet.[15] Chinese leaders did so anyway and explosively prospered.[16]

By the early 2000s, determined to achieve its "rightful place" at the center of the globe's nations as defined by its massive population, China had already begun its aggressive control of its internal internet and surpassed its democratic adversaries technologically. Over the next two decades, democratic political and corporate leaders would repeatedly downplay manifold Chinese use of the five advantages coupled with its scale. China profitably and secretly pursued—and vigorously denied publicly—its massive campaigns of "patriotic" hacking or stealing from democratic firms and economies.[17] Its economic and government actors engaged in rampant violations of international rules or norms on cybered and physical intellectual property theft to meet ambitious economic and technological five-year plans and guidance from senior Chinese Communist Party leaders. Buoyed by massive and obscured state-subsidized investments, China's corporations rocketed to prominent positions globally in key technology industries. They "dumped" deliberately underpriced goods to dominate markets and strategically used their market scale to reinforce the coercive power of their bad business practices of bullying, bribing, blackmailing, and hostile buyouts.[18] Due to the lure of its demographically huge market size, China was not challenged by industrialized democratic leaders, even when its government or corporations used funds or threats to coerce democratic corporate entities or smaller states, punished them for their home nations' political decisions, or exploited cyber thefts to build its own technology and take over markets.[19]

By the late 2010s, Chinese leader Xi Jinping, confident of China's rise and wealth, openly rejected the unregulated liberal nature of the democratic internet. By then, his diplomats were asserting that their massive state would be a "rule-maker, not rule-taker" in the global order.[20]

Likewise, other adversaries have declined to comply with the democracies' naive assumptions. Russian criminals discovered and exploited the five offense advantages of the substrate early on. By the mid-2010s, Russia hosted the bulk of the more sophisticated organized cyber gangs, with the government contracting these proxies to pursue theft and political disruption in extended and damaging cyber campaigns.[21] Russia, Iran, and others engage in the same externally aggressive cyber behaviors as China but with less demographic scale to support widespread campaigns. North Korea is widely believed to be supporting its rogue nuclear weapons program and its economy through a large, organized army of skilled hackers stealing, laundering gains, and arranging smuggling. These bad actors work directly for the state but are often located overseas to hack more easily; some even falsely advertise themselves as South Korean computer experts available for corporate or consulting IT jobs, with the potential for very lucrative future hacking accesses.[22]

Only in the past few years have the forty or so consolidated democracies—a minority among the globe's more than two hundred nations—realized the enormity of their twenty-year mistake, especially in terms of China and, to a lesser extent, Russia.[23] (See discussions by Kania and Work in this volume.) This massive complacency, greed, naivete, and hubris nurtured the conditions responsible for the development of the globally dangerous great systems conflict emerging between large opposing cyber-competent states and dragging navies into cyber warfare.

↦ CYBERED CONFLICT TO CYBER WARFARE TO GREAT SYSTEMS CONFLICT

When governments engage in malicious cross-border cyber exploitation themselves or through proxies, "cybered conflict" emerges.[24] It is a spectrum of struggle stretching from peace through kinetic war that is built on the cybered insecurity of modern societies. In this case, the term "cybered" emphasizes the systemic shaping and likely cumulatively strategic effects far beyond networks and throughout society in peace, crisis, and warfare.[25] When large states elevate the base level of cybered conflict to major operations for their own purposes to harm or manipulate the cybered systems of other nations, cyber warfare emerges. "Cyber warfare" is a cumulative term capturing the processes, organizations, strategies, tools, techniques, and contestations enabled by cybered conflict's technologies and techniques and employed by states in campaigns against key societal systems of opposing states along the full spectrum of peace to kinetic war.

As these campaigns become recognized and begin to shape the assumptions about, and rankings within, the global distribution of whole-of-society power and likely outcomes, Great Systems Conflict (GSC) emerges. Cyber warfare accelerates, even if secretly, and the largest states in the world intensify their efforts and expand organizations meant to systemically exploit, expand, and evolve the five offense advantages into coercive campaigns against their adversary states.[26] While espionage has always been useful, a critical characteristic of GSC is the persistent hunt for entrée into adversaries' cybered systems. Access starts everything in cybered conflict; without it, no tool can be applied, offense advantage employed, or effect achieved.[27] Knowing at all times—to the extent possible—what systems the defender uses with which vulnerabilities or what tools attackers could employ is crucial to whether any cybered operations in offense or defenses will work. When the major global states have risen to this level of constant, deceptive, and obscurable conflict, defenders must assume adversaries are ubiquitous and seeking to find the cyber vulnerabilities of their and other states' key systems, even if only to stockpile these "zero days"—unseen exploitable weaknesses—for later use.

Furthermore, newer technologies will not necessarily help to change the ubiquity, intensity, or persistence of this rising interstate struggle. Future evolutions of cybered warfare will inevitably involve "cyber's offspring" such as artificial intelligence, quantum, nano, space, or other electronics in autonomous, robotic systems.[28] However, as of today, the foundations of these innovations will still be built on unsafe languages and free code off the internet. Barring greater systemic defensive changes to the digital industries and economies of democracies, the five cyber offense advantages will, for the foreseeable future, still allow attackers to corrupt newer cyber-dependent technologies as well.[29] Any as-yet-unseen technology found in the near future will be the same. If a new technology is easy, useful, and available, it will be widely commercialized on the cheap and adopted, and its vulnerabilities inherited for adversaries and criminals to exploit.[30]

⊢• NAVIES, CYBERED WARFARE, GSC, AND THE COLLECTIVE CYBER RESILIENCE OF THE NATION

Inevitably, naval forces, their societies, and the wider maritime environment will be involved in Great Systems Conflict. There are currently no inherently dampening systemic forces to prevent its expansion and persistence across all segments of opposing digitized national systems, including the highly digitally insecure maritime world. (See deWitte and Lehto, Kavanagh and Leconte, Hilger, Pugh, and Sandhoo in this volume.) Navies have several aspects that makes this integration inevitable, including their roles as military organizations being attacked or tasked to respond, as a service with unique competencies evolved for the ocean domain, and as the nation's geostrategic actor defending national supply chains, seabeds, and ports.

As a major national military service as well as the specialized sea service, navies will be expected to be able to defend themselves while being tasked to support cyber warfare offensive or defensive operations requiring, for example, far forward locations, underwater accesses, and even distant loitering with exquisite and digitally enabled capabilities. (See Pugh, Cleary, Brutzman and Kline, and Long and Vaughan in this volume.) By definition, the closer the GSC struggle moves toward the onset of traditionally understood kinetic exchanges, the more cyber competence will be expected of digitized navies as the armed and forward-deployed maritime military services. Unique access capabilities specific to maritime operations will be integrated into cyber warfare. (See related discussions in this volume by Jones and Tangredi.)

But it is when navies act in peace as defenders of rights to economic supply lifelines in a deeply cybered global system that naval involvement in cyber warfare is ensured long before the missiles are launched. As it matures and deepens, Great Systems Conflict disrupts, and forces the reordering of, the existing global system's political, technological, and economic arrangements in peacetime. Navies will be drawn into this intensifying cyber warfare simply because the sea is no longer a cyber-free commons. As of today, the maritime environment has become one of the front lines of GSC. As cyber-enabled campaigns multiply throughout the oceans, expanding manipulation of sensors, satellites, cables, undersurface and seabed operations, and commercial maritime activities or ports, navies will have no choice but to respond. Allowing Great Systems Conflict to evolve toward, and resolve with, an authoritarian global hegemon is existentially untenable for democracies and their navies.

In their geoeconomic role, navies of democracies in particular will be part of the cyber defense solution organized to stop a major adversary from holding hostage the sea-relevant critical national systems or economies of individual democracies. For a minority group of states, a collective defense solution is the only viable alternative; individual democracies cannot prevail alone against the scale of likely major adversaries. Already emerging among democratic states' policy and defense communities are the rudiments of a new narrative recognizing the rise of Great Systems Conflict, the minority status of democracies in the world, and collective cybered defense as the only viable strategy for the long-term survival of democratic systems.[31] A new organizing concept is also needed, such as the whole-of-society Cyber Operational Resilience Alliance.[32] Its overarching mission is to scale up democracies, buy time by collectively defending the "democratic IT" infrastructure of these nations, and transform the shoddy cyber substrate into a securable foundation for prosperous democracies.[33]

Integral to the modern history of industrialized navies, fleets can be usefully viewed as a systemic, collective solution to the vulnerabilities of fighting with a relatively small number of vessels, each carrying a dense concentration of assets. As a result, modern navies bring to the table historically success-ful experiences in pursuing collective solutions and jointly organizing for maneuver in complex shared and potentially hostile environments. As noted by Klimburg and Wells in this volume, these navies have developed and implemented nonbinding but effective coordinating operational agreements for multiparty activities at sea across multiple or free-for-all jurisdictions. Their fleets operate nearly continuously to establish presence, uphold agreements, collect information, and be ready to fight in a fluid, not always foreseeable commons with a variety of other actors. (See also discussions by Jones and Tangredi in this volume.) By virtue of this history and the fact that Great Systems Conflict now ranges across the spectrum of peace to war and from seabed to water column to ports, navies will inevitably be called upon to embed their surface, submarine, and air assets in support of future collective cyber GSC operations of allied democracies.[34]

Navies, cyber, and warfare are now intricately systemically interwoven, with naval forces squarely participants in, and defenders against, cyber warfare over the next century. The key question is how soon democracies' navies will understand, accept, develop sufficient competence in, and resource for that existential cybered fight.

NOTES

1. A belief encouraged by the U.S. government at least until 2011. See, for example, the White House, *International Strategy for Cyberspace: Prosperity, Security, and Openness in a Networked World*, May 2011, https://obamawhitehouse.archives .gov/sites/default/files/rss_viewer/international_strategy_for_cyberspace.pdf; J. P. Barlow, "A Declaration of the Independence of Cyberspace," *Humanist—Buffalo* 56, no. 3 (1996).
2. See a 1997 report for the Office of the Assistant Secretary of Defense, David S. Alperts and Daniel S. Papp, eds., *The Information Age: An Anthology of Its Impact and Consequences*, Command and Control Research Program Publication Series, 1997, https://apps.dtic.mil/sti/tr/pdf/ADA461496.pdf.
3. Barlow.
4. "Memory-safe" means the computer language itself makes it difficult to hide malicious code deep in the software running the systems. Vahid Eftekhari Moghadam et al., "Memory Integrity Techniques for Memory-Unsafe Lan-guages: A Survey," 12 March 2024, https://ieeexplore.ieee.org/document/10477384 /references#references.

5. A. Boulanger, "Open-Source versus Proprietary Software: Is One More Reliable and Secure than the Other?" *IBM Systems Journal* 44, no. 2 (2005).

6. Charles Arthur, *Digital Wars: Apple, Google, Microsoft, and the Battle for the Internet* (Kogan Page Publishers, 2014).

7. C-SPAN, "Cybersecurity Threats to the U.S.: Interview with Cybercom Commander General Keith Alexander," ed. Paul Wolfowitz, https://www.c-span.org/video/?306956–1/cybersecurity-threats-us2012.

8. Chris C. Demchak, *Wars of Disruption and Resilience: Cybered Conflict, Power, and National Security* (Athens: University of Georgia Press, 2011).

9. Ronald Deibert, "The Growing Dark Side of Cyberspace (. . . and What to Do about It)," *Penn State Journal of Law & International Affairs* 1 (2012): 260–74.

10. Melissa Hathaway, *Cyber Readiness Index 1.0* (Great Falls, VA: Hathaway Global Strategies LLC, 2013).

11. Laura DeNardis, *The Global War for Internet Governance* (New Haven: Yale University Press, 2014).

12. Francis J. Fukuyama, "Reflections on the End of History, Five Years Later," *History and Theory* (1995): 27–43.

13. Sagar Samtani et al., "Cybersecurity as an Industry: A Cyber Threat Intelligence Perspective," in *The Palgrave Handbook of International Cybercrime*, ed. Thomas J. Holt and Adam M. Bossler (London: Palgrave, 2020).

14. Pierluigi Paganini, "Cyber-Espionage: The Greatest Transfer of Wealth in History," *H+ Magazine online*, 1 March 2013, http://hplusmagazine.com/2013/03/01/cyber-espionage-the-greatest-transfer-of-wealth-in-history/.

15. James Bradley, *The China Mirage: The Hidden History of American Disaster in Asia* (London: Hachette Ltd., 2015).

16. A view still expressed with a little caution. See Larry Diamond, "Prospect for Democracy and Democratization in Chinese Societies," speech, 21 October 2017, https://diamond-democracy.stanford.edu/speaking/speeches/prospects-democracy-and-democratization-chinese-societies.

17. Jack Linchuan Qiu, "Virtual Censorship in China: Keeping the Gate between the Cyberspaces," *International Journal of Communications Law and Policy*, no 4 (Winter 1999/2000).

18. Robert D. Atkinson and Stephen Ezell, "False Promises: The Yawning Gap between China's WTO Commitments and Practices" (Washington, DC: Information Technology and Innovation Foundation, 2015).

19. See U.S. House of Representative report, Committee on Rules, *Examining China's Coercive Economic Tactics*, 10 May 2023.

20. James Laurenceson, "Rising China as a Rule-Taker or Rule-Maker?" *Australian Institute of International Affairs*, 27 November 2017.

21. João Marcos Barbosa Oliveira, Eduardo Stefani, and Ivanir Costa, "Silent Skirmishes: Cyber Warfare's Erosion of Westphalian Principles in the Prelude to the 2022 Russian-Ukrainian War," *Journal Revista Contemporânea* 3, no. 9 (2023).

22. Seongjun Park, "Evading, Hacking, and Laundering for Nukes: North Korea's Financial Cybercrimes and the Missing Silver Bullet for Countering Them," *Fordham Journal of International Law* 45 (2021).

23. Del Quentin Wilber, "China 'Has Taken the Gloves Off' in Its Thefts of U.S. Technology Secrets," *Los Angeles Times*, 16 November 2018.

24. Peter Dombrowski and Chris Demchak, "Cyber War, Cybered Conflict, and the Maritime Domain," *Naval War College Review* 67, no. 2 (2014): 70.

25. Chris Demchak, "Cybered Conflict vs. Cyber War," Atlantic Council Issue Brief, 2010, https://www.atlanticcouncil.org/blogs/new-atlanticist/cybered -conflict-vs-cyber-war/.

26. Robert D. Blackwill and Jennifer M. Harris, *War by Other Means* (Cambridge, MA: Harvard University Press, 2016).

27. Blake E. Strom et al., *Mitre Att&Ck: Design and Philosophy*, MP180360R1 (McLean, VA: The MITRE Corporation, 2020).

28. Chris C. Demchak, "What Corrodes Cyber, Infects Its Offspring: Unlearned Lessons for Emerging Technologies," *Cyber Defense Review* 7, no. 13 (2022), https://cyberdefensereview.army.mil/Portals/6/Documents/2022_winter /16_Demchak_CDR_V7N1_WINTER_2022.pdf.

29. George Galdorisi and Sam J. Tangredi, *Algorithms of Armageddon: The Impact of Artificial Intelligence* (Annapolis, MD: Naval Institute Press, 2024), 186–94.

30. Samuel Gibbs, "Mobile Web Browsing Overtakes Desktop for the First Time," *The Guardian*, 2 November 2016, https://www.theguardian.com/technology /2016/nov/02/mobile-web-browsing-desktop-smartphones-tablets; Kevin Zhu, Kenneth L. Kraemer, and Sean Xu, "The Process of Innovation Assimilation in Different Countries: A Technology Diffusion Perspective on E-Business," *Management Science* 52, no. 19 (October 2006): 1557–76.

31. Victor Cha, "How to Stop Chinese Coercion: The Case for Collective Resilience," *Foreign Affairs* 102 (2023).

32. Amy Chang, *Warring State: China's Cybersecurity Strategy* (Washington, DC: Center for a New American Security, December 2014).

33. Personal observation by Dr. Sandro Gaycken, Digital Society Institute, European School of Management and Technology, Berlin, Germany, 8 December 2014; Chris C. Demchak, "We Need a NATO/EU for Cyber Defense ('Cora')," *Defense One*, 24 March 2019.

34. Chang.

2 Cyber Threats to Commercial Maritime Order

BRUCE JONES

Crises can be revealing. When the *Ever Given* ran aground in the Suez Canal in March 2021, consumers worldwide saw images of bulk ships lined up for miles at the entrance to that key global chokepoint. It did more than any library of analyses to explain how globalization works. Amid the COVID-19 disruption to global markets, Americans experienced an education in U.S. reliance on global supply chains through inflation as container ships stacked up off California's coast. The threat of global famine caused by Black Sea combat illuminated global world food markets. And each of these crises highlighted the same vital point: global supply chains move by sea.

Globalization is primarily a maritime enterprise. Eighty-five percent of the world's trade moves by sea, as does two-thirds of the world's supply of oil and gas.[1] One-third of American gross domestic product and more in core allies like Britain depend on these globalized goods transport. This seaborne global economy is a gargantuan target for offensive cyber operations.

Relative to the potential massive economic damage, the system is digitally underprotected. Three dynamics of the maritime industry are shaping the issue: its increasing technological adoption from a low base, partial centralization, and rapid growth in the number and sophistication of cyber attacks.

⊢• TECHNOLOGIC STATE OF THE GLOBAL MARITIME SYSTEM

Far more so than any national navy, the commercial shipping enterprise draws on a complex mix of ship builders, owners, and operators; freight forwarders and local transport companies; port operators, stevedores' associations, crane operators, and pilots; and global multinationals. It operates through myriad authorities at the local, state, national, transnational, and global level. And as many as a dozen insurance regimes cover different aspects of the movement of goods by sea.

For this system to function smoothly, dozens of information systems interact on an hour-by-hour (and in some cases, minute-by-minute) basis occurring over hundreds of ports worldwide, in more than 150 countries, each with their own information systems, regulations, and sovereign authorities. It is a complex, multisector, multidomain, multinational "system of systems of systems" operating at a genuinely global level. (See related discussion of the global cyber substrate by Demchak and of the maritime transportation system by deWitte and Lehto in this volume.)

That complexity means that there are hundreds of thousands of potential entry points for cyber penetration or attack because this massive maritime transportation system (MTS) is also surprisingly low-tech beyond the engine rooms or navigation software of modern container ships. But the sector is slow to adopt new technologies, especially in the handling of cargo where bills of lading may be filled by hand and shared by fax or by exchanging thumb drives. Even the most high-tech ship must be able to interact with that low-tech system. The more sophisticated large global shipping companies that dominate the system have operated essentially as intermediaries between freight forwarders, port authorities, and local transporters. Nonetheless, some of those information management systems are rudimentary, and manual uploading of software is routine.[2]

⊢• PARTIALLY CENTRALIZED DATA MANAGEMENT

A fluid network that globally links international MTS over hundreds of thousands of individual transponders and receivers is not managed by a central authority. It operates within standards set by the International Maritime Organization (IMO), but there is no coordinated effort among international coast guard authorities or globally enforceable formal mechanisms to enforce digital security such as encryption or verification protocols.[3] And it relies on many intermediate receivers operated by low-tech ports and local boating clubs, and occasionally staffed by volunteers.

For example, integrated into most global shipping is the global positioning system–based and ship-identifying automated information system (AIS) transponder by which almost all commercial ships send maritime very high-frequency (VHF) data to nearby ships, ground-based receivers, and satellites.[4] (Naval ships turn them on and off as needed.) The AIS system is one of the most consequential and most vulnerable points of entry for cyber attack.

AIS transmits the name, number, location, speed, and heading of the ship every several seconds while sailing and every few minutes at anchor, and periodically sends additional information such as the ship's IMO identification number, dimensions, and estimated time at destination. With at least eighty thousand ships at sea at any one time, each sending around ten pieces of data every six seconds, the AIS system shares billions of pieces of data per day.[5] A VHF antenna attached to the International Space Station supports the network.[6]

The maritime commercial sector becomes more centralized in the five mega-firms accounting for 70 percent of all global shipping. Maersk, Mediterranean Shipping Company, CMA/CGM Group, Cosco Shipping Holdings Company, and Hapag-Lloyd are highly sophisticated entities themselves. Within their own centralized conglomerates, then, they are able to drive technological advances.[7]

⊢• RISING CYBER THREATS TO MARITIME OPERATIONS

Estimates are that by 2023, there had been a 400 percent increase in cyber attacks by nonstate actors since 2020.[8] In July 2018 COSCO suffered an attack on its phone and email systems that disrupted business operations in North America.[9] In the same time period, a virus infected the main software system of DNV Maritime, the world's largest provider of classification, software, and certification systems to the commercial shipping fleet.[10] A malware attack hit the Mediterranean Shipping Company in April 2020, causing its main data center in Geneva to be closed for six days, at a cost to the company of several hundred million dollars.[11] An early 2023 ransomware attack came from the notorious group LockBit, which took possession of all of the data of the port of Lisbon and threatened to release that data if a ransom was not paid.[12]

The largest cyber disruption to the commercial maritime industry so far, however, originated with a state actor—Russia. The 2017 NotPetya campaign was a Russian attack on Ukrainian tax management software (MeDoc), but the malware spread to other nations' commercial entities like the massive Danish shipping firm Maersk.[13] From there, it infected the entirety of the world's largest shipping firm, which moved one in five containers representing roughly 15 percent of global trade. Unusable for several days were fifty thousand laptops, four thousand servers, and seventeen terminals globally, with $10 billion in damages over all affected entities.[14] The company itself estimates $300 million in direct losses from the attack, not including later information technology (IT) upgrade spending and expanding from eight hundred to six thousand IT personnel.[15] A two-minute cyber attack on Maersk's systems cost more than all Somali piracy attacks combined.[16]

Maersk, both as primary victim and largest entity in the system, began efforts not just to recover from the attack but also to build a sophisticated system for the entire industry, TradeLENS.[17] Built in collaboration with IBM Blockchain, it aimed to provide a one-stop, cloud-based data center for ports, port operators, ship operators, and commercial maritime networks. If fully adopted, TradeLENS would have put two well-resourced, sophisticated entities at the heart of cyber defense for the global maritime industry. However, it would also mean far greater centralization in the industry, reversing its low-tech, distributed feature, which, under some circumstances, provides a source of resilience for highly complex systems. (See discussions of systemic cyber resilience in this volume by Ross and Warner, and Demchak.) In any event, the industry was not ready to adopt a system-wide platform, and in November 2022, Maersk and IBM quietly shelved the program.[18] Interviews with shipping executives suggest that a major obstacle was industry hesitation to share data into a pooled system—a continuing challenge common across all collective cyber defense proposals.

Beyond NotPetya, the Houthis' Red Sea navigation attacks, and the Russian-Ukrainian war, no other significant deliberate state-based cyber attacks on a major shipping firm are known in open sources. One possible deterrent is that the average container ship carries cargo from different economies via complex global supply chains, and, for the most part, ship operators do not know what is on their ships (the exception is hazardous material).[19] Though detailed data on these attacks is classified, however, port operators and international coast guard officials note increasing Chinese, Russian, North Korean, and Iranian cyber probes of U.S. and Western ports to test cyber defenses and gather data. Others are in effect "test runs" at wider attacks on critical infrastructure.

In the United States, with its complicated system of different authorities for foreign defense and domestic law enforcement, the Coast Guard performs an important bridging function: operating as an armed service and part of the Department of Defense (DOD) cyber defense (and increasingly, offense) infrastructure with its own Coast Guard Cyber Command but also within the Department of Homeland Security system for homeland cyber protection. (See chapter in this volume by Koch.) The ability to move between foreign and domestic authorities is particularly useful in the world of commercial shipping. The lines of global shipping ownership, however, are generally transnational, and at any given time, less than 10 percent of the ships docked in U.S. harbors are American-owned. And most democratic countries' economies rely heavily on the flow of goods in and out of ports on ships they do not own or regulate. Of course, any national authority can stipulate host port privileges to insist on various safety—including cyber safety—protocols for ships entering their waters. But that is a far weaker tool than direct regulatory authority.

Indeed, the genuinely global and transnational nature of the industry poses a serious challenge for regulation and cyber defense.

⊢• ISSUES FOR RESEARCH AND POLICY

Initiating effective regulation and maritime cyber defense requires solving a number of technical and policy issues. Leading cyber experts and institutions lie outside of, and are largely "sea-blind" to, the unusual configuration and specific threats to the global maritime system. So many cyber threats to terrestrial infrastructure exist that a focus on maritime activities seems a lower priority. But effects at sea inevitably become critical effects ashore, generating a series of critical questions unanswered for sea or even land. One is whether responses should be centralized or decentralized to keep up with the increasing sophistication of attacks.

While very large economic entities are potential targets for consequential attacks, these sophisticated, well-resourced actors are also on the front lines of cyber defense.[20] Taking more advantage of their central systemic role and economic weight, for example, could be key to improved maritime-oriented innovations in cyber defenses. Policy action is needed for other issues including gaps in the IMO's legal framework for stronger cyber protection standards, training, and hygiene,[21] stronger national cyber legislation,[22] encryption and verification mechanisms for AIS,[23] and reviewing liability standards in maritime insurance, especially for incidents deemed to be "war-related."[24] An add-on maritime treaty has been proposed. While there are downsides to a treaty approach, it would create a single reference point through which several of the above elements could be advanced.[25] (See chapter in this volume by Klimburg and Wells.)

The second central question is, who could drive this agenda (or elements of it)? The IMO is that rare international institution where the United States is not a powerhouse because it is a commercial shipping featherweight. Two things give the United States more power (albeit informally): a reputation for driving safety standards at sea, and the vital role of access to the U.S. market in global economics.

Together with friendly countries that have greater roles in shipping per se—for example, Denmark and Norway—the United States and a "group of friends" could work to advance this agenda. But the extensive power of China within the IMO supports its hesitation to accept the expense of cyber upgrades as well as its far laxer standards in maritime safety.

More centralized cyber responses could be explored as well. One idea that has been floated: the use of a clearing house where companies, ports, and countries can share their experiences with attacks and defense—much like the well-developed global Cyber Rapid Response System for information sharing about internet attacks.[26] This entity would likely be housed by the IMO or the U.S. Coast Guard or by some sort of hybrid entity that draws on their respective authorities and capacities. The limit on this is companies' willingness to share proprietary software and defense techniques, but at the very least, information on attacks can be shared with such a mechanism. And there are existing examples across other sectors such as national computer emergency response teams and, in the United States, the sector information-sharing and analysis centers. It might also be necessary to create a pooled fund on which low-capacity ports and firms can draw to upgrade their capabilities, which the European Union routinely does in other sectors.

An alternative approach is to incentivize the major shipping firms to take a more central role in upgrading the sector's defenses. This could be financed via the Group of Seven large economy nations or even the expanded Group of Twenty. While Maersk/IBM's experience is a cautionary tale, it is probably the case that other firms were leery of adopting a unified software package that they may have believed gave Maersk a competitive advantage. However, if several major firms were incentivized to train and equip their respective partners, it could generate a significant, industry-wide improvement in standards, training, and responses.

This idea is also behind the formation of the Cyber Resilience Alliance by major commercial IT capital goods firms. This concept is particularly relevant today, as a subset of the shipping "majors" increasingly take on "home-to-home" roles in vertical integration business strategies. They increase their leverage on the entire system for control and possibly security by absorbing freight forwarders and land-based transports into seamless global supply networks that go from initial customer all the way to final consumer.

This alternative could potentially be complemented by an expansion into the cyber realm of two existing programs run by the U.S. Coast Guard. One is the Container Security Initiative—which puts Coast Guard personnel physically and informationally present in several major ports worldwide—to enhance defenses.[27] At a maximum, this existing initiative could be turned into a container security and cyber initiative, where the same incentives (access to the U.S. market) and penalties (denials thereof, or delays) created powerful reasons for ports and their respective partners to upgrade their cyber defenses. The second initiative is the International Port Safety Program, whereby the United States helps partners develop port safety measures.[28] A limitation on this program is that it is reciprocal—if the United States wants to inspect a partner port, it is thereby also granting the right for a reciprocal inspection.

Still, the relationships developed through program partners could be used to offer an add-on cyber support within an adjusted framework that would limit other countries' access to U.S. cyber defense.

⊢• CONCLUSION

The global commercial shipping system—the MTS—is both the major artery of the global economy and a soft target for cyber attack. Upgrading both defenses and response capacity will warrant sustained attention, significant personnel, time, and money. There are a number of issues that need to be resolved—many of which parallel concerns of cyber networks ashore but have their own specific aspects. However, one can argue that cyber networks ashore cannot be separated from the maritime networks on which the land supply chain depends.

A primary issue is the attractiveness and effectiveness of centralized as opposed to decentralized responses. While centralization could logically appear more efficient (but possibly less resilient), there are significant business reasons why commercial shipping firms and their supporting contractors are reluctant to embrace it. This hesitation seems to put the burden of regulation onto governments, the IMO, or the U.S. Coast Guard (leading efforts by other coast guards, as noted by Kim in this volume). But it is not clear how to add effective regulation without stifling maritime competition and technical development. An intensified dialogue between the U.S. Coast Guard, other leading coast guards, and the five global shipping majors could be a starting point for fleshing out answers.

If maritime supply provides 85 percent of global trade, it should be no surprise that protecting it from cyber threats is a mammoth task, and one in which navies must be involved. The risks here are simply too large to ignore or underfund. Sustained attention to the problem by industry, governments, scholars, the cyber community overall—as well as navies—is a critical first step.

NOTES

1. Rose George, *Ninety Percent of Everything: Inside Shipping, the Invisible Industry That Puts Clothes on Your Back, Gas in Your Car, and Food on Your Plate* (Metropolitan Books, 2013); Mark Levinson, *The Box: How the Shipping Container Made the World Smaller and the World Economy Bigger* (Princeton University

Press, 2008); Daniel Yergin, *The New Map: Energy, Climate, and the Clash of Nations* (Penguin Press, 2020).

2. "Chinks in the Armor: Software and Communication Vulnerabilities on Ships," *GTMaritime*, 11 January 2023, https://www.gtmaritime.com/security/; Bruce Jones, *To Rule the Waves: How Control of the World's Oceans Shapes the Fate of the Superpowers* (Scribner, 2011), 110–23.

3. Syed Khandker et al., "Cybersecurity Attacks on Software Logic and Error Handling within AIS Implementations: A Systematic Testing of Resilience," *IEEE Access*, no. 10 (2022): 29493–29505, https://doi.org/10.1109/ACCESS.2022.315894.

4. Malik Shahzad Kaleem Awan and Mohammed A. Al Ghamdi, "Understanding the Vulnerabilities in Digital Components of an Integrated Bridge System (IBS)," *Journal of Marine Science and Engineering* 7, no. 10 (October 2019): 350, https://doi.org/10.3390/jmse7100350.

5. Marine Traffic, 21 October 2021, https://www.marinetraffic.com/en/ais/home/centerx:-115.2/centery:26.7/zoom:4. On 21 October 2021 Marine Traffic reported monitoring two hundred thousand ships. This was unusual; eighty thousand to one hundred thousand is the more typical number.

6. European Space Agency, "AIS on ISS," https://www.esa.int/Enabling_Support/Space_Engineering_Technology/AIS_on_ISS.

7. Chronis Kapalidis et al., "A Vulnerability Centric System of Systems Analysis on the Maritime Transportation Sector Most Valuable Assets: Recommendations for Port Facilities and Ships," *Journal of Marine Science and Engineering* 10, no. 10 (October 2022): 1486, https://doi.org/10.3390/jmse10101486.

8. Jasmina Ovcina Mandra, "Naval Dome: 400% Increase in Attempted Hacks since February 2020," *Off-shore Energy*, 5 June 2020, https://www.offshore-energy.biz/naval-dome-400-increase-in-attempted-hacks-since-february-2020/. The U.S. Coast Guard cites it in its updates on cyber protection: "Northern California Area Maritime Security Committee Cyber Security Newsletter," January 2022, https://www.sfmx.org/wp-content/uploads/2022–01_AMSC-Cyber-Newsletter.pdf.

9. The ownership structure here is illustrative of the industry. Shanghai-based COSCO Holdings is the parent company of COSCO Shipping North America, which in turn owns COSCO SHIPPING Terminals Shipping (North America) Inc. That entity formed a joint venture with Stevedoring Services of America and CMA Terminal Links; the resulting entity is called Pacific Maritime Services. That joint venture supplies terminal services to the Pacific Container Terminal, which is itself owned by SSA Marine, which is a subsidiary of CARRIX, a Seattle-based maritime services company, which owns the gantry cranes in the port. The port itself is a department of the City of Los Angeles, but governed by the Los Angeles Board of Harbor Commissioners, which operates as its

landlord, overseeing more than two hundred leaseholders. See Edwin Lopez, "How COSCO Responded to a Cyberattack on its Systems," *Supply Chain Drive*, 31 July 2018, https://www.supplychaindive.com/news/COSCO-cyberattack-response-timeline/529008/; "Cosco Reports Cyberattack at its U.S. Operations," *The Maritime Executive*, 25 July 2018, https://maritime-executive.com/article/cosco-reports-cyberattack-at-its-u-s-operations.

10. Mike Schuler, "DNV Confirms Ransomware Attack Impacting 1,000 Ships," *gCaptain*, 16 January 2023, https://gcaptain.com/dnv-confirms-ransomware-attack-impacting-1000-ships/; Damien Black, "Maritime Software Company Admits to Cyberattack," *Cybernews*, 10 January 2023, https://cybernews.com/news/maritime-software-company-cyberattack/.

11. George Grispos and William R. Mahoney, "Cyber Pirates Ahoy! An Analysis of Cybersecurity Challenges in the Shipping Industry," *Journal of Information Warfare* 21, no. 3 (August 2022): 59–73, https://arxiv.org/abs/2208.03607; Shefali Kapadia, "3 Years, 3 Cyberattacks on Major Ocean Carriers. How Can Shippers Protect Themselves?" *Supply Chain Drive*, 29 April 2020, https://www.supplychaindive.com/news/ocean-carrier-cybersecurity-maersk-msc-cosco/576754/.

12. Rakin Rahman, "Cyber Attack Threatens Release of Port of Lisbon Data," *Port Technology*, 3 January 2023, https://www.porttechnology.org/news/cyberattack-threatens-release-of-port-of-lisbon-data/; Matt Burgess and Lily Hay Newman, "The Unrelenting Menace of the LockBit Ransomware Gang," *Wired*, 24 January 2023, https://www.wired.com/story/lockbit-ransomware-attacks/. In that instance, the ransom demanded was trivially small by comparison to the sector—$1.5 million. Cyber defense officials interviewed for this chapter note that this is an important compliance challenge: the costs of paying off attackers can be far lower than the IT and training upgrades necessary for more effective cyber defense. Confidential interview, U.S. Government, Washington, DC, 8 February 2023.

13. Ellen Nakashima, "Russian Military Was behind 'NotPetya' Cyberattack in Ukraine, CIA Concludes," *Washington Post*, January 12, 2018, https://www.washingtonpost.com/world/national-security/russian-military-was-behind-notpetya-cyberattack-in-ukraine-cia-concludes/2018/01/12/048d8506-f7ca-11e7-b34a-b85626af34ef_story.html.

14. Josephine Wolff, "How the NotPetya Attack Is Reshaping Cyber Insurance," Brookings Institution, 1 December 2021, https://www.brookings.edu/techstream/how-the-notpetya-attack-is-reshaping-cyber-insurance/.

15. Grispos and Mahoney; Nakashima.

16. Grispos and Mahoney.

17. Caroline Donnelly, "Maersk Employs Cloud-First Strategy to Disrupt Competition and Build Innovation," *Computer Weekly*, 26 June 2019, 7–9, https://www .computerweekly.com/news/252465699/Shipping-giant-Maersk-on-taking-a -cloud-first-approach-to-disrupting-the-competition; author's notes, Maersk HQ, October 2019.

18. "A. P. Moller—Maersk and IBM to Discontinue TradeLENS, a Blockchain-Enabled Global Trade Platform," Maersk, 29 November 2022, https://www maersk.com/news/articles/2022/11/29/maersk-and-ibm-to-discontinue-tradelens.

19. Notwithstanding the rhetoric of deglobalization and de-linkage, 2022 marked an all-time high in U.S.-Chinese trade volumes. "Global Trade Outlook and Statistics," World Trade Organization, 5 April 2023, 19, https://www.wto.org /english/res_e/booksp_e/trade_outlook23_e.pdf.

20. Shashi K. Shah, "The Evolving Landscape of Maritime Cybersecurity," *Review of Business* 25, no. 3 (2004): 30–36.

21. Md Saiful Karim, "Maritime Cyber Security and the IMO Legal Instruments: Sluggish Response to an Escalating Threat?" *Marine Policy*, no. 143 (September 2022), https://doi.org/10.1016/j.marpol.2022.105138; Juan Ignacio Alcaide and Ruth Garcia Llave, "Critical Infrastructures Cybersecurity and the Maritime Sector," *Transportation Research Procedia*, no. 45 (March 2020): 547–54, https:// doi.org/10.1016/j.trpro.2020.03.058.

22. Chan Yan Jau, "Cyber Attacks as an Evolving Threat to Southeast Asia's Maritime Security," in *Evolving Threats to Southeast Asia's Maritime Security*, Asia Maritime Transparency Initiative, Center for Strategic and International Studies, December 2022, https://amti.csis.org/cyber attacks-as-an-evolving-threat-to -southeast-asias-maritime-security/; Dimitris Amprazis, "Top 11 Maritime Security Compromises of All Time," *Threatspan*, 27 December 2017, https:// threatspan.com/2017/12/29/top-11-maritime-security-compromises-of-all-time/.

23. Khandker et al.

24. V. A. Greiman, "Defending the Cyber Sea: Legal Challenges Ahead," *Journal of Information Warfare* 19, no. 3 (2020): 68–82, https://www.jstor.org/stable/27033633.

25. Brendan Sullivan, "A Tale of Two Treaties: A Maritime Model to Stop the Scourge of Cybercrime," *Boston University International Law Journal* 39, no. 2 (Summer 2021): 143–80, https://heinonline.org/HOL/P?h=hein.journals/builj39&i=155.

26. William Loomis et al., *Raising the Colors: Signaling for Cooperation on Maritime Cybersecurity*, Atlantic Council, October 2021, https:// www.atlanticcouncil.org/in-depth-research-reports/report/raising-the -colors-signaling-for-cooperation-on-maritime-cybersecurity/.

27. U.S. Customs and Border Protection, "CSI: Container Security Initiative," https:// www.cbp.gov/border-security/ports-entry/cargo-security/csi/csi-brief.

28. U.S. Coast Guard—Pacific Area, "International Port Security Program," https://www.pacificarea.uscg.mil/Our-Organization/District-14/D14-Units/Activities-Far-East-FEACT/FEACT-Maritime-Security/.

3 Maritime Transportation System and Cyber Threats

PAULA deWITTE and MARTTI LEHTO

Maritime transportation is today an increasingly technologically advanced automated process in which computers are employed in every stage from navigation and communication to cargo handling and customs in both operational technology and information technology systems. More than 80 percent of the world's cargo is carried by vessels that are themselves becoming increasingly complex and dependent on the extensive use of digital communication technologies throughout their operational life cycle. Further, maritime transport operates under an international framework for legal requirements and compliance. The international maritime transportation system (MTS) relies on these cybered systems for all aspects of its operation and management. As a result, the entire process—from ports, vessels, and supply chains through both onshore and offshore infrastructure—is vulnerable to cyber attacks. To create a credible assessment framework for cyber security management of the MTS, it is critical to examine the entire system in some detail and how it manages cyber threats and vulnerabilities in systemic, decision-making, and organizational terms.

⊢• THE (DIGITAL) MARITIME TRANSPORTATION SYSTEM

Maritime digital transformation is accelerating, widely embracing automation including in the traffic systems. With approximately fifty thousand vessels at sea or in port at any one time, the deeply digitized maritime transport industry is highly vulnerable to cyber attacks by nation-state and criminal attackers. The maritime transportation system as a geographically and physically complex and diverse system consists of:

- ship manufacturing
- shipping companies
- maritime operators
- ports and harbors
- logistics operators
- customers and other stakeholders.[1]

The MTS technical environment is a highly interconnected global system combining the multiple diverse systems of vessels, fairways, and ports. Securing the cyber aspects of these interconnected systems hosted, owned, and operated by multiple stakeholders requires a system-of-systems view in cyber security. The maritime and port operating environments involve cyber-physical systems equipped with intelligent machines, robots, and other corresponding products. They can independently create and exchange information, perform different functions, and control each other.

Each of these functions makes the maritime environment a target-rich opportunity for hackers. A 2022 U.S. Coast Guard Cyber Command report on cyber security trends in the maritime environment highlighted the "exponentially" rising significance of cyber hygiene, detection, and response. The year 2022 saw a 68 percent increase in reported maritime cyber incidents, with the Coast Guard Cyber Command having to ramp up its efforts to ensure maritime facilities are complying with cyber regulations.[2]

Thus, the MTS is best viewed as a system of systems in which the actions of multiple dispersed, independent, component systems influence the larger, more complex system. (See related chapter by Jones in this volume.) In this case, a system is a group of interacting, interrelated, and interdependent information technology (IT) and operational technology components that form a complex and unified whole. The goal of a system-of-systems view is to get maximum value out of a large system by an understanding of how each of the smaller systems works, interfaces, and is used. Such designs require systems thinking—a holistic approach to cyber security analysis focused on comprehensive cyber security in the maritime environment.[3]

⊢• MTS INFORMATION TECHNOLOGY SYSTEMS

IT systems in maritime environments are the traditional company IT systems that might include workstations, laptops, and mobile devices with software, email, calendars, business analytics, and financial systems (accounts), and with data for administration, personnel information, maintenance and service (plans, spares, work permits), electronic manuals, and certificates. There are many IT systems, components, vendors, jurisdictions, and manufacturers, as well as organizational policies, procedures, and requirements within the MTS.

The MTS and maritime industry comprise the following components:[4]

- seaport operations, including vessel control and traffic management, personnel management and screening, passenger management and passport control, Wi-Fi, and physically wired networks
- cargo and shipping, including logistics, supply chain, routing, scheduling, tracking loading/offloading, and loss management
- manufacturing, supply chain, payment systems, software, and hardware
- vessel traffic management, including ship management, routing, location management, and communication
- shipping line operations, including passenger information, reservation systems, communication, baggage and cargo handling, maintenance, catering, and payment systems
- vessel operations, including the ship's onboard network architecture providing interconnection between the bridge navigation, communication, mechanical, ship monitoring and security, cargo handling and other specialized systems, and communication with external networks with regard to vessel traffic management, ports, and shipping lines
- unmanned/autonomous vehicles, including remote control and monitoring systems.

The maritime industry's digital transformation has led to widespread cloud adoption to manage personnel information, enterprise resource planning, customer relationship management, and other corporate functions. IT also refers to the technical assets that are used in managing information processing, including software, hardware, and communication technologies.[5]

↦ VESSEL SYSTEM OF SYSTEMS

Maritime environments and vessels have increasingly become targets for cyber attacks. Operational technology (OT) encompasses the computing systems that manage industrial operations. These systems likewise support both human-to-machine and machine-to-machine interfaces with industrial processes, often to promote efficiency and automation.[6] OT includes the industrial control systems (ICS) linking equipment and software.

As depicted in figure 3-1, ICS are the interfaces where virtual commands generate physical reality in industrial environments. ICS provide real-time, two-way data flow between sensors, workstations, and other networked devices throughout a system. They allow continuous and distributed monitoring and control. ICS include supervisory control and data acquisition system, distributed control system, and programmable logic control software.[7] The distributed control system is a particular type of process control system that connects controllers, sensors, operator terminals, and actuators.

Vessels' systems do not need to be attacked physically or directly. An attack can arrive via a company's shore-based IT systems and relatively easily penetrate a ship's critical onboard OT systems. (See related discussion by Hilger

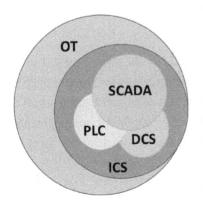

FIGURE 3-1. Environment of Industrial Control Systems (ICS), Supervisory Control and Data Acquisition (SCADA), Distributed Control Systems (DCS), Programmable Logic Control (PLC), and Operational Technology (OT) *Source: Formulated by authors based on Kessler and Shepard, 2022*

in this volume.) Systems such as inertial navigation systems and satellite communications are used for a variety of purposes, including access control, navigation, traffic monitoring, and information transmission, and they offer considerable opportunities for attacks.[8]

OT enables cyber-physical operations on board. Such functions and systems include, among others, power management, remote support for engines, data loggers, cargo management and control, sensors, pumps, actuators, hydraulics, cranes, and on-board measurements and control. The global maritime distress system, propulsion control system, integrated bridge systems, machinery management, and power control systems are other key elements of the automation systems on board a ship.[9]

Inertial navigation systems comprise the hardware and software technology in the bridge of the vessel where all functions related to navigation and communication are directed. Inertial navigation systems include, among others, electronic chart display and information systems, radar, automatic identification systems, echo sounder, sonar, and NAVTEX. Global navigation satellite systems deliver precise timing and positioning.[10] A cyber attack on any one system can lead to a catastrophic failure of the entire inertial navigation system.

Communication systems (satellite communications, Fleet Broadband, 3G/4G/5G, Wi-Fi) are vulnerable. For high-speed data transmission rates throughout maritime operations, most modern vessels are equipped with the maritime very small aperture terminal, which acts as a ground station for satellite data transmission. This terminal offers a variety of communication and security services, but it can also be a single point of failure.

⊢• MTS CYBER THREATS AND VULNERABILITIES

Although the interconnectivity and utilization of the cyber-physical systems facilitate transportation, they also present opportunities for illegal exploitation, increasing the risk for the MTS.[11] Poor cyber security could lead to significant loss of customer and/or industry confidence, reputational damage, potentially severe financial losses or penalties, and litigation affecting the companies involved.

Maritime transportation cyber risk refers to a measure of the extent to which a technology asset could be threatened by a potential circumstance or event that may result in shipping-related operational, safety, or security failures due to information or systems being corrupted, lost, or compromised. Cyber risk management means the process of identifying, analyzing, assessing, and communicating a cyber-related risk and accepting, avoiding, transferring, or mitigating it to an acceptable level, considering costs and benefits of actions taken to stakeholders.[12]

The motivations of cyber attackers can be organized as a practical threat taxonomy. The threats included in this model are applicable to all of the different scenarios that can be experienced. This threat model is a sixfold classification based on hacker motivational factors:[13]

1. cyber vandalism
2. cyber crime
3. cyber espionage
4. cyber terrorism
5. cyber sabotage
6. cyber warfare

⊢○ Cyber Vandalism

Cyber vandalism encompasses cyber anarchy, illegal hacking, and hacktivism. Hackers find interfering with computer systems an enjoyable challenge. Hacktivists wish to attack companies for political or ideological motives. Cyber vandals can deface websites, disrupt a company's services, or delete databases.

The impacts of cyber vandalism can be significant and long-lasting. For example, a port that has its computer systems brought down by a denial-of-service attack could see vital operations postponed or canceled, leading to serious disruptions in the supply chain.

⊢○ Cyber Crime

Cyber criminals are interested in making money through fraud or from the sale of valuable information. The Commission of the European Communities defines cyber crime as "criminal acts committed using electronic communications networks and information systems or against such networks and systems."[14] (See related discussion by Tiirmaa-Klaar in this volume.)

In 2018 Australian shipbuilder and defense contractor Austal was the subject of a cyber security breach and extortion attempt. The Austal data management system had been targeted by an unknown offender. Some staff email addresses and mobile phone numbers were accessed. The attacker tried to sell some of the stolen material online and engage in extortion.[15]

The Death Kitty ransomware disrupted TransNet's container and trucking operations in July 2021. Other impacts detected by cyber security service provider Ensign InfoSecurity throughout 2021 include the theft of data that could be sold by threat actors, as well as serious disruptions to companies involved in logistics and supply chains.

⊢○ Cyber Espionage

Cyber espionage can be defined as an action aimed at obtaining secret information (sensitive, proprietary, or classified) from individuals, competitors, groups, governments, and adversaries for the purpose of accruing political, military, or economic gain by employing illicit techniques on the internet, networks, programs, or computers. Cyber espionage is a potent and inexpensive way to access a significant volume of information that is intended to be confidential.[16]

⊢○ Cyber Terrorism

Cyber terrorists utilize networks in attacks against critical infrastructure systems and their controls. The purpose of the attacks is to cause damage and raise fear among the public, and to force the political leadership to give in to the terrorists' demands. Although cyber terrorist attacks against the MTS have not yet materialized, an increased level of "know-how" on the part of terrorists will make them more likely to occur.[17]

⊢○ Cyber Sabotage

Cyber sabotage is an activity in which an attacker (a state actor or a state-sponsored group) operates below the threshold of war or executes military operations other than war. The goals may be to cause instability in the target country, to test one's own offensive cyber attack capabilities, to prepare for hybrid operations, or to prepare warfare actions.[18]

In June 2017 the NotPetya malware was intended by Russian actors to harm Ukraine, but the malicious code leaked into other systems. The variant infected the IT systems of the world's largest shipping company, Maersk, with six hundred container vessels handling 15 percent of the world's seaborne trade. The breakdown affected all business units at Maersk, including container shipping, port and tugboat operations, oil and gas production, drilling services, and oil tankers. Maersk reported up to $300 million in losses.[19] Fortunately, data backup from a Maersk company system in Ghana that was unintentionally disconnected from the internet allowed Maersk to recover.[20]

In 2023 pro-Russian hackers attacked the largest Japanese port of Nagoya with ransomware, shutting the port for over two days and causing major manufacturers like Toyota to suspend operations temporarily.[21]

⊢─○ Cyber Warfare

Cyber warfare is an umbrella term for the operations of state actors in cyberspace. It is typically defined as an act of war using internet-enabled technology to perform an attack on a nation's infrastructure (civilian or military).

On February 24, 2022, armed forces of the Russian Federation launched an invasion of Ukraine. One day earlier massive cyber attacks began targeting different organizations of the Ukrainian government, financial sector, energy sector, and several others. During the war, destructive wiper malware known as WhisperGate was used to attack several Ukrainian organizations. WhisperGate malware overwrites the master boot record of a system and creates a fake ransom note. Additionally, it downloads another malware (WhisperKill) from a Discord server to corrupt local files.[22]

Throughout the conflict, such wiper and similar attacks have continued against Ukrainian facilities, including all shipping. In addition, Russian attacks on satellite ground equipment of Ukraine leaked outside to affect other ground stations in Europe. Russia has also jammed and spoofed global positioning system equipment, all of which is used by the MTS in Ukraine and other countries. The entire MTS will be a cyber target in wartime.

⊢• CYBER VULNERABILITIES

Vulnerability is the inherent weakness in a system that increases the probability of an occurrence or exacerbates its consequences. These affect all maritime systems just as they imperil land-based systems. Each critical infrastructure contains specific vulnerabilities in IT/OT systems. The primary causes of vulnerabilities fall into three general categories: the human element, configuration issues, and insecure design.[23] Vulnerabilities can also be divided into those that exist in people's actions, in systemic processes, or in technologies.[24]

People like to click website links. Most cyber security threats are due to employee errors. Many reports indicate that employee errors accounted for 90 to 95 percent of all breaches that cause financial losses. Employees are often victims of social engineering tactics and may end up unknowingly providing attackers with login credentials or classified organization data.[25] Mariners also access the internet insecurely.

Processes in organizations and across networks are key to the implementation of effective cyber security measures. Processes are crucial in defining how the MTS stakeholder's activities, roles, and documentation are used to mitigate the risks. Process vulnerabilities among others are caused by a lack of written security policy, poor regulating policy, lack of security awareness and training, poor adherence to security, lack of access control, and nonexistence of disaster/contingency plans.[26] Many shipping firms have poorly secured processes.

Technology solutions protect against cyber risks that may arise from network vulnerabilities; however, the designs and operations of technology itself contain vulnerabilities in both hardware and software. So, technological vulnerabilities are security holes in a system, especially the aging systems widely found throughout the MTS.

Hardware vulnerabilities are often very difficult to identify. In January 2018 the entire computer industry was put on alert by two new processor vulnerabilities, dubbed Meltdown and Spectre, that defeated the fundamental operating system security boundaries separating kernel and user space memory.[27] The MTS would not have been immune and might have been affected, but shipping firms are notoriously secretive about such attacks, making the overall system hard to defend.

⊢• CONCLUSION: SECURING, DEFENDING, AND RESILIENCE

Cyber security for the maritime transportation system overall is particularly complex and challenging. (See related discussion by Jones in this volume.) There are many different classes of vessels, all of which operate in very different environments with varying levels of digital sophistication, vulnerabilities, and requirements for resilience. (See also related discussions by Hilger, and Falcone and Panter.)

The MTS's cyber security operations require comprehensive awareness on the system level of the potential for cyber attacks and sudden losses. Appropriate awareness thus supports cyber risk management and, more extensively, the evaluation of whole cyber capability. The combination of system views, decision-making levels, and an organization's cyber structure can be considered a framework for evaluating cyber security management.

There is a need for effective cyber security education and training for ship and port personnel, owners, management, stockholders, and policymakers. Studies have indicated that people are the largest source of cyber security vulnerabilities. There are currently several cyber security solutions and technical tools available to meet the needs of the MTS. However, they also present challenges such as the fragmentation of technology, problems at the practical level of implementation and maintenance of new security elements, and measures that may lead to an increase in the complexity of the entire functional system and add to the difficulty of managing the whole.

In securing and defending the MTS from cyber attacks, system-of-systems resilience is needed, as noted by Ross and Warner, Demchak, and others in this volume. Cyber resilience is a concept that brings business continuity, IT/OT security, and organizational resilience together. By being resilient, organizations can reduce the impact of an attack and ensure that they can continue to operate effectively. In the maritime environment, resiliency requires information communications technology and operations technology systems to have the capability to protect themselves and to detect, respond to, and recover from cyber attacks.

NOTES

1. U.S. Department of Homeland Security, "2014 Sector Risk Snapshots," *DHS Science and Technology* website, 1 January 2015, https://www.dhs.gov/science-and-technology/2014-snapshot-archives; Robert C. Bronk and Paula DeWitte, "Maritime Cyber Security: Meeting Threats to Globalization's Great Conveyor," in Martti Lehto and Pekka Neittaanmäki, eds., *Cyber Security: Critical Infrastructure Protection* (Barcelona: Springer, 2022).

2. Bridget Johnson, "Maritime Cyber Incidents Increased at Least 68 Percent in 2021, Coast Guard Reports," *Government Technology and Service Coalition (GTSC) Homeland Security Today*, 26 August 2022, https://www.hstoday.us/featured/maritime-cyber-incidents-increased-at-least-68-percent-in-2021-coast-guard-reports/.

3. Gary C. Kessler and Stephen D. Shepard, *Maritime Cyber Security: A Guide for Leaders and Managers* (self-published, February 2022).

4. Gary C. Kessler, "Cyber Security in the Maritime Domain," *U.S. Coast Guard, Proceedings of the Marine Safety & Security Council* 76, no. 1 (Spring 2019): 34–39, https://commons.erau.edu/cgi/viewcontent.cgi?article=2377&context=publication; International Maritime Organization, *Guidelines on Maritime Cyber Risk Management*, MSC-FAL.1/Circ.3, 5 July 2017, https://wwwcdn.imo.org/localresources/en/OurWork/Facilitation/Facilitation/MSC-FAL.1-Circ.3-Rev.1.pdf.

5. William Loomis et al., *Raising the Colors: Signaling for Cooperation on Maritime Cybersecurity* (Washington, DC: Atlantic Council, October 2021), https://www.atlanticcouncil.org/wp-content/uploads/2021/10/Raising-the-colors-Signaling-for-cooperation-on-maritime-cybersecurity.pdf.

6. Stavros Karamperidis, Chronos Kapalidis, and Tim Watson, "Maritime Cyber Security: A Global Challenge Tackled through Distinct Regional Approaches," *Journal of Maritime Science and Engineering* 9, no. 12 (2021): 1323, https://doi.org/10.3390/jmse9121323; Scott A. Weed, *U.S. Policy Response to Cyber-Attack on SCADA Systems Supporting Critical National Infrastructure*, Perspectives on Cyber Power 7 (Maxwell Air Force Base, AL: Air University Press, 2017).

7. "What's the Difference between OT, ICS, SCADA, and DCS?" *Securion*, 1 May 2019, https://www.securicon.com/whats-the-difference-between-ot-ics-scada-and-dcs/; Kessler and Shepard.

8. U.S. Department of Homeland Security.

9. Frank Akpan et al., "Cybersecurity Challenges in the Maritime Sector," *Network* 2, no. 1 (2022): 123–38, https://www.mdpi.com/2673–8732/2/1/9.

10. Akpan et al.

11. Martti Lehto, "Cyber Security in Aviation, Maritime and Automotive," in Pedro Diez et al., eds., *Computation and Big Data for Transport*, (Barcelona: Springer, 2020), 19–32, https://content.e-bookshelf.de/media/reading/L-13389949 -06ea9dd94c.pdf.

12. International Maritime Organization, "Maritime Cyber Risk," June 2017, https:// www.imo.org/en/OurWork/Security/Pages/Cyber-security.aspx.

13. Martti Lehto, "Cyber-Attacks against Critical Infrastructure," in Lehto and Neittaanmäki, eds., 255–86.

14. European Union Commission, *Communication from the Commission to the European Parliament, the Council and the Committee of the Regions: Towards a General Policy on the Fight against Cybercrime* (Brussels, 22 May 2007), 267.

15. Jane Norman, "Defence Shipbuilder Austal Hit by Cyber Security Breach and Extortion Attempt," Australian Broadcasting Company, 1 November 2018, https://www.abc.net.au/news/2018-11-01/defence-shipbuilder-austal -subject-of-a-cyber-security-breach/10458042.

16. Finnish Security and Intelligence Service (SUPO), "SUPO Also Combats Cyber Espionage," 2022, https://supo.fi/en/cyber-espionage.

17. Christopher Beggs, "Proposed Risk Minimization Measures for Cyber-Terrorism and SCADA Networks in Australia," National Defence College, Helsinki, Finland, 1–2 June 2006; Interpol, *The Protection of Critical Infrastructures against Terrorist Attacks: Compendium of Good Practices*, compiled by CTED and UNOCT, 2018, https://www.un.org/counterterrorism/sites/www.un.org .counterterrorism/files/eng_compendium-cip-final-version-120618.pdf.

18. Joshua Rovner, "Sabotage and War in Cyberspace," *War on the Rocks*, 19 July 2022, https://warontherocks.com/2022/07/sabotage-and-war-in-cyberspace/.

19. Jacob Gronholt-Pedersen, "Maersk Says Global IT Breakdown Caused by Cyber-Attack," *Reuters*, 27 June 2017, https://www.reuters.com/article/us -cyber-attack-maersk-idUSKBN19I1NO.

20. Daniel E. Capano, "Throwback Attack: How NotPetya Accidentally Took Down Shipping Giant Maersk," *Industrial Cybersecurity Pulse*, 30 September 2021, https://www.industrialcybersecuritypulse.com/threats-vulnerabilities /throwback-attack-how-notpetya-accidentally-took-down-global-shipping -giant-maersk/.

21. "Toyota to Suspend Packaging Line after Cyberattack on Japan Port," *Reuters*, 6 July 2023, https://www.reuters.com/business/autos-transportation/japans -biggest-port-plans-resume-operations-thursday-after-cyberattack-2023-07-06/.

22. Microsoft, *Defending Ukraine: Early Lessons from the Cyber War*, 22 June 2022, https://aka.ms/June22SpecialReport.

23. Weed.

24. Martti Lehto, "Phenomena in the Cyber World," in Lehto and Neittaanmäki, eds., 3–29.

25. AIG, *Human Cyber Risk: The First Line of Defence*, 2022, https://www.aig.co.uk content/dam/aig/emea/united-kingdom/documents/Insights/cyber-human -factor.pdf.

26. Federal Communications Commission, *Cyber Security Planning Guide*, 2014, https://www.fcc.gov/sites/default/files/cyberplanner.pdf; E. Hess, Helical, Inc., "People, Process, and Technology: The Trifecta of Cyber Security Programs," *DEV*, 23 October 2019, https://dev.to/helicalinc/understanding-the-trifecta-of -cyber security-programs-kaj.

27. Lucian Constantin, "37 Hardware and Firmware Vulnerabilities: A Guide to the Threats," *CSO*, 11 August 2011, https://www.csoonline.com/article /3410046/hardware-and-firmware-vulnerabilities-a-guide-to-the-threats .html; Jane Chong, "Why Is Our Cyber Security So Insecure?" *The New Republic*, 11 October 2013, https://newrepublic.com/article/115145/us-cyber security-why-software-so-insecure.

4 Cyber Threats to Warships

RYAN HILGER

n September 1997 the USS *Yorktown* (CG 48) found itself dead in the water after a new networked engineering control system attempted to divide by zero. For nearly three hours, *Yorktown* drifted off the Virginia coast due to an operator entry that prompted the buffer overflow, causing a catastrophic loss of power.[1] Barely a decade later, Michael Assante, a cyber security engineer and a former Navy officer, destroyed a diesel generator with a mere thirty lines of code, as officials from the Department of Homeland Security, the Department of Energy, and the North American Electric Reliability Corporation and other electric utilities looked on in shock.[2] Another decade later in 2017, Chief of Naval Operations Adm. John Richardson launched Operation Orion Hammer to determine if a cyber attack could have caused the collision between the USS *John S. McCain* (DDG 56) and the merchant vessel *Alnic MC*.[3]

Even in the wake of its 2019 *Cybersecurity Readiness Review*, the U.S. Navy remains decidedly vulnerable to adversary cyber attacks against the fleet and its supporting infrastructure and programs.[4] Cyber security is imperative for overall unit readiness, and the Navy's sailors and officers should understand how cyber attacks will be launched against them. This chapter outlines the threats to ships across shipboard networks, the combat and engineering systems, and the ship's crew, and concludes with recommendations on how shipboard leadership can improve their cyber readiness and unit resilience.

⊢• WARSHIPS AND THE CYBER KILL CHAIN

Orders of battle and tactical planning often consider only the combat capabilities a warship brings to bear against our forces. The combination of these networks and combat systems, with a competent and proficient crew, can generate significant capabilities for an operational commander, but this perspective obscures how warships and their crews are vulnerable to sustained cyber campaigns from advanced persistent threats (APTs). Placing the ship and the crew in the context of the cyber kill chain shines a light on how threats may reach the ship and degrade or destroy combat readiness and effectiveness.

From a cyber perspective, *a warship is simply a collection of networks, sensors, effectors, and people, all of which can be exploited.* Industry and academia consider the networks, sensors, and effectors broadly to be cyber-physical systems, but for our purposes, the italicized definition helps differentiate the individual categories of systems and their common exploitation methods. Figure 4-1 shows how networked cyber-physical systems have proliferated through modern warships, touching every major system needed for unit readiness, combat effectiveness, and seaworthiness.[5]

Each of these systems is exploitable, and planners should assume that many of these systems will already have been compromised long before they deploy on a ship, possibly during the design or construction. The Navy's core platforms—aircraft carriers, destroyers, submarines, aircraft, and major combat and weapons systems—have existed for decades as physical platforms, often constructed and maintained by the same defense contractors. Since 1980, which many of the Navy's core platform designs predate, the defense industrial base has consolidated from more than fifty defense and aerospace contractors to approximately six, with a concurrent reduction and consolidation of physical facilities, network infrastructure, and production capacity.[6] In cyber terms, the systems of interest have remained surprisingly static, but the defense industrial base has consolidated into several large prime contractors supported by more than three hundred thousand subcontractors.[7] Russian,

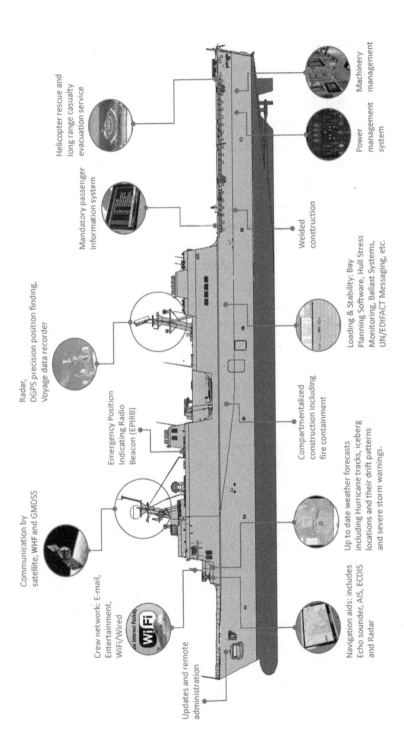

FIGURE 4-1. Automation Systems for Modern and Autonomous Ships

Source: Frank Akpan et al., "Cybersecurity Challenges in the Maritime Sector," Network 2, no. 1 (March 2022): 123–38, https://doi.org/10.3390/network2010009. Used by permission.

Chinese, Iranian, and other advanced persistent threats can now tailor and focus their cyber operations against these few, highly lucrative targets that integrate systems and information into a single repository. They have been doing so successfully for years.[8] (See discussions related to adversary capabilities by Kania, Work, and Demchak in this volume.) Additionally, these highly capable threat actors are moving deeper into the supply chains—the small and medium businesses with lamentable cybersecurity practices, which accounted for more than 60 percent of cyber breaches in 2021.[9] The civilian maritime sector continues to see increasing trends in cyber attacks against shipbuilders, ports, and the ships themselves as well.[10] Every aspect of a warship's life cycle is under attack daily from capable adversaries.

Within its programs, the Department of Defense continues to struggle with modernizing system architectures, refactoring software code bases, and improving software and hardware development cycles to industry standards. (See related discussions by Dombrowski, Cleary, Brutzman and Kline, Bebber and White, and, for artificial intelligence, Long and Vaughan in this volume.) In 2022 the Government Accountability Office (GAO) reported that of thirty-eight major defense acquisition programs surveyed, only six had achieved software delivery time frames under three months, and only one in under one month, despite all thirty-eight programs reporting the use of modern software development methods.[11] Thus, once a cyber vulnerability or exploited system is detected in the fleet, it may take the program half a year or more to deploy a patch.

Cyber attacks move through a kill chain, which defense industry corporation Lockheed Martin conceptualizes as reconnaissance, weaponization of the vulnerability, payload delivery, exploitation, installation, command and control, and follow-on exploitation.[12] Each phase requires new information and actions, which are not confined to a specific system. For example, social engineering tactics against a sailor on board a destroyer may yield technical information and a vulnerability, which can then be weaponized through prior persistent access at the defense contractor and then pushed through normal fleet means for installation and subsequent use across all ships. While this falls into long-standing espionage practices, the rapid incorporation of information into actionable payloads makes the threat markedly different. Command and control and exploitation of this new cyber payload may not require real-time access, as in the case of the Stuxnet attack, or cause catastrophic results. An attacker's intention may be to degrade or deny capabilities, or to time attacks to create larger geopolitical or strategic effects.[13]

THREATS TO SHIPBOARD NETWORKS

Shipboard networks control nearly every aspect of a ship's capabilities, and today's navies have come to rely on them as the primary means of conducting daily operations and controlling the ship. Thus, shipboard networks are the most lucrative and exploitable target for adversary action. This section considers all networks on board except the industrial control systems and weapons.

Shipboard networks resemble those in many organizations worldwide: servers, end points, printers, cabling and physical infrastructure, switches, and so on. These devices, and the software that runs them, are largely commercial off-the-shelf products across all layers of the open systems interconnection model.[14] This commercial sourcing means that many of the issues the wider cyber security community reports daily can also directly impact a ship's networks. These vulnerabilities do not have to be exquisitely designed and executed attacks from APTs against the ship's networks, and indeed are more likely to be common weaknesses. The Open Web Application Security Project's (OWASP's) top ten highlights the simplistic nature of the vulnerabilities that plague networks: broken access controls, insecure design, security misconfigurations, vulnerable and outdated components, identification and authentication failures, security and logging failures, and more.[15] The GAO found that the Department of Defense lags significantly in understanding and remediating cyber vulnerabilities in weapons systems, a statement it reiterated in 2021.[16] The GAO's 2018 report highlights how easily most major weapons systems could be compromised by a red team, using many of the same vulnerabilities reported by OWASP.[17]

For the ship's crew, the vulnerabilities to shipboard networks arrive with contractor installation. (See related discussions of port cyber insecurity by deWitte and Lehto, and Vogt and Kollars in this volume.) This adds a layer of uncertainty, since the defense industrial base's networks are vulnerable to the same issues indicated above, allowing APTs to infiltrate and potentially load malware or other cyber payloads into systems during development and production. Recently, the cyber security community increased attention to supply chain security. As security measures improve, adversaries will look deeper into the supply chains to compromise software and hardware in the hopes that vulnerabilities will pass through security testing. Increasingly, this appears to be working.[18]

Vulnerabilities can also come from the crew and their practices as well: poor account and privilege management, common logins for work centers, poor password requirements and enforcement, poor patching practices, and so on. The Navy's own 2019 *Cybersecurity Readiness Review* highlighted the poor state of training and management practices as a critical factor in the service's overall poor cyber readiness.[19]

Finally, the long-held belief that simply operating under emissions control, or unconnected to the internet in real time (air-gapping), will keep a ship safe has not been a valid assumption, particularly since the Stuxnet incident in 2009. Adversary patterns of defense industrial base exploitation point to a safer assumption—crews should assume that all networked systems on board, including sensors and weapons, are already compromised. These infections may elude routine monitoring until the adversary's conditions for payload execution are met. Indeed, this is the foundational premise of zero trust principles and program architecture design.[20]

Shipboard networks are the backbone of a ship. They link operational technologies, weapons, and sensors into an effective fighting platform. Degrading or disabling these networks can have substantial impacts to combat readiness or seaworthiness, though compromising industrial control systems and operational technologies requires additional skill and information.

⊢• THREATS TO SENSORS, EFFECTORS, AND ENGINEERING SYSTEMS

Attacks to sensors, effectors, and industrial control systems differ from cyber attacks against traditional networks primarily in the physical effects of the attack.[21] Effects can range from wiping the system to catastrophic damage—the Aurora Generator Test or Iranian uranium centrifuges, for example.[22] As attacks against operational technologies proliferate and become easier, events like the 2017 collision between the USS *John S. McCain* (DDG 56) and

Alnic MC, the grounding of the *Ever Given* in the Suez Canal, or the capsizing of the *Golden Ray* in St. Simon Sound may become more commonplace when security breach–related command and control threats exacerbate the problems.[23]

APTs have the motivation, capability, and resources and opportunities to engineer far more devastating attacks to warships by exploiting the industrial control systems, sensors, and weapons, even if normally disconnected from the central shipboard networks. The maritime industry and navies heavily leverage existing industrial control systems to operate complex ships in harsh environments. While executing these attacks is not trivial, these types of attacks have been a regular occurrence since Stuxnet in 2009 and are increasing in frequency worldwide.[24]

Attacking these types of systems requires significant resources and planning in the intelligence and reconnaissance phase of the cyber kill chain. Unlike ransomware or more mainstream attacks on traditional systems, in these attacks each system is different. Operational technologies, like programmable logic controllers (PLCs), supervisory control and data acquisition systems (SCADA), and other industrial control systems, are highly specialized devices that often combine unique hardware designs, proprietary firmware, control signals, or data formats, and custom software designs to create the physical controls required. The PLC controlling the gas turbines will be completely different from the PLC or supervisory control and data acquisition system monitoring and controlling electrical power distribution. To exploit even one of these systems requires an attacker to acquire tremendous amounts of information to enable them to tailor the payload for that specific design. In the case of Stuxnet, the payload targeted Siemens PLCs, but only if running the correct firmware versions and connected to the specific centrifuges known to be in operation in Iran's uranium enrichment operations; it caused no harm in all other cases.[25]

As previously noted, APTs from China and Russia have penetrated the defense industrial base and potentially compromised many of the U.S. Navy's major weapons systems. While information exfiltration may have been a primary goal, it is also possible that these adversaries maintain enduring access to contractor networks and develop custom payloads.

THREATS TO (AND FROM) SAILORS

The crew represents the largest cyber threat to a warship.[26] Verizon's long-running annual *Data Breach Investigations Report* notes that 82 percent of identified cyber breaches involved the human element, whether from stolen credentials, system misuse or improper access, or outright error.[27] Utilizing human mistakes continues to play such an outsized role in cyber attacks for one simple reason: it works. People can overcome nearly any technical control put in place. People, whether sailors on board a destroyer or cleared defense contractors developing the system, are prime targets for adversary exploitation. Both Russia and China have been active in various social engineering attacks for more than a decade.[28]

Sailors are present at all primary points along the cyber kill chain, and leadership must understand that no amount of training or supervision will prevent a skilled adversary from exploiting one of them to gain information or access. Open-source intelligence techniques allow anyone with a modicum of basic training to amass sufficient information to track individuals—or whole ships—to extort or blackmail them or their families. This will only get worse as the costs to produce deep fakes and artificial intelligence–assisted programs that produce false but believable materials drop, and the potential impact against unit readiness and security rises.[29] On board, sailors can be either passive threats, such as potential victims of spear-phishing or whaling, or more active through regular maintenance and operations activities or as insider threats to deliver hidden payloads.[30]

FIGHTING THE SHIP

Producing resilient combat capabilities on a warship requires a different mindset than the traditional approach. Under the current engineering- and training-centric combat readiness paradigm, if a ship's systems were functioning properly and the crew is trained, the ship is considered combat-ready. However, given the cyber security vulnerabilities mentioned earlier, a ship could be the best one in her squadron yet struggle to get off the pier. As the president of the United States has already directed, this requires leaders to embrace the concept of "assume breach" and be proactive and involved cyber defenders.[31] In this case, assume systems already contain hidden payloads and that at least one or more of the ship's sailors and the ship are being tracked by open-source intelligence techniques.

Sailors are a major part of the problem, but they can also be part of the solution. Warships are not fully autonomous systems, and it is the people that make them resilient. Resilience is the ability to "prepare and plan for, absorb, recover from, and more successfully adapt to adverse events."[32] Thus, leaders can exercise backup plans and begin planning for and practicing how to fight through cyber attacks taking systems offline. The starting point involves two questions. Could you put to sea with all systems running on manual, backup procedures, and networks down? If already at sea, do you know at what point you become a liability rather than a combat-capable asset?

In all cases, leaders must assume that the sailors lack sufficient training, requisite skills, and access to the right technical data to effectively respond to network outages or restore functionality. High-assurance practices like two-person control and pair programming offer immediately actionable tactics to reduce a single person's access to critical systems.[33] Finally, granting a sailor privileged access to networks or critical systems is a decision commensurate with qualifying a sailor to stand an armed watch. Just because the sailor arrives on board with a security clearance and the requisite training does not mean that leaders should blindly grant access to systems. It is incumbent on leaders to understand and continually assess a sailor's suitability for continued privileged access and act commensurate with the principle of least privilege.[34]

⊢• CONCLUSION

To understand the extent of the maritime cyber threats, one must reconceptualize a warship as a collection of networks, sensors, effectors, and people, all of which can be exploited by a determined adversary. Generating credible combat capability requires people to recognize the various threats to the networks, systems, and sailors, and how threats to those systems may reach an operational fleet via the cyber kill chain. The cyber battlefield at sea is becoming increasingly complex, but embracing the "assume breach" mindset and developing resilience will allow ships and their crews to limit the effect of adversary action and provide more enduring combat power for the nation.

NOTES

1. Gregory Slabodkin, "Software Glitches Leave Navy Smart Ship Dead in the Water," *GCN.com*, 13 July 1998, https://gcn.com/1998/07/software -glitches-leave-navy-smart-ship-dead-in-the-water/290995/.

2. Andy Greenberg, "How 30 Lines of Code Blew Up a 27-Ton Generator," *Wired*, 23 October 2020, https://www.wired.com/story/how-30-lines-of-code-blew -up-27-ton-generator/.

3. Sam LaGrone, "Navy 'Orion Hammer' Investigation into USS *John McCain* Collision Has Turned Up No Evidence of Cyber Attack," *USNI News*, 25 August 2017, https://news.usni.org/2017/08/25/navy-orion-hammer-investigation-uss -john-mccain-collision-turned-no-evidence-cyberattack.

4. U.S. Department of the Navy, *Secretary of the Navy Cybersecurity Readiness Review*, March 2019, https://www.wsj.com/public/resources/documents /CyberSecurityReview_03–2019.pdf?mod=article_inline.

5. F. Akpan et al., "Cybersecurity Challenges in the Maritime Sector," *Network* 2, no. 1 (March 2022): 123–38, https://doi.org/10.3390/NETWORK2010009.

6. "Final Report of the Commission on the Future of the United States Aerospace Industry," 2002, https://history.nasa.gov/AeroCommissionFinalReport. pdf; U.S. Department of Defense, "Department of Defense Report State of Competition within the Defense Industrial Base," 2022, https://media.defense. gov/2022/Feb/15/2002939087/-1/-1/1/STATE-OF-COMPETITION-WITHIN -THE-DEFENSE-INDUSTRIAL-BASE.PDF; R. Carril and M. Duggan, "The Impact of Industry Consolidation on Government Procurement: Evidence from Department of Defense Contracting," *Journal of Public Economics* 184 (April 2020): 104141, https://doi.org/10.1016/J.JPUBECO.2020.104141; U.S. Department of Defense, "Securing Defense-Critical Supply Chains: An Action Plan Developed in Response to President Biden's Executive Order 14017," February 2022, https:// media.defense.gov/2022/Feb/24/2002944158/-1/-1/1/DOD-EO-14017-REPORT -SECURING-DEFENSE-CRITICAL-SUPPLY-CHAINS.PDF.

7. Joseph Marks, "The Cybersecurity 202: Defense Contractors Are Yet Another Sector Highly Vulnerable to Hacking, Study Finds," *Washington Post*, 22 June 2021, https://www.washingtonpost.com/politics/2021/06/22/cybersecurity -202-defense-contractors-are-yet-another-sector-highly-vulnerable-hacking -study-finds/.

8. U.S. Cybersecurity and Infrastructure Security Agency, *Russian State-Sponsored Cyber Actors Target Cleared Defense Contractor Networks to Obtain Sensitive U.S. Defense Information and Technology*, 16 February 2022, https://www.cisa .gov/uscert/ncas/alerts/aa22–047a; Ellen Nakashima and Paul Sonne, "China Hacked a Navy Contractor and Secured a Trove of Highly Sensitive Data on

Submarine Warfare," *Washington Post*, 8 June 2018, https://www.washingtonpost
.com/world/national-security/china-hacked-a-navy-contractor-and-secured
-a-trove-of-highly-sensitive-data-on-submarine-warfare/2018/06/08/6cc396fa
-68e6–11e8-bea7-c8eb28bc52b1_story.html; U.S. Federal Bureau of Investigation,
The China Threat, https://www.fbi.gov/investigate/counterintelligence/the-china
-threat; U.S. Cybersecurity and Infrastructure Security Agency, *Chinese State-Sponsored Cyber Operations: Observed TTPs*, 20 August 2021, https://www.cisa.
gov/uscert/ncas/alerts/aa21–200b.

9. Verizon Corporation, *Data Breach Investigations Report 2022*, 2022, https://
   www.verizon.com/business/resources/reports/dbir/.

10. P. H. Meland et al., "A Retrospective Analysis of Maritime Cyber Security
    Incidents," *TransNav: The International Journal on Marine Navigation and
    Safety of Sea Transportation* 15, no. 3 (September 2021): 519–30, https://doi.org
    /10.12716/1001.15.03.04.

11. U.S. Government Accountability Office (GAO), *Weapons Systems Annual Assessment: Challenges to Fielding Capabilities Faster Persist*, GAO-22–105230, 8 June
    2022, https://www.gao.gov/products/gao-22–105230.

12. Lockheed Martin Corporation, "Cyber Kill Chain® | Lockheed Martin," https://
    www.lockheedmartin.com/en-us/capabilities/cyber/cyber-kill-chain.html.

13. Ralph Langner, "Stuxnet: Dissecting a Cyberwarfare Weapon," *IEEE Security
    and Privacy* 9, no. 3 (May 2011): 49–51, https://doi.org/10.1109/MSP.2011.67.

14. M. M. Alani, "OSI Model," *Springer Briefs in Computer Science*, no. 9783319051512
    (2014): 5–17, https://doi.org/10.1007/978–3-319–05152–9_2/FIGURES/3.

15. Open Web Application Security Project (OWASP) Foundation, "OWASP Top
    Ten," https://owasp.org/www-project-top-ten/.

16. U.S. GAO, *Weapon Systems Cybersecurity: DOD Just Beginning to Grapple with
    Scale of Vulnerabilities*, GAO-19–128, October 2018, https://www.gao.gov/assets
    /gao-19–128.pdf; U.S. GAO, *Weapon Systems Cybersecurity: Guidance Would Help
    DOD Programs Better Communicate Requirements to Contractors*, GAO-21–179,
    March 2012, https://www.gao.gov/assets/gao-21–179.pdf.

17. U.S. GAO, *Weapon Systems Cybersecurity*.

18. U.S. Department of the Navy, *Secretary of the Navy Cybersecurity Readiness
    Review*, March 2019; U.S. Department of Defense, *Securing Defense-Critical
    Supply Chains*; David Nothacker, "Supply Chain Visibility and Exception
    Management," in *Disrupting Logistics* (30 January 2021): 51–62, https://doi
    .org/10.1007/978–3-030–61093–7_5; Sevedmohsen Hosseini, Dmitry Ivanov,
    and Alexandre Dolgui, "Review of Quantitative Methods for Supply Chain
    Resilience Analysis," *Transportation Research Part E: Logistics and Transportation Review* 125 (May 2019): 285–307, https://doi.org/10.1016/j.tre.2019.03.001;

Jeffrey Engstrom, *Systems Confrontation and System Destruction Warfare: How the Chinese People's Liberation Army Seeks to Wage Modern Warfare*, RR-1709 (Santa Monica, CA: RAND Corporation, 2018), https://www.rand.org/pubs/research_reports/RR1708.html; A. Ghadge et al., "Managing Cyber Risk in Supply Chains: A Review and Research Agenda," *SSRN Electronic Journal* 25, no. 2 (July 2019): 223–40, https://doi.org/10.2139/ssrn.3426030; Joseph Robertson and Michael Riley, "The Long Hack: How China Exploited a U.S. Tech Supplier," *Bloomberg*, 12 February 2021, https://www.bloomberg.com/features/2021-supermicro/; Charles Clancy et al., *Delivery Uncompromised: Securing Critical Software Supply Chains* (MITRE Corporation, January 2021), https://www.mitre.org/sites/default/files/2021-11/prs-21-0278-deliver-uncompromised-securing-critical-software-supply-chain.pdf.

19. U.S. Department of the Navy, *Secretary of the Navy Cybersecurity Readiness Review*.

20. U.S. National Institute of Standards and Technology, *Zero Trust Architecture*, Special Publication 800–207, February 2020, https://nvlpubs.nist.gov/nistpubs/SpecialPublications/NIST.SP.800–207-draft2.pdf.

21. Bonnie Zhu, Anthony Joseph, and Shankar Sastry, "A Taxonomy of Cyber Attacks on SCADA Systems," in *2011 IEEE International Conferences on Internet of Things, and Cyber, Physical and Social Computing* (2011): 380–88, https://doi.org/10.1109/iThings/CPSCom.2011.34.

22. Greenberg; Thomas M. Chen and Saeed Abu-Nimah, "Lessons from Stuxnet," *Computer* 44, no. 4 (April 2011): 91–93, https://openaccess.city.ac.uk/id/eprint/8203/1/.

23. LaGrone; U.S. National Traffic Safety Board, *Capsizing of Roll-on/Roll-off Vehicle Carrier Golden Ray, St. Simons Sound, Brunswick River, Near Brunswick, Georgia, September 8, 2019*, Marine Accident Report NTSB/MAR-21/03, 26 August 2021, https://www.ntsb.gov/investigations/AccidentReports/Reports/MAR2103.pdf; Kit Chellel, Matthew Campbell, and K. Oanh Ha, "How the Billion-Dollar *Ever Given* Cargo Ship Got Stuck in the Suez Canal—Bloomberg," *Bloomberg*, 23 June 2021, https://www.bloomberg.com/news/features/2021-06-24/how-the-billion-dollar-ever-given-cargo-ship-got-stuck-in-the-suez-canal.

24. Chen and Abu-Nimah; Robert M. Lee, Michael J. Assante, and Tim Conway, *German Steel Mill Cyber Attack*, SANS Industry Control Systems Defense Use Case, 30 December 2014, https://assets.contentstack.io/v3/assets/blt36c2e63521272fdc/bltc79a41dbf7d1441e/607f235775873e466bcc539c/ICS-CPPE-case-Study-2-German-Steelworks_Facility.pdf; Nozomi Networks, "Executive Summary," *OT/IoT Security Report Cyber War Insights, Threats and Trends, Recommendations 2022*, August 2022, https://www.cisa.gov/uscert/sites/default/files

/ICSJWG-Archive/QNL_SEP_22/Nozomi-Networks-OT-IoT-Security-Report -ES-2022–1H_508c.pdf; Robert M. Lee, Michael J. Assante, and Tim Conway, *Analysis of the Cyber Attack on the Ukrainian Power Grid*, SANS Industry Control Systems/Energy Information Sharing and Analysis Center Defense Use Case, 18 March 2016, https://africautc.org/wp-content/uploads/2018/05/E -ISAC_SANS_Ukraine_DUC_5.pdf; Alessandro di Pinto, Younes Dragoni, and Andrea Carcano, *TRITON: The First ICS Cyber Attack on Safety Instrument Systems Understanding the Malware, Its Communications and Its OT Payload* (presented at *Black Hat USA 2018*, distributed by Nozomi Networks), 2018, https://scadahacker.com/library/Documents/Cyber_Events/Nozomi%20-%20 TRITON%20-%20The%20First%20SIS%20Cyberattack.pdf; U.S. Cybersecurity and Infrastructure Security Agency, *Chinese Gas Pipeline Intrusion Campaign, 2011 to 2013*, 21 July 2021, https://www.cisa.gov/uscert/ncas/alerts/aa21–201a; U.S. Cybersecurity and Infrastructure Security Agency, *Understanding and Mitigating Russian State-Sponsored Cyber Threats to U.S. Critical Infrastructure*, 11 January 2022, https://www.cisa.gov/uscert/ncas/alerts/aa22–011a; William Turton and Kartikay Mehrotra, "Colonial Pipeline Cyber Attack: Hackers Used Compromised Password," *Bloomberg*, 4 June 2021, https://www.bloomberg. com/news/articles/2021–06–04/hackers-breached-colonial-pipeline-using -compromised-password; Andy Greenberg, "A Hacker Tried to Poison a Florida City's Water Supply, Officials Say," *Wired*, 8 February 2021, https://www.wired .com/story/oldsmar-florida-water-utility-hack/.

25. Kim Zetter, "An Unprecedented Look at Stuxnet, the World's First Digital Weapon," *Wired*, 3 November 2014, https://www.wired.com/2014/11/countdown to-zero-day-stuxnet/.

26. Joe Payne, Mark Wojtasiak, and Jadee Hanson, *Inside Jobs: Why Insider Risk Is the Biggest Cyber Threat You Can't Ignore* (New York: Skyhorse, 2020).

27. U.S. Federal Bureau of Investigation, "The China Threat."

28. U.S. Cybersecurity and Infrastructure Security Agency, *Russian State-Sponsored Cyber Actors Target Cleared Defense Contractor Networks to Obtain Sensitive U.S. Defense Information and Technology*; U.S. Office of Personnel Management, *Cybersecurity Incidents*, n.d. (2015), https://www.opm .gov/cybersecurity/cybersecurity-incidents/; Fatima Salahdine and Naima Kaabouch, "Social Engineering Attacks: A Survey," *Future Internet 2019* 11, no. 4 (April 2019), 89, https://doi.org/10.3390/FI11040089; and U.S. Federal Bureau of Investigation, *Clearance Holders Targeted on Social Media*, n.d., https://www.fbi.gov/investigate/counterintelligence/the-china-threat /clearance-holders-targeted-on-social-media-nevernight-connection.

29. U.S. Federal Bureau of Investigation, *Clearance Holders Targeted on Social Media*; Christopher Bronk, Gabriel Collins, and Dan Wallach, *Cyber and Information Warfare in Ukraine: What Do We Know Seven Months In?* Center for Energy Studies Issue Brief, Rice University Baker Institute for Public Policy, 6 September 2022, https://www.bakerinstitute.org/research/cyber-and-information-warfare -ukraine-what-do-we-know-seven-months; "Social Media Poses a Real Threat to Military Cybersecurity," *Army Technology*, 29 June 2022, https://www.army technology.com/comment/social-media-threat-military-cybersecurity/.

30. Lavi Lazarovitz, "Deconstructing the SolarWinds Breach," *Computer Fraud & Security*, no. 6 (January 2021): 17–19, https://doi.org/10.1016/S1361–723(21)00065–8, https://doi.org/ 10.1016/S1361–723(21)00065–8.

31. The White House, "Executive Order on Improving the Nation's Cybersecurity," May 2021, https://www.whitehouse.gov/briefing-room/presidential-actions/2021/05/12 /executive-order-on-improving-the-nations-cybersecurity/.

32. Alexander Kott and Igor Linkov, "Fundamental Concepts of Cyber Resilience: Introduction and Overview," in *Cyber Resilience of Systems and Networks*, eds. Alexander Kott and Igor Linkov (Cham Springer, 2019), 1–25, http://www .springer.com/series/13439.

33. U.S. National Institutes of Standards and Technology, Cyber Security Informa-tion Center, "Glossary: Two Person Control," n.d., https://csrc.nist.gov/glossary /term/two_person_control.

34. F. B. Schneider, "Least Privilege and More," *IEEE Security and Privacy* 1, no. 5 (September 2003): 55–59, https://doi.org/10.1109/MSECP.2003.1236236.

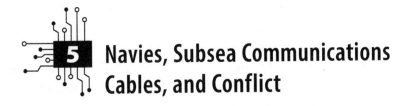 Navies, Subsea Communications Cables, and Conflict

CAMINO KAVANAGH and RAYNALD LECONTE

Global communications heavily rely on subsea communications cables, which transmit over 95 percent of all intercontinental voice and data traffic. This dependence is not simply convenience; subsea fiber-optic cables can move greater amounts of high-bandwidth data more rapidly than wireless means, and they continue to outpace satellites in cost, reliability, capacity, and latency.

Navies have played historic roles in subsea cable deployment, applying their surveying skills to sounding and mapping the seabed; their engineering and innovation edge to testing, laying, maintenance, and repair; and their intelligence edge for uses of strategic, operational, and tactical value. Additionally, they have critical roles in protecting the cables, including collaboration with commercial entities and with allies around the world to ensure the security and resilience of both privately owned and military-specific cable systems.

The past decade has seen an enormous shift in the cable industry—including in cable system technologies and architectures—and in the array of participants involved in subsea cable communications. All of this is emerging against the backdrop of an enormous shift in the international order, with the United States no longer the predominant power, a rising, assertive China, and a belligerent, resurgent Russia.

The effects of these changes are evident in activity beneath the waters and on the seabed. They are demonstrated in policy and regulatory decisions affecting cable routing, financing, and investments; and in investments in cable repair capabilities and in maritime deterrence capabilities, including for subsea monitoring and surveillance. Some of these developments may give the United States an immediate advantage, but they also risk making the systems more vulnerable. In situations of crisis and particularly during conflicts, navies will be deeply involved in defending this nationally critical cyber infrastructure.

⊢• HISTORICAL BEGINNINGS

In the mid-1850s, Great Britain extended its first successful subsea cables across the English Channel. At the same time, American financier Cyrus Field requested that the United States Naval Observatory (previously the U.S. Navy Department of Charts and Instruments) investigate whether a cable link could be laid from St. John's, Newfoundland, across the Atlantic to Valentia Island off the coast of Ireland.[1]

Field's proposal coincided with a recent survey of ocean winds and currents in the Atlantic carried out by Lt. Otway H. Berryman, USN, commanding the USS *Dolphin*, which included soundings of the ocean floor taken at intervals of thirty miles.[2] The analysis of the soundings confirmed Field's view that the seabed between Newfoundland and Ireland was ideal terrain for a cable. From that point on, the U.S. Navy played a pivotal role in the laying of the (short-lived) 1858 transatlantic cable and those that followed across the Atlantic and the Pacific. As the cables gradually stretched across the oceans, their value to power projection (along with their vulnerabilities) became increasingly evident.

Throughout the latter half of the nineteenth century, Britain, France, and Germany each sought to establish its own cable system. All efforts were entirely independent of each other and heavily subsidized by the colonial governments of the time. The projects had immense value during peacetime, connecting newly acquired colonial territories and centralizing control of diplomatic and financial affairs, and were even more so during conflict. Private companies in the United States soon followed suit, establishing a Pan-American system connecting Washington with Mexico as well as Central and South America. Their system was established with much diplomatic encouragement but with limited financial support from government.[3]

⊢• VULNERABILITY IN WAR: CUTTING CABLES

The vulnerabilities of cables, however, became more evident in conjunction with their expanding use and criticality. Terrestrial and subsea cable systems and the data transiting them were increasingly viewed as targets by belligerents. Cable tapping, sabotage, and disruption became major tactics of both regular and irregular warfare from the mid-1800s onward. The capabilities required to cut and repair cables were formally introduced into company-level military training as well as war planning by the major powers in the early 1900s.[4]

The first major international conflict to feature subsea cables was the Crimean War (1853–56). The laying of a cable three hundred nautical miles in length from Varna to Balaklava in the Black Sea and establishing its terrestrial links during a live conflict were a major feat.[5]

For the United States, the Spanish-American War of 1898 sealed the importance of subsea cables in wartime and drew attention to the "impracticality" of laying such cables by contract or having civilians operate them during conflict. It also highlighted the country's almost complete lack of preparedness for the communications aspect of the war, both in terms of ensuring connectivity with the U.S. mainland once in Cuba, and in ensuring the necessary grappling and repair capabilities for cables on the seabed. Nonetheless, under constant risk of fire, the Army's Signal Corps worked aboard a chartered ship to sever the Spanish cable section connecting Santiago and Guantánamo and to establish communications between U.S. Army operations in Cuba and the U.S. Navy in Key West, Florida, and, later, the White House war room in Washington, DC.[6] The value of these actions—along with the legal manipulation that enabled the seizure of what was a French-owned cable system (New York–Santiago via Haiti)—was inestimable to U.S. wartime efforts.

This first overseas war also brought the United States across the Pacific to the Philippines, then a Spanish colony, advancing the U.S. Army's cable laying, cutting, and sabotage capabilities and expertise. Indeed, upon defeating the Spanish fleet in the Philippines, one of the first steps taken was to refit a captured Spanish ship as the U.S. Army's first cable-laying ship. It was replaced by another after it ran aground on Corregidor Island while laying a cable.[7] These ships allowed the Army Signal Corps to lay 250 nautical miles of cables, connecting the principal islands in the Philippines and, subsequently, lay the Alaska cable connecting the northwestern coast of the continental United States (Washington State) to the southern point of the U.S. Alaskan territories.

The skills required to lay and repair the cables in hostile contexts were outlined in the U.S. Signal Corps *Handbook of Submarine Cables*, published in 1905. Its foreword noted that "rapid cable laying in time of war for friendly use, and the prompt interruption of hostile cables are recognized as military operations of primary importance . . . [essential for] successful campaigning as are telegraphic and telephonic systems for land operations."[8]

A decade later, Britain's severing of Germany's cables connecting to North America was one of the first belligerent acts of World War I, cementing the role of cable cutting in conflict.[9]

⊢• TECHNOLOGY AND DIPLOMACY

Over the same period, Germany, France, and the United States began to use diplomatic and legal means to challenge British domination of subsea cables and related supply chains. The United States, for example, tried to challenge British dominance of the cable industry, including the supply of gutta-percha, the Malay gum critical to insulating and protecting the cables.[10]

The first cable-related governance regimes had already started to emerge in Europe in the late 1800s. Governments utilized these codifying efforts to introduce common standards and rules on questions of interoperability and tariffs and to end other states' dominance of the data flowing through the cables, particularly news and stock prices. As a result, those strategic interests thwarted efforts to protect the telegraphic cable infrastructure from belligerent state action (such as cable cutting) in the negotiations leading to the 1884 Convention for the Protection of Submarine Telegraphs and in the 1907 Hague Convention negotiations.[11]

The centrality of subsea cables to the post–World War I peace settlement negotiations in Paris confirmed their strategic and geopolitical value. The peace treaty stipulated that neither Germany nor German nationals could maintain ownership of the submarine cables (or portions thereof).[12]

At the same time, the lengthy high-level debates over the fate of Germany's cables confirmed the legitimacy of cable cutting as a tactic of war. They also ensured that extant territorial practices would not be extended to information technologies. Instead, the growing global infrastructure would be viewed as a "common good" for which more equitable arrangements would need to be developed. (See chapter by Klimburg and Wells on the distinction between a common good versus a resource.) The United States was largely behind these proposals, its motives strongly influenced by strategic and geopolitical interests, particularly postwar territorial arrangements in the Pacific that favored Japan and placed U.S. strategic communications links in the Pacific at risk.[13]

Cable sabotage and tapping continued to play an important role in both the interwar years and during World War II. One of the first moves of that war was the Allies' cutting of German cables connecting Emden to Lisbon and New York via the Azores. French cable stations infiltrated by Germany were closed.[14] Telegraphic communications were gradually surpassed by radio, although their value for interception and surveillance persisted into the Cold War, as did concerns of their possible sabotage. These concerns were seldom met with calls for international legal restraints, however.[15]

⊢ CABLES FOR INTELLIGENCE AND SURVEILLANCE

By the mid-1900s single-wire cables were replaced with coaxial cables, many of which were passed through repeaters to extend their reach. By this time, naval submarine capabilities had significantly advanced, including for subsea interception and surveillance purposes. In the late 1950s the Office for Naval Research sought the support of AT&T to establish a deep-sea surveillance system to detect and track Soviet submarine systems.[16]

This sound surveillance system (SOSUS) established listening posts at strategic points in the North Atlantic by stringing hydrophones along lengths of the subsea communications cables on the seabed.[17] The hydrophones were, in turn, connected by cables to terrestrial naval operational processing facilities. The system was viewed as "a key, long-range early warning asset for protecting the United States against the threat of Soviet ballistic missile submarines . . .

and also provided vital cueing information for tactical, deep-ocean anti-submarine warfare."[18] The U.S. Navy operated thirty such undersea surveillance sites during the Cold War.[19] A Soviet submarine reportedly sabotaged the cables connecting one of the undersea listening posts in the 1970s.[20]

Little else was publicly revealed about the systems until it was discovered that a U.S. National Security Agency employee had been selling information on an operation code-named Ivy Bells to the KGB. Implemented in the 1970s, the operation involved placing hydrophones to tap into a Soviet undersea cable running parallel to the Kuril Islands off Russia and serving as a critical communications link between two major Soviet naval bases.[21] Although the tapping of Soviet military cables was not directly connected to the SOSUS system, information on SOSUS itself leaked out.[22]

At around the same time that the U.S. underwater surveillance system was being established, Britain turned its attention to the potential targeting of submarine cables by the Soviet Union as well as landlines and radio circuits critical to the North Atlantic Treaty Organization (NATO) Allies' strategic communications.[23] There was evidence that the Soviet Union was investing in identifying them and that it had the capabilities to conduct sabotage and electronic countermeasures.[24]

⊢• CONTEMPORARY DEVELOPMENTS

In light of "increasingly worrisome submarine activity on the part of potential adversaries," the United States continues to make enormous efforts to enhance the Navy's undersea surveillance capabilities, establishing SOSUS-like networks to monitor Chinese submarine activity in the East and South China Seas, as well as upgrading its fixed and other maritime surveillance systems.[25]

An indication of the continued value of subsea cables for intelligence-gathering purposes in the post–Cold War era was the repurposing of the USS *Jimmy Carter* to "carry crews of technicians to the bottom of the sea so they could tap fiber optic lines," reportedly using "a special floodable chamber to perform such operations" at a cable system's "regeneration points," the points where the signal passing through the fibers is amplified and pushed forward.[26] Other NATO members are also investing in similar capabilities.[27]

Tapping cables on land, however, has proved much easier, as revealed in 2013, and news of which continues to emerge.[28]

Other naval powers, too, have invested in subsea surveillance and intelligence-gathering capabilities. For instance, the *Yantar*, officially a Russian oceanographic research vessel, is reportedly equipped with manned and unmanned deep-sea submersibles capable of operating at a depth of six thousand meters, and reportedly has the capabilities to "connect to top-secret communications cables."[29] Russia has also invested significantly in upgrading its submarines for advanced surveillance capabilities and to facilitate its clandestine cable activities.[30] For its part, the Chinese government and the People's Liberation Army have been advancing research and development across a range of relevant areas, including in optical transmission and sensing technologies and underwater optical networks, and advancing efforts to build a maritime surveillance system in the South China Sea.[31]

The Russian Federation's invasion of Ukraine witnessed a spike in suspicious activity relevant to subsea cables and involving Russian vessels such as the *Yantar* in the territorial waters or exclusive economic zones of other nation-states.[32] The 2022 Nord Stream explosions as well as the cutting of cables in the Norwegian Sea in October 2023 and in the Baltic Sea in November 2024 have accelerated concerns about the security and resilience of subsea communications cables (as well as energy pipelines and other underwater infrastructure), especially considering the limited available repair capabilities.[33]

The global number of cable repair ships remains low, with operations often constrained by resource, contractual, and regulatory issues. It can take one to three weeks to repair a single major cable break if vessel availability, cable supplies, weather, and vessel access to the relevant waters all come together rapidly. While U.S. repair capabilities have increased, including through the U.S. Cable Security Fleet established in 2021, other challenges affecting the industry are daunting.[34] These include ensuring a steady and secure supply of cable system components and spare parts and guaranteeing the physical and cyber security of depots, repair facilities, and other terrestrial infrastructure, as well as that of automated or remote network management systems—all of which increase complexity and consequences during crisis and conflict.

⊢• STATE OF THE CABLE INFRASTRUCTURE

Today, over 530 fiber-optic subsea cable communications systems are operational or planned. This number does not include dedicated military cables. Those already operational add up to 1.4 million kilometers of cable lying on the seabed. Some recent builds stretch as far as 45,000 kilometers, and others are projected to transmit data at a rate of 540 terabytes per second.

Private companies still own and operate most of the cable systems and maintenance and repair ships. In the past, most commercial cable projects followed a consortium model, involving carriers and suppliers from a handful of countries. This ownership pattern is changing, bringing an end to the era of a telecommunications monopoly over subsea cable systems. Hyperscalers and over-the-top media services such as Google, Meta, Microsoft, and Amazon are building their own cable systems to meet capacity demands, with significant impact on the industry. In addition, a number of independent infrastructure providers have also emerged and are taking on a growing number of cable projects. Chinese companies, too, rapidly expanded into the cable industry in the decade leading to 2019, from manufacturing and supply of core components to cable laying, maintenance, and repair (although maintenance and repair are largely constrained to Asian waters).[35]

Today's cables are made up of multiple pairs of optical fibers, roughly the diameter of a human hair, embedded in cable systems with multiple exploitable points. The fibers are covered in silicone gel and sheathed in varying layers of plastic, steel wiring, and copper. To shield the cable against potential external aggression, additional layers of steel wire—the thickness of which is determined by sea depth and proximity to commercial marine activity—are applied to the outside. Burial of the cables is more common closer to shore, where there tends to be more activity. Optical receivers (still referred to as repeaters) are laid approximately every one hundred kilometers. The cables reach shore at a beach manhole and from there are channeled to a cable landing station, from which the data is transited to a point of presence and on to relevant facilities. In newer "open" builds, the cables can be run directly to data centers. Remote network management systems are used to control operations.

⊢• FUTURE OF CABLE SECURITY

Barring major conflict, the reliability of commercial subsea cables, engineered in accordance with the "five nines standard" (available 99.999 percent of the time), remains high. While faults do occur, the rate has not increased with the growth and capacity extension of the cables. Organizations such as the International Cable Protection Committee currently consider that there is enough diversity in the international submarine cable network to maintain a secure level of protection.

Risk management and mitigation are reportedly introduced at every step of the design, development, deployment, and operation of subsea cable systems, according to the commercial owners of cables. Innovations in optical transmission technologies, monitoring and sensing techniques, and machine learning are also said to be allowing for greater prevention and detection of potential threats or interference with the fibers and related submerged and terrestrial components.[36] Advances such as distributed acoustic sensing for line and component monitoring may also provide an additional way to detect suspicious activity on or around the cables.[37]

The physical and cyber security of cable systems' land infrastructure and components is also being hardened, including through advanced encryption of data transiting cables and by applying zero-trust security controls and technologies across other core elements (identity, end points, apps, infrastructure, and networks).[38] So, too, is the cybersecurity of remote network management systems and related software since vulnerabilities were publicly reported a decade ago.[39] There is also more awareness of critical nodes such as internet exchange points and data centers, the vulnerabilities of which were brought to light in recent years.[40] Navy systems are surely applying many of these same risk management approaches, not least since they also rely on commercial hardware, software, and contractors for all aspects of cable system development and operations.

Complementing these efforts is a visible increase in maritime situational awareness and broader maritime deterrence capabilities. This includes patrols and exercises (often with NATO and other partners) in relevant waters above, on, and below the surface using a range of technologies and capabilities, as well as new coordination structures such as NATO's recently announced Undersea Infrastructure Coordination Cell and its Maritime Center for the Security of Critical Undersea Infrastructure.[41] It also includes investments in upgrading maritime vessels and underwater surveillance technologies and systems, as well as the Navy's investment in new capabilities for laying and repairing Department of Defense–specific cables that connect to the global information grid.[42]

The United States is also using its policy and regulatory power, as well as its diplomatic clout, to influence cable routing and investment decisions. Many of these are aimed at curbing the perceived risks to U.S. national security of Chinese involvement in the laying of commercial cables, notably with regard to cables landing or linking to the U.S. mainland or to any of the U.S.-controlled "strategic switching points" in the Pacific, thus limiting China's access to submarine cables and related land infrastructure for surveillance, espionage, and other such purposes.[43]

Will these efforts make subsea cables more resilient to intentional damage and to the surveillance and espionage efforts of other nation-states? Perhaps, in peacetime. History, however, is a great mirror for reflecting on the advantages of and risks to these systems—notably when considered in conjunction with vulnerabilities (cyber, physical, electromagnetic) in other critical communications systems—and illuminates what this, in turn, means for naval operations in crisis and conflict.

NOTES

1. Ainissa Ramirez, "A Wire across the Ocean," *American Scientist* 103, no. 3 (May–June 2015): 180, https://www.americanscientist.org/article/a-wire-across-the-ocean.
2. See Daniel R. Headrick, *The Invisible Weapon: Telecommunications and International Politics, 1851–1945* (Oxford: Oxford University Press, 1991).
3. See report of Col. James Allen, chief signals officer, Army of Porto Rico (Puerto Rico), *Of the Operations of the Signal Corps on the South Coast of Cuba*, Headquarters of the Army in the Field, Ponce, Porto Rico, 1 September 1898, https://atlantic-cable.com/Cables/1888Santiago-Guantanamo/index.htm.
4. "From Australia to Zimmermann: A Brief History of Cable Telegraphy during World War One," Oxford University Educational Resources, Innovation-in-Combat-educational-resources-telegraph-cable-draft-1.pdf.

5. Walter Peterson, "The Queen's Messenger: An Underwater Cable to Balaclava," *History of the Atlantic Cable and Undersea Communications*, April 2008, https://atlantic-cable.com/Cables/1855Crimea/.

6. Report of Col. Allen.

7. Bill Glover, "CS *Hooker*," *History of the Atlantic Cable and Undersea Communications*, 23 August 2015, https://atlantic-cable.com/Cableships/Hooker/index.htm.

8. Brig. Gen. A. W. Greely, chief signal officer, U.S. Army Signal Corps, foreword to *Handbook of Submarine Cables* (Washington, DC: Government Printing Office, 1905, republished 2012 by Forgotten Books).

9. Gordon Corera, "How Britain Pioneered Cable Cutting in World War One," *BBC*, 15 December 2018, https://www.bbc.com/news/world-europe-42367551.

10. See Helen Godfrey, *Submarine Telegraphy and the Hunt for Gutta Percha* (Leiden: Brill, 2018).

11. Camino Kavanagh, *Wading Murky Waters: Subsea Communications Cables and Responsible State Behaviour* (Geneva: United Nations Institute for Disarmament Research, 2023), 20, https://unidir.org/publication/wading-murky-waters-subsea-communications-cables-and-responsible-state-behaviour/.

12. Treaty of Versailles Article 244 and Annex VII. In addition, the value of privately owned cables (or portions of them) was credited to Germany in the reparation account.

13. George H. Blakeslee, "Japan's New Island Possessions in the Pacific: History and Present Status," *The Journal of International Relations* 12, no. 2 (October 1921): 185–87.

14. Association des Amis des Cables sous Marins, *Bulletin #11*, January 1999, https://www.cablesm.fr/bulletins (in French).

15. Kavanagh, 27–28.

16. Tara Davenport, "Submarine Cables, Cybersecurity, and International Law: An Intersectional Analysis," *Catholic University Journal of Law and Technology* 21 (December 2015): 94.

17. Davenport.

18. "Sound Surveillance System (SOSUS): The Fish Hook that Catches Chinese Submarines," *Global Defense Corp*, 15 January 2020, https://www.globaldefensecorp.com/2020/01/15/sound-surveillance-system-sosus-the-fish-hook-that-catches-chinese-submarines/.

19. Steven Stashwick, "U.S. Navy Upgrading Undersea Sub-Detecting Sensor Network," *The Diplomat*, 4 November 2014, https://thediplomat.com/2016/11/us-navy-upgrading-undersea-sub-detecting-sensor-network/.

20. Laurence Peter, "What Makes Russia's New Spy Ship *Yantar* Special," *BBC*, 3 January 2018, https://www.bbc.com/news/world-europe-42543712.

21. For a concise discussion of Ivy Bells, see Matthew Carle, "The Mission behind Ivy Bells and How It Was Discovered," *Military.com*, 7 February 2017, https://www.military.com/history/operation-ivy-bells.html.

22. Perhaps the most detailed revelation of previously classified information on covert submarine operations, including Ivy Bells, is Sherry Sontag and Christopher Drew, *Blind Man's Bluff: The Untold Story of American Submarine Espionage* (New York: Public Affairs, 1998),

23. Michael Goodman and Huw Dylan, "British Intelligence and the Fear of a Soviet Attack on Allied Communications," *Cryptologia* 40, no. 1 (January 2016): 15–32.

24. Goodman and Dylan, 19.

25. Joseph Trevithick, "The Navy Wants a Rapidly Deployable Version of Its Cold War Era Submarine Monitoring Network," *The War Zone/The Drive*, 21 February 2020, https://www.thedrive.com/the-war-zone/32319/the-navy-wants-a-containerized-sub-tracking-sonar-that-can-be-left-at-sea-for-long-periods.

26. Sebastien Roblin, "Russian Spy Submarines Are Tampering with Undersea Cables That Make the Internet Work. Should We Be Worried?" *The National Interest*, 18 February 2018, https://nationalinterest.org/blog/buzz/russian-spy-submarines-are-tampering-undersea-cables-make-internet-work-should-we-be; Olga Khazam, "The Creepy, Long-Standing Practice of Undersea Cable Tapping," *The Atlantic*, 16 July 2013, https://www.theatlantic.com/international/archive/2013/07/the-creepy-long-standing-practice-of-undersea-cable-tapping/277855/; Associated Press, "New Nuclear Sub Is Said to Have Special Eavesdropping Ability," *New York Times*, 20 February 2005, https://www.nytimes.com/2005/02/20/politics/new-nuclear-sub-is-said-to-have-special-eavesdropping-ability.html.

27. U.K. Ministry of Defense, "First of Two MROS Ships Arrives in the UK," *Naval News*, 19 January 2023, https://www.navalnews.com/naval-news/2023/01/first-of-two-mros-ships-arrives-in-the-uk/. France, too, is making such investments, some of which were hinted at in its Seabed Warfare Strategy launched in February 2022. See Xavier Vavasseur, "France Unveils New Seabed Warfare Strategy," *Naval News*, 16 February 2022, https://www.navalnews.com/naval-news/2022/02/france-unveils-new-seabed-warfare-strategy/.

28. Khazam; Sebastian Moss, "Danish Whistleblower Details NSA Collaboration, Submarine Cable Spying, Surveillance Data Center," *DataCenterDynamics*, 18 November 2020, https://www.datacenterdynamics.com/en/news/danish-whistleblower-details-nsa-collaboration-submarine-cable-spying-surveillance-data-center/.

29. Alexander Andrev, "The Special Mission Ship 'Yantar' Entered the Mediterranean Sea," Federal Assembly of the Russian Federation, 8 October 2017, https://www.pnp.ru/politics/korabl-specnaznacheniya-yantar-voshyol-v-sredizemnoe-more.

html. See also H. I. Sutton, "Yantar: Russian Ship Loitering Near Undersea Cables," *Covert Shores*, 13 September 2017, http://www.hisutton.com/Yantar.html.

30. Sean Ali et al., *The Rise of Russia's Military Robotics* (Tallinn: International Centre for Defence and Security, 2021); Heinrich Lange et al., *To the Seas Again: Maritime Defence and Deterrence in the Baltic Region* (Tallinn: International Centre for Defence and Security, 2019); Henrick Beckvard, ed., *Strategic Importance of, and Dependence on, Undersea Cables*, NATO Cooperative Cyber Defence Centre of Excellence, 2019, 2–3, https://www.ccdcoe.org/uploads/2019/11/Undersea-cables -Final-NOV-2019.pdf; Garrett Hinck, "Evaluating the Russian Threat to Undersea Cables," *Lawfare*, 5 March 2018, https://www.lawfaremedia.org/article/evaluating-russian-threat-undersea-cables.

31. Catherine Wong, "'Underwater Great Wall': Chinese Firm Proposes Building Network of Submarine Detectors to Boost Nation's Defence," *South China Morning Post*, 19 May 2016, https://www.scmp.com/news/china/diplomacy-defence /article/1947212/underwater-great-wall-chinese-firm-proposes-building; Lane Burdette, "Leveraging Submarine Cables for Political Gain: U.S. Responses to Chinese Strategy," *Journal of Public and International Affairs*, 5 May 2021, https://jpia.princeton.edu/news/leveraging-submarine-cables-political-gain-us -responses-chinese-strategy; Huong Le Thu and Bart Hogeveen, *UK, Australia, and ASEAN Cooperation for Safer Seas*, Australian Strategic Policy Institute, 2022, https://www.aspi.org.au/report/uk-australia-and-asean-cooperation -safer-seas; "What Lies Beneath: Chinese Surveys in the Maritime Sea," Asia Maritime Transparency Initiative, 1 March 2022, https://amti.csis.org/what -lies-beneath-chinese-surveys-in-the-south-china-sea/; James Griffiths, "Beijing Plans Underwater Observation System in South China Sea," *CNN*, 30 May 2017, https://www.cnn.com/2017/05/29/asia/south-china-sea-underwater-observation -system/index.html.

32. U.S. Office of the Director of National Intelligence, *Annual Threat Assessment of the U.S. Intelligence Community*, February 2022, https://www.dni.gov/index.php /newsroom/reports-publications/reports-publications-2022/3597–2022-annual-threat-assessment-of-the-u-s-intelligence-community; Sebastien Seibt, "Threat Looms of Russian Attack on Undersea Cables to Shut Down West's Internet," *France24*, 23 March 2022, https://www.france24.com/en/europe/20220323-threat -looms-of-russian-attack-on-undersea-cables-to-shut-down-west-s-internet; "UK Military Chief Warns of Russian Threat to Vital Undersea Cables," *The Guardian*, 10 January 2022, https://www.theguardian.com/uk-news/2022/jan/08/uk -military-chief-warns-of-russian-threat-to-vital-undersea-cables; Rishi Sunak, *Undersea Cables: Indispensable, Insecure* (London: Policy Exchange, November 2017),

https://policyexchange.org.uk/wp-content/uploads/2017/11/Undersea-Cables
.pdf. Note that the claim in the Sunak report relating to the Kerch Strait cable
was fact-checked and rebuffed by DataCenterDynamics. See Sebastian Moss,
"Fact Check: Russia Did Not Cut Submarine Cable When It Invaded Crimea,"
DataCenterDynamics, 3 February 2022, https://www.datacenterdynamics.com/en
/news/fact-check-russia-did-not-cut-submarine-cable-when-it-invaded-crimea/.

33. Atle Staalesen, "'Human Activity' behind Svalbard Cable Disruption," *The Barents
Observer*, 11 February 2022, https://thebarentsobserver.com/en/security/2022/02
/unknown-human-activity-behind-svalbard-cable-disruption; European Commission, "Statement by President von der Leyen on the Investigation into the
Damaged Gas Pipeline and Data Cable between Finland and Estonia," 10 October
2023, https://ec.europa.eu/commission/presscorner/detail/en/statement_23_4888;
Ministry of Defence, Sweden, "Damaged Telecommunications Cable between Sweden and Estonia," 19 October 2023, https://www.government.se/articles/2023/10
/damaged-telecommunications-cable-between-sweden-and-estonia/.

34. In 2019 the U.S. National Defense Authorization Act for Fiscal Year 2020 (Public
Law No. 116–92 [12/20/2019]) provided for the establishment of a Cable Security
Fleet (Sec. 3521). It is now part of 46 U.S. Code Chapter 532: Cable Security
Fleet, https://uscode.house.gov/view.xhtml?path=/prelim@title46/subtitle5
/partC/chapter532&edition=prelim. For a discussion on challenges relevant
to operationalizing the fleet, see Douglass R. Burnett, "Repairing Submarine
Cables Is a Wartime Necessity," U.S. Naval Institute *Proceedings* 148, no. 10
(October 2022): 38–43, https://www.usni.org/magazines/proceedings/2022
/october/repairing-submarine-cables-wartime-necessity.

35. Kavanagh; Hilary McGeachy, "The Changing Strategic Significance of Submarine
Cables: Old Technology, New Concerns," *Australian Journal of International
Affairs* 76, no. 2 (March 2022): 161–77, https://www.tandfonline.com/doi/full
/10.1080/10357718.2022.2051427; Matthew P. Goodman and Matthew Wayland,
Securing Asia's Subsea Network: U.S. Interests and Strategic Options (Wash-
ington, DC: Center for Strategic and International Studies Briefs, April 2022),
https://csis-website-prod.s3.amazonaws.com/s3fs-public/publication/220405_
Goodman_SecuringAsia_SubseaNetwork_0.pdf.

36. M. Mazur et al., "Transoceanic Phase and Polarization Fiber Sensing Using
Real-Time Coherent Transceiver," *2022 Optical Fiber Communications Conference
and Exhibition,* San Diego, CA, 2022, 1–3.

37. The automatic identification system (AIS) was never designed as a tracking
tool, nor was it created as a security or risk solution. See "AIS Spoofing: New
Technologies for New Threats," Windward, 4 December 2022, https://windward
.ai/blog/ais-spoofing-new-technologies-for-new-threats/; Andrej Androjna et al.,

"AIS Data Vulnerability Indicated by a Spoofing Case-Study," *Applied Sciences* 11, no. 11 (May 2021): 5015, https://doi.org/10.3390/app11115015.

38. Microsoft, "Guiding Principles of Zero Trust," 14 June 2023, https://learn.microsoft.com/en-us/security/zero-trust/zero-trust-overview; Microsoft, "Submarine Cables Require Improved International Protections," February 2023 (now unavailable).

39. Michael Sechrist, *New Threats, Old Technology: Vulnerabilities in Undersea Communications Cable Network Management Systems* (Cambridge, MA: Harvard Kennedy School, 2012), https://www.belfercenter.org/sites/default/files/legacy/files/sechrist-dp-2012-03-march-5-2012-final.pdf.

40. Yuval Shavitt and Chris C. Demchak, "Unlearned Lessons from the First Cybered Conflict Decade—BGP Hijacks Continue," *Cyber Defense Review* 7, no. 1 (Winter 2022): 193–205, https://cyberdefensereview.army.mil/Portals/6/Documents/2022_winter/20_Shavitt_Demchak_CDR_V7N1_WINTER%20 2022.pdf.

41. The center will cover all nature of undersea infrastructure, not just communications. See "NATO Stands Up Undersea Infrastructure Coordination Cell," North Atlantic Treaty Organization (NATO), 15 January 2023, https://www.nato.int/cps/en/natohq/news_211919.htm. This follows the earlier announcement of a joint European Union (EU)–NATO taskforce: "NATO and the EU Set Up Taskforce on Resilience and Critical Infrastructure," NATO, 11 January 2023, https://www.nato.int/cps/en/natohq/news_210611.htm.

42. Kelly Agee, "Baltimore Firm Wins $39 Million Navy Contract for Undersea Cable Work," *Stars and Stripes*, 28 January 2022, https://www.stripes.com/theaters/asia_pacific/2022-01-28/transoceanic-cable-navy-contract-defense-department-4441296.html.

43. These are American Samoa, Guam, and Hawai'i. See Geoffrey L. Irving, "Leaning on the Big Switch in the Pacific: Why the United States Dominates Pacific Telecom Infrastructure," Center for International Maritime Security, 1 February 2023, https://cimsec.org/leaning-on-the-big-switch-in-the-pacific-why-the-united-states-dominates-pacific-telecom-infrastructure/.

6 Global Agreements, Cyber, and the Sea

ALEXANDER KLIMBURG and LINTON WELLS II

O f all the domains of human action, the sea has been the most dynamic in terms of its relationship with international law and governance. The beginning of international law is often dated to the discussions of sovereignty and territorial waters by Hugo Grotius and his contemporaries that predated the vaunted Peace of Westphalia of 1648. Similar to the fashion in which the treaties of Westphalia defined state sovereignty—and were influenced by thinking on naval matters—modern-day treaties and the evolving international law on cyber can benefit from the sea as well.[1] As both academic literature and personal experience have shown, international naval agreements played a marked role in the de-escalation of tensions during the Cold War.[2]

Given that geopolitical tensions today are comparable in many ways to Cold War levels, it is urgent that we closely consider the naval lessons about the power of norms—even if often neglected—of nonbinding military-to-military agreements, and of a "commons-based" global strategy. Navies have, in essence, developed and demonstrated in use in the past all the tools needed today for cyber policymaking nationally and globally and for deterring future cyber warfare.

WHY APPLY MARITIME LEGAL AND REGULATORY APPROACHES TO CYBER ISSUES?

Maritime legal and regulatory approaches are a potentially excellent fit for examining cyber issues on several grounds. First, they traditionally have evolved from practical technical procedures to specific policy concepts. Second, they have applied local and regional solutions to general problems. Third, maritime activities typically occur in complex shared sovereignty/ domains where governments are not the only actors.

Naval experiences have been applied to both bilateral and multilateral fora to help evolve regional practices into politically binding arrangements that might eventually become legally binding. They have been used both as confidence-building measures and to reduce the likelihood of escalation. The naval experience demonstrates that norms and procedures can alter common practice leading to new policy, and the lessons learned could apply to cyber. Admittedly, the analogies are not exact—the pace of technological change in cyber is much more rapid than at sea, and the major participants today have fundamentally different views of the desired end state. But the similarities are worth investigation.

EVOLUTION OF MARITIME TREATIES AND REGULATIONS

Maritime treaties and regulations have been refined through the centuries since Grotius outlined his *Mare Liberum* (Freedom of the Seas) in 1608. The development of the law of the sea is intimately tied to three principles— freedom, sovereignty, and a commons or shared sovereignty—in particular, what later become known as the "common heritage of mankind." A crucial development stage before reaching the level of legally binding law are so-called norms, sometimes defined as "soft law" and representing what is known as accepted practice or even "rules of the road."[3] The development of the 1972 Convention on the International Regulations for Preventing Collisions at Sea (COLREGs) is one such example of how norms can proceed to political agreements and final legally binding treaties.[4]

The current version of the COLREGs was introduced by the International Maritime Organization in 1972 and was adopted in 1977. It is effectively a handbook on accepted maritime navigation behavior, stipulating forty-one common "rules of the road." The COLREGs themselves evolved over many years, adapting from informal sailing ship–focused national and regional rules to steamship-focused acts of the U.S. Congress and the British Parliament in the 1830s and 1840s, to more international discussion in the 1960s.[5] COLREGs represented an important reference point for the Third United Nations Convention on the Law of the Sea (UNCLOS III).

UNCLOS III is the most complete international agreement on the law of the sea. It was the result of "the longest, largest, and most complex formal negotiation ever attempted."[6] After preparations between 1966 and 1972, the convention took place between 1973 and 1982 and was opened for signature on 10 December 1982. Including UNCLOS I, which convened in 1958, and UNCLOS II in 1960, it represented fundamental transformations in thinking in diverse areas ranging from territorial seas to resource rights to dispute resolution.[7] A sweeping reinterpretation of the Grotian systems of ocean law, it incorporated or drew on a number of regional agreements and operational standards. This included military-to-military agreements, some of which were arguably the most important attempts to draft commonly accepted norms in otherwise unregulated space.

⊢• EFFECTS OF NAVAL OPERATIONAL PRACTICES

For many years, navies have combined legal frameworks with operational practices to develop agreements such as the bilateral U.S.-Soviet Incidents at Sea (INCSEA) agreement and the multinational Code for Unplanned Encounters at Sea (CUES) in the Western Pacific. While not legally binding, and while not always successful, overall these approaches have been useful in reducing the likelihood of accidental escalation stemming from maritime disputes.[8]

The INCSEA agreement, signed in 1972, was a breakthrough in military-to-military (actually navy-to-navy) agreements and reduced the number of incidents at sea resulting from close—usually deliberate—encounters between Soviet and North Atlantic Treaty Organization ships and aircraft, primarily those of the United States.[9] Already during the Cuban Missile Crisis of 1962, it became apparent to both navies that an accident—such as a collision or an accidental weapons launch—might actually precipitate the outbreak of conflict. INCSEA provided a set of norms to which both navies adhered, including stand-off distances that vessels were to maintain during encounters as well as communication practices. It is widely considered one of the most successful confidence-building measures in the maritime domain.

The maritime experience points to the crucial importance of having an agreed document such as INCSEA that specifies permissible behavior as a starting point. Lacking such a foundation, previous attempts to formulate operational agreements for communication on international cyber security issues have often floundered from the outset at the practical "points of contact" stage—that is, agreeing on which government official would be responsible for communicating with other governments on specific incidents.[10] As challenging as determining the basic points of contact question can be, agreeing on which topics could be open for discussion is even harder.

The evolution of the INCSEA agreement and its articles offers possible applicability in cyberspace.[11] For example, INCSEA's Article II invokes the predecessor of COLREGs as the basic rules of the road. This wording has been applied to the collection of cyber norms drafted by the 2015 Report of the United Nations Group of Governmental Experts on Developments in the Field of Information and Telecommunications in the Context of International Security (UN GGE). The UN GGE cyber norms have the unique distinction of having been endorsed by the UN General Assembly and are therefore considered politically binding.[12]

Similarly, CUES may offer some practical guidance for cyber norm and agreement creation. CUES is a nonbinding Australian initiative based on COLREGs to ensure that navy ships and aircraft follow the rules of the road when they encounter each other.[13] The most recent CUES was concluded in April 2014 at the Western Pacific Naval Symposium in Qingdao after more than a decade of development. While it has the potential to be effective as an incident avoidance mechanism and therefore has some cyber applicability, it is not as comprehensive or as mutually observed as was INCSEA.

Less successful has been the U.S.-China military maritime consultative agreement (MMCA) that was signed in 1998 "to facilitate consultations . . . for the purpose of promoting common understandings regarding activities undertaken by their respective maritime and air forces." The MMCA largely has not been met with comparable enthusiasm in execution.[14] One notable omission in the 1998 agreement is any mention of COLREGs and agreed rules of the road.

A general pattern that may be inferred from these three examples is that political agreements that reference commonly agreed norms or rules of the road may be more likely to succeed than those that do not. This pattern suggests that the eleven UN GGE cyber norms could form a basis of a future political agreement that avoids the potential trap of a legally binding agreement where one side may be much more inclined to adhere to it than the other. Treating the UN GGE norms as akin to COLREGs may therefore prove to be a key to success in building confidence in cyberspace.

⊢• SOVEREIGNTY, GLOBAL PUBLIC GOODS, AND GLOBAL PUBLIC RESOURCES

Sovereignty in cyberspace is unclear. As Vice Adm. T. J. White, USN (Ret.), points out, "Sovereignty always has been contentious . . . but perhaps not always for a common reason."[15] For the last three centuries, charts and maps have been mostly in common agreement between states because they depict observable phenomena (mountain ranges, coastlines, etc.). Sailors can locate where they are based on navigational coordinates. However, there are no particular, permanent, observable locations for information traveling via the internet. Identifying the location of actors in cyberspace is seldom possible to the degree that a naval actor's physical location can be determined. Ascertaining their real identity is often even harder. To a degree, much like espionage, many of the actors would like it to stay that way.

Unlike purely terrestrial regimes, maritime activities can take place under several different types of sovereign regimes—from inland waters to territorial seas, to exclusive economic zones, to the high seas.[16] The boundaries among these regimes are geographically based and hence observable. In cyberspace, different levels of assumed sovereignty have in practice been observed. Concepts such as "active cyber defense" and "hunt forward operations" have been sketched out in direct topologies, where there are notable operational differences between "blue space" (national or governmental networks), "green space" (allied networks), "red space" (adversary networks), and "gray space" (undetermined networks).[17]

Unfortunately, in this model, gray space can be allocated to either a subordinate or even an irrelevant role, a dangerous assumption as it effectively can include the entirety of the internet outside of the zone of the belligerents. Worse, some of the gray networks might even be crucial to the operation of the internet as a whole. In that, there is a meaningful parallel to be drawn to the concept of the high seas as a "common" and some sort of public good—the protection of which should be of equal interest not only to all belligerents, but especially to the uninvolved neutrals. Unsurprisingly, the concept of both the commons and associated notions of global public good and global public resources is firmly rooted in the law of the sea, and in particular in UNCLOS III.

The differences between a global public good (such as clean air) and a global public resource (such as the mineral riches of the deep seabed) are important in this context. Global public *goods* are "non-rivalrous" ("my use does not limit your use") and are regulated by international norms and agreements between nations or simply self-enforced by the community. Global public *resources*, in contrast, are potentially "rivalrous" ("my use *can* limit your use") and thus preferably regulated centrally by a distribution agency. The International Seabed Authority in Kingston, Jamaica, was set up specifically to manage deep-sea resource extraction under UNCLOS III.[18]

The common heritage of mankind (CHM) concept is one of the three basic principles of UNCLOS and explicitly addresses a global public resource (the deep seabed). However, the CHM principle has proven to be relatively malleable and has been applied to the idea of global public goods as well as global public resources. This dual usage was evident in later attempts to bring the CHM into the Antarctic Treaty System, as well as its adoption within the Moon Treaty (1979).[19] Most recently, the UN High Seas Treaty (2023) explicitly recognized the entire high seas as part of the CHM, further pushing the definition of CHM away from a global public resource to that of a global public good.

In cyber terms, the potential implications of viewing (parts of) the internet as a global public resource or global public good are stark. Defining the internet as a public good aligns with the argument that the current multi-stakeholder model for managing internet resources is sufficient, with non-state bodies like the Internet Corporation for Assigned Names and Numbers and the Internet Engineering Task Force, as well as the many private companies, in the lead.[20] In contrast, a public resource definition strengthens the argument that a single intergovernmental organization should be responsible for managing internet resources. Therefore, the United States and the like-minded group of liberal democracies have largely argued for the former, while Russia and China have supported the latter interpretation.

One cyber version of a global public good has been identified as the "public core of the global internet." Much of the norm-setting for this concept was undertaken by a multi-stakeholder initiative—the Global Commission on the Stability of Cyberspace (GCSC).[21] The GCSC defined the public core of the internet as being those components that were crucial to the integrity and availability of the global internet as a whole, including the regular function of the "packet routing and forwarding, naming and numbering systems, the cryptographic mechanisms of security and identity, and physical transmission media."[22]

The GCSC called on all actors to refrain from interfering in the public core.[23] This concept was first advocated by the Netherlands and France, but later was taken up by many other democratic nations that have signed the "Paris Call for Trust and Security in Cyberspace," where the protection of the public core is a key principle.[24] It has also entered legislation in the European Union Cyber Security Act, and parts of the concept were adopted in the 2021 UN Open-Ended Working Group and 2022 UN GGE reports. As such, it represents an early and still unconcluded attempt to frame parts (in this case, the core operating elements) of the internet as the basis of a global public good and help address some of the more consequential questions regarding sovereignty in cyberspace.

⊢• RECONCILING THE NAVAL AND CYBER EXPERIENCE

To paraphrase a famous saying, policy developments in the cyber and maritime realms are not equal, but they may well rhyme. Certain concerns, like the centrality of international law along with the reality of operational and political considerations, remain the same. Rule-abiding nations are always wary of committing to legal constraints that less law-abiding nations will likely covertly eschew, and their avoidance will be difficult to prove. Equally, the applicability of existing international law to cyberspace remains a hotly contested issue, as discussed in the chapter by Higson and Passerello.[25] The challenge of avoiding a "lawfare" trap is compounded by operational and tactical considerations—committing to a set of norms that preclude the use of operational abilities that are useful for uncertain gain may well seem a doubtful trade-off. But the history of maritime law shows us that the national interest is sometimes best served by taking an international perspective.

First, norms are useful instruments in both domains. At best, they are politically binding, not legally binding, and therefore provide a helpful hedge against "lawfare" practices. The evolution of COLREGs shows that, while norms may well contribute to binding international law (for example, UNCLOS III), they also can stand on their own. The UN GGE norms may well prove to be the COLREGs of the future—an agreed rules-of-the-road document that is increasingly expanded upon and made more coherent with existing international law over time and experience.

Second, even non–legally binding military-to-military (or like-to-like) agreements need to have a common "hymn sheet" to be effective. There is little point in having a naval process like the U.S.-China MMCA (or a cyber process like the Open-Ended Working Group point-of-contact agenda point) if there is not a clear definition of the rules of the road to guide disputes when needed.[26] The Chinese use of their coast guard and maritime militia (which are not subject to CUES) as the main instruments in the South China Seas, however, also shows how important it is that the points of contact and rules of the road actually have been agreed.

Third, norms do not need to be adhered to be powerful. While it is true that most of the eleven UN GGE norms were violated within months of the 2015 agreement, "violations of the norm help reinforce the norm," as a former U.S. diplomat often noted.[27] Arguably, the often-reported Russian violations of the UN GGE norms over the preceding seven-odd years helped make the case that Russia was systemically a "bad actor," something that was most visibly borne out in Russia's March 2022 invasion of Ukraine. Although COLREGs were not applied to MMCA, they continued to exist, and while China has managed to avoid applying CUES to coast guard activity in the South China Sea, COLREGs are still in effect there as well and provide a yardstick with which to judge China's behavior.

Fourth, the long-term political benefits of a commons-based global strategy outweigh the short-term cost—if there is even a cost. For instance, the public core norm was not welcomed with much enthusiasm by the United States when it was first fielded in UN GGE discussions in 2015.[28] One of the purported reasons for this rejection was the concern that adhering to the norm would curtail certain types of intelligence-gathering. A closer understanding of the norm, as well as relevant international humanitarian law, may have helped addressed this concern, and, since signing the Paris Call in 2021, the United States can be considered a supporter of the norm.

Given that the United States is often accused of monopolizing much of the global internet, its support for defining the basic core of the internet as a global public good goes some way to undermine the monopolizing argument—when it is well understood.[29] In that, the U.S. calculus should not be too dissimilar to that of the United Kingdom when it first supported the "freedom of the seas" provision at a time when the Royal Navy reigned supreme.[30] The best way to enshrine the principles of the rules-adhering Pax Britannica was to internationalize them. Perhaps the same enlightened self-interest should apply to forward-looking national cyber policies in our age as well.

NOTES

1. On the application of Westphalian principles to cyberspace, see Chris C. Demchak and Peter Dombrowski, "Rise of a Cybered Westphalian Age," *Strategic Studies Quarterly* 5, no. 1 (Spring 2011): 32–61.
2. As a naval officer, Linton Wells II witnessed the effects of the 1972 Incident at Sea Agreement (INCSEA). A series of freedom of navigation and trailing operations involving the Soviets in the Eastern Mediterranean and the Black Sea in 1971 were marked by constant attempts at intimidation, near-collisions, and generally belligerent attitudes. A decade later, similar operations in the Western Pacific were conducted under INCSEA procedures in a thoroughly professional manner, and concluded with an underway presentation of gifts to the escorting Soviet frigate.

For a discussion on the relevance of INCSEA for cyber, see Alexander Klimburg, *Of Ships and Cyber: Transposing the Incidents at Sea Agreement* (Washington, DC: Center for Strategic and International Studies, 28 September 2022), https://www.csis.org/analysis/ships-and-cyber-transposing-incidents-sea-agreement.

3. As described in the chapter by Higson and Passerello, certain areas such as the Law of Armed Conflict, space law, international aviation agreements, critical infrastructure, and trade pacts relate to norms as well.

4. International Maritime Organization, "Convention on the International Regulations for Preventing Collisions at Sea, 1972 (COLREGs)," https://www.imo.org/en/About/Conventions/Pages/COLREG.aspx.

5. The first International Maritime Conference was convened in 1889 "to consider regulations for preventing collisions," and this led to the International Convention for the Safety of Life at Sea, which began to be promulgated regularly in 1914 following the loss of the *Titanic*. See Jeff Werner, "The History of the Rule of the Road," 26 January 2017, https://www.allatsea.net/the-history-of-the-rule-of-the-road/.

6. Robert L. Friedheim, *Negotiating the New Ocean Regime* (Columbia: University of South Carolina Press, 1993), 26.

7. P. Hoagland, J. Jacoby, and M. E. Schumacher, "Law of the Sea Overview," in *Encyclopedia of Ocean Sciences*, ed. J. H. Steele, S. A. Thorpe, and K. K. Turekian (London: Academic Press, 2001), 1481–92, provide a variety of other authoritative sources as well as an overview.

8. On INCSEA, see U.S. Department of State, "Agreement between the Government of the United States of America and the Government of the Union of Soviet Socialist Republics on the Prevention of Incidents on and over the High Seas" (Incidents at Sea Agreement), 25 May 1972, https://2009–2017.state.gov/t/isn/4791.htm. On CUES, see "Document: Code for Unplanned Encounters at Sea," *USNI News*, 22 August 2016, https://news.usni.org/2014/06/17/document-conduct-unplanned-encounters-sea. Concerning lack of success, see Pete Pedrozo, "The U.S.-China Incidents at Sea Agreement: A Recipe for Disaster," *Journal of National Security Law and Policy* 6 (2012): 207–26, https://jnslp.com/wp-content/uploads/2012/08/07_Pedrozo-Master.pdf; and Phil Stewart, "U.S. Navy Says China Unreliable after Meeting No-Show; Beijing Says U.S. Twisting Facts," *Reuters*, 17 December 2020, https://www.reuters.com/world/us/us-navy-says-china-unreliable-after-meeting-no-show-beijing-says-us-twisting-2020-12-17/.

9. Although the INCSEA agreement was only signed by the United States and the Soviet Union on a navy-to-navy basis (by Secretary of the Navy John Warner and Fleet Admiral of the Soviet Union Sergey Gorshkov), the other North Atlantic Treaty Organization navies also complied. For a succinct discussion

of INCSEA's history and possible future, see Richard Moss, "Revisit Incidents at Sea," U.S. Naval Institute *Proceedings*, March 2018, https://www.usni.org/magazines/proceedings/2018/march/revisit-incidents-sea.

10. For instance, the Organization for Security and Cooperation in Europe 1039 Process Confidence Building Measure 9, as well as the 2023 UN Open-Ended Working Group points of contact agenda item.

11. Klimburg.

12. Michael Schmitt, "The Sixth United Nations GGE and International Law in Cyberspace," *Just Security*, 10 June 2021, https://www.justsecurity.org/76864/the-sixth-united-nations-gge-and-international-law-in-cyberspace/.

13. James Manicom, "Confidence, Trust, and the CUES," Centre for International Governance Innovation, 21 May 2014, https://www.cigionline.org/articles/confidence-trust-and-cues/.

14. Pedrozo.

15. Vice Adm. T. J. White, USN (Ret.), personal communication with authors, March 2023.

16. "An international regime is the set of principles, norms, rules, and procedures that international actors converge around. Sometimes, when formally organized, it can transform into an intergovernmental organization." See Stephen D. Krasner, "Structural Causes and Regime Consequences: Regimes as Intervening Variables," *International Organization* 36, no. 2 (Spring 1982): 185–205.

17. Erica Borghard, "U.S. Cyber Command's Malware Inoculation: Linking Offense and Defense in Cyberspace," Council on Foreign Relations blog, 22 April 2020, https://www.cfr.org/blog/us-cyber-commands-malware-inoculation-linking-offense-and-defense-cyberspace.

18. See International Seabed Authority, "About ISA," https://www.isa.org.jm/about-isa/; Marjorie Ann Brown, *The Law of the Sea Convention and U.S. Policy*, CRS-IB95010 (Washington, DC: Congressional Research Service, 16 June 2006), https://www.gc.noaa.gov/documents/gcil_crs_2006_report.pdf. For the U.S. and Chinese position on ISA, see John Marek, "U.S.-China International Law Disputes in the South China Sea," *Wild Blue Yonder Online Journal*, 9 July 2021, https://www.airuniversity.af.edu/Wild-Blue-Yonder/Article-Display/Article/2685294/us-china-international-law-disputes-in-the-south-china-sea/; Oriana Skylar Mastro, "How China Is Bending the Rules in the South China Sea," *The Interpreter*, 17 February 2021, https://www.lowyinstitute.org/the-interpreter/how-china-bending-rules-south-china-sea.

19. The Antarctic Treaty System (ATS) describes both the original Antarctic Treaty (1959) and its many revisions and supplemental agreements. While it can be argued that the "freezing of territorial claims" (rather than the outright rejection

of them) in the ATS undermines the CHM, the Antarctic Treaty does make reference to a "common interest of mankind," and there have been repeated attempts to make this synonymous with the CHM principle. For text of the Antarctic Treaty, see "The Antarctic Treaty," Secretariat of the Antarctic Treaty official website, https://www.ats.aq/e/antarctictreaty.html.

20. On the Internet Corporation for Assigned Names and Numbers, see "One World, One Internet," https://www.icann.org/. On the Internet Engineering Task Force, see "About," https://www.ietf.org/.

21. Alexander Klimburg was the director of the GCSC.

22. "Advanced Cyberstability," Global Commission on the Stability of Cyberspace, November 2019, https://cyberstability.org/report.html#item-8.

23. "Statement on the Interpretation of the Norm on Non-Interference with the Public Core," The Hague Centre for Strategic Studies, 22 September 2021, https://hcss.nl/news/statement-on-the-interpretation-of-the-norm-on-non-interference-with-the-public-core/.

24. "Paris Call for Trust and Security in Cyberspace," *Paris Call 11.12.2018*, https://pariscall.international/en/.

25. Lauren M. Cherry and Peter P. Pascucci, "International Law in Cyberspace," American Bar Association, 27 July 2023, https://www.americanbar.org/groups/law_national_security/publications/aba-standing-committee-on-law-and-national-security-60-th-anniversary-an-anthology/international-law-in-cyberspace/. This American Bar Association document (written by two U.S. Navy Judge Advocate General officers in a private capacity) provides a summary of some of the most important national statements between 2012 and 2022.

26. "EU Statement—UN General Assembly Open-Ended Working Group on ICT: Points of Contacts Directory," Delegation of the European Union to the United Nations in New York, 5 December 2022, https://www.eeas.europa.eu/delegations/un-new-york/eu-statement-%E2%80%93-un-general-assembly-open-ended-working-group-ict-points-contacts-directory_en?s=63.

27. Former Department of State official Michele Markoff, discussions in multiple settings, 2015–22.

28. Much of this account of the GGE is taken from Alexander Klimburg, *The Darkening Web: The War for Cyberspace* (New York: Penguin Books, 2018), particularly 117–22.

29. In 2021 and 2023 the Russian representation at the International Telecommunication Union exploited a lack of understanding of the public core norm to put forward its own "endorsement" of the norm, saying, incorrectly, that it made the case for governments to have the final say on matters pertaining to internet governance. This was countered by the former director of the GCSC (Klimburg)

in a press release: https://hcss.nl/news/statement-on-the-interpretation-of-the
-norm-on-non-interference-with-the-public-core/.

30. The Freedom of the Seas provision in the 1908 Declaration of London would
have both strengthened the right of neutrals as well as curtailed the ability
to enforce a "distant blockade." The fact that Germany had not ratified the
declaration by the outbreak of World War I gave the United Kingdom a pretext
to pursue a "distant blockade" against Germany. At the same time, the United
States insisted on the rights of neutrals as outlined in the declaration. After
World War I, refusal of all major powers except the United States to entertain
the issue led it to be effectively mute until UNCLOS reintroduced it. See also
https://encyclopedia.1914–1918-online.net/article/freedom_of_the_seas.

7 International Law and Cyber Warfare in the Maritime Environment

DANIELLE HIGSON and ROBERT PASSERELLO

As emerging technology, complex networks, and the internet are interwoven in virtually every human endeavor—from banking, healthcare, and communications to naval warfare—it is critical to understand the existing international legal framework that governs this evolving domain called cyberspace. First, one must look to the principle of *jus ad bellum* to understand how a cyber operation could be the lawful basis to enter an armed conflict. Once hostilities begin, the law of armed conflict (LOAC), which aims to regulate the conduct of hostilities, applies to all forms of warfare, regardless of domain.

Whether armed conflict occurs between states or between states and terrorist groups, and whether it occurs at sea, on land, by air, in space, or in cyberspace, the LOAC applies to all states. Accordingly, it requires planning and execution consistent with a complex body of international laws and domestic policy. This chapter argues that lawful cyber warfare delivering effects in furtherance of military or naval objectives cannot occur before policy and legal concerns are addressed concerning lowering authorities for offensive cyber operations by units such as warships.

⊢• "CYBER ATTACKS" LEADING TO WAR

In the maritime environment, the United Nations Charter on the Law of the Sea, whether adhered to by treaty ratifiers or as a matter of customary international law, provides the international legal consensus on operations that emanate from or on the sea.[1] (See Klimburg and Wells in this volume.) Whether on the high seas, in economic exclusive zones, in contiguous zones, or on territorial seas, cyber operations may only be conducted for peaceful purposes unless an accepted international legal basis authorizes the "use of force." When a cyber operation is of such nature, scale, and effect amounting to "use of force" or considered an "armed attack"—as in every other domain—the LOAC applies. However, cyber operations below the level of armed conflict, which some describe as gray zone conflict and which may cause harm to states, organizations, corporations, and individuals, are not clearly prohibited by or addressed within the law of war and instead rely on enforcement of domestic criminal law or the other instruments of national power.

When might a cyber operation with specific effects provide the legal justification for armed conflict? *Jus ad bellum* is a legal concept of just war theory that provides two instances where nations may legitimately and legally go to war, consistent with international law and the United Nations Charter (UNC) in particular. Under the UNC, a nation's military may engage in war to defend itself in accordance with Article 51 or as part of a United Nations–authorized security council action pursuant to Article 42. Outright war, an armed attack, or a use of force—whether at sea, undersea, air, ground, space, or cyberspace—is legally prohibited unless one of these two exceptions exists.

Article 2(4) of the UNC establishes the prohibition of the threat or use of force. Specifically, it states, "All Members shall refrain in their international relations from the threat or use of force against the territorial integrity or political independence of any State or in any other manner inconsistent with the Purposes of the United Nations." Article 2(4)'s general prohibition is aimed at preventing war, resolving disputes through peaceful means, and protecting the sovereignty and national integrity of all nations. As a warfare component, cyber effects would be prohibited by international law if deemed a use of force or the threat thereof.[2]

⊢• USE OF FORCE IN CYBERSPACE

What constitutes a use of force in cyberspace? The UNC does not determine or define what constitutes specifically a "use of force." Nonetheless, the non-binding Tallinn Manual II composed by a group of reputable international scholars states that "a cyber operation constitutes a use of force when its scale and effects are comparable to non-cyber operations rising to the level of a use of force."[3]

Some actions amounting to a use of force are obvious, such as a hostile military force entering territorial waters, national airspace, or land without the consent of the sovereign nation. Similarly, a missile launched from land systems, from the air or sea, from one territory into another, or the insertion of a clandestine force intending to cause physical harm all amount to a clear use of force.

But what about interrupting banking transactions, the flow of electricity and water, or disrupting or denying a government or corporation access to their critical data? Depending on the impact, one could certainly argue that the harm, pain, and injury of stopping the flow of water (as an example) is at least equivalent to a poorly aimed missile that enters and strikes an open field where no one is killed. As commanders, planners, and operators think about cyber effects and their legal implications, it is important to give due consideration to the nature of the effect intended.

When a use of force amounts to an "armed attack," Article 51 of the UNC allows a state to respond with force in self-defense. Article 51 recognizes the inherent right of individual or collective self-defense in the case of an "armed attack" against a member of the United Nations. However, the term "armed attack" is not explicitly defined in the UNC, leading to debates and discussions about its scope and interpretation. While an armed attack may be somewhat obvious when one nation kinetically attacks the navy of another, launches missiles from one territory into another, or uses ground forces to invade, it is less clear in cyberspace.

Nevertheless, customary international law is coalescing. Traditional notions of armed attacks were developed in the context of kinetic force in the physical domain. In cyberspace, the effects of a particular cyber operation are often, but not always, nonphysical and, in most instances, do not necessarily involve physical destruction as in a traditional armed attack. However, as cyber capabilities and actors have become more sophisticated and effective, there is growing recognition that the effects of certain cyber operations will rise to the level of a use of force or an armed attack, triggering the right to self-defense under international law. The effects will resemble kinetic attacks, causing death and destruction.

Understanding whether a cyber operation seeking to achieve particular effects is a use of force or an armed attack, as the UNC prohibits, depends on the cyber operation's scale and ultimate impact or effect. Key considerations derived from a helpful framework within Tallinn Manual II in determining whether a cyber incident constitutes an armed attack include effects and consequences, scale and intensity, attribution, intent, and context.[4] Ultimately, the analysis and determination of whether a cyber operation constitutes an armed attack is highly fact-specific and subject to interpretation.

Who decides if an act is an armed attack? The victim state decides. Were the effects of the cyber operation to such a level that the state wants to use force in response and go to war? If the victim state does not want to use force in response, then there is no reason to deem it an armed attack. The victim state can still deem the behavior wrongful and use other instruments of national power to respond. For example, in the case of the Sony cyber intrusion by North Korea, the United States responded with sanctions. Other options might include a diplomatic demarche, criminal investigations and prosecution, or export controls and other economic costs.

⊢• "CYBER ATTACKS" IN THE MARITIME DOMAIN

To illustrate what might constitute an armed attack delivered through cyber effects in the maritime domain, it is worth analyzing the collisions at sea by the USS *Fitzgerald* and the USS *McCain*. Both guided-missile destroyers collided with commercial ships in June and August 2017, respectively. When these incidents occurred less than three months apart, both within the vicinity of the South China Sea, suspicion arose as to the underlying cause of the fatal collisions.[5] Were the accidents caused by human error, mechanical malfunction, or the nefarious actions of an advanced adversary employing cyber means that led to an intentional or unintentional navigational or steering change? The answer would be critical in understanding whether the death and destruction were the result of an armed attack and informing the U.S. response.

As officials conducted the investigation, it was known that a well-delivered "cyber attack" could impact the steering of the ships, given the known vulnerabilities of vessels relying on networked operating systems, including navigation, propulsion, and steering. (See Hilger in this volume.) If these systems are compromised through a cyber attack, the ship's crew could lose some degree of control of its directional movement and/or speed, causing a deadly collision.

In both collisions, the incidents' ultimate cause was determined to be human error, exacerbated by gaps in leadership, training, and policy. Had the investigation shown evidence of cyber attacks that caused the navigation systems, data displays, or other critical systems to err, and those actions were attributable and intentional (foreseeable), it is clear that—given the loss of life—the U.S. government could have concluded that a use of force amounting to an armed attack had occurred and, accordingly, could have lawfully responded in self-defense pursuant to Article 51 of the UNC. Policy considerations may drive the decision whether to respond with force and call the malicious cyber effect a cyber attack. Still, under international law, such an event would have justified kinetic military actions in self-defense.

This example also demonstrates the complexity of determining if an incident that caused death and destruction resulted from a cyber attack. At this time, it is hard to imagine a ship's commanding officer being able to determine with certainty that a critical system on the ship was targeted and destroyed by a cyber attack by another state. Without the ability to make this determination and positively attribute it to a particular state, it would not be possible for the ship to lawfully respond in self-defense. Analyzing such a situation inevitably takes time, and the response will be determined at the highest levels. As a matter of U.S. policy, while all passive defensive measures are authorized—such as shutting the system down, generating additional barriers or firewalls, or instituting policies that make it difficult to hack our systems—the equivalent of firing back (assuming you could attribute the attack) is considered a cyber effect and requires authorization at the secretary of defense level or higher.

⊢ CYBER ATTACK OR CYBER EFFECT?

Precise use of language is always important; however, in describing cyber operations, it is imperative to be precise with word choice, given the significance under international law and within the U.S. government. The term "cyber attack" should not be used loosely to describe the multitude of malicious cyber activities, but should be reserved for situations where the effects cause a level of death and destruction equivalent to a kinetic attack.

During peacetime, potential opponents may seek to have impactful cyber effects such as degrading, denying, or manipulating the enemy's ability to communicate, command and control, fundraise, promulgate propaganda, or take other actions that impose nonlethal or destructive costs on the adversary. Under U.S. policy, a cyber effect can be of diverse types, and while every cyber attack is also a cyber effect, the reverse is not true—every cyber effect is not a cyber attack and may not even come close.

Actions that create noticeable denial effects in cyberspace or manipulation that leads to denial effects, including denial, degradation, disruption, destruction, or manipulation (of data), would all be considered cyber effects.[6] Nonetheless, it is likely that only a cyber operation designed to destroy a network, server, or computer that completely, irreversibly, and permanently denies its use or renders it inoperable would be considered a use of force under Article 2(4).

A cyber effect to include actions that simply degrade, disrupt, or manipulate in a temporary and reversible manner would likely not amount to a use of force. If it is not a use of force, it certainly is not an armed attack. Putting the word "attack" after the word "cyber," in most instances, may feed the sense of decisive action being taken, consistent with the military's bias for decisive and impactful actions. However, it complicates matters under both law and policy. In fact, one might argue that for many reasons, one should never publicly describe a cyber operation as an attack unless the president has determined it to be an armed attack and wants to respond with force.

Some would argue that red lines need to be drawn so it can be clearly understood which actions in cyberspace will be considered an armed attack. But this can be a dangerous paradigm since if red lines are crossed, the United States needs to be ready to back them up with force. If it does not, credibility is destroyed, and future red lines may not have the desired result. This is not to say that some very high-level lines could not be drawn, such as cyber operations that impact our nuclear command and control networks. However, lines drawn for less impactful adversary cyber operations, such as a cyber operation that impacts an operating network of a U.S. Navy vessel or jams our communication or surveillance systems, may unnecessarily tie our hands and be escalatory in nature.

During peacetime, what guides the commanding officer of a U.S. warship as to when the ship can respond to an armed attack with force? Unless there are mission- or theater-specific rules of engagement (ROEs), the standing rules of engagement (SROEs) provide the clearest expression of U.S. policy concerning the right and obligation to act in self-defense. The SROEs provide that military units and the individuals that compose those units may defend themselves from a hostile act or demonstrated hostile intent.[7] As previously discussed, a hostile act is an attack or other use of force (which could be cyber) against the United States, U.S. forces, or other designated persons or property. On the other hand, hostile intent requires additional observations and analysis of indications and warnings that a hostile act is imminent. The SROEs define hostile intent as "the threat of imminent use of force against the United States, U.S. forces, or other designated persons or property." Hostile intent is the imminence of the "use of force" before it occurs, such as a fire control radar locked on target.

⊢ CYBER SELF-DEFENSE

Self-defense in cyberspace is complex. As a matter of international law, a state that is the target of a cyber effect that rises to the level of an armed attack may exercise its inherent right of self-defense. Passive defensive actions, such as firewalls or multifactor authentication for access, aimed at making an adversary's cyber attack, act of espionage, or theft of intellectual property more difficult are legally uncomplicated. Instead, complications arise when determining whether a cyber event is occurring or has occurred and attributing the actions. If it were possible for a ship to determine that malicious cyber activity was occurring, that it was imminently likely to cause a loss of life, and that it could be attributed to a particular source, the commanding officer could lawfully respond with kinetic force under the self-defense theory. Of course, the same caution and de-escalatory strategy that would apply in the physical domain would apply in response to a cyber attack.

If the capability for attribution existed on board a ship, one might expect supplemental ROEs to provide guidance to the commanding officer. Currently, a specific cyber response action aimed at targeting an adversary who has committed a cyber attack is treated as a matter of policy as an offensive cyber operation—requiring the deliberate planning and complex interagency approval process under National Security Policy Memorandum 13 (2018).[8] This makes it impractical for a ship to defend itself against a cyber attack beyond passive defensive measures.

Once passive defensive measures fail, given the speed and possible harm a cyber attack could cause a ship in the middle of the ocean, there is a clear justification for maintaining the expertise, policies, tools, and authorities necessary for units to identify and attribute cyber attacks, as well as the ability to defend themselves from an ongoing cyber attack that could cause death, serious bodily harm, or destruction of military equipment or impede the accomplishment of a critical mission. However, significant policy hurdles and current resource constraints at the tactical level preclude specific and limited preapproved responses to a current cyber attack. Given this reality, the U.S. Navy must develop more sophisticated passive defense measures. (See related chapter by Dombrowski in this volume.) While from a legal and policy perspective, preapproved self-defense measures in response to specific triggers that identify hostile acts in cyberspace are sensible, there are still likely to be resource, manpower, and tool gaps at the tactical level that pose insurmountable challenges—in the short term—to effective self-defense response actions in cyberspace.

⊢• CYBERSPACE AND GRAY ZONE CONFLICT

Although the triggers that represent a use of force or an armed attack are different when delivered via cyber means rather than kinetic ones, the analyses are similar and subject to the same international legal framework under the UNC and law of war. Although cyber effects constituting use of force or armed attack have occurred, they remain rare and represent a very small percentage of the uncountable daily malicious cyber activities we face.

Currently, most cyber intrusions relate to espionage, intellectual property theft, financial scams, or denial of service actions. While they do not amount to a use of force or armed attack, they do impact the stability and security of individuals, organizations, corporations, and states. The concept of gray zone conflict relates to this intermediate stage below the level of armed conflict, low-level cyber conflict, and daily confrontation. At this time, the most effective ways of responding to these threats are defensive passive measures such as complex firewalls, multifactor authentication for access, password protocols, encryption rules, and other barriers and policies that ensure cyber hygiene and prevent mistakes that enable intruders to access systems.

Gray zone conflict in cyberspace is a daily threat that causes economic, social, and informational injury, but international law has yet to effectively regulate these activities or provide the appropriate mechanism to hold individuals and/or states responsible. The domestic law of most countries would characterize these actions (gray zone conflict) by states or their surrogates as criminal in nature; however, there are geopolitical, diplomatic, and jurisdictional hurdles that make a transnational criminal justice or coordinated diplomatic/economic response system ineffective. While many nations and international organizations work hard to agree upon norms of accepted behavior in cyberspace, there remain long-standing concerns and disagreements. At a minimum, the significant gap between the United States, People's Republic of China, European Union, and Russia with respect to open access to information, privacy rights, and intellectual property theft will likely ensure that there will be little agreement in the near term between the largest and most influential nations.

⊢• CYBERSPACE AND THE LAW OF ARMED CONFLICT

Once gray zone activity turns into recognized armed conflict, all belligerents must abide by *jus in bello*, as exemplified by the LOAC, to afford rights to combatants and protect civilians and civilian objects. It does not matter who started the conflict or whether it was lawful. If this mattered, all parties would claim to be the victim. The LOAC has four main principles: military necessity, distinction, proportionality, and unnecessary suffering. Although these principles are based on traditional kinetic strikes, there is fair consensus that the LOAC applies to cyber operations.

However, there is little granularity on exactly how the principles apply in cyber operations. Military necessity is straightforward, even as it applies to cyber. The target of any strike, whether prosecuted by kinetic or cyber means, must be of some military benefit. Belligerents are not allowed to strike purely civilian targets without military benefit, and accordingly, cyber targets where an effect is sought must be validated as a military objective. But the application of the other LOAC principles is not as clear.

Distinction requires that belligerents distinguish between military forces/objects and civilians and civilian objects. Cyber targets are often dual-natured, meaning they are used by civilians and military forces. For example, one server could hold both military and civilian data. The LOAC requires armed forces to wear uniforms to distinguish themselves from civilians. While they technically could, cyber packets do not distinguish themselves as belligerents or even identify with the flag of their state.

The principle of proportionality requires that the military advantage of a particular strike or cyber effect be greater than the harm to civilians. In kinetic strikes, the harm to civilians is death and destruction of property. Cyber operations often may not cause death or destruction directly, but second- and third-order effects may lead to death as a consequence of the cyber effect. A cyber operation that takes out the power for a period to allow belligerents to carry out operations in the dark or to prevent the other side from communicating would not directly cause any deaths. But without power, civilians could die in a hospital because their medical equipment is not able to function. Thus, it is hard to assess the military advantage of a cyber operation against the possible harm that might occur.

Finally, the principle of unnecessary suffering prohibits the infliction of superfluous injury. In some ways, cyber operations may be preferred or even required by this principle since most would not cause any civilian physical suffering or death in comparison to kinetic means. Nonetheless, as civilian infrastructure becomes more dependent on being connected via cyber means, could it be considered unnecessary suffering if a civilian cannot use their internet or cell phones for hours or even days to conduct actions they need to survive? While these principles do not neatly apply to cyberspace operations, they need to be considered.

⊢• ROEs FOR CYBER WARFARE?

How would ROEs apply to cyber operations in an armed conflict? It is difficult to say. ROEs, which are a statement of policy, generally restrict action further than the limitations of the LOAC and can never authorize actions prohibited by them. ROEs are more restrictive in a war with limited objectives (i.e., counterterrorism strikes in a country with which we are not at war compared to a war with relatively unlimited objectives [such as World War II]). In a war of unlimited objectives in which a state is fighting for survival—sometimes referred to as a war of necessity—or seeks to defeat the other side decisively, one would not expect much more ROEs than declaring the hostile force. It is current U.S. policy that offensive cyber operations are closely controlled and approved at the highest levels. They are only conducted by units directly under the operational control of U.S. Cyber Command. This virtually nullifies any need for supplemental ROEs for cyberspace operations. In the future, could this be different? Certainly.

In any armed conflict, offensive cyber operations will still have unique considerations. By the nature of cyberspace operations, it can be difficult to contain the collateral damage of a large-scale cyber effect and how it ultimately affects the civilian population. There are also concerns over poorly defined red lines for adversaries in cyber and the concern of tripping those lines and escalating a conflict.

These policy and legal concerns must be addressed before the authority to approve offensive cyber operations is lowered and/or maritime units such as warships can execute offensive cyber operations. In the meanwhile, cyber operations—whether in the maritime domain or elsewhere—will remain tightly controlled.

NOTES

1. Customary international law is a legal concept that refers to the development of legal principles and norms through the consistent and general practice of states, accompanied by a belief that such practices are legally required (*opinio juris*). Unlike treaties, which are formal agreements between states, customary international law arises from the customary behavior and beliefs of states over time.

2. United Nations, "The U.N. Charter," https://www.un.org/en/about-us/un-charter/full-text.

3. Michael N. Schmitt, "Rule 69," in *Tallinn Manual 2.0 on the International Law Applicable to Cyber Operations* (Cambridge: Cambridge University Press, 2017), 330; "The U.N. Charter."

4. Schmitt, "Rule 71 (Discussion)."

5. See discussion in Chris Demchak, Keith Patton, and Sam J. Tangredi, "Why Are Our Ships Crashing? Competence, Overload, and Cyber Considerations," Center for International Maritime Security, 25 August 2017, http://cimsec.org/ships-crashing-competence-overload-cyber-considerations/33865.

6. Joint Publication 3-1, *Cyber Operations* (Washington, DC: The Joint Staff, June 2018), 40.

7. Chairman of the Joint Chiefs of Staff Instruction 3121.01B, "Standing Rules of Engagement/ Standing Rules for the Use of Force by U.S. Forces," June 2005.

8. National Security Policy Memorandum 13 is the presidential-level interagency policy that sets forth the coordination requirements and approval process necessary to authorize specified cyber effects, which are defined as the denial, degradation, disruption, destruction, or manipulation of a cyber network or system executed by cyber means. Gary P. Corn, "National Security Decision-Making in the Age of Technology: Delivering Outcomes on Time and on Target," *Journal of National Security Law & Policy* 12, no. 61 (2021), https://digitalcommons.wcl.american.edu/cgi/viewcontent.cgi?article=3001&context=facsch_lawrev.

8 Secrecy, Deception, Cyber, and Navies

MICHAEL POZNANSKY

Whether it is spies, covert operations, or other deceptive actions, secrecy has long played an important role in the maritime domain. The maturation of cyberspace over the last couple of decades has introduced novel ways to employ secrecy for convenience, efficiency, plausible deniability, and often effectiveness in obtaining otherwise unobtainable outcomes. It is now easier than ever for states to illicitly acquire information, deceive opponents or victims, and conduct covert action at varying scales to support offensive and defensive operations that shape the maritime environment as well as the entire global international system.[1]

Cybered warfare in particular is rife with tools and opportunities for creating misleading and obscured effects.[2] This chapter argues that any system heavily reliant on cyber, including those using artificial intelligence or operating in space, is vulnerable to state-engendered deception. Consequently, cybered warfare and secret statecraft inevitably have a major and direct effect on navies.

⊢• SECRET STATECRAFT IN CONTEXT

Statecraft refers to "the organized actions governments take to change the external environment in general or the policies and actions of other states in particular to achieve the objectives set by policymakers."[3]

There are two main types of secret statecraft. The first is espionage, or spying. The means are many, ranging from signals intelligence to human assets, satellite imagery, and more. The second type of secret statecraft is covert action. At the broadest level, covert action refers to operations in which the sponsor seeks to conceal their identity entirely or at least achieve plausible deniability while engaging in otherwise obfuscated activities.[4]

Deception is central to both forms of secret statecraft. This can involve fooling another actor (or system) into believing a false or incomplete narrative or accepting as true inaccurate elements of a larger picture. Spies use dead drops, ciphers, and cover stories to prevent foreign governments from learning their identity, their connection with foreign agents, and the information they have stolen. Covert operators use proxies, front organizations, and other means to create a layer of deniability between the sponsor and the actions they are affecting.

Intelligence agencies thrive on secrecy and deception, but militaries also practice it through the use of camouflage, feints, decoys, and false signals. Navies routinely employ deception to protect fleets.[5]

⊢• THE EVOLUTION OF SECRET STATECRAFT IN THE CYBERED ERA

In the pre-cyber era, governments were most concerned with physical means of deception, especially espionage. To catch spies seeking to personally steal classified secrets, governments themselves used deception and lures. In the late 1970s, for example, the Federal Bureau of Investigation employed a Navy lieutenant commander to act as a double agent, resulting in the arrest of two KGB officers.[6] In a more recent case in 2022, a Federal Bureau of Investigation sting operation caught a Navy nuclear engineer attempting to provide secrets related to submarine technology and nuclear propulsion to a foreign adversary.[7]

Alongside espionage, covert operations have been a key part of secret state-versus-state competition involving deception, especially in the maritime domain where ships are accessible in foreign ports. Sabotage, defined as "a mission . . . to secretly disarm, obstruct, or destroy enemy war materiel or infrastructure for military advantage," has been especially prevalent.[8] A report from the Center for Naval Analyses identifies more than twenty cases of maritime sabotage since World War II involving solely online open-source materials.[9]

Maritime sabotage, a form of covert action, has important parallels to—and key differences with—cyber operations, which are often deployed toward similar ends. Much like offense using cyberspace, what makes sabotage so appealing is that it has "the potential to achieve effects without the dedication of large amounts of resources" and, often in history, countermeasures were difficult to implement.[10] Second, while collateral damage to third parties could entail significant costs in political backlash for the perpetrator if correctly identified, the difficulty of accurate attribution in cyberspace may conversely reduce such costs. (See Demchak in this volume.) Third, while retaining the element of surprise was not necessarily critical to the success of conventional sabotage, it is in cyberspace, at least as long as it takes to gain access to the target system and to execute the intended payload dynamic, which is less obviously applicable to cyberspace.[11]

States now enjoy new and different opportunities using cyberspace for both espionage and covert action in secret statecraft. One of the defining features of cyberspace is that it has fundamentally altered covert action's problem of scale. Whereas covert operations typically "had to remain small" if they were to have any chance of achieving "plausible deniability," cyberspace enables actors to conduct covert activities on a much larger scale while still hiding behind the veil of anonymity.[12]

Cyberspace has also enabled other new forms of deception—and with it, potentially the pursuit of new ends. Old-fashioned attempts at selling, and attempting to buy, blackmail for, or grab secrets have not gone away; rather, they have evolved. A now-common tactic across cyberspace is for government officials to digitally impersonate criminals and foreign spy handlers to groom or catch those wanting to sell secrets.

⊢• ESPIONAGE IN THE CYBERED ERA

The defense community writ large is a prime target of modern-day cyber network exploitation. Some of the biggest threats include cyber attacks against the defense industrial base with the aim of, among other objectives, stealing valuable intellectual property.[13] One of the earliest openly discussed incidents, Moonlight Maze, occurred in the late 1990s.[14] A foreign power—later identified as Russia—penetrated a wide range of American military networks. The attackers purportedly used a variety of hop points across cyberspace to conceal their identity.[15] Russian actors have perpetrated a large number of successful attacks since then.

The maritime environment is a particularly attractive target for digital espionage. As the People's Republic of China has risen to having the largest navy in the world, its efforts to digitally steal naval secrets now form a significant part of its cybered statecraft. In 2018 Chinese hackers successfully accessed the computer network of an unnamed U.S. Navy contractor to extract sensitive undersea warfare plans including development of a submarine-launched anti-ship cruise missile. This work was contracted with the Naval Undersea Warfare Center in Newport, Rhode Island.[16] In 2019 the *Wall Street Journal* reported that "Chinese hackers have targeted more than two dozen universities in the U.S. and around the globe as part of an elaborate scheme to steal research about maritime technology being developed for military use." The victims were either "research hubs focused on undersea technology" or places where professors had relevant expertise.[17]

The Chinese group responsible, commonly known as Advanced Persistent Threat (APT) 40, has been active for over a decade. The cybersecurity firm Mandiant notes that "the group has specifically targeted engineering, transportation, and the defense industry, especially where these sectors overlap with maritime technologies."[18] They have also exploited stolen maritime platforms to their advantage. For instance, this same Mandiant report notes that after capturing an unmanned underwater vehicle in the South China Sea in 2016, "APT40 was observed masquerading as [an unmanned underwater vehicle manufacturer], and targeting universities engaged in naval research." The use of varying forms of deception—to include spear phishing and compromised web shells—is among their primary techniques.

⊢• DECEIVING THE DECEIVERS IN CYBERSPACE

Deception is routinely used in return against digitally enabled espionage to the extent affordable. Traps are laid that enable the victim to either track the attacker or even inject malware back into the attacker's systems. Defensive deception means potential perpetrators always have to worry about whether a virtual minefield has been entered.[19]

In cyberspace, a deceptive digital tool commonly used against attackers is called a "honeypot." Online attackers are allowed to discover access to a secretly controlled network containing what seems to be interesting, possibly classified, files. As the spies are lured away from real operational networks into accessing the false network, information about their methods, origins, apparent intents, and so on is collected for analysis, possible later arrest, and, at the very least, denial of success in this attempt.

The case of Moonlight Maze illustrates how this works in practice. A major reason the Russians got caught was the deployment of a honeypot. Operators created fake files, including "directories, documents, usernames, and passwords," misleading the Russian hackers into believing they were real and subsequently stealing them, thereby enabling the United States to track them.[20] Reportedly, the U.S. Defense Advanced Research Projects Agency developed a capability wherein unauthorized access to certain systems triggers the proliferation of fake data, making it hard for the attacker to distinguish what is real or fake.[21]

What all of this suggests is that cyber espionage against navies or assets in the maritime environment more broadly is also vulnerable to clever defensive deception methods by would-be victims even in cyberspace.

⊢• COVERT ACTION IN THE CYBERED ERA

As the second overarching form of secret statecraft, covert operations impacting the maritime domain have also undergone an important evolution and transformation in the cybered world. Although sometimes conflated, there are at least two major types of activity worth distinguishing: physical disruption that impacts cyber-enabling capabilities on the one hand, and cyber disruption that impacts both physical and digital systems on the other.

A major maritime concern in the current environment is the disruption via sabotage of infrastructure such as undersea fiber-optic cables that are essential to internet access and the flow of data. (See Kavanagh and Leconte in this volume.) Although there is some redundancy when it comes to undersea cables, damage to the right ones at the right time will cause disruptions and harm to societal functions.[22] Moreover, attributing attacks on undersea infrastructure, to include cables, can be exceedingly difficult. This, in turn, makes opaqueness in the originators of the cable breaks an attractive option for the cable-destroying states seeking to retain some semblance of deniability as a means of competing below the level of armed conflict.[23]

This threat is not merely hypothetical. In 2022, as Vladimir Putin was massing troops on Ukraine's border before eventually invading, there were concerns that a planned Russian naval exercise near Ireland—which also happened to be "above vital subsea communications cables"—was meant to send a message about Russia's capacity to interfere with them if it wished.[24] More generally, Russian submarines and "oceanographic research vessels" have been observed probing undersea cables, causing alarm among North Atlantic Treaty Organization allies.[25] For its part, China was accused in March 2023 of cutting cables to Matsu, an island controlled by Taiwan.[26] Many similar incidents have taken place in recent years.

A second variant of covert operations impacting navies and the wider maritime environment is subversion of both digital and physical functions critically dependent on cyber-related capabilities. In the event of a conflict, for example, adversaries could covertly attempt to affect the sealift of U.S. forces by leveraging deceptive, covert capabilities—disrupting deployment and shipping schedules.[27]

In recent years, malicious actors have already demonstrated the ability to target critical shipborne navigational systems such as the automatic identification system and the global positioning system (GPS). The intent is to deceive ships about the identity of other ships or their own location, called "spoofing." A 2019 report identifies "extensive Russian GPS spoofing" affecting maritime navigation, especially in the Black Sea.[28] Of note, such disruption is now possible because ships are cyber vulnerable; this would have been impossible in the pre-cyber era without physically commandeering ships.

Malicious actors have also targeted operational technology used in ports and on ships, including their supervisory control and data acquisition systems, to cause damage and disruption (as described by Hilger in this volume).[29] In 2017 pirates hacked the navigation system of a container ship, attempting to steer it to a location where it could be easily boarded. Without steering control, the captain turned off propulsion, denying the pirates success but also sitting dead in the water for ten hours waiting for information technology help to arrive by helicopter.[30]

Malicious actors can also affect otherwise purely commercial maritime digital systems in ways that significantly impact the maritime domain and transport of essential resources. Sometimes this effect spills over from the original target to subvert the wider global system. The 2017 NotPetya attack remains the major case in point.[31]

⊢• LOOKING AHEAD

Secret statecraft is pervasive in the cybered era from peace through war. Its wide-ranging impacts on the maritime domain mean that cyber warfare is part of a defending navy's mission. U.S. Cyber Command's concept of persistent engagement and recognition of the fluidity of cyberspace are both extremely familiar to maritime services (as described by Tangredi in this volume). At the same time, the fact that much of what happens in cyberspace takes place in the shadows—what this chapter has called secret statecraft—is different from things like freedom of navigation operations, which prioritize overt demonstrations to show presence. Grappling with these similarities and differences is a key task moving forward.

Additionally, the relevance of deception and secrecy will only continue to grow as militaries continue to lean into a range of emerging technologies. For example, while an increased usage of autonomous systems brings a number of potential benefits, the threat of sabotage and subversion of these cyber-enabled platforms remains a major risk.[32] The same goes for artificial intelligence capabilities, which are deeply dependent on cyberspace.[33] In short, any systems that rely on cyber capabilities—and there are many—are potentially vulnerable. Coming to terms with the pervasiveness of deception in this environment is imperative.

NOTES

1. Michael Warner, "A Matter of Trust: Covert Action Reconsidered," *Studies in Intelligence* 63, no. 4 (December 2019): 33–41.
2. Chris Demchak, "Defending Democracies in a Cybered World," *The Brown Journal of World Affairs* 24, no. 1 (Fall/Winter 2017): 139–58.

3. Quoted in Stacie E. Goddard, Paul K. MacDonald, and Daniel H. Nexon, "Repertoires of Statecraft: Instruments and Logics of Power Politics," *International Relations* 33, no. 2 (2019): 304.

4. Ronald Reagan, "Executive Order 12333—United States Intelligence Activities," December 1981, https://www.archives.gov/federal-register/codification/executive -order/12333.html.

5. Chris C. Demchak and Sam J. Tangredi, "'Sea Hacking' Sun Tzu: Deception in Global AI/Cybered Conflict and Navies," in *AI at War: How Big Data, Artificial Intelligence, and Machine Learning Are Changing Naval Warfare*, ed. Sam J. Tangredi and George Galdorisi (Annapolis, MD: Naval Institute Press, 2021), 295.

6. FBI, "Operation Lemon Aid Spy Case," https://www.fbi.gov/history/famous-cases /operation-lemon-aid-spy-case.

7. Julian E. Barnes, David E. Sanger, and Brenda Wintrode, "U.S. Navy Engineer Charged in Attempt to Sell Nuclear Submarine Secrets," *New York Times*, 10 October 2021, https://www.nytimes.com/2021/10/10/us/politics/espionage-nuclear-submarine-fbi.html.

8. Alexander Powell et al., *Maritime Sabotage: Lessons Learned and Implications for Strategic Competition*, N00014–16-D-5003 (Arlington, VA: Center for Naval Analyses, October 2021), 5, https://www.cna.org/archive/CNA_Files/pdf /maritime-sabotage-lessons-learned-and-implications-for-strategic-competition .pdf.

9. Powell et al.

10. Powell et al., 9.

11. Powell et al., 24.

12. Warner, 33.

13. David Vergun, "DOD Focused on Protecting the Defense Industrial Base from Cyber Threats," *DOD News*, 7 February 2022, https://www.defense.gov /News/News-Stories/Article/Article/2926539/dod-focused-on-protecting-the -defense-industrial-base-from-cyber-threats/.

14. Fred Kaplan, "How the United States Learned to Cyber Sleuth: The Untold Story," *Politico*, 20 March 2016, https://www.politico.com/magazine/story/2016/03 /russia-cyber-war-fred-kaplan-book-213746/.

15. Ben Buchanan and Michael Sulmeyer, "Russia and Cyber Operations: Challenges and Opportunities for the Next U.S. Administration," Carnegie Endowment for International Peace, December 2016, https://carnegieendowment.org/2016/12/13 /russia-and-cyber-operations-challenges-and-opportunities-for-next-u.s. -administration-pub-66433.

16. "China Hacked Sensitive Undersea Warfare Plans—*Washington Post*," *Reuters*, 8 June 2018, https://www.reuters.com/article/us-usa-china-cyber/china -hacked-sensitive-u-s-navy-undersea-warfare-plans-washington-post-idUSKC N1J42MM.

17. Dustin Volz, "Chinese Hackers Target Universities in Pursuit of Maritime Military Secrets," *Wall Street Journal*, 5 March 2019, https://www.wsj.com /articles/chinese-hackers-target-universities-in-pursuit-of-maritime-military -secrets-11551781800?mod=article_inline.

18. Fred Plan et al., "APT40: Examining a China-Nexus Espionage Actor," *Mandiant*, 10 August 2023, https://www.mandiant.com/resources/blog/apt40 -examining-a-china-nexus-espionage-actor.

19. Erik Gartzke and Jon Lindsay, "Weaving Tangled Webs: Offense, Defense, and Deception in Cyberspace," *Security Studies* 24, no. 2 (2015): 338–39.

20. Kaplan.

21. Gartzke and Lindsay, 340–41.

22. Justin Sherman, "Cord-Cutting, Russian Style: Could the Kremlin Sever Global Internet Cables?" *Atlantic Council: New Atlanticist* (January 2022), https:// www.atlanticcouncil.org/blogs/new-atlanticist/cord-cutting-russian-style-could -the-kremlin-sever-global-internet-cables/.

23. Tim McGeehan, "Tumult in the Deep: The Unfolding Maritime Competition over Undersea Infrastructure," Center for International Maritime Security, 19 October 2023, https://cimsec.org/tumult-in-the-deep-the-unfolding -maritime-competition-over-undersea-infrastructure/.

24. Conor Gallagher and Simon Carswell, "Russian Naval Drill to Still Take Place over Vital Cables, Experts Believe," *Irish Times*, 31 January 2022, https://www .irishtimes.com/news/environment/russian-naval-drill-to-still-take-place -over-vital-cables-experts-believe-1.4789421.

25. Garrett Hinck, "Evaluating the Russian Threat to Undersea Cables," *Lawfare*, 5 March 2018, https://www.lawfareblog.com/evaluating-russian -threat-undersea-cables.

26. Huizhong Wu and Johnson La, "Taiwan Suspects Chinese Ships Cut Islands' Internet Cables," *Associated Press*, 18 April 2023, https://apnews.com/article /matsu-taiwan-internet-cables-cut-china-65f10f5f73a346fa788436366d7a7c70.

27. Jason Ileto, "Cyber at Sea: Protecting Strategic Sealife in the Age of Strategic Competition," Modern War Institute, 10 May 2022, https://mwi.westpoint.edu /cyber-at-sea-protecting-strategic-sealift-in-the-age-of-strategic-competition/.

28. "Study Maps 'Extensive Russian GPS Spoofing,'" *BBC*, 2 April 2019, https:// www.bbc.com/news/technology-47786248#.

29. William Loomis et al., "A System of Systems: Cooperation on Maritime Cyber-security," Atlantic Council Cyber Statecraft Initiative, October 2021, https://www.atlanticcouncil.org/in-depth-research-reports/report/cooperation-on-maritime-cybersecurity-a-system-of-systems/. For a discussion of potential mitigation strategies, see Jandria Alexander et al., "Cyber Attacks on Navy Port Supply Operations," Booz Allen Hamilton Perspectives, https://www.boozallen.com/markets/defense/indo-pacific/cyberattacks-on-navy-port-supply-operations.html.

30. "Hackers Took 'Full Control' of Container Ship's Navigation Systems for 10 Hours—IHS Fairplay," Resilient Navigation and Timing Foundation, 25 November 2017, https://rntfnd.org/2017/11/25/hackers-took-full-control-of-container-ships-navigation-systems-for-10-hours-ihs-fairplay/.

31. Andy Greenberg, "The Untold Story of NotPetya, the Most Devastating Cyberattack in History," *Wired*, 22 August 2018, https://www.wired.com/story/notpetya-cyberattack-ukraine-russia-code-crashed-the-world/.

32. Tyson B. Meadors, "Cyber Warfare Is a Navy Mission," U.S. Naval Institute *Proceedings* 148, no. 9 (September 2022): 68–73, https://www.usni.org/magazines/proceedings/2022/september/cyber-warfare-navy-mission.

33. Sungbaek Cho et al., "Cybersecurity Considerations in Autonomous Ships," NATO Cooperative Cyber Defence Centre of Excellence, 2022, https://ccdcoe.org/uploads/2022/09/Cybersecurity_Considerations_in_Autonomous_Ships.pdf.

SECTION 2

OPERATIONS

The Dawn and Disquiet of Naval Cyber

NORMAN FRIEDMAN

It has now been more than sixty years since the U.S. Navy opened the cyber age at sea by adopting the naval tactical data system (NTDS) in 1959.[1] Looking back at that system, so simple by modern standards, we can understand a similar set of the issues behind the later deployment of cyber (and now artificial intelligence [AI]) in naval systems. The U.S. Navy adopted a computer command system because it was impossible for unaided humans to keep track of rapidly developing tactical situations, particularly air attacks. The core command function involved was the creation and maintenance of a tactical picture upon which decisions could be based. In the most stressful case, mass air attack, the decisions were allocation of defending fighter aircraft and their direction once assigned to incoming raids.

Prior to automation, the picture was maintained by plotters as a vertical plot in a ship's combat information center (CIC). When a radar operator detected a target, he reported it to a teller, who in turn reported it to a plotter. This chain of reporting imposed time lags in the picture created on the vertical plot, which in turn was the basis for decisions. The more aircraft were detected, the longer the lags.

The key point was that the ship's fighters were directed based not on observed reality but on a picture created below decks in the CIC. No one in the CIC could tell how far the picture lagged reality—there was no automatic source of "ground truth." Once World War II ended, both the U.S. Navy and the Royal Navy tested then-current CIC procedures to measure lags—the unreality of the picture—as the number of attackers increased. The results were not encouraging, and it was obvious at the time that the situation would worsen as attackers' speeds increased with the advent of jet aircraft. The history of how the U.S. Navy's digital technologies could fail to provide ground truth illuminates what naval cyber failures could look like when under attack in future conflicts.

⊢• NTDS AND THE DIGITAL ERA

NTDS was the result of early 1950s Sixth Fleet full-scale exercises in the Mediterranean, with particularly unhappy results. It was inspired by the first U.S. computer-aided air defense system, the semi-automatic ground environment (SAGE), which was conceived for North American strategic air defense. In its case, as later in the case of NTDS, the air defense problem seemed hopeless until computers were brought in. In the North American case, before SAGE the justification for radars monitoring the air approaches to the United States was that they would enable U.S. bombers to get off the ground before they could be obliterated by Soviet attacks. Protection of the United States was deemed impossible. Post-SAGE, a real defense of North America was considered possible, just as post-NTDS, it seemed that a carrier task force could in fact survive a Soviet attack.

At the outset, NTDS employed a large and very expensive computer, and it was limited to major fleet units (planned widespread installation was drastically slowed as the Vietnam War ate the money required). As Moore's law crushed the size and cost of computers, it and its equivalents spread through the fleet. However, a major issue was to what extent allied navies would buy compatible computer command systems. Another subtler issue was how visible computerization was to the fleet.

The answer may be somewhat depressing.[2] The Navy never faced the saturation attacks that had originally justified creating NTDS and, later, Aegis. The system's first major test came in Vietnam, when an NTDS-equipped ship monitored air traffic above the Tonkin Gulf. Monitoring was needed at least partly to distinguish friendly, enemy, and civilian air traffic, so that friendlies and, apparently above all, airliners would not be shot down. In the course of the Vietnam War, the Navy's concept of air control using computer-maintained air pictures expanded to employ other resources, such as fixed radars and even intelligence data. This development seems to have been a major reason why North Vietnamese air defenses were ineffective against naval aircraft late in the war. Additionally, a computer air picture was probably largely responsible for the success of the naval component of the air attack against Libya in 1986. There was a gap between computer displays and reality that narrowed but did not go away.

⊢• COMPUTER DISPLAYS VERSUS REALITY ("GROUND TRUTH")

A related naval computer–aided command system failed badly when the USS *Vincennes* (CG 49) shot down an Iranian airliner in 1988. The *Vincennes* was monitoring air traffic above the Persian Gulf. A safe corridor had been defined for airliners flying out of Iran. Air traffic outside the corridor was considered potentially hostile. On the theory that failure teaches far more than success, what does that incident tell us about cyber's current and future struggles with representing what is actually happening outside of the command operations center?

The first thing to remember is that a computer system is primarily a means of organizing information to support tactical decisions. It presents a picture that it has created with human assistance. To the decision-makers interpreting the display, the picture *is* reality. They do not, and cannot, constantly think about its limitations or about the assumptions built into it. As computer displays become slicker, this tendency is reinforced.

This is true for the combat computer displays of allied nations and, presumably, adversaries. Some years ago, a very experienced Royal Navy captain made just this point. He had recently helped develop the British national command system, which displayed a picture of a situation based largely on intelligence inputs. He contrasted current with past techniques. He imagined a war in the desert, in which a dying soldier staggered into the commander's tent and threw down a bloodied piece of paper. It was up to the commander who received that paper to decide if the information on the paper was valid. A modern system might incorporate the same information, but anyone using it would have to drill down some considerable distance to find out that it was no more than a bloodied piece of paper. It would still be necessary to decide how valid it really was, but those responsible for tactical decisions might not realize just how shaky the evidence behind their information might be.

Unfortunately, the picture on the screen is not reality; it is an attempt to show reality. For example, NTDS supported three classes of symbols representing objects it was tracking: friendlies, enemies, and unknowns presumed hostile. That made excellent sense in a hot war situation. In colder war situations like that in the Gulf, the absence of a category for neutrals was unfortunate (European allies later modified their command systems to embody a neutral category).

Also, NTDS and Aegis were designed to handle saturation raids. There was not much point, it seemed, for them to display details of particular targets, such as their trajectories. The first question about a potential target was whether it was actually a threat (i.e., was approaching), and the second had to be whether it could be engaged. Those monitoring the situation in the ship's combat direction center could obtain information about a particular target only through a relatively cumbersome technique, referring to its track number (which the display did not show). NTDS and Aegis were, moreover, designed to combine data from multiple ships, so their computers were always trying to merge tracks from different ships showing the same target, renumbering the tracks in the process. All of these factors were perfectly sensible—except that they reflected hot war assumptions not particularly relevant in the Gulf.

⊢• THE *VINCENNES* AND AEGIS

The *Vincennes* had a first-generation Aegis system. Her UYK-7 computers had limited capacity, particularly for generating graphics. As a consequence, instead of showing the fly-safe corridor, her displays showed the centerline of that corridor. Those in her combat direction center were aware of this, but under stress, they concentrated on what they could see. It seems fair to say that the better the display, the more operators under stress will rely entirely on it to understand what is happening.[3]

Stress was probably imposed by the situation. The *Vincennes* was new to the Arabian Gulf, so her officers were unaware that the Iranians frequently (and bombastically) threatened the U.S. Navy with annihilation but did not make serious attempts. Their intelligence briefing included the information that the Iranians had announced that this weekend—4 July—they would destroy the Americans. Not knowing that this promise was repeated every weekend was unfortunate. In addition, they had been briefed on anti-ship missile tactics, the main recent example of which was the Argentine Exocet attacks in the Falklands. Key to those attacks had been direction by a stand-off targeteer, an Argentine maritime patrol airplane. When the *Vincennes* observed an Iranian maritime patrol airplane orbiting over the Gulf, it was not difficult to connect it with a planned attack.[4] Again, experience would have shown that the Iranians often flew their P-3s over the Gulf without any consequences.

The *Vincennes* was working with the frigate USS *Sides* (FFG 14), which spotted the Iranian airliner first.[5] The ships traded target data, as their systems were intended to. Also as intended, both ships adopted the track number assigned by the frigate. The system on board the *Vincennes* never announced that it had changed track numbers, because that would have been a distraction in the situation for which the *Vincennes* was designed. Unfortunately, it seems that the track number *Vincennes* initially assigned to the airliner was later assigned by a nearby battle group to an aircraft landing on its carrier. The two groups were close enough that their data link nets apparently merged. Again, that was not apparent to those aboard the *Vincennes*. Ironically, she had been assigned to the Gulf partly to clean up sloppy data link practices.

Further complicating the situation was the reality, common in the Middle East, that military and civilian aircraft often operated from the same airfields, so that the point of origin of a flight could not indicate what sort of airplane it was.

Those in the combat direction center saw an unknown aircraft flying off the line displayed on their screen indicating the safe corridor. They did what they were supposed to do: they tried to use the international radio distress channel to contact the approaching airplane. It later turned out that commercial pilots never monitored that channel, so that "you are standing into danger" brought no response.

The remaining means of deducing the identity of the unknown approaching aircraft was to monitor its behavior. An officer in the combat direction center queried that by track number—but did not realize that a different number had been assigned to the airliner. He saw the aircraft's altitude running down rapidly. Not surprisingly, he called out that it was diving. Given other Iranian behavior, he might reasonably imagine that the unknown airplane was about to crash into his ship. Reality was very different; the airliner was just pulling out of its climb to cruising altitude. Not surprisingly, the ship fired a missile in self-defense. The result was a horrific error.

⊢• LESSONS FOR CYBER SYSTEMS

What does the disaster say about cyber systems? First, it is important to think about the assumptions buried in their design. Aegis was conceived as a fleet air defense system to deal with mass air and missile attacks. It was not conceived as a means of monitoring crisis situations, but it was used for that because of its very superior radar detection and tracking capacity.[6]

Second, under stress, whatever the display shows—without immediately available contrary information—is likely to be taken as true by operators. Whatever the system did not display was invisible and insignificant. Displays were and are typically two-dimensional, although from time to time, holographic three-dimensional displays are tried out. In the case of the *Vincennes*, it would have made an enormous difference if those in the combat direction center had been able to interrogate track data by using a trackball instead of a numerical display linked to a track number.

An important goal of cyber in command systems is to take more and more raw information into account, so that the decision-maker is better informed. That leaves open the question of how the underlying cyber system reaches its conclusions. That lack of "explainability" is also a very difficult issue for AI. (See related discussions by Long and Vaughan, and Pugh in this volume.) Some years ago, a "knowledge wall" was used in a war game at the Naval War College. Its creators emphasized that a commander who questioned what he saw could always drill down to see where the information originated. That evaded the question of whether a commander under stress would generally do so. Cyber command systems are conceived to integrate an increasing amount of data quickly enough for it to be used. The *Vincennes* incident is a sobering reminder that system designers must be explicit in process and physical terms about how they assume their systems will be used. Everyone must be aware that these systems will often be employed under unexpected circumstances.

Another factor is the quality of input information. For *Vincennes*, there was little question of quality; her radar was excellent and its output, precise. In fact, *Vincennes* incorporated a very primitive form of AI intended to filter out some air targets as inappropriate—things like birds. Inescapably, however, large-scale command systems have to employ fuzzier information, typically intelligence data, to be able to accurately process complex situations where exquisitely precise data may not be enough. Some information is classed as sensitive intelligence because interpretation—for example, identification of emitters—involves sensitive sources. In other cases, interpretation is more difficult, and conclusions are not as certain. A commander under pressure to reach a quick decision needs to see machine analysis based on a variety of accurate data sources—a problem that the emerging AI-based systems also face.

⊢• NETWORK-CENTRIC OPERATIONS AND INDIVIDUAL RESPONSIBILITY

Another side of modern cyber-mediated warfare is network-centric operations. It is based on a picture of the situation created by the maximum possible number of sensors. Potential targets are located precisely, and the natural means of attack is global positioning system (GPS)–guided weapons. (See related discussions by Brutzman and Kline, and Cleary in this volume.) Again, failure may be instructive. During the war against Serbia, a U.S. bomber dropped a GPS-guided bomb on the Chinese embassy in Belgrade. GPS guidance is the obvious complement to a network-centric tactical picture; the picture defines the position of the target, and the bomb gets there. In this case, however, it got to the wrong address.

The Chinese said, furiously, that their embassy was clearly marked, with flags flying in front: How could the attack have been anything but deliberate? How could the bomber crew have struck? The bomber flying too high to see flags on buildings, however, attacked a target as indicated by coordinates developed by collaborative interpretation of intelligence data. Apparently, the intended target was a Serbian arms office at a particular street address; the GPS address seems to have been deduced from the related intelligence analysis.

Individual responsibility for lethal acts is a very important military virtue. There is now considerable debate over how that does or does not comport with new types of loitering munitions that independently choose their targets. How does individual responsibility fit into a world of collaborative targeting of precision munitions? In the Chinese case, someone certainly decided to hit whatever was at the location of the Serbian office. But it is unlikely that an individual found the street address and worked out coordinates from city maps. And it is really unlikely that the crew of the bomber can or should be held responsible in any way. How much responsibility is attached to the intelligence unit that decided where it was? And to whomever associated an address in Belgrade with GPS coordinates? It seems unlikely that anyone walked through Belgrade to establish them. It was later suggested that, as in many cities whose road grids were established hundreds of years ago, Belgrade street addresses were somewhat confusing. It is likely that whoever decided to hit that location was unaware of these detailed "ground truth" issues.

⊢• INFORMATION AND CYBER ATTACKS

In this case, the picture was based on a mixture of what could be seen directly—sensor data—and what could be deduced—intelligence data. Those making tactical decisions under pressure are unlikely to have probed down into the details to find out the origin and reliability of information. If they normally had done so, the speed of decision inherent in cyber—in automation—would have been lost. For decades, it has been known that fast decision-making is a key to success in combat. That is, after all, why cyber is so attractive.

Neither of these examples embodies an important current cyber theme: how to deal with enemy cyber attacks (or, for that matter, imposing cyber attacks on the enemy's cyber systems). When systems like NTDS and Aegis were conceived, electronic attack generally meant jamming or deception. (See related discussions by Pugh and Poznansky in this volume.) The data links associated with NTDS and Aegis were designed to overcome jamming by a combination of encryption and, later (in Link 16), frequency-hopping. Encryption was particularly important for NTDS because its data link carried computer commands, such as "engage this target" or "enter this new track into the database."

A final observation concerns the Navy's adoption of AI in dealing with enemy cyber attacks. There seems to be a real threat that, even against cyber defenses including AI, a sufficiently sophisticated attacker could seize control of a target system, perhaps even launching its weapons. (See related discussions on naval shipboard systems by Falcone and Panter in this volume.) If that attack happens, how can responsibility for any digitally guided firing of weapons be attributed or later be justified with substantive digital evidence? That will be a particular issue for armed but unmanned vehicles, which already exist as aerial platforms (unmanned aerial vehicles). AI developers, promoters, and users have yet to solve this problem. Widespread AI use might even make the problem of cyber and knowing ground truth in conflict more difficult.

NOTES

1. My account of early naval command systems and of the *Vincennes* incident is taken from my book, *Network-Centric Warfare: How Navies Learned to Fight Smarter through Three World Wars* (Annapolis, MD: Naval Institute Press, 2009). The sudden shift in optimism about U.S. strategic air defense can be traced to a 1952 proposal to exploit the Navy-sponsored Whirlwind computer, which had been conceived as a training tool. It seems to have been the first computer that could accept input data while running. See my *The Fifty-Year War: Conflict and Strategy in the Cold War* (Annapolis, MD: Naval Institute Press, 2001), 446. My explanation of the *Vincennes* incident is based on research by an Air Force officer studying at the Naval Postgraduate School: Kristen Ann Dotterway, *Systematic Analysis of Complex Dynamic Systems: The Case of the USS* Vincennes, unpublished master of science in systems technology thesis (Monterey, CA, Naval Postgraduate School, June 1992). I find it a lot more persuasive than the combat stress explanation initially offered by the U.S. Navy. For more details of the use of computer air control in Vietnam, see my *U.S. Naval Attack Aircraft* (Annapolis, MD: Naval Institute Press, 2021).

2. For example, projects to install computer combat systems in *Charles F. Adams*–class destroyers stalled twice. Four of the destroyers were transferred to Greece—but only two had the new systems. This is presumably a parallel to all the current cases in which managers seem oblivious to either the capabilities of computer systems or the need to keep them current.

3. Discussions of the effects of stress and complexity in the incident include Nancy C. Roberts, *Reconstructing Combat Decisions: Reflections on the Shootdown of Flight 655*, Technical Report NPS-AS-93-008 (Monterey, CA: Naval Postgraduate School, October 1992), https://apps.dtic.mil/sti/tr/pdf/ADA259045.pdf. For an overall discussion of complexity in military systems, see Chris C. Demchak, *Military Organizations, Complex Machines: Modernization in the U.S. Armed Services* (Ithaca, NY: Cornell University Press, 1991).

4. The *Vincennes* commanding officer's perspective is contained in Will Rogers and Sharon Rogers with Gene Gregson, *Storm Center: The USS* Vincennes *and Iran Air Flight 655* (Annapolis, MD: Naval Institute Press, 1992).

5. In September 1989 the commanding officer of the USS *Sides*, who decided not to shoot, questioned the "unrestrained" and "consistently aggressive" attitude of the *Vincennes* crew (the ship's nickname was "Robo-Cruiser") and suggested that a general atmosphere of needing "to prove the viability of Aegis [technology] in the Persian Gulf" contributed to the mistake, provoking a six-month acrimonious discussion in the pages of U.S. Naval Institute *Proceedings*. See David R. Carlson, "Comment and Discussion," U.S. Naval Institute *Proceedings* 115, no. 9 (September 1989): 87–89, 92, and *Proceedings* "Comment and Discussion" from November 1989 through April 1990.

6. See supporting remarks by an officer involved in Aegis design, M. Eckhart, "Comment and Discussion," U.S. Naval Institute *Proceedings* 116, no. 3 (March 1990): 32.

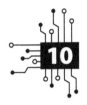# 10 U.S. Naval Forces and Cyber
Personnel, Organization, Operating Principles

ROBERT "JAKE" BEBBER and T. J. WHITE

Naval forces operate in an unforgiving domain. To survive and win, navies must be professionalized forces that utilize dynamic operating procedures and must constantly innovate, adopt, and integrate new technologies into naval operations. The U.S. Navy has long proven successful in its nearly 250 years of service, especially in adopting and optimizing technology in the electromagnetic spectrum and information sciences.

Despite the U.S. Department of Defense determination in 2011 that cyberspace is a warfighting domain, the U.S. Navy risks falling behind key adversaries as well as sister services in operationalizing cyberspace.[1] It has failed to expand its cyber operating forces and accelerate its cyber maneuver capability. To understand this lag requires an overview of how the U.S. Navy has organized and trained its cyber forces up to the present, how they are employed now, and what must be done if it expects to compete and win.

⊢• ANTECEDENTS OF NAVY CYBER

When charting the progression of cyber mission forces in the U.S. Navy, one can begin noting the service has nearly one hundred years of experience as an early mover in operationalizing the electromagnetic spectrum; its forward-focused personnel, organization, and operating principles produced early successes. For example, to avoid operational and technical surprise, the Navy established the Office of Naval Intelligence in 1882 to gain a better understanding of foreign navies.[2] In 1899 the first official Navy wireless message was sent from a steam ship to shore at Highland Station in New Jersey.[3] During the interwar years (1919–39), it experimented with and ultimately adopted several different technologies, including long-range naval gunnery (analog mechanical fire control computing), search and fire control radar, and long-haul communications for command and control of unit and fleets across the world's oceans.[4]

The combination of effective intelligence and a deep knowledge of wireless communications led directly to the 4–6 June 1942 victory in the Battle of Midway. Brilliance, hard work, and no small measure of luck were joined by skilled exploitation of signals intelligence and the prior decisions by the Navy to invest (operating principles) in individuals such as Edward Layton and Joe Rochefort (personnel) to develop an expert cultural knowledge of Japan and technical plus operational understanding of the Imperial Japanese naval threat (organization).[5]

Throughout the Cold War (1945–91), both the American and Soviet fleets understood the value of the electromagnetic spectrum for maneuver and decision advantage at sea. Each sought to develop new technologies and apply them to fleet operations while simultaneously disrupting and denying the spectrum, and thus spectrum-dependent weapons, to their adversary. At the same time, the United States was applying lessons learned from establishing combat information centers at sea, and the Navy began adopting tactical data links, integrated combat systems (Aegis), and over-the-horizon weapons (Tomahawk, Harpoon), and utilizing networked sensors, large-scale computing resources, and real-time information synthesis to drive military campaign assessment. (See detailed discussion by Friedman in this volume.) These new technologies and operational concepts were central to the victory of coalition forces during Operation Desert Storm and constituted the infancy of the Navy's cyber-driven operations.

In 2004 the Navy established the cryptologic technician networks rating to meet fleet requirements to perform computer network operations. This was followed in 2005 by the disestablishment of the Naval Security Group and its missions being assumed by a new Naval Network Warfare Command.[6] That same year, the Navy expanded the core competencies of its special-duty cryptology officers to include both information operations and related capabilities in electronic warfare, military information support operations (formerly psychological operations), operational security, military deception, and cyberspace operations.[7]

This early reorganization brought together those experts charged with operating and defending the Navy's command, control, and communications (C3) networks with those who exploit and attack adversary C3 networks. At this point the Navy was (perhaps) best postured institutionally to make the programmatic and technical innovations necessary to complement talent reorganization and maintain its decisive edge over future competitors in electromagnetic operations.

After the establishment of U.S. Cyber Command (USCYBERCOM) in 2010 as a four-star military command to undertake global synchronization and execution of full-spectrum cyberspace operations, all the military services—including the U.S. Navy—established formal service components and forces assigned for employment to USCYBERCOM.

⊢• DEVELOPMENT OF CYBER PERSONNEL

In 2009 the Navy established the information warfare community, originally titled the information dominance community, to manage officers, enlisted, and civilian professionals who possess extensive skills in vital information-related fields, including intelligence, meteorology and oceanography, information technology and network administration, communications, cryptology, space operations, and cyberspace operations.[8] The Navy has reorganized enlisted rates and officer designators since then and has sought to rapidly grow its cyber-related cadre of active-duty and reserve component personnel.

Among the enlisted rates within the information warfare community, those that work extensively or exclusively in cyberspace operations are information systems technicians, with an approximate strength in 2023 of 11,000 sailors, and cyber warfare technicians (CWTs) (formerly known as cryptologic technician networks), with an approximate strength in 2023 of 2,300 sailors.[9]

While other rates certainly provide support to cyberspace operations, such as intelligence specialists, the information systems technician and CWT rates will most often be performing as on-net operators conducting offensive and defensive operations, technical analysts, or network maintenance and system administration. In 2024 a robotics rating was approved to build that expertise in the enlisted corps. There is no officer equivalent at this writing.

In 2010 the Navy established the cyber warrant officer program to identify, develop, and commission by warrant technically proficient sailors to operate, analyze, plan, and direct full-spectrum cyber operations. It followed up in 2019 by reestablishing the warrant officer 1 rank to retain and promote sailors with cyber skills at the E-5 rank.[10] The commissioned officer fields that lead the Navy's cyberspace mission efforts include cryptologic warfare (CW) officers, with an approximate strength in 2023 of 1,200 officers, cyber warfare engineers (CWEs), with an approximate strength in 2023 of 80 officers, and information professional (IP) officers, with an approximate strength in 2023 of 1,100 officers.[11]

The 2023 National Defense Authorization Act required the Secretary of the Navy to "establish a cyber operations designator [for officers] and rating [for enlisted]," which led to the creation of a maritime cyber warfare officer (MCWO) designator and the enlisted cyber warfare technician rate.[12] This officer community was initially staffed by the conversion of approximately 120 officers from the current CW and IP fields. MCWOs, CWs, CWEs, and IPs are restricted line officers, which means they are not eligible for command at sea (surface ship, submarine, aircraft squadron, special warfare, explosive ordnance disposal). Cyber warfare designations are still evolving and will undoubtedly be renamed in the future as roles and responsibilities respond to changing circumstances of conflict.

⊢• DEVELOPMENT OF NAVY CYBER ORGANIZATIONS

The Navy has three principal service organizations responsible for cyber mission forces and support. The first, Fleet Cyber Command (FCC), was established in 2010 and is the main cyber operational command tasked with network operations, signals intelligence, cyberspace operations, and space operations. The FCC commands the Navy Cyber Warfare Development

Group that for thirty years has served as the Navy's center for cyber warfare innovation—for example, establishing in 2020 a cyber "foundry" to accelerate the development of offensive cyber capabilities. At the same time, the Navy also reactivated the World War II–era U.S. Tenth Fleet (C10F) as the cyber force provider to the service and the joint force, also serving as the naval component to USCYBERCOM. Since its establishment in 2010, FCC/C10F has grown into an operational force of "19,000 Active and Reserve Sailors and civilians organized into 26 active commands, 40 Cyber Mission Force units, and 29 reserve commands around the globe."[13] FCC/C10F is a dual-hatted Echelon II command with a vice admiral serving as commander of both entities.[14]

The second principal organization is Naval Information Forces (NAVIFOR) command, an Echelon III command under U.S. Fleet Forces, which handles "all Navy IW force generation and delivery to naval and joint operational commanders; IW doctrine, policy and governance; training requirements; and community management. [As of 2023,] NAVIFOR directs 600 military and civilian employees to generate IW readiness across the fleet, including direct administrative control of over 85 commands and activities manning [approximately] 20,000 billets across the globe."

NAVIFOR is the type command for meteorology and oceanography, cryptology, cyber, electronic warfare, information operations, intelligence, information networks, and space disciplines.[15] Like all type commands, this is the manpower, training, modernization, and maintenance component for these disciplines. In 2014 the commander of naval information forces was designated as the information warfare community leader. NAVIFOR is commanded by a vice admiral.[16]

Most of the enlisted sailors and officers in cyberspace operations receive initial training at learning sites located in Pensacola, Florida (Information Warfare Training Command Corry Station), and Virginia Beach, Virginia (Information Warfare Training Command Virginia Beach). These two learning sites are Echelon IV commands reporting to the Center for Information Warfare Training, an Echelon III learning center command for Naval Education Training Command, headquartered in Pensacola.

For both ITs and CWTs, the initial training pipeline can take a year or more, before going to their first duty station. As of 2023 an IP officer will go through twenty weeks of training at Virginia Beach (after their commissioning source training), followed by a first operational tour, usually as the communications officer or information security officer on a warship. A cryptologic warfare officer, including warrant officers, will receive twelve weeks of training at Corry Station before heading to their first command, usually a shore activity.[17] As of this writing, the MCWO cadre is sourced through conversions and transfer of officers in other warfare career fields until a new officer training pipeline is established.

Finally, in 2019 the Navy reorganized the Space and Naval Warfare Systems Command into the Navy Information Warfare Systems Command (NAVWAR), reflecting its broader mission to provide the Navy with "capable and secure communications and networks that span platforms and facilities."[18] NAVWAR is one of five major Department of the Navy systems acquisition commands that conduct "research and development, systems engineering, testing and evaluation, technical, in-service and support services" for the Navy.[19]

Ultimately, resource decisions (that is, funding) concerning all organizations fall to the Chief of Naval Operations (with the concurrence of the Secretary of the Navy). Within the Office of the Chief of Naval Operations (OPNAV) is the Deputy Chief of Naval Operations (DCNO) for information warfare (N2/N6), commonly referred to as OPNAV N2/N6. OPNAV N2/N6 is one of a few resource sponsors on the headquarters staff. In 2009 the Navy reorganized the OPNAV staff by merging the former DCNO for intelligence (N2) with the DCNO for command, control, communications, computers, intelligence, surveillance, and reconnaissance (N6) to better orchestrate the recognized importance and value proposition of information to drive both decision and combat advantage alongside the newly established information warfare community.[20] N2/N6 is the Navy's primary office for resourcing intelligence capabilities, cyber warfare, command and control, electronic warfare, battle management, oceanography, and meteorology. The OPNAV N2/N6 mission is to "provide end-to-end accountability for Navy information requirements, investments, capabilities and forces."[21] The DCNO for information warfare also formally serves as the director of naval intelligence and is a vice admiral in rank.[22]

By 2020 the Navy had organized its cyber forces like its other warfare communities. It had a professional cadre of officers, enlisted, and civilian personnel; an OPNAV resource sponsor or "platform baron"; a type command; a systems command; and uniquely, a dedicated operational command.[23] The necessary pieces had been placed on the board and the organizations had been stood up, structured, and aligned. In terms of warfighting structure, resourcing, and organization, Navy cyber maneuver forces and operational capabilities were now organizationally equal with the rest of the Navy's warfare communities, such as surface, undersea, and air warfare.

⊢• UNINTENDED CONSEQUENCES OF MISALIGNED EARLY OPERATING PRINCIPLES

The fact that intelligence services were the earliest to develop and use cyberspace, principally as a means of espionage, led to the early uses of cyberspace capabilities being highly selective, secretive, and cloistered at the highest levels of government—analogous to perceptions of strategic nuclear weapons deterrence/missions. Keeping cyber operations compartmented from conventional military planning and operations resulted in the military intelligence culture conflating "cyber equals nuclear" and "cyber equals compartmented." Cyber issues were left occupying the narrow intellectual space reserved for strategic nuclear deterrence and sensitive intelligence collection (with an occasional toe dipped in special operations). Cyber employment decisions were reserved for the highest levels in government. Indeed, this was institutionalized by U.S. policymakers when USCYBERCOM was established in 2010 as a subunified command under U.S. Strategic Command (where strategic nuclear forces are principally controlled); collocated at the National Security Agency headquarters (where sensitive signals intelligence collection is conducted); and with its commander being dual-hatted as the director of the National Security Agency and commander, U.S. Cyber Command.

These misaligned policies and perceptions depressed the development of information strategic resources in support of traditional military operations and competitive strategies during key early years. Conversely, adversaries were already employing cyberspace operations and fundamentally reshaping global power to their advantage.

Only in 2018 did USCYBERCOM, as directed by the policy community at the Department of Defense and White House upon recommendation of USCYBERCOM, adopt new cyberspace operating principles and approaches that better align with the reality of competition and conflict in cyberspace today. Instead of operating solely as a reaction force, waiting to be attacked and holding a "deterrence by punishment" framework that sought to prevent attacks by threatening to impose retaliatory costs (a nuclear approach), U.S. cyber forces shifted to an "initiative-persistent strategy aimed at thwarting and frustrating adversaries" by "defending forward" to identify, disrupt, or halt malicious cyber activity "at the source."[24] U.S. cyberspace operations teams would now "persistently contest malicious cyber activity in day-to-day competition."[25]

More to the point of this chapter, this conceptual shift in cyberspace operations mirrors the long-standing core conventional naval strategy of "forward presence," whereby forward-deployed combat-credible forces serve U.S. national security interests by operating daily in the maritime commons to secure free trade and conduct engagement with partner nations and allies. (See chapter by Tangredi in this volume for more elaboration of this point.) If necessary, these forces are prepared to conduct combat operations forward.[26]

This correction of the original misalignment allows, in principle, for more vigorous integration of cyber with Navy operations. The Navy has since adopted a "cyberspace superiority vision" guided by the three principles of *secure*, *survive*, and *strike*, and an "information superiority vision" built upon three efforts: *modernize*, *innovate*, and *defend*. These principles and efforts encompass Navy cyberspace activities across the entire competition continuum, from day-to-day operations to crisis and conflict. Superiority is not possible without security, which includes all information technology, networks, data, critical infrastructure, weapons systems, and combat platforms. Security requires that the Navy keep its best cyber talent and cultivate a professional cyber security workforce and cyber warfighting culture. Superiority demands a Navy that can "fight hurt" in a contested or denied electromagnetic and networked environment and that is postured to conduct combat operations in and through cyberspace.[27]

In combat at sea, there simply are no successful combat operations without assured cyberspace. No success will be possible without modernizing the Navy's information and operational technology infrastructure, leveraging advanced decision-support technology, and transforming cyber security culture service-wide and within the defense industrial base from compliance-centered to readiness-centered.[28]

For Navy commanders, whether a fleet commander or the commanding officer of a ship, cyberspace superiority requires a set of capabilities that recognize anomalies, threats, and unknowns, and that can identify and neutralize the event while delivering cyber-physical combat effects. In addition, the nature of joint cyberspace is that the Army, Air Force, Marines, Space Force, Coast Guard, and allies must also recognize and neutralize their own anomalies, threats, and unknowns. Allies and joint forces all leverage shared strengths and suffer shared weaknesses and vulnerabilities. In 2022 then-Chief of Naval Operations Adm. Michael Gilday released his Navigation Plan 2022 (NAVPLAN 2022), prioritizing readiness, capability modernization, the generation of cost-effective capacity to achieve warfighting risk, and investment in a trained, resilient, and educated combat force that delivers to Navy commanders what they need to fight and win.[29]

To implement NAVPLAN 2022 and future force design imperatives, the Navy pursues four capability objectives. These aims are tied to the ability of the Navy to achieve its cyberspace superiority vision. These goals include long-range fires (how the Navy shoots), counter–command, control, communications, computers, cyber, intelligence, surveillance, and reconnaissance (how the Navy maneuvers), terminal defense (how the Navy defends), and contested logistics (how the Navy supplies). Enabling these goals are live, virtual, and constructive training, naval operational architecture, artificial intelligence, and unmanned aerial systems.

Table 10-1 summarizes the main concepts of the Navy documents related to cyberspace operations. The Department of the Navy information superiority vision, prepared by the Navy's chief information officer, focuses on network operations and defense of networks, in which the Navy cyber force will obviously play a role.[30] The Navy chief information officer capstone design is

TABLE 10-1. Main Concepts of Navy Documents Related to Cyberspace Operations

Chief Information Officer Information Superiority Vision	Chief Information Officer Capstone Design	Cyberspace Superiority Vision	Navigation Plan 2022
Modernize	1 x Goal	Secure	Long-Range Fires
Innovate	2 x Outcomes	Survive	Counter–Command, Control, Communications, Computers, Cyber, Intelligence, Surveillance, Reconnaissance, and Targeting
Defend	3 x Objectives	Strike	Terminal Defense
	4 x Attributes		Contested Logistics
			Live Virtual Constructive Training
			Naval Operations Architecture
			Artificial Intelligence
			Unmanned Systems

effectively an update to the vision.[31] Importantly, all capability objectives are dependent on cyberspace operations.

⊢• ASSESSMENT AND RECOMMENDATIONS: WHERE DO WE GO FROM HERE

Despite these laudable additions, updates, and reorganizations, the Navy still finds itself in the position of playing "catch-up" to its sister services, as well as its principal adversaries. How did this happen after being at the leading edge in the early 2000s?

Conceptually, the Navy suffered for twenty years from a form of "institutional Alzheimer's" in how to manage and defend its own spectrum, conduct counter-targeting operations, and maneuver in cyberspace to support fleet operations. The service had abandoned its requirement to conduct war at sea in a contested electromagnetic environment in favor of overland strike in an information-rich benign environment. Its post-2003 over-the-horizon targeting was built to "find and fix" non-state actors who lacked spectrum disruption and denial capabilities.

The result is that, right now, the Navy is only a resource provider to the joint force and remains short of the cyber capabilities it needs. The cyber and electromagnetic spectrum "voice" within the Navy's warfare integration efforts needs to be elevated. To succeed, the Navy will need its own cyberspace operations forces capable of conducting its Title 10 cyber-physical military operations in support of fleet operations. This organic force, here referred to as maritime cyber teams (MCTs), must focus on generating the accesses to support the outcomes envisioned by the information superiority vision, the cyberspace superiority vision, and NAVPLAN 2022:

- The MCTs must be resourced by OPNAV N2/N6 with necessary and sufficient talent, infrastructure, and tools.
- The type commander, NAVIFOR, remains responsible for force generation but should not be limited to capability and tactics, techniques, and procedures development.
- The MCTs should be operationally assigned under commander, FCC/C10F, and aligned to forward-deployed naval forces missions synchronized to the joint force and component commander's integrated priorities and targets that are not being actioned by the joint force.
- The MCT mission must directly support fleet maneuver and warfighting. This requires that they be under tactical control of numbered fleet commanders.

The creation, employment, and resourcing of maritime cyber teams, however, must not come at the expense of the joint force. In that regard, the Navy must look to the other services to model its resourcing since it has previously underinvested in cyber capabilities—particularly in comparison to the other services. While the Navy should prioritize resourcing to conduct operations against its peer competitor, China, it should also ensure sufficient resources for global fleet operations. The Navy no longer has the luxury of underinvesting when its peer is now operating globally.

Maritime cyber teams will require their own cyberspace operations infrastructure and an expansion of resources to the Navy Cyber Warfare Development Group. This also includes funding more billets for cyber warfare engineers, since eighty is inadequate. These three improvements will permit the Navy to access, exploit, and act on targets that support its maritime mission to fight and win at sea. Importantly, these abilities in turn require the maritime cyber teams to develop the tactics, techniques, and procedures, rules of engagement, and additional training requirements that will nest within ship battle orders and fleet operational plans and deploy strike group preplanned responses. Integrating with these established orders and responses also demands close collaboration with fleet staffs and component commanders throughout development.

Leading these efforts at a carrier strike group or an amphibious ready group that constitutes the core of an expeditionary strike group is the information warfare commander (IWC). While the IWC has an important role in synchronizing information-related and cyber capabilities across the carrier strike group or amphibious ready group, they do not have equivalent "weapons release" authorities that fellow composite warfare commanders—such as the surface warfare commander or air warfare commander—possess. Granting the IWC weapons release authority is critical when it comes to network defense and emissions control, and demands serious attention to network insecurities, signal radiation, and frequency deconfliction, as well as conducting forceful corrective actions. An effective IWC will also require the authority to execute military cyberspace operations in support of the commander's priorities—no different than an air warfare commander executing air operations.

To support the joint force, the Navy must fully resource Joint Force Headquarters–Cyber Navy and integrate it with the recently established Fleet Information Warfare Command Pacific.[32] The Navy should add billets as well as leverage Marine Forces Pacific and Marine Forces Cyber. The Navy's shift to a single information environment (Flank Speed) must be completed to include overseas information environments.[33] This would support the efforts outlined in the information superiority vision and improve cyber security readiness by adopting a "zero trust" cloud architecture. To ensure maritime maneuver and assured command and control, the Navy will have to successfully integrate Project Overmatch within its Consolidated Afloat Network Enterprise System (the information backbone on naval platforms). Project Overmatch is the Navy effort to support the larger Defense Department joint all-domain command and control effort to reliably connect U.S. and allied forces across land, air, sea, and space via cyberspace.[34]

Most importantly, the Navy will need to recognize that it must regain and retain the support of the U.S. Congress. Recent media reports of infighting in the Pentagon over fleet size and maritime capabilities have frustrated Congress as it seeks to resource the Navy at a time when China's navy has already surpassed the U.S. service in size and scale of capabilities.[35]

The above recommendations provide useful navigation for the voyage the Navy must take while adopting a meaningful sense of urgency—one that measures time horizons in weeks and months, not years or decades. Time is not on our side, and we have none to lose.

NOTES

1. Mike Lennon, "Department of Defense: Cyberspace Is a New Warfighting Domain," *Security Week*, 14 July 2011.
2. Jeffery Dorwart, *Dorwart's History of the Office of Naval Intelligence, 1865–1945* (Annapolis, MD: Naval Institute Press, 2019).
3. *U.S. Naval Communications Chronological History*, 2006, https://www.navy -radio.com/manuals/NAVCOMM-history-2006.pdf.
4. See Vincent P. O'Hara and Leonard R. Heinz, *Innovating Victory: Naval Technology in Three Wars* (Annapolis, MD: Naval Institute Press, 2022).
5. Elliot Carlson, *Joe Rochefort's War: The Odyssey of the Codebreaker Who Outwitted Yamamoto at Midway* (Annapolis, MD: Naval Institute Press, 2013).
6. From 1935 to 2005, the Naval Security Group was the organization within the U.S. Navy tasked with signals intelligence, cryptology, information assurance, and denial of intelligence to adversaries. It was replaced by the Navy Network Warfare Command.
7. U.S. Naval Academy, "Information Warfare: Cryptologic Warfare History," https://www.usna.edu/InformationWarfare/history/Cryptological_Warfare _History.php.
8. U.S. Naval Academy, "Information Warfare: Cryptologic Warfare History."
9. "Information Systems Technician (IT)," *MyNavy HR*, https://www.mynavyhr. navy.mil/Career-Management/Community-Management/Enlisted/Information- Warfare/IT/; "Cyber Warfare Technician (CWT)," *MyNavy HR*, https://www .mynavyhr.navy.mil/Career-Management/Community-Management/Enlisted /Information-Warfare/CWT/.
10. Ben Werner, "Navy Brings Back Warrant Officer-1 Rank for Cyber Sailors," *USNI News*, 13 June 2018.

11. "Cryptologic Warfare (1810)," *MyNavy HR*, https://www.mynavyhr.navy.mil/Career-Management/Community-Management/Officer/Active-OCM/Restricted-Line/Cryptologic-Warfare/; "Information Professional (1820)," *MyNavy HR*, https://www.mynavyhr.navy.mil/Career-Management/Community-Management/Officer/Active-OCM/Restricted-Line/Information-Professional/; "Cyber Warfare Engineering (1840)," *MyNavy HR*, https://www.mynavyhr.navy.mil/Career-Management/Community-Management/Officer/Active-OCM/Restricted-Line/Cyber-Warfare-Engineering/.

12. Mario Vulcano, "Establishment of Cyber Operations Designator and Rating for the Navy?" *Station Hypo*, 21 June 2022; Chris Demchak, Michael Poznansky, and Sam J. Tangredi, "A Divorce between the Navy and CyberCommand Would be Dangerous," *War on the Rocks*, 23 August 2023.

13. U.S. Fleet Cyber Command/U.S. Tenth Fleet, "Command Description," https://www.fcc.navy.mil/#:~:text=U.S.%20Tenth%20Fleet%20is%20the,at%20Fort%20George%20Meade%2C%20Md.

14. U.S. Fleet Cyber Command/U.S. Tenth Fleet. An Echelon II command reports directly to the Chief of Naval Operations.

15. U.S. Navy type commands perform administrative, personnel, and operational training functions in the Navy for a "type" of naval weapons platform, such as surface (ship) warfare, submarine warfare, and naval aviation, formerly within a fleet organization, but currently reporting to Fleet Forces Command.

16. U.S. Navy Information Forces (NAVIFOR), "Mission," https://www.navifor.usff.navy.mil/About-Us/Mission/.

17. "Center for Information Warfare Training," *MyNavy HR*, https://www.netc.navy.mil/CIWT/.

18. Naval Information Warfare Systems Command, "About," https://www.navwar.navy.mil/.

19. Naval Information Warfare Systems Command.

20. Command, control, communications, computers, intelligence, surveillance, and reconnaissance (C4ISR) has recently become C5ISR with the addition of "cyber."

21. "OPNAV N2/N6," https://mrr.dawnbreaker.com/portals/phase3/opnav-resource-sponsors/opnav-n2-n6/.

22. "OPNAV N2/N6."

23. Prior to 1991, the term "platform baron" referred to the Deputy Chief of Naval Operations for a particular warfare area, such as surface warfare, undersea warfare, and naval aviation. At the time, each Deputy Chief of Naval Operations functioned as the senior-most decision-maker for their respective warfare community. These positions were subsequently downgraded.

24. Emily O. Goldman, "Paradigm Change Requires Persistence—A Difficult Lesson to Learn," *The Cyber Defense Review* 7, no. 1 (Winter 2022): 114.

25. Goldman.

26. Thomas G. Mahnken, "Forward Presence in the Modern Navy: From the Cold War to a Future Tailored Force," Naval History and Heritage Command, 16 August 2017, https://www.history.navy.mil/research/library/online-reading -room/title-list-alphabetically/n/needs-opportunities-modern-history-us-navy forward-presence-modern-navy-cold-war-future-tailored-force.html.

27. Department of the Navy, *Cyberspace Superiority Vision*, October 2022, https:// media.defense.gov/2023/Aug/15/2003281352/-1/-1/0/DON%20CYBERSPACE%20 SUPERIORITY%20VISION.PDF.

28. "From the Report (February 2020 version)," *USNI News*, 21 February 2020.

29. U.S. Chief of Naval Operations, *Navigation Plan 2022*, 26 July 2022, https:// media.defense.gov/2022/Jul/26/2003042389/-1/-1/1/NAVIGATION%20PLAN%20 2022_SIGNED.PDF.

30. Department of the Navy, *Information Superiority Vision*, February 2020, 1, DONInformationSuperiorityVisionFINAL14Feb20.pdf.

31. Department of the Navy Chief Information Officer, "Capstone Concept for Information Superiority," 6 September 2022, https://www.doncio.navy.mil /(2cb4hzjjevo4ch45uageewao)/ContentView.aspx?id=15864#:~:text=This%20Cap stone%20Design%20Concept%20for,order%20to%20realize%20Information%20 Superiority.

32. Mike Pomerleau, "Navy Provides New Details on Information-Warfare-Task Force for Pacific," *Fedscoop*, 7 April 2022.

33. Adam Stone, "Flank Speed Moves Navy to a Cloud-Based Microsoft Office 365 Solution," *FedTech*, 27 May 2022.

34. Megan Eckstein and Colin Demarest, "Project Overmatch: U.S. Navy Preps to Deploy Secretive Multidomain Tech," *Defense News*, 8 December 2022.

35. Lara Seligman, Lee Hudson, and Paul McLeary, "Inside the Pentagon Slugfest over the Future of the Fleet," *Politico*, 24 July 2022; Brad Lendon, "China Has Built the World's Largest Navy. Now What's Beijing Going to Do with It," CNN, 5 March 2021, https://www.cnn.com/2021/03/05/china/china-world-biggest-navy -intl-hnk-ml-dst/index.html.

11 U.S. Marine Corps and Cyber Operations

THOMAS MORSE

yber warfare in the U.S. Marine Corps today is shaped by maneuver warfare doctrine, new service concepts, and a desire for synchronized unity of effort across the service.[1] Cyberspace operations in the Marine Corps are considered full-spectrum operations that could be conducted to defend and protect its systems, to retain the ability to execute command and control, as well as to deliver nonlethal fires in cyberspace to place the adversary into a combined arms dilemma.[2]

The service is challenged with adapting to a rapidly evolving dimension of warfare that may, however, be viewed by many vocal former senior leaders of the Marine Corps as counter to service culture and the established way of doing business. All these forces have significant impacts on units and on employment of cyberspace operations by the Marine Corps.

⊢• CYBER FORCE TRANSFORMATION

The Marine Corps established Marine Forces Cyberspace Command (MARFORCYBER) in October 2009 in response to the establishment of U.S. Cyber Command (USCYBERCOM).[3] In 2014 MARFORCYBER underwent a transformation as it began to mature and build cyber teams. This trans-formation was the result of the warfighting ethos of its leadership, Maj. Gen. Daniel J. O'Donohue, the new commander of MARFORCYBER, and Col. Ryan Heritage, the deputy commander. Both infantry officers, Major General O'Donohue and Colonel Heritage brought a honed "maneuverist" mindset to an organization populated by intelligence and communications professionals.

Major General O'Donohue often referenced the combat mission teams (CMTs) as his maneuver elements and its leaders as his maneuver element commanders. This was a marked change in how the organization viewed itself and its cyber teams. As the CMTs were built, the idea of maneuver was intrinsically valuable, as the Marines viewed cyberspace in the same way ground, air, and naval forces view their respective domains. The teams sought out the gaps in the adversary's defenses, avoiding the hardened surfaces. This maneuvering was often referenced as swimming upstream or downstream, depending on the orientation to the objective. Once adversary gaps were exploited, cyber forces could maneuver, by swimming up- or downstream, to a more advantageous position avoiding a hardened defense or surface.

Several years later, Maj. Gen. Matthew G. Glavy, a Marine aviator, served as commander of both MARFORCYBER and Joint Task Force Ares.[4] He demonstrated the maneuverist mindset and combined arms approach that the service sought. In an interview discussing operations, he stated that "while Ares has been hacking into [the Islamic State of Iraq and Syria] in cyberspace, forces on the ground have driven the group out of most of Syria and Iraq."[5]

Marine Corps Doctrinal Publication 1, *Warfighting*, defines combined arms as "the full integration of arms in such a way that to counteract one, the enemy must become more vulnerable to another. We pose the enemy not just with a problem, but with a dilemma—a no-win situation."[6] As future wars are conducted, this mindset with a clear combined arms philosophy will increase the service's lethality.

⊢• MARFORCYBER STRUCTURE

The Marine Corps, like other services, has centralized its cyber units. Most Marine cyber units fall under MARFORCYBER, which is commanded by a major general and located at Fort Meade, Maryland, the same base as

USCYBERCOM and the National Security Agency. In fact, MARFORCYBER provides thirteen cyber units to USCYBERCOM's Cyber Mission Force, which includes cyber protection teams, combat mission teams, national mission teams, and combat support teams.[7]

Adding to the challenges facing Marine Corps cyber operations is the fact that they support multiple joint combatant commanders: "MARFORCYBER is the component command entrusted with providing direct cyber operations support to U.S. Special Forces Command."[8]

MARFORCYBER has two subordinate commands, Marine Corps Cyberspace Operations Group and Marine Corps Cyberspace Warfare Group (MCCYWG). Each of these units is commanded by a Marine colonel. Titles of the groups indicate their different responsibilities in defensive and offensive cyber operations. As officially described, "[Marine Corps Cyberspace Operations Group] executes Marine Corps Department of Defense Information Network (DODIN) Operations and Marine Corps Defensive Cyberspace Operations in order to enhance freedom of action across warfighting domains, while denying the efforts of adversaries to degrade or disrupt this advantage through cyberspace."[9] In contrast, "MCCYWG organizes, trains, equips, provides administrative support, manages readiness of assigned forces, and recommends certification and presentation of Cyber Mission Force Teams to U.S. Cyber Command. The MCCYWG plans and conducts full spectrum cyberspace operations as directed by [commander], MARFORCYBER in support of service, combatant command, joint, and coalition requirements."[10]

The warfighting mindset displayed by the MARFORCYBER commanders shaped how Marines assigned to MARFORCYBER viewed cyberspace operations. As the Marine cyber workforces grew, Marines initially assigned to MARFORCYBER on cyber protection teams, combat mission teams, national mission teams, and combat support teams began to rotate back to the Fleet Marine Forces. Throughout this transition, they maintained the "maneuverist" mindset developed while at MARFORCYBER.

⊢• CHANGES IN MISSION AND ORGANIZATION

When the Marine Corps emerged from wars in Iraq and Afghanistan, geopolitical changes shifted the Department of Defense's threat focus, codifying this shift within the National Defense Strategy. The focus of the Marine Corps became a return to the sea and littoral operations. Title 10 of the U.S. Code directs that "the Marine Corps shall be organized, trained, and equipped to provide fleet marine forces of combined arms, together with supporting air components, for service with the fleet in the seizure or defense of advanced naval bases and for the conduct of such land operations as may be essential to the prosecution of a naval campaign."[11] To fulfill its Title 10 requirements, the Marine Corps needed to review its organization to prepare for the next conflict. This required a change in a service structure that became optimized for persistent land campaigns in Central Asia. In reassessing the mission, Commandant of the Marine Corps Gen. David H. Berger developed *Force Design 2030* as an implementation plan. *Force Design 2030* directed extensive changes in organization and capabilities to meet the intent of the National Defense Strategy and to be completed by 2030. In his defense of *Force Design 2030*, General Berger summarized the imperative for change: "for the sweeping changes the Marine Corps needs to make to meet the principal challenges facing the institution: effectively playing our role as the nation's naval expeditionary force-in-readiness while simultaneously modernizing the force to play its necessary roles in the operating environment described in the National Defense Strategy."[12]

Prior to the implementation of *Force Design 2030*, the Marine Corps had already started significant organizational changes, including the creation of the 17XX cyberspace occupational field (OCCFLD) and the position of deputy commandant for information, as well as adding information as the seventh warfighting function, alongside command and control, fires, force protection, intelligence, logistics, and maneuver. The creation of the 17XX OCCFLD was directed by the commandant during the March 2017 executive offsite of Marine Corps flag officers.[13] This guidance was formalized with the publication of Marine Administrative Message 136/18 and was intended to create a highly skilled workforce capable of employing cyberspace capabilities.[14] As the Marine Corps grew a cyber workforce, a deputy commandant position was created to coalesce the intelligence, cyber, and communications fields and enhance and synchronize unity of effort.

Prior to the creation of the 17XX OCCFLD, cyberspace missions in the Marine Corps were typically conducted by different units across the service, often siloed by separate staff sections. Furthermore, these missions were conducted by separate occupational fields disjointedly. Although initially opposed by some information warfare personnel, the merger of these cyber-related OCCFLDs led to an increased unity of effort and complementary effects across multiple fields. With the merger of offensive and defensive cyber military occupational specialties into a single OCCFLD—although generating some adversarial tensions—the Marine Corps is well on its way to creating unified and complementary effects across multiple OCCFLDs.

In 2021 the Marine Corps took another step toward unity of effort by merging the 1711 cyberspace effects operator military occupational specialty, with the current 1721 cyberspace defensive operator, to become a new 1721 specialty, now known as a cyberspace warfare operator.[15] Previously, the service siloed enlisted Marines into either offense or defense specialists until they reached the rank of master sergeant. Now, the same Marine can conduct both offensive and defensive actions in support of friendly schemes of maneuver.

These changes also addressed joint requirements as those listed in Joint Publication 3–12, *Cyberspace Operations*, which describes the three types of cyberspace missions as offensive cyberspace operations, defensive cyberspace operations, and Department of Defense information network operations.[16] The Marine Corps decided that there was little need to have separate occupational fields for these closely related functions.

FLEET MARINE FORCE CYBER EXPANSION

As the service's cyber workforce has grown and matured, the number of cyber units has increased. The Marine Corps has established cyber units within the Marine Expeditionary Forces (MEF), the largest units of the Fleet Marine Force, and at various installations. On 1 October 2018 the Marine Corps activated the first of its cyber units in the operating forces to support I MEF (based in Camp Pendleton, California), the Defense Cyberspace Operations–Internal Defensive Measures (DCO-IDM) company.[17]

Capt. Benjamin Opel, the unit's first commander, succinctly articulated how this new unit increased the lethality of the MEF: "The added security provides the ability to command and control through lines of communication in cyberspace giving the commanding general flexibility to employ Marines without concern of being compromised."[18] The creation of DCO-IDM companies provided their respective MEFs with their first organic cyber units. These companies can then be task-organized for specific missions and support packages based on MEF prioritization, and not the consolidated priorities at the service level.

Each MEF, commanded by a lieutenant general, now has cyberspace warfare Marines. All command elements down to the Marine expeditionary unit, commanded by a colonel, have cyber planners to integrate cyberspace operations in support of the scheme of maneuver. These planners are mostly senior staff noncommissioned officers, with some commissioned officers. Within the MEF, the communications battalions (containing the DCO-IDM company), and the separate radio battalions have cyberspace warfare operators. Based on geography and assigned missions, each MEF has organized its cyber Marines in different formations, but within the new general scheme.

⊢• CHALLENGES TO MARINE CORPS CYBER

For all the success cyberspace reorganizations have achieved in the Marine Corps, it continues to face several challenges that range from the vocal former senior leaders opposing many changes within the service, to issues with talent management and retention. At the macro level, the challenges faced by the current commandant with the implementation of *Force Design 2030* are indicative of the challenges faced by cyber Marines at the micro level.

While the service prides itself on adaptability and innovation, public dissent by many former senior Marine leaders continues. According to James Webb, "Twenty-two retired four-star Marine generals signed a nonpublic letter of concern to Gen. Berger, and many others have stated their support of the letter."[19] Additionally, Lt. Gen. Paul Van Riper, USMC (Ret.), although well known for creative thought, wrote in *Marine Corps Times* that "I'm saddened beyond belief knowing that our Marine Corps soon will no longer be the ready combined-arms force that our nation has long depended upon when its interests were threatened. . . . In the end the Corps will have more space experts, cyber warriors, influence specialists, missileers and others with unique skills—many of which already are provided by other elements of the joint force. But it will only have them because it gave up Marines prepared to close with and destroy the enemy."[20]

The Marine Corps prides itself on its ability to fight in traditional warfare domains. However, this mentality can come with shortfalls, as Gen. Tony Zinni, USMC (Ret.), points out: "If we fail to adapt, fail to innovate, fail to develop and grow, we will find ourselves forever reacting and struggling. How do we adapt? When do we realize that the old models do not work anymore?"[21]

Although cyberspace is hard to see or visualize, we should recognize that adversaries are probing the cyber front lines and attempting to gain access to interior lines. Adversaries can relentlessly reconnoiter from remote overseas positions, gaining the intelligence they need to defeat U.S. forces in other domains. Unless the service wants to revert its command and control model to that of typewriters and hand-carried communication, it must find a way to adapt and compete with the adversary in cyberspace.

The opposition to changes at the service level will inevitably impact the retention and talent management of cyber Marines. The Marine Corps and cyberspace operations have a paradoxical relationship in which conflicts over organizational changes are similar to those occurring at the service level. Though the Marine Corps prides itself on initiative and adaptation, the disruptive changes that may result are often disorienting and agitating. The individual Marines and small-unit leaders have done exactly what the service prides itself on—adapting and becoming more lethal against the opposing will of the adversary. However, to do what is expected remains risky and hard in the face of tradition. There are numerous examples of how this paradoxical relationship results in punishing Marines for doing what was expected.

As a service, the Marine Corps struggles with making sense of how to evaluate these cyber war Marines and define career paths that optimize the lethality of the force. Furthermore, promotion boards have lacked the promised precept language that would properly recognize the scope of work performed by these Marines. Only a few 1702 cyber warfare officer billets reside in the Fleet Marine Force, and the number is even lower for field-grade officers (major through colonel). Traditionally, Marine officers are told that in order to remain competitive for promotion, they should perform well in a key billet, in grade, and out in the fleet. Given the few existing fleet cyber warfare billets and the larger number of cyber warfare Marines that would need to rotate through these billets to stay competitive, the service needs to determine how best to direct promotion boards in promoting and retaining those with expertise but without service in the Fleet Marine Force.

Discussions concerning retention and talent management for cyber Marines frequently focus on pay and benefits. Often, the perception of senior leaders is that service compensation cannot compete with the high salaries that many of these Marines would receive in the commercial sector. Hence, retention is almost impossible. However, countless interviews with the highest performing enlisted Marines leaving the service indicate that money was never the sole or primary reason for their exit.[22] In fact, many of these Marines simply wanted to be listened to or respected for what they contributed. In their view, decisions affecting cyber operations were often made by senior personnel with no experience with them.

Given the recent establishment of cyber-related occupational specialties, most of the expertise resides in junior personnel and in the enlisted ranks. Within the joint cyber community, it was common for Marine staff sergeants and gunnery sergeants to attend meetings on behalf of USCYBERCOM senior executive service civilian leaders who could not attend. These senior leaders generally understood and appreciated the impact these Marines had for the nation better than uniformed service leaders, and thus were more comfortable in granting junior personnel greater authority than their counterparts in other Marine Corps branches, particularly on technical matters.

Inevitably, this caused conflict over who represented the Marine Corps in dealing with the senior-most officials in the Department of Defense. In one notable example, two expert staff sergeants were requested to attend a meeting with the secretary of defense and chairman of the joint chiefs to discuss current operations. The size of the particular meeting space did not allow for the typical number of more senior staff officers. The uproar that occurred within MARFORCYBER over two mid-grade enlisted Marines briefing the senior-most defense decision-makers and not being supervised in doing so was so extreme that at least one of these Marines decided to exit the service shortly after the incident.[23]

Nevertheless, the service has made improvements in more recent years. Now, "CMT commander billets are designated as O-5 [lieutenant colonel] command equivalent" to the traditional arms.[24] But this step requires others. For the Marine Corps to remain the most lethal combined arms force that has ever existed, it must first get its policies on cyber personnel in better order.

FUTURE OF MARINE CORPS CYBER OPERATION

In future operations, Marines will need to conduct operations in cyberspace to both defend against and attack the adversary. Equipment from generators to aircraft is networked, creating multiple avenues of approach for adversary cyber maneuver. In a manner similar to the prioritization of fires support, in cyberspace Marines will prioritize the defense of operational technology in accordance with the discrete systems necessary for success during individual phases of an operation. For example, during a maritime prepositioning force offload, logistics systems would be given a higher priority than fires systems. Conversely, in kinetic combat, cyber defense of fires systems would be assigned a higher priority.

As a part of the stand-in force, Marines may need to deliver cyber munitions as a part of a lethal and nonlethal package, creating a combined arms dilemma for the adversary. This package will need to combine all available weapons in every domain to defeat the adversary to enhance the effectiveness of lethal fires and force protection. The fundamentals of combined arms fires supporting friendly maneuver to defeat the adversary are still valid. These fundamentals do not simply change or stop being true because they involve zeroes and ones and are harder to visualize. Failing to bring to bear all available fires in a combined arms approach is counter to the service's foundational doctrine.

In future wars, the Marine Corps will use a combined arms philosophy and maneuverist mindset, leveraging cyberspace operations to seek, close with, and destroy the adversary. The Marine Corps prides itself on fighting in any clime and place, and today that includes cyberspace.

NOTES

1. "Maneuver warfare is a warfighting philosophy that seeks to shatter the enemy's cohesion through a variety of rapid, focused, and unexpected actions which

create a turbulent and rapidly deteriorating situation with which the enemy cannot cope. Rather than wearing down an enemy's defenses, maneuver warfare attempts to bypass these defenses in order to penetrate the enemy system and tear it apart. The aim is to render the enemy incapable of resisting effectively by shattering his moral, mental, and physical cohesion—his ability to fight as an effective, coordinated whole—rather than to destroy him physically through the incremental attrition of each of his components, which is generally more costly and time-consuming. Ideally, the components of his physical strength that remain are irrelevant because we have disrupted his ability to use them effectively." Marine Corps Doctrinal Publication (MCDP) 1, *Warfighting* (1997), 73, https://www.marines.mil/Portals/1/Publications/MCDP%201%20 Warfighting.pdf.

2. Full-spectrum operations can be defined as "air, land, maritime, and space domains, electromagnetic spectrum, and information environment (which includes cyberspace)." Recent versions of the *DOD Dictionary of Military and Associated Terms* (as of 2017), 97, https://www.tradoc.army.mil/wp-content /uploads/2020/10/AD1029823-DOD-Dictionary-of-Military-and-Associated -Terms-2017.pdf, have replaced full-spectrum operations with "full spectrum superiority." However, such operations can be conducted without assuming superiority. Hence, the original term is used in this chapter.

3. U.S. Marine Corps Forces Cyberspace Command, "About Us," https://www .marforcyber.marines.mil/About/.

4. Joint Task Force-Ares was created in 2016 to combat the militant organization online as a complement to the global coalition fighting against the group's grip on power in Iraq and Syria. The task force has since undergone several changes. The Army's cyber component was originally tasked to lead the joint cyber effort, but in 2018, responsibility shifted to Marine Corps Forces Cyberspace Command, which allowed the team to focus not just on the Islamic State group, but more broadly on counterterrorism efforts globally. Mark Pomerleau, "Cyber Command Shifts Counterterrorism Task Force to Focus on Higher-Priority Threats," *C4ISRNET*, 4 May 2021, https://www.c4isrnet.com/cyber/2021/05/04 /cyber-command-shifts-counterterrorism-task-force-to-focus-on-higher -priority-threats/#:~:text=Joint%20Task%20Force%2DAres%20was,has%20 since%20undergone%20several%20changes.

5. Dina Temple-Rasten, "How the U.S. Hacked ISIS," NPR, 26 September 2019, https://www.npr.org/2019/09/26/763545811/how-the-u-s-hacked-isis.

6. MCDP 1.

7. "Cyber 101: U.S. Marine Corps Forces Cyberspace Command (MARFORCY- BER)," https://www.cybercom.mil/Media/News/Article/3254942/cyber101-us

-marine-corps-forces-cyberspace-command-marforcyber/; "Establishment of the Cyberspace 1700 Occupational Field (MARADMIN 136/18)," 1 March 2018, https://www.marines.mil/News/Messages/Messages-Display/Article/1454562/establishment-of-the-cyberspace-1700-occupational-field-occfld/.

8. "Cyber 101: U.S. Marine Corps Forces Cyberspace Command (MARFORCYBER)."

9. U.S. Marine Corps Forces Cyberspace Command, "About Us."

10. U.S. Marine Corps Forces Cyberspace Command.

11. U.S. Marine Corps, *Force Design 2030*, March 2020, https://www.hqmc.marines.mil/Portals/142/Docs/CMC38%20Force%20Design%202030%20Report%20Phase%20I%20and%20II.pdf. The document is periodically updated.

12. Gen. David H. Berger, "The Case for Change," *Marine Corps Gazette*, June 2020, https://mca-marines.org/wp-content/uploads/The-Case-for-Change.pdf.

13. The 17XX OCCFLD subsequently became the information maneuver OCCFLD, adding space and psychological operations military occupational specialties.

14. "Establishment of the Cyberspace 1700 Occupational Field (MARADMIN 136/18)."

15. "Cyberspace Operations Occupational Field (OCCFLD 17) (MARADMIN 164/18)," 17 March 2018, https://www.marines.mil/News/Messages/Messages-Display/Article/1469004/cyberspace-operations-occupational-field-occfld-17/; "Update to FY 2022 MOS Manual for the 17XX Occupational Field (MARADMIN 399/21)," 3 August 2021, https://www.marines.mil/News/Messages/Messages-Display/Article/2717969/update-to-fy22-mos-manual-for-the-17xx-occupational-field/.

16. Joint Publication 3–12, *Cyberspace Operations*, 19 December 2022, https://www.jcs.mil/Portals/36/Documents/Doctrine/pubs/jp3_12.pdf.

17. "First Defensive Cyberspace Operations Internal Defensive Measures Company Activation," 1 October 2018, https://www.imef.marines.mil/Media/News/News-Article-Display/Article/1743397/first-defensive-cyberspace-operations-internal-defensive-measures-company-activ/).

18. "First Defensive Cyberspace Operations Internal Defensive Measures Company Activates," 1 October 2018, https://www.dvidshub.net/video/633120/first-defensive-cyberspace-operations-internal-defensive-measures-company-activation.

19. James Webb, "Momentous Changes in the Marine Corps Deserve Debate," *Wall Street Journal*, 25 March 2022, https://www.wsj.com/articles/momentous-changes-in-the-marine-corps-deserve-debate-reduction-david-berger-general-11648217667.

20. Lt. Gen. Paul K. Van Riper, USMC (Ret.), "Jeopardizing National Security: What Is Happening to Our Marine Corps?" *Marine Corps Times*, 21 March 2022, https://www.marinecorpstimes.com/opinion/commentary/2022/03/21/jeopardizing-national-security-what-is-happening-to-our-marine-corps/.

21. U.S. Marine Corps, *Force Design 2030.*

22. Based on my own knowledge and experience with conducting exit interviews and counseling high-performing Marines.

23. Personal interview.

24. "Fiscal Year 2023 Combat Mission Team Commander Selection Board Announcement (MARADMIN 363/22)," 19 July 2022, https://www.marines. mil/News/Messages/Messages-Display/Article/3097285/fiscal-year-2023-combat-mission-team-commander-selection-board-announcement/.

12 U.S. Coast Guard and Cyber Operations

BRYAN KOCH

The U.S. Coast Guard has drastically evolved its operations in cyberspace over the past decade. The service established Coast Guard Cyber Command (CGCYBER) in 2013 as a flag-level command subordinate to the assistant commandant for intelligence and dual-hatted with CG-6, the Coast Guard's assistant commandant of command, control, communications, computers, and information technology (C4IT). For the first several years after its establishment, CGCYBER operated with a small complement consisting of a cyber security operations center, a vulnerability assessment team, and a certification and authorization team.

All these functions were inherited from other Coast Guard units within CG-6. Over the past decade, while the U.S. Coast Guard has evolved considerably in employing its unique defense, offense, and law enforcement authorities, it still has challenges in its security contributions, multi-mission role, public-private information sharing, and interagency coordination.

⊢• FIRST COAST GUARD CYBER STRATEGY

In 2015 the commandant of the Coast Guard released the service's first cyber strategy.[1] The *Coast Guard Cyber Strategy* established cyberspace as an operational domain within the Coast Guard and outlined three strategic priorities on which to focus efforts: defending cyberspace, enabling operations, and protecting infrastructure.

The "defending cyberspace" priority specifically targeted multiple internally oriented goals and objectives focused on decreasing risk, establishing a cyber workforce and culture, and concentrating cyber defense activity around enabling Coast Guard missions. The "enabling operations" priority further expanded Coast Guard efforts to develop cyber capabilities, incorporate cyber operations into mission planning and execution, and develop both intelligence support to cyber operations and cyber support to existing Coast Guard operational activities. The "protecting infrastructure" priority focused on updating the Coast Guard's port risk management tools and methodologies to incorporate cyber security, improving information sharing with industry, reducing vulnerabilities at port facilities and on vessels, and incorporating cyber education and training for mariners.

⊢• COAST GUARD CYBER ALIGNS WITH DEPARTMENT OF DEFENSE ON CYBER

Following the 2015 U.S. Office of Personnel Management data breach, the U.S. Coast Guard launched a cyber crisis action team to respond to the Department of Defense (DoD) *Cybersecurity Implementation Plan*.[2] The team led to a formal agreement between the Department of Homeland Security (DHS) and DoD, acknowledging the Coast Guard's alignment under DoD for cyber security policy and operations.

The immediate effect of this agreement severed the Coast Guard from dual reporting of cyber security incidents to and tasking from the DHS office of the chief information officer in addition to DoD's Joint Force Headquarters–Department of Defense Information Network (JFHQ-DoDIN). The *DoD Cybersecurity Implementation Plan* mandated all departments and services to implement strong authentication, harden devices, reduce their attack surface, and align all systems and networks to a supporting DoD-certified cyber security service provider (CSSP). However, the Coast Guard quickly realized that many internal organizational challenges encumbered its ability to take the necessary action to fulfill the requirements of this plan. This sparked a multiple-year effort to reorganize the Coast Guard's cyberspace forces.

In 2017 the Coast Guard made significant organizational changes to operationalize its cyber functions. Coast Guard leadership chartered the Cyber–Chief Information Officer–C4IT Transformation Project Implementation Office (C3T PIO) to retain chief information officer responsibilities and consolidate all information technology (IT) program management functions under CG-6, establish a DoD-certified CSSP and cyber protection team (CPT) within CGCYBER, promulgate a cyberspace workforce model in alignment with the DoD cyber workforce framework, and fully align all DoD enterprise services management framework functions under CGCYBER or CG-6.

⊢• NEW OPERATIONAL COMMAND AND ORGANIZATIONAL CHANGE

The new mission of the C3T PIO resulted in the elevation of CGCYBER as an operational command reporting directly to the commandant of the Coast Guard, with administrative functions aligned under the deputy commandant for operations. The C3T PIO also spearheaded further organizational change by restructuring the C4IT service center's centralized service desk—responsible for entry-tier IT support—and its subordinate command's enterprise service operation branch—accountable for Tier 2 and Tier 3 IT support—into CGCYBER. This same reorganization effort also realigned the differential global positioning system and nationwide automatic identification system operations and monitoring functions from the Coast Guard navigation center into the existing enterprise operations center within the enterprise service operation branch to create the Coast Guard's network operations and security center.[3]

During this realignment, CGCYBER formally established its first CPT and expanded its vulnerability assessment elements into a DoD-recognized "blue team." The network operations and security center's and blue team's expanded capabilities accelerated CGCYBER's establishment and certification as a CSSP. This realignment further allowed a clear bifurcation between CGCYBER and CG-6 with CGCYBER managing all "secure, operate, and defend" functions under the DoD enterprise services management framework while CG-6 retained responsibilities for all "design, build, and configure" functions. To separate the management of the cyber workforce, operational capabilities, and strategy from the programmatic functions of CG-6, the Coast Guard also established the office of cyberspace forces independent from CG-6 and CGCYBER under the assistant commandant for capabilities. In 2019 the Coast Guard officially split the roles of assistant commandant of C4IT and commander of CGCYBER. That same year, the Coast Guard's first CPT reached initial operational capability per DoD standards.

⊢• FIRST NATIONAL MARITIME CYBERSECURITY PLAN

In 2019 heightened concerns around cyber risks in the maritime environment reached new levels of visibility, culminating in the White House releasing its first *National Maritime Cybersecurity Plan*.[4] The plan outlined ten priority action items related to risks and standards, information and intelligence sharing, and creation of a cyber security workforce. To focus efforts related to risk and standards, the plan directed the National Security Council to deconflict the roles in maritime cyber security across twenty federal agencies, tasked the Coast Guard to develop cyber risk modeling standards, directed the General Services Administration to strength cyber security requirements in government contracts with port facilities, and tasked DHS to identify, prioritize, mitigate, and investigate cyber security risks in critical ship and port systems.

To improve information sharing, they also tasked the Coast Guard, the Cybersecurity and Infrastructure Security Agency (CISA), the Federal Bureau of Investigation, and the intelligence community to collaborate to exchange information with industry and to share cyber intelligence with nongovernment entities, and they tasked the director of national intelligence to prioritize appropriate collection to defend the maritime transportation system (MTS). To build the maritime cyber workforce, the National Maritime Cybersecurity Plan tasked the Coast Guard to develop career opportunities for a competent cyber workforce, directed the Coast Guard and U.S. Navy to develop personnel exchanges with industry and national laboratories, and charged the Coast Guard to develop and deploy CPTs to prevent and respond to cyber incidents in the MTS.

↦ SHIFT IN PRIORITIES AND SECOND CYBER STRATEGY

These action items ignited a shift in prioritization within the Coast Guard. Its focus moved from internal cyber security efforts for defending itself to concentrating on the cyber defense of critical public infrastructure.

The 2021 National Defense Authorization Act amended the Coast Guard's statutory mission for port, harbor, and coastal facility security to not only take measures to prevent and respond to acts of terrorism or transportation security incidents in the marine environment but also prevent and respond to cyber incidents, transnational organized crime, and foreign state threats in the MTS.[5] The fiscal year 2021 and 2022 budgets also each resourced the Coast Guard with an additional CPT. In addition, the fiscal year 2021 budget resourced the service with personnel and resources to build the Coast Guard's first offensive cyber capability.

To refocus internal efforts across the service, the Coast Guard superseded its cyber strategy with the *2021 Cyber Strategic Outlook*, which listed three priorities: defend and operate the enterprise mission platform (EMP), protect the MTS, and operate in and through cyberspace.[6]

The first priority, defend and operate the EMP, reiterated the mission-focused nature of cyber defense of the Coast Guard. This priority highlighted the fact that not only is cyberspace an operational domain for the Coast Guard, but the Coast Guard's IT systems (the EMP) also are in themselves an operational asset for the Coast Guard, similar to a cutter or aircraft. It also closely aligns the Coast Guard with the updated concept of operations of the Defense Department's JFHQ–DoDIN to secure, operate, and defend the DoDIN.[7] This placed a command-centric focus on cyber defense operations.[8] Rather than describing cyber security and information technology as a cost center for the Coast Guard, this priority clearly outlines how the Coast Guard views the EMP as an operational platform vital to mission success.

Second, to protect the MTS, the Coast Guard outlined multiple efforts to update risk frameworks, reporting standards, and existing Coast Guard operating procedures in alignment with the 2019 *National Maritime Cybersecurity Plan*. These efforts also highlighted the concept of employment for CPTs and the need for improved information sharing and partners both within the government and with other key stakeholders, including industry and partner nations.

Third, to prioritize the ability to operate in and through cyberspace, the Coast Guard will build partnerships with the intelligence community and DoD partners, develop offensive cyber capability, and equip Coast Guard operational commanders with the ability to integrate offensive and defensive cyber capability with traditional Coast Guard missions.

SIGNIFICANT FUNDING CHALLENGES BUT ADVANCES NONETHELESS

Despite significant advancements in its ability to secure, operate, and defend the EMP, the Coast Guard continues to face a myriad of challenges in this domain. It struggles with obtaining resources for desired cyber security investments and planning at the IT system level. Many legacy IT applications were not designed to be able to incorporate the necessary security controls to meet today's best practices. Cyber security requirements compete with functionality requirements over a finite pool of resources, and the Coast Guard is programmatically aligned to focus on mission-related outcomes normally associated with enhanced functionality. The harsh reality of the situation too often requires either a mandate from JFHQ–DoDIN, immediate annualized cost savings, or strong executive advocacy within Coast Guard leadership in order to further advance internal cyber security measures. However, CGCYBER has persisted in gaining support of this effort including milestones such as certifying both its CSSP and its red team to DoD standards and credentialing its command cyber readiness inspection team to meet JFHQ–DoDIN standards in inspecting Coast Guard commands.

COLLABORATION IN MARITIME CYBER RISK REDUCTION

As of 2022 the Coast Guard had two CPTs that met the DoD standards for full operational capability, and it has resourced and is building a third CPT. To fully integrate cyber operations in the MTS, the Coast Guard also created the maritime cyber readiness branch (MCRB) within CGCYBER and staffed every Coast Guard area, district, and sector command with a maritime transportation system specialist–cyber (MTSS-C). CGCYBER's MCRB is comprised of Coast Guard personnel with backgrounds in contingency planning, facilities inspections, or port security operations gained through field tours at Coast Guard sectors and marine safety units, as well as those with an aptitude for cyber operations. The MTSS-Cs added cyber-trained personnel to every Coast Guard operational unit's facilities inspection department. The addition of both the MCRB and the MTSS-Cs created a natural interface between CGCYBER, other Coast Guard commands, and the port facilities and vessel operators throughout the United States. In 2021 the MCRB directly supported CG units in their response to forty-seven cyber security incidents throughout the country.[9] Collaborative partnerships built during these responses further led to over a dozen deployments by CGCYBER CPTs for assessment, hunt, or incident response missions.[10]

The initial operationalization of the relationship between CGCYBER CPTs, the MCRB, and existing Coast Guard units swiftly produced results to decrease the cyber risk to the MTS. As CGCYBER began to field its first CPT missions, U.S. port facility operators were working toward updating their facility security assessments and facility security plans. In February 2020 the commandant of the Coast Guard issued clarifying guidance on Coast Guard regulations (Title 33, Code of Federal Regulations 105 [Maritime Security: Facilities] and 106 [Marine Security: Outer Continental Shelf Facilities]) requiring facilities to assess and document vulnerabilities associated with their computer systems and networks in their facility security assessments and facility security plans.[11]

While assessing the risks in these ports, CGCYBER CPTs documented and reported multiple patterns of common vulnerabilities including weak access control and authentication due to weak password policies and a lack of multi-factor authentication implementation, unnecessary user and administrative privileges in contrast to the cyber security principle of "least privilege," and a deficiency in system maintenance evidenced by a lack of software patching and prolific instances of unsupported computer operating systems.[12]

↦ BECOMING A FULL MEMBER OF CYBER COMMAND

During this same period, the Coast Guard also established a cyber mission team, its first offensive cyberspace capability. As with CPT development, the Coast Guard is building its cyber mission team to the DoD standard for combat mission teams and national mission teams. As of 2023 Coast Guard cyber mission team members were conducting "early operations as augmentees to the Cyber National Mission Force."[13] Although heavily reliant on DoD resources to enable operations, the Coast Guard is continuing to rapidly develop its cyber workforce to prepare for future operations.

The Coast Guard recently reached significant workforce milestones. In 2022 the Coast Guard Academy graduated the first cohort of cyber systems majors from its ranks.[14] The Coast Guard also has created a direct commission officer program for entry into the Coast Guard officer corps for individuals with cyber skills.[15] Also established are enlisted and warrant specialties aligned to Coast Guard cyber missions, adding distinct career paths across all Coast Guard accession sources. CGCYBER is also developing a program with the Coast Guard Auxiliary to leverage its volunteer force in support of Coast Guard cyber operations.[16]

⊢• WIDENING ROLE IN THE FUTURE: OFFENSIVE WITH DEFENSIVE

Despite massive advancements in cyberspace for the Coast Guard over the last decade, the service will continue to evolve through the implementation of its *2021 Cyber Strategic Outlook*. Within the EMP, the Coast Guard is currently transitioning to a performance-based infrastructure managed services contract, which will transform the backbone of the EMP into a "hybrid-cloud, managed service delivery model" platform.[17] This change in procurement strategy is intended to force the Coast Guard to address its "technical debt" (that is, the costly maintenance of cheaply constructed software or hardware buried in the older, less capable digital infrastructure supporting Coast Guard systems) by transferring this responsibility to their contractor and incentivizing efficient delivery of both functionality and security.

The Defense Information Systems Agency's zero-trust cyber security initiative, known as Project Thunderdome, will also drastically impact how Coast Guard systems handle security control implementation.[18] Under Thunderdome, DoD and Coast Guard systems will move to a zero-trust model that "assumes that entities already operating inside a network can't automatically be trusted."[19] The initiative will force Coast Guard systems to embrace the necessary security controls to validate trust internal to the EMP and the DoDIN, further decreasing risk to mission-critical systems.

Protecting the MTS will require further development of the Coast Guard's multi-mission role, including as a regulatory agency and as a cyber-capable agency within DHS. The Coast Guard will need to further explore how it will adapt its existing regulations to address the cyber risk to the MTS directed in the 2021 *Cyber Strategic Outlook*. This closely aligns with the White House's *National Cyber Strategy*, which lists regulation as a key component of "Strategic Objective 1.1: Establish Cyber Security Requirements to Support National Security and Public Safety."[20]

The Coast Guard will also need to revamp efforts to promote information sharing through public-private collaboration with the MTS. The Coast Guard is successful in building trust and cooperation within its area maritime security committees at the sector level, and the number of cyber incidents reported to the Coast Guard's National Response Center has slowly increased from 2020 to 2023. However, the Coast Guard believes that many incidents remain unreported, as businesses and organizations remain cautious about reporting cyber incidents to the Coast Guard. In 2022 the Coast Guard issued a bulletin urging organizations to lower their reporting threshold and submit more reports.[21] The Coast Guard will need to streamline and prioritize how it fulfills its sector risk management agency goals to "realize . . . real-time, actionable, multi-directional sharing" to effectively thwart threats to the MTS.[22]

Interagency coordination is another challenge that the Coast Guard must address. It will need to better integrate with the federal cyber security centers to leverage the Coast Guard's unique array of authorities to act in cyberspace. The Coast Guard will need to work with a myriad of agency partners including the National Cyber Investigative Joint Task Force, which leads investigations into cyber crime and counterintelligence threats in cyberspace, CISA's Joint Cyber Defense Collaborative, which coordinates cyber response across sector risk management agencies, and various components of the intelligence community to build toward intelligence-driven, threat-informed operations.[23] The Coast Guard will also need to build this collaboration into its incident response planning to align new procedures under the Cyber Incident Reporting for Critical Infrastructure Act of 2022, which centralizes coordination of critical infrastructure reporting at CISA.[24]

As the Coast Guard's cyber mission team reaches maturity and achieves full operational capability within the joint force, the Coast Guard will need to work with the DoD, DHS, and Department of Justice to find the proper niche for the Coast Guard's offensive capabilities to thwart, disrupt, and dismantle threat actors. As both a military branch and a law enforcement agency, the Coast Guard is well positioned to fulfill a unique role in targeting the malicious cyber actors whose origins and affiliations are ambiguous and could be either nation-state or non-state criminal actors threatening U.S. critical infrastructure. (See also chapter in this volume by Kim on the Korean coast guard and similar challenges.) The U.S. Coast Guard presence within DHS provides an opportunity for DHS leadership to align resources to their priorities. This DHS umbrella—if properly supported—will enable CGCYBER to deliver cyber effects without disrupting "cyber norms" and without leading to unnecessary conflict escalation with near-peer adversaries.

NOTES

1. U.S. Coast Guard, *United States Coast Guard Cyber Strategy*, June 2015, https://www.uscg.mil/Portals/0/Strategy/Cyber Strategy.pdf.

2. U.S. Department of Defense, *DoD Cybersecurity Discipline Implementation Plan*, October 2015, https://dodcio.defense.gov/portals/0/documents/cyber/cyberdis-impplan.pdf.

3. The differential global positioning system (DGPS) was designed as a workaround for the reduced signals accuracy (random offset) implanted by the U.S. Department of Defense in the civilian public signals from the military satellite global positioning system (GPS). Other U.S. departments insisted that DoD allow the military-grade signals for commercial use, but DoD demurred. The U.S. Coast Guard was a lead agency in developing DGPS as a replacement for radio-transmitted maritime positioning systems such as the long-range navigation system, which it argued was too expensive to maintain. President Bill Clinton directed DoD to eliminate the difference between military and civilian GPS in 2000. However, DGPS is still widely used since DGPS adds ground-based stations to satellite GPS, providing better accuracy than GPS alone. For a short description, see "Differential GPS: What It Is and How to Use It," *GISGeography*, 4 November 2023, https://gisgeography.com/differential-gps/. The nationwide automatic identification system is based on the internationally sanctioned automatic identification system, but with additional features to facilitate Coast Guard monitoring of ship traffic. See U.S. Coast Guard Acquisition Directorate, "Nationwide Automatic Identification System," November 2022, https://www.dcms.uscg.mil/Portals/10/CG-9/Acquisition%20PDFs/Factsheets/NAIS.pdf.

4. U.S. Executive Office of the President, *2023 National Maritime Cyber Strategy*, December 2019, https://trumpwhitehouse.archives.gov/wp-content/uploads/2021/01/12.2.2020-National-Maritime-Cybersecurity-Plan.pdf.

5. USC 70116: Port, Harbor, and Coastal Facility Security, 4 March 2023, https://uscode.house.gov/view.xhtml?req=46+usc+70116&f=treesort&num=3&edition=prelim#:~:text=46%20USC%2070116%3A%20Port%2C%20harbor%2C%20and%20coastal%20facility,References%20In%20Text%20Codification%20Prior%20Provisions%20Amendments%20%C2%A770116.

6. U.S. Coast Guard, *2021 Cyber Strategy Outlook*, August 2021, https://www.uscg mil/Portals/0/Images/cyber/2021-Cyber-Strategic-Outlook.pdf.

7. A description and history of JFHQ–DoDIN is available on its official website, https://www.jfhq-dodin.mil/About-Us/.

8. Sarah Sybert, "DoD Improves Command-Centric Operational Framework; Paul Fredenburgh Quoted," *ExecutiveGov*, 7 December 2020, https://executivegov.com/2020/12/dod-improves-command-centric-operational-framework-paul-fredenburgh.

9. Coast Guard Cyber Command, *2021 Cyber Trends and Insights in the Marine Environment Report*, 19 August 2022, 5, https://www.dco.uscg.mil/Portals/9/2021CyberTrendsInsightsMarineEnvironmentReport.pdf.

10. *2021 Cyber Trends and Insights*, 10.

11. Commandant, U.S. Coast Guard, Navigation and Vessel Inspection Circular No. 01–20: "Guidelines for Addressing Cyber Risks at Maritime Transportation Security Act (MTSA) Regulated Facilities," 26 February 2020, https://www.dco.uscg.mil/Portals/9/DCO%20Documents/5p/5ps/NVIC/2020/NVIC_01–20_CyberRisk_dtd_2020–02–26.pdf?ver=2020–03–19–071814–023.

12. Coast Guard Cyber Command, *2021 Cyber Trends and Insights in the Marine Environment*, 6.

13. Robert K. Ackerman, "Coast Guard Cyber Moves Closer to Defense Department," *The Cyber Edge by Signal*, 1 March 2023, https://www.afcea org/signal-media/cyber-edge/coast-guard-cyber-moves-closer-defense-department#:~:text=The%20U.S.%20Coast%20Guard%20is%20expanding%20its%20cyber,cyber%20activities%20overseas%20in%20conjunction%20with%20foreign%20partnerships.

14. Erica Moser, "Coast Guard Academy Graduates First Cyber Systems Majors," *The Day* (New London, CT), 18 May 2022, https://www.govtech.com/education/higher-ed/coast-guard-academy-graduates-first-cyber-systems-majors.

15. Kathy Murray, "New Direct Commissioning for Coast Guard Cyber Officers Offers New Opportunities to Serve," *MyCG*, 14 January 2022, https://www.mycg

.uscg.mil/News/Article/2898718/new-direct-commissioning-for-coast-guard
-cyber-officers-offers-new-opportunitie/.

16. U.S. Coast Guard Auxiliary, "AUXCYBER Augmentation Program," n.d., https://
wow.uscgaux.info/content.php?unit=C-DEPT&category=auxcyber.

17. "USCG Infrastructure Managed Services (IMS)" (Federal Contract Pre-
Solicitation), *GOVTRIBE*, 31 May 2019, https://govtribe.com/opportunity
/federal-contract-opportunity/uscg-infrastructure-managed-services-ims
-70z0791905312019.

18. Jon Harper, "DISA Setting Direction for Thunderdome Cybersecurity Initiative,"
FEDSCOOP, 27 April 2022, https://fedscoop.com/disa-setting-direction-for
-thunderdome-cybersecurity-initiative/.

19. Harper.

20. Office of the President, *2023 National Cyber Strategy*, 2 March 2023, 8–9, http://
www.whitehouse.gov/wp-content/uploads/2023/03/National-Cybersecurity
-Strategy-2023.pdf.

21. U.S. Coast Guard, Maritime Security Information Bulletin, "Cyber Security
Awareness and Action," 11 April 2022, https://www.dco.uscg.mil/Portals/9
/DCO%20Documents/5p/MSIB/2022/USCG-MSIB-02–22-Cybersecurity
-Awareness-and-Action.pdf.

22. *2023 National Cyber Strategy*, 10.

23. See "Sector Risk Management Agencies," *Cybersecurity Infrastructure and
Security Agency* official website, n.d., https://www.cisa.gov/topics/critical
-infrastructure-security-and-resilience/critical-infrastructure-sectors
/sector-risk-management-agencies.

24. *2023 National Cyber Strategy*, 12.

13 Maritime and Civilian Collective Cyber Defense in Europe

HELI TIIRMAA-KLAAR

European militaries today recognize the need to rebuild modern naval capabilities depleted during the post–Cold War era, but these long-awaited increases in annual budgets need to include increased investment in cyber defense capabilities. Such developments would help balance individual national efforts and contribute to greater, more effective cooperation among North Atlantic Treaty Organization (NATO) Allies, including in defense of their maritime operations. Larger investments in cyber defense are critical to better address the growing threat of high-intensity maritime and cyber warfare.

More effective investment requires a different division of labor in securing critical information and telecommunications links in Europe. By custom, European capitals are individually responsible for their own cyber incident response, cyber defense, cyber intelligence, and attribution of cyber operations. While the European Union (EU) has taken the lead in many areas of European policy—and has adopted a regulatory framework for civilian cyber security—all operational cyber competencies, both military and civilian, remain strictly in the hands of individual nations.

Cyber defense cooperation between NATO Allies is, by policy, based on multinational cooperation frameworks and initiatives among the cyber defense organizations of the Allied governments. NATO's actual cyber posture is also based on national cyber defense capabilities. Building a coherent approach to collective cyber defense among NATO Allies (involving both military and civilian actors) that are also EU member states will require additional efforts if it is to be more than merely the sum of the individual parts. Understanding the major features of cyber security cooperation between the nations of the EU and the European NATO allies is necessary to build a coherent approach to collective cyber defense among NATO Allies (involving both military and civilian actors). It requires additional efforts that are not yet in progress.

⊢• EUROPEAN NAVIES AND CYBER DEFENSE

Healing Europe's Achilles' heel—the defense spending gap in Europe that has grown over the past thirty years—is difficult. The major powers on the continent downgraded their Cold War militaries in the post–Cold War years, restructuring their armed forces from territorial defense to expeditionary out-of-area operations. Apart from the United Kingdom and France, the defense spending of the other major European countries declined between 1991 and 2023. As a result, NATO's expeditionary missions have been almost exclusively led and supported by superior U.S. military forces and capabilities. Financial and Eurozone crises in the 2000s resulted in further decline across the spectrum of defense capabilities.

European navies collectively lost 32 percent of their at-sea combat firepower during this period. Despite maintaining overall defense spending levels, even France and the United Kingdom dramatically reduced their naval capability. The resulting strategic capabilities gap has put European defense in a dangerous position.

After the start of the Russian war of aggression against Ukraine in 2022, however, the European Defense Agency reported an unprecedented increase in European defense spending, beginning to reverse the previous chronic underinvestment in military capabilities. But it remains difficult for countries to support Ukraine or any other state with arms and ammunition while trying to replenish their own defense forces and supplies.

This turnaround, however, could be an optimistic sign for the cyber defense community. This rapid modernization of armaments and capabilities allows for the integration of cutting-edge technologies into European defense structures and the recruitment of new cadres with specialized expertise, such as cyber defense professionals.

⊢• MODERNIZING EUROPEAN NAVAL AND CYBER FLEETS

During the last three decades, all major European navies have undergone significant changes in their capabilities, strategies, and missions, developing over time what appears to be a division of labor according to budgets and expertise.

While shifting its focus to global maritime security and power projection, Britain's Royal Navy decommissioned many older ships and has sought to replace them with fewer but more modern vessels equipped with advanced technologies. The sea service specifically invested scarce resources heavily in submarine technology, creating one of the most technologically advanced attack submarines (*Astute* class). The United Kingdom also prioritized joint operations between the navy and other branches of the armed forces, enhancing cooperation with NATO and other allies.

The French navy also shrank and modernized its fleet as budgets declined. With a focus on power projection and expeditionary warfare, the French navy introduced new amphibious assault ships and advanced naval aviation, including the development of the Rafael carrier-based fighter and the NH90 helicopter.

The Italian navy emphasized local sea control, international peacekeeping, humanitarian aid, and disaster relief operations. It prioritized anti-submarine warfare and mine countermeasures technologies, as well as new amphibious assault ships and helicopter carriers.

Over the same period from the 1990s to 2022, the focus of the German navy shifted toward a more expeditionary role while also significantly reducing the size of the fleet.[1] It emphasized modernization, interoperability, and enhanced capabilities for crisis response operations.

Due to the increased intensity of cyber operations against European civilian and military targets associated with Russia's 2022 war of aggression against

Ukraine, greater attention is on digital threats, including maritime vulnerabilities. European militaries now accept that they are facing cyber and hybrid threats including network intrusions, espionage, supply chain vulnerabilities, malware, satellite communications jamming, and social engineering. After the explosion of the Nord Stream gas pipeline in 2022, they also began to prioritize undersea warfare capabilities and the cybersecurity of undersea infrastructure.

European navies are now developing capabilities to counter sophisticated cyber operations. The Royal Navy has established a cyber security operations center that monitors threats in real time and organizes mitigation and response in accordance with the principles of the United Kingdom's 2022 cyber doctrine and the all-source threat assessments and actions from the National Cyber Force. The Joint Cyber Reserve Unit, which includes experts from the private sector, also supports the Royal Navy's cyber operations.[2] The French navy has established the Naval Cyber Defense Group, which is responsible for protecting its networks and communications infrastructure from cyber threats.[3] The German Bundeswehr operates a joint support and enabling service that provides cyber services to all branches of the German Armed Forces, including the navy, to detect and respond to cyber threats, as well as to provide training.[4] Italy has a dedicated cyber emergency response team (CERT) for the navy to provide incident response services and training.[5]

Today, all major European navies have plans for further modernization and technological advancement, including unmanned underwater vehicles, unmanned surface vessels, artificial intelligence–enabled capabilities, network protection, and cyber defense.[6]

⊢• NAVAL DEPENDENCE ON CIVILIAN MARITIME AND TELECOMMUNICATIONS INFRASTRUCTURE

Risks to ports and civilian infrastructure also affect navies with such threats as the compromise of sensitive information, disruption of communications and navigation systems, and remote or embedded hacking and other malicious or state-sponsored cyber operations.[7] Like many other navies, European navies rely heavily on civilian ports and civilian digital and telecommunications infrastructure including navigation, communication, and data exchange capabilities, and logistics. To mitigate these risks, European militaries and navies must work closely with civilian port authorities and service providers to ensure the cyber security of naval forces.

Civilian cyber standards are regulated at the European level through the various EU cyber policies and directives, while cyber security requirements for European militaries are both set separately by each country and coordinated within the larger NATO defense interoperability frameworks. EU cyber security regulations now increasingly include the transport sector, including all maritime infrastructure and ports, and the wider telecommunications infrastructure—all of which are not necessarily consistent with naval cyber security requirements at present.

Nonetheless, European governments and the private sector have begun to invest heavily in maritime cyber security protocols. Since the 2017 NotPetya ransomware incident, which severely disrupted the massive Danish Maersk shipping operations globally,[8] the EU has increased its focus on maritime cyber security and related cooperation mechanisms.[9] As the EU's external trade by sea accounts for more than 50 percent of its total trade volume, its civilian cyber security agency published guidelines and best practices for port cyber security in 2019, and the European Maritime Safety Agency now promotes online courses on cyber security and engages with the civilian maritime sector on cyber issues.[10] Both the NATO and EU efforts suggest policy foundations already exist that could be productively used for more cooperative cyber defense arrangements with naval forces and civilian maritime stakeholders.

⤏ THE FRAGMENTED CYBER SECURITY AND DEFENSE ARCHITECTURES IN EUROPE

Cyber security and defense architectures in Europe consist of several layers of coordination and cooperation between a large number of public and private sector actors. This provides, in principle, an institutional environment useful for more cyber defense cooperation in the maritime environment. However, achieving cyber resilience in Europe requires a major coordination and cooperation effort across four distinct, functional public sector cyber communities that exist in all European countries and are also part of the respective EU or NATO cooperation frameworks. Unfortunately, no single point of contact or directory to reach all European cyber stakeholders at the same time exists.

First, there is a large cyber incident response and resilience community—consisting of both technical and policy experts—involved in incident response, information sharing, early warning, and related coordination activities to protect critical information infrastructure. The second community consists of representatives of law enforcement agencies, prosecutors, judges, and other experts from European criminal justice systems focused on cyber crime.[11] The third community is the cyber intelligence and diplomacy community with its own specific cooperation and information-sharing structures that deal with state-sponsored (or -organized) cyber operations.[12] Finally, there is the defense community, whose primary mission is to defend the cyber networks of defense forces. This community also engages in defense cooperation bilaterally, multilaterally, or within the larger NATO framework.[13] Furthermore, many governments use numerous private companies for cyber intelligence gathering, early warning, and response, complicating this already convoluted picture.

In this large pan-Europe network, several bubbles of cooperation and information sharing at different levels already exist. First, there are several institutional and political policy coordination frameworks and mechanisms in place within EU and NATO. Second, there is the operational-technical level of coordination taking place between civilian cyber incident response entities. Third, there is the less visible but active cooperation on a bilateral level between European countries, including classified information and intelligence sharing. Plus, all cyber communities must work closely with the private sector, which owns and operates about 85 percent of the cyber security infrastructure on the European continent.

Nonetheless, all intelligence-, defense-, and national security–related cyber activities remain the prerogative of individual national governments. There are smaller trusted circles and cooperation agreements between a number of European countries that share more sensitive information within the intelligence, defense, and incident response communities, but most serious cyber incidents and their mitigation and response as well as cyber operations' attribution decisions remain national. Isolated serious cyber incidents involving defense have been identified, but only in a few cases has solidarity with other European nations been sought to attribute the attacks, such as the Viasat hack in the beginning of the 2022 Russian invasion of Ukraine.[14]

While some major events may result in coordinated EU statements and policy responses, even when private sector actors are involved, however, malicious cyber operations often remain hidden within the closed confines of national incident response or intelligence circles.

↦ KEY SHARING ROLE OF THE CYBER INCIDENT RESPONSE COMMUNITY IN EUROPE

As a result, the large but fragmented civilian cyber incident response community remains the main forum for the exchange of information on cyber threats in Europe. There are many formations within this community. First, there is an official CERT cooperation group of EU member states (Computer Security Incidence Response Teams Network) set up by the European Commission and some sectoral cyber response groups in pan-European sectors such as the European Centre for Cybersecurity in Aviation.[15] Each EU member state has its national and governmental CERTs, which all also belong to a global CERTs organization called the Forum of Incidence Response and Security Teams. Each country also has a dedicated military CERT that protects the separate military and defense networks built for effective command and control in wartime. In principle, military and civilian CERTs in each nation share information and coordinate on a regular basis. NATO nations' military CERTs do share information with NATO headquarters in Brussels and its operational NATO Computer Incident Response Capability (NCIRC) Technical Center in Mons, Belgium.[16]

There are also civilian sectoral CERTs in larger countries, and most large private sector companies have their own cyber teams. Companies falling within the scope of the EU Network and Information Systems 1.0 and 2.0 directives must report cyber incidents to national CERTs. Large consultancies also provide cyber services to industry and have their own dedicated incident response teams. Finally, global technology companies well established in the European market also have significant information about routine cyber incidents that occur on the continent.

In recent years, a small group of European nations that work more closely together have formed a "trusted cyber nation group." They have coalesced around the issues of cyber stability, coordinated attribution, and threat information sharing at the policy and operational levels. Roughly the same number of nations are also working closely with the U.S./U.K.-led intelligence partnership, which was instrumental in leading the ad hoc international cyber coalition that defended Ukraine from Russian cyber attacks during the war. These groups provide the necessary examples demonstrating the benefits of collective cyber defense.

⊢• COMPETENCY LIMITED ROLE OF EU AGENCIES IN PROMOTING EUROPEAN CYBER SECURITY

To understand the way the EU's role in strengthening Europe's cyber posture has evolved, it is necessary to understand that the EU can only act within the competencies conferred on it by the EU treaties.[17] In practice, this means that the European Commission has the right of initiative mainly in the customs union, monetary policy, internal market, economic policy, civil protection, and some areas of home affairs.

While not specifically one of the rights of initiative, however, cyber security affects all these areas of EU competence at the same time. In its "classical" competence areas, the EU has built up an impressive history of cyber regulation and policy since the adoption of its first cyber security strategy in 2013 under the competence area of the internal market. The majority of existing EU cyber policies and legislative initiatives aim to increase overall cyber resilience and strengthen the union's cyber ecosystem by fostering cooperation, improving technological capabilities, and creating a higher level of cyber preparedness in EU member states. The two editions of the EU Network and Information Systems Security directives aim to set higher cyber standards for key economic actors and public administrations across the union.[18]

The EU Cyber Certification Framework and the Cyber Resilience Act aim to provide more trustworthy technology, while the Cyber Competence Centers Network aims to channel additional resources into cyber innovation and research in all EU member states. Another set of EU mechanisms includes legislation to promote the fight against cyber crime, law enforcement cooperation, and the collection of electronic evidence.[19] A myriad of related EU agencies and cooperation working groups participate in the day-to-day implementation of all these initiatives. Foreign policy, national security, and defense, however, remain formally the exclusive competence of individual EU member states.

├• SPECIFIC MANDATES AND EU INTERGOVERNMENTAL NATIONAL CYBER SECURITY AND DEFENSE

The EU's Common Foreign and Security Policy remains intergovernmental—meaning that the EU's high representative for foreign affairs and security policy and its External Action Service can coordinate and represent the union in foreign policy matters only if they have a mandate from the member states. Relying on the leadership and contribution of the member states, since 2017, the EU has adopted several common strategies to respond to malicious cyber activity and a cyber sanctions regime.[20]

A joint framework for responding to malicious cyber activities, the "Cyber Diplomacy Toolbox," has imposed horizontal sanctions on entities and individuals organizing cyber operations against EU interests.[21] Several joint statements attributing and condemning cyber attacks have been issued by the EU. The European External Action Service's nascent EU Intelligence and Situation Center has coordinated information sharing among European countries to provide analysis and syndicated intelligence to support joint decision-making on cyber attribution and the application of sanctions.

On the cyber defense side, the EU has focused on its military and civilian missions and operations under the Common Security and Defense Policy, as well as on capability development projects under the mandate of the European Defense Agency.[22] A 2022 EU Cyber Defense Policy aims to strengthen European cyber security capabilities, increase military and civilian cooperation, close potential security gaps, reduce strategic dependencies, and develop cyber capabilities.[23] These efforts must be implemented by EU member states, including their navies, with additional funding available through EU instruments.

The EU is currently conducting two maritime missions under the Common Security and Defense Policy.[24] The Irini mission is intended to implement the United Nations arms embargo on Libya in the Mediterranean.[25] The Atalanta European naval operation combats piracy off the Horn of Africa and in the western Indian Ocean.[26] EU member states' navies use their national cyber capabilities to achieve the mission objectives.

⊢• NATO'S ROLE: WHAT STEPS TOWARD COLLECTIVE DEFENSE IN CYBERSPACE?

Following the massive 2007 Russian cyber attacks against Estonia, NATO's 2009 Strategic Concept recognized cyber threats as a potential source of disruption and destabilization. In its most recent 2022 Strategic Concept, NATO confirms that "a single cumulative set of malicious cyber activities . . . could rise to the level of an armed attack and could lead the North Atlantic Council to invoke Article 5 of the North Atlantic Treaty."[27] Furthermore, at the Warsaw Summit in 2016, NATO recognized cyberspace as an operational domain equal to air, land, sea, and space. Over the previous decade, NATO paid particular attention to defending its own networks and operations in cyberspace. In 2016, Allies adopted a Cyber Defense Pledge to provide support in the form of increased resilience, improved information sharing, and mutual assistance. In 2021 the fourth edition of the NATO Cyber Defense Policy states that its cyber defense posture is to support the Alliance's core missions of collective defense, crisis management, and cooperative security.

In 2018 a cyberspace operations center was established as part of NATO's enhanced command structure. A small group of Allies have committed their national cyber capabilities to NATO missions for use in situations where the Alliance needs to conduct a computer network operation. The NATO Defense Planning Process guides the development of NATO-wide cyber defense capabilities, like all other NATO defense capabilities. NATO maintains contact with Allies' national civilian cyber authorities through the information exchange established by the voluntary memorandum of understanding frameworks.[28]

Furthermore, NATO has established a straightforward cyber governance structure with clear lines of command. Composed of Allied representatives and reporting to the North Atlantic Council, NATO's Cyber Defense Committee advises the council on political and strategic aspects of cyber defense and prepares high-level political decision drafts on cyber issues for adoption. Other parts of NATO's structures help internally coordinate cyber defense and responses. These include the NCIRC Technical Center in Mons, the NATO C3 Board, the NATO military authorities, the NATO Communications and Information Agency, and the Allied Command Transformation unit planning the annual Cyber Coalition Exercise conducted by the Center of Excellence on Cooperative Cyber Defense in Tallinn.[29]

As a military organization, NATO practices its cyber response and related decision-making in advance and is increasingly integrating cyber in its crisis management exercises. The annual Locked Shields cyber technical exercise is conducted by the Center of Excellence on Cooperative Cyber Defense involving experts from thirty-two nations.[30] Cyber is expanding in the many annual and regional naval exercises such as BALTOPS in the Baltic Sea.

⊢• BUILDING A COHERENT COLLECTIVE CYBER DEFENSE POSTURE IN EUROPE

Despite the substantial number of actors and the extreme fragmentation of the European cyber defense landscape, there are nonetheless several foundations on which to build a collective defense posture including navies, but it will not be easy. The main obstacle is the uneven level of cyber resilience, coordination, and capabilities among individual nations. European underinvestment in overall defense also contributed to the poor state of military cyber defense in many NATO countries, including navies. On the positive side, European nations are on the way to modernizing their cyber capabilities as defense spending increases.

At least three major actions should be taken to achieve a more robust naval cyber defense posture through better cooperation between the various civilian and military cyber actors across the European continent and among NATO Allies.

The priority for NATO Allies should be to evaluate the possibilities to upgrade the unequal cyber capabilities among NATO Allies that hamper collective activities. For example, NATO could establish a peer learning mechanism among Allies to level the playing field. Together with the EU and its defense fund, specific programs could be created to build cyber defense capabilities with a maritime focus. In addition, dedicated cyber education and training opportunities for European cyber defense personnel could address the shortage of experts and the skills gap in this area. Additional investment in innovation and research will also increase opportunities to better integrate innovative technologies into modern naval warfare.

Second, NATO and its Allies should also prioritize civil-military coopera-tion efforts in Europe and within NATO to include key civilian counterparts of all Allies. For example, both civilian and military agencies should be involved in preparing the decisions necessary to invoke NATO's Article 5 collective defense. In peacetime, the civil-military cooperation should involve regular coordination on cyber security requirements established for all actors across the maritime domain, as well as in supporting domains, such as the telecommunications sector.

A third key area for improvement could be the development of crisis management mechanisms and cooperation on cyber issues such as a dedicated EU-NATO permanent cyber incident response mechanism. It should bring together different cyber communities from governments and the private sector, in particular key critical maritime infrastructure such as ports and the incident response teams of major shipping companies. For example, NATO's Cyber Incident Response Center should coordinate with relevant national civilian, intelligence, and military cyber authorities to identify and mitigate potential vulnerabilities for naval forces and subsea infrastructures in NATO countries.

The increasing defense budgets of European countries must support the additional focus on cyber defense in the overall modernization of European naval forces as well. Given the many actors involved and the criticality of the cyber domain to European security, this additional effort to ensure collective cyber defense across civilian and military forces—including navies—is essential to address the growing threat of high-intensity maritime and cyber warfare facing NATO and EU nations.

NOTES

1. Jeremy Stöhs "Into the Abyss? European Naval Power in the Post–Cold War Era," *Naval War College Review* 71, no. 3 (Summer 2018).
2. "Joint Cyber Reserve Force," https://www.gov.uk/government/groups /joint-cyber-reserve-force.
3. Vivian Machi, "Four Questions with France's Military Cyber Mission Lead," *C4ISRNET*, 8 November 2022.
4. Bundeswehr, "20 Years of the Joint Support and Enabling Service," https://www.bundeswehr.de/en/about-bundeswehr/history/history-joint -support-and-enabling-service.
5. Luigi Garafalo, "'Secure, Survive, Strike,' la strategia cyber del Dipartimento della Marina Usa fa eco alla nuova normativa italiana," *CYBERSECURITYITALIA*, 2 November 2022.

6. Pierre Morcos and Colin Wall, "Are European Navies Ready for High-Intensity Warfare?" *War on the Rocks*, 31 January 2022, https://warontherocks.com/2022/01/are-european-navies-ready-for-high-intensity-warfare/.

7. NATO Cooperative Cyber Defense Center of Excellence (CCDCOE), *Military Movement: Risks from 5G Networks* (Tallinn: NATO CCDCOE, 2022), 25–28, 41–48.

8. European Maritime Safety Agency, "The EU Maritime Profile—Overview of the EU Maritime Economy," https://www.emsa.europa.eu/eumaritimeprofile/section-1-overview-on-the-eu-maritime-economy.html.

9. Mark McQuade, "The Untold Story of NotPetya, the Most Devastating Cyberattack in History," *Wired*, 22 August 2018.

10. European Union Agency for Cybersecurity, *Port Cybersecurity—Good Practices for Cybersecurity in the Maritime Sector*, November 2019, https://www.enisa.europa.eu/publications/port-cybersecurity-good-practices-for-cybersecurity-in-the-maritime-sector/; European Maritime Safety Agency, "Awareness in Maritime Cybersecurity," https://www.emsa.europa.eu/contact/advanced-search/item/3477-cybersec.html.

11. EUROPOL, "Cyber Intelligence," 7 December 2021, https://www.europol.europa.eu/operations-services-and-innovation/services-support/information-exchange/intelligence-analysis/cyber-intelligence.

12. European Parliamentary Research Service, "Understanding the EU's Approach to Cyber Diplomacy and Cyber Defense," *EU Policy—Insights*, PE651.937, May 2020, 5–9.

13. European Parliamentary Research Service, 10–11.

14. Council of the EU, "Russian Cyber Operations against Ukraine: Declaration by the High Representative on Behalf of the European Union," 10 May 2022.

15. European Union Aviation Safety Agency, "European Center for Cyber Security in Aviation," https://www.easa.europa.eu/en/eccsa.

16. NATO, "Cyber Defense," 14 September 2023, https://nrdc-ita.nato.int/operations/allied-reaction-force/nato-cyber-operation-centre.

17. "Division of competences within the European Union," EUR-Lex, https://eur-lex.europa.eu/EN/legal-content/glossary/division-of-competences.html.

18. European Commission, "Directive on Measures for a High Common Level of Cybersecurity across the Union (NIS2 Directive)," https://digital-strategy.ec.europa.eu/en/policies/nis2-directive.

19. European Commission, "Cyber Resilience Act," 15 September 2022, https://digital-strategy.ec.europa.eu/en/policies/cyber-resilience-act; European Cybersecurity Competence Center and Network, https://cybersecurity-center.europa.eu/index_en.

20. European Council, "Cyber-Attacks: Council Extends Sanctions Regime until 18 May 2025," 16 May 2022, https://www.consilium.europa.eu/en/press /press-releases/2022/05/16/cyber-attacks-council-extends-sanctions-regime -until-18-may-2025/.
21. Erica Moret and Patryk Pawlak, "The EU Cyber Diplomacy Toolbox: Towards a Cyber Sanctions Regime?" European Union Institute for Security Studies, 12 July 2017, https://ethz.ch/content/dam/ethz/special-interest/gess/cis/center -for-securities-studies/resources/docs/EUISS-Brief_24_Cyber_sanctions.pdf; European Council, "Russian Cyber Operations against Ukraine: Declaration by the High Representative on Behalf of the European Union," 10 May 2022, https://www.consilium.europa.eu/en/press/press-releases/2022/05/10/russian -cyber-operations-against-ukraine-declaration-by-the-high-representative-on -behalf-of-the-european-union/.
22. European Defense Agency, "Cyber," https://eda.europa.eu/what-we-do /capability-development/cyber.
23. European Commission, "Cyber Defense: EU Boosts action against Cyber Threats," 10 November 2022, https://ec.europa.eu/commission/presscorner/ap i/files/document/print/en/ip_22_6642/IP_22_6642_EN.pdf.
24. Diplomatic Service of the European Union, "CSDP Missions and Operations," 23 January 2023.
25. European Union Naval Forces Mediterranean, "Operation Irini," EUNAVFOR MED Irini, https://www.operationirini.eu/.
26. EU Naval Force Operation ATALANTA, "Mission," https://eunavfor.eu/mission.
27. NATO, "Strategic Concepts 2022," 18 July 2022, https://www.nato.int/cps/en /natohq/topics_56626.htm.
28. NATO, "Cyber Defense."
29. NATO Cooperative Cyber Defense Center of Excellence, https://ccdcoe.org/
30. NATO Cooperative Cyber Defense Center of Excellence, "Locked Shields," https://ccdcoe.org/exercises/locked-shields/.

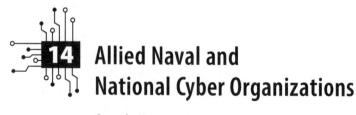

14 Allied Naval and National Cyber Organizations

South Korea

SO JEONG KIM

Since 2017 there has been a 900 percent increase in cyberattacks on various operational technology systems worldwide.[1] Maritime cyber incidents have also been steadily increasing. Control systems and operational systems in the maritime sector, which account for a large part of global logistics movement, have rapidly become more reliant on information and communication technology, particularly as the integration of recent technologies from the Fourth Industrial Revolution is actively taking place.[2]

At the same time, the risks associated with information technology have also exposed vulnerabilities in information and communication systems used in the maritime sector, resulting in increased attention to maritime cyber security. The introduction of autonomous ships that apply cutting-edge digital technology and artificial intelligence in the shipbuilding and maritime industry, for example, has raised the need for security system preparation across the entire maritime sector beyond cyber security requirements for ships alone.[3] In anticipation of new environmental changes, critically needed are policy clarifications of roles, greater inclusion of cyber security in maritime response plans, more interagency information sharing, and, finally, increased support for the naval services, including the Korean Coast Guard, currently acting proactively to fill maritime cyber security gaps.

⊢• KOREA AND MARITIME CYBER SECURITY

Despite the continuous need for maritime cyber security, its importance was not recognized in the Republic of Korea (ROK) until relatively recently, and the issues raised did not address the entire maritime sector but only responded to cyber threats to ships. (See discussion of ship cyber risks by Hilger in this volume.) The 2022 Korean Indo-Pacific Strategy acknowledges the importance of the cyber domain and specifies the reinforcement of cyber capabilities in the Indo-Pacific region, but it does not connect it to the reinforcement of cyber capabilities in the maritime sector.[4] Nor does the 2019 Korean National Cyber Security Strategy mention any related content.[5] The 2024 revised National Cybersecurity Strategy similarly lacks specific mention of maritime and port cyber security.[6] Instead of emphasizing efforts to ensure supply chain security, though, this content is also limited to security measures within critical infrastructure control systems.

One explanation for Korea's focus on ship cyber security rather than the wider maritime issues stems from the central influence of the International Maritime Organization (IMO), a specialized agency under the United Nations. Its development and implementation standards for cyber security focus on standardizing safety management regulations for ships, not on wider port operations, for example.[7] Korea has adopted the international community's guidelines and resolutions to support safe transportation while maintaining its own maritime operational flexibility for cyber risks.

After establishment of a cyber systems panel in 2016, the International Association of Classification Societies—a nongovernmental organization established to standardize and regulate merchant ship "classes"—published a recommendation for twelve key technologies to ensure the safety of ship cyber systems in 2018.[8] Accordingly, Korean companies that own ships are now required to comply with maritime cyber security standards due to the necessity of following international standards for the operation of ships. Therefore, the current focus of maritime cyber security issues is limited to cyber security threats that can occur on ships, and the awareness of improving cyber security levels for the port and maritime sectors as a necessary protection area for national security is not highly prioritized.

Examining cyber security incidents in the maritime sector in Korea—and the current state of cyber security efforts by the Korean government, military, and related agencies—leads to recommendations for future policy directions and technical actions for the ROK.

⊢• MARITIME CYBER SECURITY INCIDENTS IN KOREA

Korean awareness of maritime cyber threats lags that in the United States. According to the U.S. Coast Guard Cyber Command, risks in ports include facility access control, terminal headquarters data management, ransomware response, operational system protection, location-based system protection, and ship security, among other areas. As elaborated by Koch in this volume, the U.S. Coast Guard's cyber command emphasizes the ability of its organization to perform tasks such as information, operations, and evaluations in response to the complexity and breadth of cyber risks in maritime environments.

For example, a specific company's data breach may be dealt with from a commercial confidentiality protection standpoint, or it may be handled from the perspective of defense contractors' more regulated confidentiality protection. According to data from the U.S. Coast Guard Cyber Command, requiring the confidential sharing of information on data breaches at major port services falls within the scope of the command's responsibilities involving maritime protection.

Conversely, the most significant maritime-related cyber security incident in Korea was not publicized—perhaps not even detected until five years later. On 21 June 2021 it was revealed that defense industry companies, including Daewoo Shipbuilding and Marine Engineering, which builds submarines, were subject to hacking attempts. Daewoo Shipbuilding and Marine Engineering is a key defense company that builds ROK flagship submarines, including the Dosan Ahn Chang-ho submarine, Korea's first three-thousand-ton class submarine. In 2016 Daewoo's submarine construction bureau was hacked by a suspected North Korean hacker group, and more than sixty classified military secrets including internal data of forty thousand documents related to submarine core technology were stolen.[9]

Few such cyber threats of maritime and defense systems have been publicly identified in Korea. Perhaps companies fear that—unlike procedures of the U.S. Coast Guard—data breaches may not be kept confidential by government authorities. Presumably, such revelations might provide business advantages to competitors.

⊢• KOREAN CYBER SECURITY STRATEGIES

⊢○ Indo-Pacific Strategy of 2022

The South Korean government recognizes the strategic importance of the Indo-Pacific region and aims to maintain regional stability. In December 2022 it announced the "Free, Open, and Prosperous Indo-Pacific Strategy" as one of its specific implementation strategies to become a pivotal global state under the Yoon Seok-yeol administration.[10]

Unlike in the past, where South Korea's foreign policy was limited to the Korean Peninsula and Northeast Asia due to the North Korean nuclear issue, the scope of its foreign policy has been greatly expanded. South Korea's Indo-Pacific strategy emphasizes the achievement of a vision of freedom, peace, and prosperity in the region and calls for efforts to strengthen a rules-based order built on universal values and peaceful resolution of conflicts through dialogue. To reduce conflicts and tensions by complying with universally accepted international laws and norms and fostering stable international relations, South Korea seeks to achieve this goal through comprehensive cooperation, including in the cyber security field.

However, there is no direct mention of strengthening capabilities in the maritime cyber security sector in the strategy document.

⊢○ National Cybersecurity Strategy of 2024

The ROK National Cybersecurity Strategy is the top-level strategic document designed to enhance national cyber security. The 2019 National Cybersecurity Strategy was the first publicly available cyber strategy, and it recently was revised in 2024. While the structure of the 2024 strategy is quite similar to its predecessor, it has several distinctive characteristics. First, it has clearly articulated the need to identify threat actors—the Democratic People's Republic of Korea and others—in cyberspace and to secure proactive capabilities to counter their malicious cyber activities. Second, while asserting its role as a global pivotal state in the international community, it has committed to enhancing cooperation as responsible users of cyberspace and specifying measures for identifying and deterring malicious actors. Third, it has outlined concrete internal cyber security governance mechanisms to implement these measures and has specified institutional improvements related to this.[11]

However, just like the 2019 version, the document makes no direct mention of cyber security in the maritime sector or specifically tasks any ministry or agency to address maritime-related cyber threats.

⊢• ROK MARITIME CYBER SECURITY POLICIES AND GOVERNANCE

Despite the silence in the national policies, the National Cyber Security Center, the Navy, and the Maritime Police are each establishing respective response organizations in their efforts to strengthen maritime cyber security. The Korea Coast Guard is the national organization responsible for safeguarding the maritime sovereignty of the Republic of Korea and maintaining the safety and security of its citizens at sea, but it is meant to work in collaboration with the National Cyber Security Center and Navy. The National Cyber Security Center oversees maritime and port cyber security from the perspective of protecting key infrastructure, while the Navy, having transformed the Cyber Protection Center established in 2015 into a direct subordinate unit in 2019, is assigned the role of a cyber operations control tower. The Maritime Police are slated to pursue cyber investigations, prevent and mitigate maritime cyber crime, and apprehend offenders, although they are reported to suffer from severe workforce shortages.[12]

The Korea Coast Guard, however—unlike other countries' maritime law enforcement agencies or organizations—also possesses general law enforcement authority on land. While its unique historical and organizational characteristics separate it from other police forces, and it possesses exclusive general law enforcement jurisdiction in the maritime domain, investigation of all crimes in all areas is a powerful feature not found in other countries' maritime law enforcement organizations.

Maritime crimes, such as drug trafficking using ships, have increased in recent years and are characterized by their international and wide-ranging nature and extensive scope of damage, unlike ordinary crimes. As cyber crime in the maritime domain continues to evolve into a unique form of information and communication network infringement crime that utilizes the specialized area of the ocean, it is becoming increasingly sophisticated.

Cyber threats to advanced technologies used in the maritime industry, especially the modernization of equipment using autonomous navigation ships, satellites, drones, and the development of networks that connect them, are expanding. South Korea as a whole is increasing its interest in, and preemptive response to, cyber crime through related investigations and information cooperation organizations.

With the development of advanced technologies, the maritime environment itself is also undergoing rapid changes. The diversification of energy sources used in renewable energy or ship propulsion is bringing changes not only to our waters but also to the global logistics and maritime transportation environment. The advancement of autonomous navigation ship technology imposes changes in the maritime environment that the maritime industry, accustomed to traditional navigation techniques, has not experienced before.

The expanding unmanned vehicle aircraft environment, such as represented by drones, is forcing the gradual adaptation of the Coast Guard's work environment to a new digitized paradigm, rather than human resources and face-to-face contact. This need for adaptation will increase as unmanned surface and unmanned undersea vehicles proliferate.

The Korea Coast Guard's major task plan for 2024 focuses on efforts to enhance public convenience through the use of modern technologies such as artificial intelligence and big data, rather than on securing cyber-related personnel and organization. The development of the Korea Coast Guard's information system in 2022 combined advanced information technology and "scientific information" with an integration platform.

Port and related maritime facilities are designated by the "Law in Critical Information Infrastructure Protection and National Cybersecurity Management" decree. Concrete guidelines such as the "Maritime Security System Guidelines (GC-24-K, 2021)" aimed at enhancing vessel system security have been established and implemented. Additionally, the "Maritime Cyber Safety Management Guidelines" released by the Ministry of Oceans and Fisheries outline the roles of the government and the private sector in maritime cyber security.

At the end of the day, however, there is room for improvement. Many of the guidelines are recommendations without binding force, indicating future directions for improvement. And there is a continuing lack of specificity regarding maritime cyber security at the strategic and policy levels, necessitating the future development of policies and strategies tailored better for the current maritime environment.

RECOMMENDATIONS FOR INCREASING MARITIME CYBER SECURITY[13]

Although the necessity of cyber security in the maritime sector has grown in emphasis internationally, its importance has been recognized relatively late in Korea. Thus far, the issues raised have been limited to responses to cyber security threats in ships rather than the entire maritime sector. As a result, cyber security as an essential national security protection area for the maritime sector has not been given a high priority. In order to enhance cyber security in the maritime sector in the future, the following proposals are recommended.

First, it is necessary to clarify the required functions and missions for maintaining cyber security in ports and to specify the vision and objectives for each function. Policy direction should be made clear through various methods such as strategies, plans, strategic outlooks, and environmental assessments, and the momentum for policy implementation should be gained by sharing them with relevant stakeholders.

Second, cyber operations using information and communication technology should be positively considered within the scope of the duties of maritime organizations, and the organizations should be fully supported in performing cyber operations using their resources. Cyber technology plays a role as a means and a tool, and also as a protected target. In setting the scope of cyber security to include Korean maritime ports, both aspects should be considered. In addition, a systemic framework that can specify the enhancement of comprehensive capabilities, such as complementary strategies and policies, reorganizing the tasks of related agencies, sharing standards and best practices, presenting risk modeling methodologies, considering cyber security in contracts with third parties, establishing procedures for risk response, promoting information sharing, and developing human resources, should be secured.

Third, the scope of information sharing should be expanded, to include the private sector, in collecting, utilizing, and sharing relevant information. Information should be provided to private enterprises using maritime facilities to help eliminate cyber security threats and to directly support the enhancement of practical cyber security and national security capabilities. Recently, the National Intelligence Service has been actively sharing threat information with private defense companies, and other government agencies in Korea have been expanding their information-sharing targets. All this suggests that consideration of providing information and technical services to private enterprises in the maritime sector for enhancing cyber security levels is necessary and should be expanded.

Fourth, there needs to be a separate evaluation and authorization department within the cyber command of the Coast Guard. Efforts to create such a department are already underway and being made to integrate it with the procurement system, in order to establish institutional and managerial procedures and justifications to support cyber security improvements in various aspects. But to be successful, the organization, budget, and workforce aspects need to be strengthened to promote all of these initiatives, and much consideration is needed for ways to train and secure specialized professionals who can handle various practical issues with a positive attitude toward the different technological solutions for these problems.

Fifth, in addition to the cyber command of the Coast Guard, other departments, such as those dealing with information and investigation, should evaluate and confirm their demands for cyber technology and threat response capabilities, and provide active ideas that can be utilized.

Finally, with regard to ship security policy proposals, several suggested measures need to be adopted, including

- consideration and application of cyber security in the design and manufacturing process of new marine vessels
- securing cyber security testing and certification technology for marine vessels

- securing vulnerability analysis technology for marine vessel systems and networks
- developing and applying security technology for control systems within marine vessels
- training personnel for cyber security in the marine vessel industry
- and providing security education for personnel in the marine vessel industry.

Additionally, international regulations and standards should be utilized to support the improvement of cyber security levels in various aspects, such as:

- the evaluation and certification of integrity and confidentiality of information systems
- the construction of integrated security systems
- the acquisition of cyber security certification technology
- the acquisition of appropriate certification technology for integrated software
- the acquisition of integrity verification technology
- the acquisition of test evaluation solutions
- and the internalization of security by establishing institutional and managerial procedures and justifications that can be implemented in practice.

The ROK is starting to recognize the threats to the overall maritime world. But it still has a long way to go in order to defeat them.

NOTES

1. Ernie Hayden, "Shipboard Operational Technology: At Risk from Human Error and Cyber Attacks," *Pacific Maritime Magazine,* https://pacmar.com/article/shipboard-operational-technology-at-risk-from-human-error-and-cyber-attacks/.
2. "What Are Industry 4.0, the Fourth Industrial Revolution, and 4IR?" McKinsey & Company, 17 August 2022, https://www.mckinsey.com/featured-insights/mckinsey-explainers/what-are-industry-4-0-the-fourth-industrial-revolution-and-4ir.

3. Shankar Nishant, "How Autonomous Ships Are Revolutionizing the Maritime Industry," *Maritime Professionals*, 15 February 2023, https://maritime-professionals.com/how-autonomous-ships-are-revolutionizing-the-maritime-industry/.

4. Ellen Kim, "Assessment of South Korea's New Indo-Pacific Strategy," Center for Strategic and International Studies, 19 January 2023, https://www.csis.org/analysis/assessment-south-koreas-new-indo-pacific-strategy.

5. So Jeong Kim and Sunha Bae, "Korean Policies of Cybersecurity and Data Resilience," in Evan A. Feigenbaum and Michael R. Nelson, eds., *The Korean Way with Data: How the World's Most Wired Country Is Forging a Third Way* (Washington, DC: Carnegie Endowment for International Peace, August 2021), 39–60, https://carnegieendowment.org/files/202108-KoreanWayWithData_final5.pdf.

6. Joon Ha Park and Shreyas Reddy, "South Korea Unveils New Cyber Strategy to Counter North Korean Threats," *NK News*, 2 February 2024, https://www.nknews.org/2024/02/south-korea-unveils-new-cyber-strategy-to-counter-north-korean-threats/?t=1712855345999.

7. International Maritime Organization, "Maritime Cyber Security," https://www.imo.org/en/OurWork/Security/Pages/Cyber-security.aspx.

8. International Association of Classification Societies (IACS), *Position Paper: Cyber Security* (London: IACS, January 2020/updated August 2023), https://iacs.s3.af-south-1.amazonaws.com/wp-content/uploads/2023/08/04171007/IACS-Cyber-Position-Paper-Rev2.pdf.

9. Oh Seok-min, "Probe Under Way into Hacking Attempts against Daewoo Shipbuilding: Gov't," Yonhap News Agency, 21 June 2021, https://en.yna.co.kr/view/AEN20210621006700325.

10. See discussion in So Jeong Kim, "South Korea's Indo-Pacific Strategy Promotes Cyber Cooperation," *Cyber Digital Europe Directions*, 4 May 2023, https://directionsblog.eu/south-koreas-indo-pacific-strategy-promotes-cyber-cooperation/.

11. So Jeong Kim, *New National Cybersecurity Strategy of ROK and Its Implications*, Institute for National Security Strategy, February 2024.

12. So Jeong Kim and Sunha Bae, "Study on U.S. Maritime Cybersecurity Strategy and Its Implications for the ROK," *Korea Association of Cyber Security* 1 (2024): 114 (in Korean), https://www.kacs.ne.kr/sub_7/7_1.php?menu=3&mode=view&year=2024&issue=1&volume=1&spage=83.

13. Certain of the recommendations are discussed in So Jeong Kim, "Maritime Cybersecurity and National Security," *Korea on Point*, 26 November 2023, https://koreaonpoint.org/view.php?topic_idx=121&idx=291.

15 Forging the Cyber Sword

The People's Liberation Army's Evolving Approach to Cyberspace Operations

ELSA B. KANIA

The Chinese People's Liberation Army (PLA) has concentrated for decades on developing asymmetric capabilities to conduct information operations, including cyberspace operations, to advance its strategic objectives in competition and conflict. In April 2024 the PLA announced another reorganization of its cyber, space, and information support capabilities.[1] This was the second notable change in force structure, less than a decade after the PLA Strategic Support Force (PLASSF, 战略支援部队) was initially created in December 2015.

Paramount leader Xi Jinping personally announced the establishment of the PLA Information Support Force (PLAISF, 信息支援部队). In parallel, the Ministry of National Defense unveiled the PLA Cyberspace Force (PLACSF, 网络空间部队) and PLA Military Aerospace Force (PLAMAF, 军事空天部队).[2] These changes are tantamount to both an elevation and a disaggregation of existing elements of the previous structure of the PLASSF.

These three forces are all likely under direct command of the Central Military Commission (CMC), which itself is directly headed by Xi Jinping, consistent with the PLA's propensity to maintain highly centralized control of strategic capabilities. Through the three newly named forces, the PLA will likely continue building capabilities to advance its competence within priority domains. The PLAISF will be responsible for enabling the network information systems and effective information integration required to enable joint operations, including through facilitating command and control and bolstering information assurance.[3] The PLACSF (which some analysts have argued could be viewed as the People's Republic of China (PRC's) military cyber command) and PLAMAF augment the PRC's posture for strategic deterrence, providing cyber and space capabilities that also offer additional flexibility for conducting coercion in peacetime competition. In any future conflict scenario, the PLA would contest information dominance (制信息权) or supremacy from the start.

Given the centralizing organizational structure of the PLA, the PLACSF will provide cyberspace and integrated cyber and electronic capabilities in support of joint operations, thereby serving as the main force conducting peacetime preparation of the battlefield, and carrying out strikes against adversary targets in any future cyber conflict involving military forces. Therefore, it is likely that the PLACSF will be responsible for cyber operations in the maritime domain as well. It is unclear what cyber warfare responsibilities the People's Liberation Army's Navy (PLAN) itself will have or retain. To provide some degree of clarity, this chapter will focus on the antecedents to, evolution of, and inferred rationales for, the PLACSF's development of those cyber warfare capabilities likely to affect the maritime domain and navies in both peace and war.

⊢• RISE AND FALL OF THE PLASSF

The PLA's approach to cyberspace and other strategic frontiers continues to be characterized by a combination of change and continuity. Traditionally, the PLA's concept of information operations has encompassed cyber, electronic, and psychological warfare, a trinity of capabilities that the PLASSF integrated and the PLACSF has now in large part inherited. To some extent, this division between "strategic" (i.e., cyber and space) and "supporting" (i.e., information as an enabler) capabilities is a logical continuation of the PLASSF's initial incubation of cyber, space, and information support capabilities under a single force, yet within separate structures.[4] Essentially, the PLASSF created a new overarching structure (and new stakeholders) rather than relegate those capabilities to the individual services (e.g., the PLAN) with responsibilities in other domains.

At the time of its creation in 2015, the PLASSF was regarded as an indicator of Xi's expanding influence as chairman of the CMC in implementing historic reforms that overcame the resistance that had impeded prior efforts. Although the division of the PLASSF could be regarded as the discarding of a model with Xi's personal imprimatur, the organization evidently became obsolete within less than a decade, and Xi's capacity to reshape the PLA remains strong.

Since its establishment, the original structure—the PLASSF—underwent continued development and expansion. Originally, it combined a number of operational units (部队) from the now-defunct General Staff Department (GSD), General Political Department, and General Armaments Department. The PLASSF's Network Systems Department (NSD) and Aerospace Systems Department (ASD) were its primary operational components. Each had its own subordinate headquarters departments that integrated and restructured a range of bases, bureaus, associated research and educational institutions, and other disparate elements.

The PLASSF's NSD appeared to have centered on the headquarters of the former Third Department of the General Staff Department (3PLA), also known as the Technical Reconnaissance Department, and possibly to have inherited elements of the electronic warfare capabilities of the former Fourth Department of the General Staff Department (4PLA), also known as the Electronic Countermeasures and Radar Department.[5] Prior to the existence of the NSD, the majority of technical reconnaissance bureaus (cyber espionage and signals intelligence capabilities) were distributed across the other armed services, including the PLAN. These bureaus were apparently subsumed within the PLA NSD structure (and now the PLACSF) and restructured as technical reconnaissance bases (技术侦察基地), likely aligned to each joint theater command.[6] However, the details of the NSD's structure are still difficult to determine based on available information.

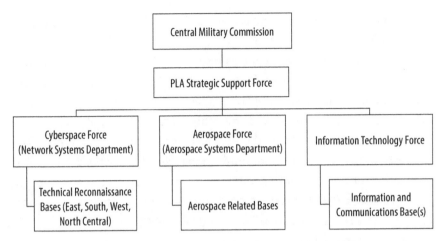

FIGURE 15-1. Previous Structure (Approximate) of the People's Liberation Army Strategic Support Force Up to 2023 *Source: Author's design*

Additional elements of this force were designed and distributed for more specialized defensive and offensive and missions, as limited references to a cyber security base (网络安全基地) suggest.[7]

The PLASSF had the potential to facilitate certain synergies, such as the doctrinal concept of integrated network-electronic warfare (网电一体战). This key element of informatized warfare has long been rhetorically emphasized but was structurally unachievable prior to the creation of the PLASSF.[8] In this regard, the PLASSF was also well situated to be foundational for the PLA's future capabilities for joint operations.

Despite decades of discussion of the importance of integrated network-electronic warfare, and while the NSD likely served as the core of the PLA's cyber forces and probably incorporated certain electronic warfare capabilities, the PLASSF did not appear to maintain a monopoly or facilitate full integration of these capabilities. For example, the former headquarters of the 4PLA, the Electronic Countermeasures and Radar Department, were possibly reconfigured within the new CMC Joint Staff Department through the new Network-Electronic Bureau (网络电子局) and Network-Electronic Countermeasures Group (网电对抗大队), seemingly a high-level joint unit, which may operate as a different echelon or be involved in some elements of coordination external to PLASSF.[9]

Beyond its cyber and space forces responsibilities, the PLASSF was also designed to act as a critical enabler for the PLA's theater commands in future joint operations. The very concept of "strategic support" from which its name originated appears to be derived from this central mission of enabling the system of systems (体系) that the PLA leverages for joint operations.[10] The PLASSF "Information and Communications Base" (信息通信基地), which originated from the former General Staff Department Information Assurance Base (信息保障基地) created in 2010, appeared to have become a critical component of the "Information Technology Force" (信息技术部队) that was the precursor to the Information Support Force.[11]

The PLA has consistently emphasized the importance of improved development of network information systems for joint operations. In practice, the PLAISF's role likely ranges from repair of military fiber-optic networks to the upgrading of military information networks to integrate new technologies. Based on the 2024 restructuring, the PLACSF is likely an expansion upon and elevation of the Network Systems Department (网络系统部) under direct command of the CMC.[12] So, too, the Military Aerospace Force is almost certainly associated with the Aerospace Systems Department (航天系统部) and likely retains much of the prior structure of bases and associated facilities.

There is not yet enough information to confidently evaluate whether the 2024 dismantling of the PLASSF will primarily change the command structure and headquarters or will correspond with further modifications to the underlying composition of units. This adjustment in nomenclature may reflect an increased openness about military cyber and space capabilities that were previously considered too sensitive or developmental to acknowledge. For years, the PLA was unwilling to admit to having military cyber forces and especially reluctant to admit to the development of offensive capabilities for the cyber domain.

Despite the rhetorical flourishes about avoiding the militarization of cyberspace that recur in PRC official statements, the more forthright references to a cyber force reveal at least an incremental transition toward greater clarity on these capabilities. This implicit acknowledgment occurs against the backdrop of increased implausibility of deniability, considering recurrent instances of the public attribution and exposure of PLA cyber threat activities, starting from the initial exposure of Unit 61398 as APT1 by Mandiant in 2013.

Considering the PLA's relative opacity and the limitations of available information, debate is likely to continue as to the drivers for and impacts of such continued changes.[13] While the PLASSF initially appeared to be designed to enable synergies and coordination across the cyber and space domains, the continued development of its operational components may have rendered a single commander and consolidated authorities to be too unwieldy.

The timing of these changes may have been impacted or potentially precipitated by recent incidents. Notably, the PLASSF was likely associated with the "spy balloon" incident that provoked a crisis in U.S.-Chinese relations in early 2023. That activity may have highlighted the imperative of closer control and increased oversight over developmental capabilities with potential international strategic implications.[14]

Moreover, the PLASSF's previous commander, General Ju Qiansheng, apparently disappeared from view in mid-2023.[15] While the reason for his disappearance and his whereabouts remain unknown, the PLASSF could be at least obliquely connected to the incidents of reported corruption that had ensnared former Minister of Defense Li Shangfu, who had himself served previously as PLASSF deputy commander.[16] Insofar as Ju was the first commander of the PLASSF to have previously risen through the 3PLA, any incidents of corruption—or other unknown problems of reliability or performance associated with his tenure—could result in more far-reaching investigations.[17] Such conditions may have provided additional motivation for this division of forces and likely changes of leadership.

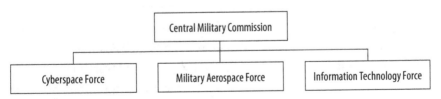

FIGURE 15-2. New Force Structure for People's Liberation Army Information Capabilities (as of April 2024)
Source: Author's design

The revised structure subordinates each of these forces directly to the CMC, potentially allowing for more centralized supervision. The PLACSF, PLAISF, and PLAMAF will each likely be aligned to support PLA joint forces based on CMC guidance, potentially through the Joint Operations Command Center.[18]

At this writing, the mechanisms of current or wartime command and control, such as the potential for delegation of authority and mechanisms of coordination with theater commands, are difficult to evaluate based on the available information.[19] However, the PLACSF's future trajectory may be influenced by the interplay of command cultures and structures with operational imperatives inherent in the character of the cyber domain, which can advantage greater flexibility and autonomy.

↦ CYBER FORCE CONCEPTS, CAPABILITIES, AND DEVELOPMENT

The PLA has tended to perceive the cyber domain as inherently offense-dominant, requiring a "strong attack mentality" and advantaging a "first strike" (先发制人) in a conflict scenario—as the PLA's information warfare strategist, Ye Zheng, once argued.[20] Indeed, the PLA National Defense University's *Science of Military Strategy* (2020) had declared, "Whoever seizes dominance in cyberspace will win the initiative in war; whoever loses this will fall into strategic passivity."[21] A "first strike" approach could enable the PLA to "offset" its disadvantages relative to a more powerful adversary such as the U.S. military, within and beyond the cyber domain. Given its missions, such lofty goals, and its structure, the PLACSF will likely continue to prioritize the integrated development of cyber reconnaissance, as well as offensive and defensive capabilities.[22]

The PLA's operational approach has therefore emphasized the importance of peacetime preparations creating accesses for capabilities that could be exploited in wartime. In practice, such preparations require the continuous development of capabilities through the process of identifying and exploiting vulnerabilities in adversaries' systems. The PLACSF is likely postured for dynamics often described as "integrated peace and wartime" (平战结合). In other words, Chinese readiness for the ongoing military struggle in this domain is orchestrated to extend across a cybered spectrum from peacetime to wartime. Such an approach leverages synergies associated with the "preparation of the battlefield" through cyber espionage, reconnaissance, and network insertions that can create persistent accesses required for future offensive operations.

The reports of PRC cyber threat activities, such as those associated with the PLA-linked Volt Typhoon hacker group, reveal how this approach appears to be playing out, with accounts of multiple incursions in critical infrastructure, such as ports, water utilities, gas pipelines, and power grids.[23] The focus of this targeting is often infrastructure in proximity to U.S. military bases, including those in Guam and Hawai'i—key centers of gravity for U.S. naval power.[24] The objective would be to establish the preconditions in peacetime for a disabling or destructive cyber attack that could impede the deployment of U.S. forces at a time and extent of the PRC's choosing.

During a conflict, the PLA would likely endeavor to attack adversaries' battle networks to paralyze their system of systems (体系) while seeking to preserve its own systems and provide resilient information support for its own joint operations.[25] Since seizing information dominance is considered an important foundation for joint operations in an era of "informatized warfare", PLA strikes against "key nodes and vital points" in an enemy's networks would require the integration of network (read: cyber) and electronic warfare with conventional operations in the course of this "confrontation of system versus system."[26] Cyber capabilities could be coordinated to combine "soft" strikes with "hard" strikes from kinetic firepower. So, too, *Science of Strategy* asserts, "destruction of the network can paralyze the enemy's combat system. Therefore, cyberspace has also rapidly developed into a combat space for high-intensity confrontation. Preventing the enemy from controlling the network guarantees victory."[27]

The PLA anticipates that cyber conflict is unlikely to remain restricted to military targets, instead expecting and probably preparing to conduct, and defend against, attacks on critical infrastructure, to include civilian targets with broader societal and economic implications. Potentially, the Cyberspace Force commander could be granted more operational authority when rapid response is required or based on predetermined courses of action.[28] In a campaign of coercion against Taiwan, for example, cyber attacks also could be aimed to have particular psychological effects.

⊢• RISING COGNITIVE AND PSYCHOLOGICAL OPERATIONS

The Cyberspace Force could be at the forefront of the PLA's exploration of new approaches to psychological operations in peacetime through wartime, such as emerging concepts of "cognitive domain operations" (认知域作战).[29] Notably, the PLACSF appears to have incorporated the component described as Base 311 (Unit 61716), previously under the auspices of the former General Political Department and, after 2016, the former PLASSF.[30] Traditionally, this unit has been known as a center for efforts in political warfare directed at Taiwan through a range of media outlets and modalities.

Since the recent military reforms, researchers associated with Unit 61716 have continued to publish research on innovative techniques for psychological warfare.[31] In particular, the PLA researchers from across a range of institutions have been evidently enthused with how exploitation of artificial intelligence can enhance the sophistication of such activities.[32] Going forward, the PLACSF is likely to play a role in continued experimentation with concepts of cognitive domain operations that will likely emphasize expansion and persistence of activities in peacetime on social media, as well as more effective integration of cyber and psychological operations.

⊢• CHINA'S CYBER SWORD AND SPEAR

As the PLA builds up its operational capabilities in the cyber domains, the Cyberspace Force will likely remain a critical strategic force that provides important emerging capabilities in support of PLA joint operations. In any future conflict scenario, the CSF would be a tip of the spear for the PLA—including for the PLAN—enabling its efforts to seize "information superiority." The PLACSF would be expected to conduct strikes against an adversary's military system of systems, while likely also targeting the homeland critical infrastructures of all allied adversaries to maximize the disruption and impediments to their military or supportive economic mobilization and defense operations globally.

As the PLA prepares to surpass U.S. naval power and support PLAN maritime operations in peacetime or conflict, the PLACSF will provide new options for coercion and incremental escalation across the maritime and all other domains.

NOTES

1. "The Ministry of National Defense convened a special press conference on the establishment of the Information Support Force" [国防部举行信息支援部队成立专题新闻发布会], *Xinhua*, 19 April 2024.

2. "The PLA Information Support Force founding meeting was convened in Beijing" [中国人民解放军信息支援部队成立大会在京举行], *Xinhua*, 19 April 2024.

3. Xiao Tianliang [肖天亮] (ed.), *The Science of Military Strategy* [战略学] (Beijing: National Defense University Press [国防大学出版社], 2020 [revision]), 182; "China's National Defense in the New Era," *Xinhua*, 24 July 2019.

4. For this argument, see, for instance, Joe McReynolds and John Costello, "Planned Obsolescence: The Strategic Support Force in Memoriam (2015–2024)," *China Brief* 24, no. 9 (26 April 2024), https://jamestown.org/program/planned-obsolescence-the-strategic-support-force-in-memoriam-2015–2024/.

5. "The Record of Grade Three Sergeant Zhou Yunxiao of a Certain Strategic Support Force Brigade" [战略支援部队某旅三级军士长赵云霄记事], *Xinhua*, 4 June 2017.

6. See also, "PLASSF Eastern Base leaders came to our institute to inspect and train non-commissioned officers" [战略支援部队东部基地领导来我院调研定向培养士官工作], 9 August 2018.

7. For one reference, see "The company's representative South Net won second place in the 2018 First Central Enterprise Cyber Security Competition of the State-owned Assets Supervision and Administration Commission" [公司代表南网获国资委2018年首届中央企业网络安全大赛第二名], FX361.com, 21 October 2018, https://m.fx361.com/news/2018/1021/8192978.html.

8. "Integrated Network-Electronic Warfare Will Smash the Battlefield Balance" [网电一体战"将打破战场天平], *China Military Online*, 3 January 2017.

9. The Joint Staff Department–Network-Electronic Bureau appears to be associated with the Network-Electronic Countermeasures Group (网电对抗大队), or Unit 31003. To what extent and whether the Network-Electronic Countermeasures Group and Cyberspace Force would coordinate or de-conflict targeting and operations remains uncertain. See "CCF Fuzhou Holds New Era Data Security and Personal Information Protection Technology Salon" [CCF福州举办新时代数据安全与个人信息保护技术沙龙], China Computer Federation, 8 November 2021.

10. According to the PLA's official dictionary of military terminology, the concept of strategic support (战略支援) is defined as "support implemented . . . to achieve a certain strategic objective," and can include providing information support. *Military Terminology of the Chinese People's Liberation Army* [中国人民解放军军语] (Beijing: Military Science Press, 2011).

11. Several notices concerning personnel recruiting introduced this new nomenclature in 2023.

12. Interestingly, early unofficial reporting did release these exact names as early as 2016, but PRC materials continued to use only the NSD and Aerospace Systems Department nomenclature until April 2024.

13. For initial commentary on the reorganization, see, for instance, J. Michael Dahm, "A Disturbance in the Force: The Reorganization of People's Liberation Army Command and Elimination of China's Strategic Support Force," *China Brief* (26 April 2024), https://jamestown.org/program/a-disturbance-in-the-force-the-reorganization-of-peoples-liberation-army-command-and-elimination-of-chinas-strategic-support-force/.

14. Chris Buckley and Amy Chang Chien, "In Its Push for an Intelligence Edge, China's Military Turned to Balloons," *New York Times*, 2 February 2023, A10, https://www.nytimes.com/2023/02/09/world/asia/china-spy-balloon-military.html.

15. Nectar Gan, "Xi's Latest Purge Targets the Military. Why Did Powerful Generals Fall Out of Favor?" *CNN*, 5 January 2024, https://www.cnn.com/2024/01/05/china/china-xi-military-purge-analysis-intl-hnk/index.html.

16. Chris Buckley and Julian E. Barnes, "China Is Investigating Its Defense Minister, U.S. Officials Say," *New York Times*, 15 September 2023, https://www.nytimes.com/2023/09/15/world/asia/xi-china-military-general-li-shangfu.html.

17. Shangguan He, "Four 'post-60s' generals were promoted to generals!" [4名"60后"将军晋升上将! 现役最年轻上将是他], *Shangguan News*, 6 July 2021.

18. See, for reference, Liu, 2016.

19. Fan Yongtao [樊永涛], Wang Jinsong [王劲松], and Li Shikai [李世楷], "Problems and Solutions to the Cyberspace Operational Command Pattern" [网络空间作战指挥方式面临的问题及对策], *Journal of Academy of Armored Force Engineering*, no. 5 (2017), 9.

20. Academy of Military Science Military Strategy Research Department [军事科学院军事战略研究部] (ed.), *The Science of Military Strategy* [战略学] (Beijing: Military Science Press, 2013).

21. Xiao, 150.

22. This is a consistent emphasis across multiple authoritative textbooks.

23. See, for instance, Microsoft Threat Intelligence, "Volt Typhoon Targets U.S. critical Infrastructure with Living-off-the-Land Techniques," 24 May 2023, https://www.microsoft.com/en-us/security/blog/2023/05/24/volt-typhoon-targets-us-critical-infrastructure-with-living-off-the-land-techniques/.

24. Ellen Nakashima and Joseph Menn, "China's Cyber Army Is Invading Critical U.S. Services," *Washington Post*, 11 December 2023, https://www.washingtonpost.com/technology/2023/12/11/china-hacking-hawaii-pacific-taiwan-conflict/.

25. "PLA Daily Commentator: Strive to Construct a Strong Modern Information Support Force" [解放军报评论员: 努力建设一支强大的现代化信息支援部队], *PLA Daily*, 20 April 2024.

26. Ye Zheng, "Lectures on the Science of Information Operations," in 2013 edition of *The Science of Military Strategy* [战略学].

27. Xiao, 403.

28. For more extensive discussion of these issues, see also John Chen, Joe McReynolds, and Kieran Green, "The Strategic Support Force: A 'Joint' Force for Information Operations," in *The PLA beyond Borders*, ed. Joel Wuthnow et al. (Washington, DC: NDU Press, 2021).

29. For reference, see Mark Stokes and Russell Hsiao, *The People's Liberation Army General Political Department* (Arlington, VA: Project 2049, 2013); and Nathan Beauchamp-Mustafaga, "Cognitive Domain Operations: The PLA's New Holistic Concept for Influence Operations," *China Brief* 19, no. 16 (6 September 2019), 6, https://jamestown.org/program/cognitive-domain-operations-the-plas-new-holistic-concept-for-influence-operations/.

30. For reference on the concept, see Wu Jieming [吴杰明] and Liu Zhifu [刘志富], *An Introduction to Public Opinion Warfare, Psychological Warfare,* [and] *Legal Warfare* [舆论战心理战法律战概论] (Beijing: National Defense University Press, 2014).

31. Liu Huiyan [刘惠燕], Xiong Wu [熊武], Wu Xianliang [吴显亮], and Mei Shunliang [梅顺量], "Some Thoughts on Promoting the Development of Cognitive Domain Combat Equipment in the Omni-Media Environment" [全媒体环境下推进认知域作战装备发展的几点思考], *National Defense Science and Technology* [国防科技] 39, no. 5 (2018): 40–42.

32. Li Bicheng [李弼程], Hu Huaping [胡华平], and Xiong Yao [熊尧], "Internet Public Opinion Guided Intelligent Agent Model" [网络舆情引导智能代理模型], *Collection* [收藏] 3 (2019).

16 Admiral Gorshkov in Cyberspace

Russia, Cyber, and Maritime Conflict

J. D. WORK

R ussian cyber operations for maritime objectives remain understudied active, persistent threats meant to contest the rules-based liberal international order. Naval matters in the cyber domain are overshadowed by political warfare, influence operations, economic espionage, covert action, and combat operations in a major regional conflict shaped by its ground and aviation dimensions.[1] Furthermore, incomplete information in the public record documenting actions in and through cyberspace distorts assessments across analyst and scholarly communities. A substantial divergence exists between the assessments of Russian capabilities and intentions provided by increasingly robust commercial cyber intelligence, and what is commonly portrayed in media coverage.

This chapter argues that the Russian naval cyber mission is intended to support continental warfare as part of the whole of the armed forces. This mission consists largely of developing and delivering effects against distant targets of military-economic potential, whether maritime or not. Due to the limits of reliable open-source analysis of the Russian fleet's cyber capabilities, this discussion will focus on the overall national and naval cyber missions, not specific units. This chapter approaches understanding the Russian naval cyber mission in four parts. The first is a review of the evolution of the overall Russian fleet mission into a strategic support force by the twenty-first century. The second is the examination of how offensive national cyber campaigns support the naval reconnaissance-strike complex. The third is a review of the national intelligence functional subset most relevant for fleet requirements—*razvedka* (intelligence-reconnaissance) against opponents' information and communications systems. The fourth is a discussion of a likely future in part influenced by the lessons of the 2022 Ukraine invasion.

⊢• TOWARD A STRATEGIC FLEET MISSION

Since at least 2010, Moscow has heavily emphasized the information domain as a key avenue to (re)achieving and maintaining Russia's status as a global power. Today, broader Russian thinking on interstate relations envisions peacetime and wartime activities not as separate campaigns, but rather as a spectrum upon which all state interactions take place. This spectrum includes military, economic, diplomatic, and cyber efforts tailored to circumstances of heightened and lowered tension.

In many ways, the evolution of the Russian Navy in the tumultuous years following the collapse of the Soviet Union was a search for relevance in the face of steady decline. This was not a unique problem, as a number of other fleets also faced policymaker demands for reductions in pursuit of a "peace dividend." But those on the Admiralty embankment also had to face the consequences of falsified communist readiness, inventory, and capabilities reporting. At the same time, the navy consistently lost out on many key funding choices between different defense recapitalization priorities throughout the opening decades of the new century.[2]

In addition to the immediate impact on the fleet itself, the maritime industrial base as a whole was in grave decline.[3] Gone was the substantively broader view of sea power within Moscow's calculus in the 1960s to 1980s. This thirty-year era led by Admiral Sergei Gorshkov built on reshaped beliefs about surprise attack, strategic strike, and decisive action at decisive moments against the enemy.[4] The Soviet Navy was reshaped from a glorified coastal defense force into a global force projector that offered critical deterrence and warfighting capabilities through conventional and nuclear options.

Recast as providing decisive contributions to influence the outcome of war, the Gorshkov-era fleet developed new strike concepts including targeting objects of enemy military-economic potential such as electrical power systems and other military industry as well as more conventional or nuclear means of attack, in addition to administrative-political centers.[5] Supporting these changes was the introduction of the submarine-launched ballistic missile that extended the reach and range of targets that could be held at risk, and the submarine and naval aviation–delivered cruise missiles.[6] Naval warfare within the fleet came to emphasize standoff distance and new options to disaggregate force employment, including the prospect that future fights would be determined by only a small number of fires salvos rather than prolonged exchanges.[7]

Gorshkov's conceptual transformations endured in Russia even as the post–Cold War period challenged his vision of power projection in the world ocean.[8] As the Soviet-era military came apart in the post–Cold War world, it was clear that the full range of sea power missions could no longer be supported—and were indeed perhaps irrelevant following what most considered defeat in the ideological and economic contest between superpowers. Yet the otherwise fraught dissolution of forces across the former republics left the fleet's own strike capabilities largely untouched.[9] Going forward, the navy would emphasize the disproportionate value of its strategic systems, especially the unique qualitative characteristics offered by flexible, low-signature submarine deployment, and would argue for recapitalization of the ballistic missile submarine (SSBN) fleet.[10]

Such exquisite acquisition programs are expensive and restricted to the highest end of the spectrum of hostilities, however, and the opportunity to generate strategic power through exploitation of the emerging internet seemed to Russia's military and intelligence leaders to be a relatively easy and low-cost additional option with lower barriers to entry.[11]

Furthermore, Russian military theorists in the 1990s extensively analyzed the late–Cold War U.S. military and its focus on network-centric warfare. Russian planners were likely aware of the U.S. government's advancing capabilities, which might threaten nuclear command and control—especially connectivity with SSBN patrols in their "bastion" concept of operations.[12] If U.S. networked operations that facilitated the speed of decision-making and precision strike would define the future of warfare, then cyber operations were deemed ideal to slow adversary decision-making, speed up one's own, and support actions in the cognitive domain of warfare. The pursuit of offensive national cyber capabilities tailored for naval purposes could therefore be seen as a logical hedging strategy to provide additional fleet force projection options under constrained budgets.

⊢→ IS THERE A RUSSIAN "FLEET CYBER"?

Russian naval cyber organization and tasking are opaque. In fact, it is unclear whether the Russian Federation Navy is responsible for organizing and executing its own cyber operations. The navy has its own cadre of network engineers, information technicians, and software developers, so presumably it has the basis for a cyber operations force. But whether they constitute what Western military forces might consider an organized cyber operations unit remains uncertain.

Indeed, likely a contested topic within the defense ministry is the extent to which possible maritime cyber missions are met by an independent "cyber service"—constituted as part of the information operations troops of the General Staff with billets assigned from the navy—or by dedicated navy-wide cyber forces or elements assigned to specific banner fleet military districts.[13] Similar debates over the role of electronic warfare components that have been recognized as contributing to cyber operations and advocated for independence within their own services are known already to occur.[14] Even from the perspective of insiders, the organization of force providers, supporting commands, and supported command relationships appears unsettled.

However, with a focus on mission rather than organization, inferences regarding the planning and execution of naval cyber operations can be drawn from unclassified commercial but credible cyber intelligence on the ongoing intrusion campaigns publicly attributed to the Russian intelligence service actors, such as the Foreign Intelligence Service, General Staff Main (Intelligence) Directorate (GRU), and Federal Security Service (FSB). Naval staffing and coordination within attributed operational units—including

FSB Center 16 and 18, GRU Main Center for Special Technologies, and 85th Main Special Service Center—remain opaque. Yet there are clearly naval priorities observed in their actions. Likewise, there is increasing indication of operational technology specialization in offensive tooling developed by attributed elements such as the Ministry of Defense and the Central Scientific Institute of Chemistry and Mechanics, and the wider contractor ecosystem including NTC Vulkan, which encompasses maritime-associated targets.[15]

These campaigns suggest that Russian cyber operations for maritime missions have two main roles: preparing and delivering a national-level strategic offensive cyber effects capability in "economic warfare," as well as missions supporting naval intelligence requirements. Since navies operate as geo-economic instruments as well as means of war, navies are capable of playing a direct role in economic warfare and thus in cyber operations (as also argued by Tangredi in this volume). Attacks on "commercial elements" of the maritime domain further have effects on naval and joint operations, particularly logistics support.

Russian "fleet cyber"—if it can be described as such—may also benefit from General Staff consideration of "special tasks." Clearly, naval expertise offering unique operational-technical competencies is required for certain cyber missions, especially signals intelligence and cryptologic roles, with an operational history traceable to the early 1920s.[16]

Furthermore, the Chinese pursuit of coercive cyber capabilities as an alternative to nuclear engagement has been embraced by Russian theorists seeking cyber options to inflict strategic damage as an alternative or supplement to nuclear operations.[17] Russian strategists envision cyber operations, or "information confrontation" (*informatsionnoyeprotivoborstvo*), as one of their tools in the deterrence/compellence/escalation tool kit, with such "factors as command and control, combat support and other types of support" in potential strategic exchanges.[18]

In Russian national strategy, cyber operations fall into two related and mutually supporting spheres. The first, "informational-technical effect," is roughly analogous to computer network operations, including computer network defense, attack, and exploitation. The second is "informational-psychological effect," which, broadly speaking, refers to efforts to change human beliefs or behavior in ways that help achieve Moscow's broader goals.[19] Efforts to create strategic influence in and through cyberspace are aimed at objects of military-economic potential as well as diplomatic, political, cultural, and religious targets uniquely conceptualized within their ideas of national will.

While the Russian Navy has not acknowledged an independent responsibility for carrying out cyber operations against potential adversaries, the naval mission is wider than the sea services alone. The manner in which Russian offensive cyber capabilities are generated and employed is inextricably interlinked with national intelligence services and likely joint naval assignments through General Staff and other specialized rotational billets. While cyber operations are not called out in Russia's maritime doctrine or naval doctrine or emphasized in the Defense Ministry's list of navy tasks, and the service lacks a Russian equivalent to the U.S. Cyber Command's Naval Component, the Tenth Fleet, it nonetheless is unlikely that maritime sector targets would be pursued absent navy interest and internal involvement.[20]

⊢• *RAZVEDKA* TECHNICAL EFFECTS FOR THE NAVAL RECONNAISSANCE-STRIKE COMPLEX

The Russian Navy was among the earliest innovators in the use of signals intelligence. Czarist Admiral A. I. Nepenin established the first OSNAZ (*Radiostantsiya Osobogo Naznacheniya*) intercept station in what is now Estonia in 1914. So it is not without precedent that cyber espionage would be pursued for the naval service.[21]

While it is difficult to distinguish specific intrusions intended to support operational preparation of the environment to deliver information-technical effects and to otherwise support the naval reconnaissance-strike complex from "pure" espionage, cyber operations against maritime targets traceable to known fleet intelligence requirements have been pursued in multiple ways since the Soviet period.[22] These included science and technology transfer through espionage intended to support fleet modernization, as well as attempts to collect against associated operational integration.

One example of this extensive program occurred in 2017 when a core Russia nexus intrusion set was observed targeting exercise Dynamic Monarch, a North Atlantic Treaty Organization–led multinational event focused on submarine search, escape, and rescue held in the eastern Mediterranean. Espionage against this exercise built upon concurrent interest in an international submarine rescue working group established after the loss of the OSCAR II/Project 949A nuclear cruise missile submarine *Kursk* in August 2000.[23] This case reflects the complex political and military value of cyber espionage for both the fleet and larger defense ministry.

On a wider spectrum, specific operational preparation of the environment incidents associated with maritime objectives have been identified with increasing frequency throughout the past decade by commercial cyber intelligence services, consistent with Russian doctrine for information-technical warfare—*razvedka*. Observed threat activity included targeting of shipping, offshore services, and extractive and energy market segments and in prior intrusions, including against coastal refinery targets.[24] Particular interest in liquefied natural gas targets has emerged over cumulative actions, including key liquefied natural gas terminals, storage enterprises, and their associated facilities,[25] suggesting at least a task-organized focus if not uniquely established objectives for distinctly maritime operational elements.

Patterns of threat activity against maritime associated targets form a subset of wider strategic-level targeting, distinctly clustered by temporal and operational characteristics.[26] For example, actions against port, ferry, and shipping targets across multiple North Atlantic Treaty Organization countries appear to be a learning campaign of stalking likely defender reactions.[27] The Russian doctrine of "reflexive control" requires considerable foreknowledge of the target's likely responses to any attack.[28] Pro-Russian "hacktivist" distributed denial of service campaigns concurrent with the ongoing conflict in Europe have provided Russia with substantial insights into the performance of maritime target networks when under network attack.

While this reconnaissance by fire has largely been limited to disruptive attack using commodity distributed denial of service capabilities, the systematic traversal of targeting across critical infrastructure sectors is distinctive. Some of the subsequent destructive intrusions against these targets were publicly labeled as criminal ransomware operations. However, other actions suspected to represent a signaling of capability are likely to be continuing Russian experimentation with proxy or other deniable capabilities.[29]

In Ukraine, cyber operations almost certainly have contributed to a range of functions, from targeting to battle damage assessment. Previously, former commander in chief of the Russian Fleet Vladimir Kuroyedov spoke of the "shift from firepower buildup to a broader use of tactical control and target designation information systems, this in order to increase the probability of successful weapon employment."[30] Other notable public examples have included contested control of surveillance camera networks supporting cruise missile and one-way attack unmanned aerial systems in the vicinity of Odessa port, and, in support of blockade operations, the compromise of Ukrainian port networks.[31] The compromise of port networks attributed by the commercial cyber intelligence industry to the Berserk Bear/Ghost Blizzard/Iron Liberty intrusion set almost certainly contributed to shipping activity targeting in support of blockade operations (whether in real time, or through pattern of life analysis).[32]

Successful intrusions may have also been leveraged to calibrate the decision to permit limited commerce under the Black Sea Grain Initiative from July 2022 to July 2023.[33] It is likely that lessons learned from blockade operations will result in further refinements in planning for employment of the naval reconnaissance-strike complex against European and other global targets.

⊢• THE FUTURE WITH RUSSIAN NAVY STRATEGIC FOCUS AND CYBER UNCERTAINTIES

The Russian Navy is essentially two navies—the old Soviet fleet and the newer Russian fleet. Older Soviet-era platforms have been upgraded over the decades, but this has occurred unevenly across individual platforms and the fleet. The Slava-class cruiser *Moskva*, sunk by the Ukrainians in May 2022, is but one example of this dynamic. A readiness report issued just before the onset of the war identified both the aging technology on board the ship as well as its poor material condition. Virtually every system on board consisted of then–state-of-the-art 1970s technology.[34] Digital capabilities were nonexistent.

Russian vessels built since roughly 2003 are generally more digitally advanced. The Russian Navy has become more reliant on automated software–driven systems in logistics, monitoring, and diagnostics, maintenance and repair, and damage control. These automated systems make it possible to plan maintenance and repair, order spare parts and identify when they are available, and speed the process of generating documentation.[35] However, the application of new technologies is uneven and subject to other design demands dictated by the Defense Ministry. Furthermore, the Russian Navy has its own cyber vulnerabilities. Shoreside administrative operations on unclassified networks are as vulnerable as any other network on the Russian internet.

The navy, like the rest of the Russian military, also operates on two separate classified networks of varying security, with higher levels of information classification having presumably higher levels of security. Still, there is no fleet-wide mandatory uniformity across new ships and submarines, and construction programs for new ships may or may not provide for the installation of advanced digital systems. Also, the navy does not provide standard software requirements for all its new vessels. This is a challenge for systems developers who may not fully understand the specifications to which they need to design a ship's software.

Conversely, this lack of uniformity of software systems across the fleet may limit the usefulness of exploits in offensive cyber fires against maritime targets, making the winding path of Russian naval cyber development a benefit.[36] Ultimately, the Russian Navy remains a strategic-level weapon. A large set of capabilities are not committed to the Russo-Ukrainian conflict and almost certainly are held in reserve for strategic engagements beyond this limited war.[37] That part of the Russian reconnaissance-strike complex oriented primarily for sea power objectives has not seen much use against targets within Ukraine. It is also significant that observed destructive operations appear increasingly to be associated with GRU-related intrusion sets as well as new unknown developmental clusters, suggesting delineation of capabilities committed in limited war versus those reserved for other strategic exchanges.[38]

It is difficult to estimate thresholds for use of these reserved capabilities, especially within the specific context of maritime military-economic potential. In early 2024 a leak from Russian military sources purportedly displayed current nuclear warfighting plans, which include triggers for nuclear use tied to percentages of combat losses of SSBNs, other submarine forces, heavy cruiser surface action groups, and command and control systems.[39] The perceived conditions for employing naval reconnaissance-strike complex information-technical effects are likely consistent with similar Russian thinking about nuclear options.[40] In any case, it is reasonable to expect the Russian Navy to increase its emphasis on strategic missions, and a less costly offensive alternative using cyberspace should remain attractive to planners in the future as well in support of national and maritime requirements.

NOTES

1. Scott Jasper, *Russian Cyber Operations: Coding the Boundaries of Conflict* (Washington, DC: Georgetown University Press, 2022); Bilyana Lilly, *Russian Information Warfare: Assault on Democracies in the Cyber Wild West* (Annapolis, MD: Naval Institute Press, 2022); Nicholas Michael Sambaluk, *Weaponizing Cyberspace: Inside Russia's Hostile Activities* (Santa Barbara, CA: Praeger, 2022); Andy Greenberg, *Sandworm: A New Era of Cyberwar and the Hunt for the Kremlin's Most Dangerous Hackers* (New York: Anchor, 2019).

2. Bora Balçay, "The Decaying Superpower: A Review of the Russian Navy," *Georgetown Security Review* 11, no. 2 (2024): 147–51.

3. Elena Efimova and Sergei Sutyrin, "Government Support for the Russian Shipbuilding Industry: Policy Priorities and Budgetary Allocations" (Turku, Centrum Balticum, May 2019).

4. Harriet Fast Scott and William Scott, *Soviet Military Doctrine: Continuity, Formulation, and Dissemination* (Boulder, CO: Westview Press, 1988).

5. Sergei Georgievich Gorshkov, "The Navy of the Soviet Union," *Soviet Military Review*, no. 6 (June 1975): 2–5; Sergei Georgievich Gorshkov, *The Sea Power of the State* (Moscow: Soviet Ministry of Defense Publishing House, 1976).

6. James J. Tritten, *Soviet Naval Forces and Nuclear Warfare: Weapons, Employment, and Policy* (Boulder, CO: Westview Press, 1986).

7. Charles Peterson, *Soviet Tactics for Warfare at Sea* (Arlington, VA: Center for Naval Analyses, November 1982).

8. Robert Whitten, "Soviet Sea Power in Retrospect: Admiral of the Fleet of the Soviet Union Sergei G. Gorshkov and the Rise and Fall of the Soviet Navy," *Journal of Slavic Military Studies* 11, no. 2 (1998): 48–79.

9. William Odom, *The Collapse of the Soviet Military* (New Haven: Yale University Press, 2008), 381–82.

10. Yu. P. Gladyshev and Yu. A. Uvarov, "Navy's Role in Strategic Deterrence," *Military Thought* 16, no. 3–4 (July–December 2007): 66–76; Victor Litovkin, "The

Bulava Missile: A Russian Military Trump Card?" *Security Index: A Russian Journal on International Security* 17, no. 2 (2011): 69–74.

11. Dorothy Denning, "Barriers to Entry: Are They Lower for Cyber Warfare?" *IO Journal* (April 2009); Max Smeets, *No Shortcuts: Why States Struggle to Develop a Military Cyber-force* (Oxford: Oxford University Press, 2022).

12. Jan Breemer, "The Soviet Navy's SSBN Bastions: Why Explanations Matter," *RUSI Journal* 134, no. 4 (1989): 33–39.

13. Joe Cheravitch, *The Role of Russia's Military in Information Confrontation* (Arlington, VA: Center for Naval Analyses, June 2021).

14. Yu. I. Lastochkin, "Problematic Issues of Creating Electronic Warfare Troops as a Branch of the Armed Forces of the Russian Federation," *Military Thought* 9 (2022).

15. Mandiant, "Contracts Identify Cyber Operations Projects from Russian Company NTC Vulkan," 30 March 2023.

16. Thomas R. Hammant, "Russian and Soviet Cryptology IV: Some Incidents in the 1930s," *Cryptologia* 25, no. 1 (2001): 61–63.

17. Fiona S. Cunningham, "Strategic Substitution: China's Search for Coercive Leverage in the Information Age," *International Security* 47, no. 1 (Summer 2022): 46–92.

18. Yu. F. Kirillov, V. I. Kuznetsov, and V. D. Roldugin, "Functional Approach to Estimation of Relative Strategic Force Ratio of Opposing Forces," *Military Thought* 14, no. 4 (October–December 2005): 115–24.

19. Defense Intelligence Agency, *Russia Military Power: Building a Military to Support Great Power Aspirations* (Washington, DC: Defense Intelligence Agency, 2017), 37–41,

20. See Anna Davis and Ryan Vest, transl., *Maritime Doctrine of the Russian Federation, 31 July 2022* (Newport, RI: Russian Maritime Studies Institute, U.S. Naval War College, n.d.),

21. David Schimmelpenninck van der Oye, "Tsarist Codebreaking: Some Background and Some Examples," *Cryptologia* 22, no. 4 (1998): 342–53.

22. Bruce W. Watson and Susan M. Watson, *The Soviet Navy: Strengths and Liabilities* (Boulder, CO: Westview Press, 1986).

23. Cyber Conflict Documentation Project, "Russia: Malicious Interest in Coalition Deep Submergence Survivability," June 2017.

24. Department of Justice, "Four Russian Government Employees Charged in Two Historical Hacking Campaigns Targeting Critical Infrastructure Worldwide," 24 March 2022.

25. Alexander Martin, "German Spy Chief Warns of Cyberattacks Targeting Liquefied Natural Gas Terminals," *The Record*, 18 September 2023.

26. Cyber Conflict Documentation Project, "Russian Nexus APT Strategic Targeting Trends," July 2017.

27. Malshare, "DDOS Monitoring against Identified Maritime Targets in Bulgaria, Denmark, Estonia, France, Finland, Greece, Italy, Poland, Sweden, and United Kingdom, February 2023 to February 2024."

28. Antti Vasara, *Theory of Reflexive Control: Origins, Evolution, and Application in the Framework of Contemporary Russian Military Strategy* (Helsinki: National Defense University, 2020).

29. Malshare, "New Target: [redacted]," 19 October 2023; Malshare, "New AlphVM victim: [redacted]," 5 November 2023.

30. V. I. Kuroyedov, "Navy Today: Main Trends in its Development and Employment," *Military Thought* 13, no. 3 (2004): 33–41.

31. Kyrylo Ovsyanyi, "Under the Supervision of the Kremlin: Russian Special Services Received Videos from Thousands of Surveillance Cameras throughout Ukraine for Years?" *Radio Free Europe/Radio Liberty*, 7 December 2023.

32. CrowdStrike, "Suspected Spear Phishing Activity Associated with BERSERK BEAR Targets Ukraine's Critical Infrastructure," 9 September 2016.

33. Antony Blinken, "Russia's Suspension of Participation in the Black Sea Grain Initiative," U.S. Department of State, 17 July 2023.

34. Igor Girkin, "Крейсер москва, вконтактике сообщают," Twitter entry, 28 April 2022, https://twitter.com/GirkinGirkin/status/1519742639922454528.

35. See corporate web page for Neotel Marine and Seascape, http://neotech-marine.ru/.

36. J. D. Work, "Offensive Cyber Operations and Future Littoral Operating Concepts," *Military Cyber Affairs* 5, no. 1 (2022).

37. Shane Huntley et al., "Fog of War: How the Ukraine Conflict Transformed the Cyber Threat Landscape," Google Threat Analysis Group, 16 February 2023.

38. Dan Black and Gabby Rancor, "The GRU's Disruptive Playbook," Mandiant, 12 July 2023.

39. Max Seddon and Chris Cook, "Leaked Russian Military Files Reveal Criteria for Nuclear Strike," *Financial Times*, 28 February 2024.

40. Dmitry Adamsky, "Nuclear Incoherence: Deterrence Theory and Non-strategic Nuclear Weapons in Russia," *Journal of Strategic Studies* 37, no. 1 (2014): 91–134.

SECTION 3

TECHNOLOGIES

17 Warfighting in the Ether

Electromagnetic Warfare— Past, Present, and Future

RANDY PUGH

O n 27 May 1905, after a seven-month, eighteen thousand–nautical–mile transit from Baltic and Black Sea ports, the Russian Fleet finally arrived in the Sea of Japan to break the Japanese siege on Port Arthur and bring the Russo-Japanese War to its conclusion.

As the ships entered the Tsushima Strait under strict radio silence, Russian radio operators reported to their officers that they were picking up Japanese signals transmitting the fleet's position to the Japanese imperial headquarters. The Russian operators offered that they might be able to disrupt or deny these communications by transmitting over them on the same frequency. The request, however, was denied by the Russian admiral.[1] Thus was the stumbling beginning of a century-plus of state-level competition across the electromagnetic spectrum (EMS) that would eventually become known as electronic warfare (EW). Eagerly embraced by navies in particular, EW is now moving into its second century, capable of fighting "smarter" when combined with artificial intelligence and cyber, but challenged by a growing need for operators skilled far beyond the naive users who dominate the services today.

⊢• EARLY ELECTRONIC WARFARE

Because of its utility, EW has been a major contributor to some of the most important military engagements in the last one hundred years, many of which still remain classified. Importantly, while a highly technical field, EW has long been appreciated by warfighters who have witnessed the exponential advantages that EW provides in combat.

The U.S. Navy was an early and enthusiastic advocate for EW. Commanders—especially at sea—constantly seek to be first to detect and engage the enemy. (See chapters on Navy and new technologies by Jones, and Bebber and White in this volume.) Since the invention of wireless communications by Guglielmo Marconi in 1896, the Navy has pursued aggressive research, development, and experimentation in radio communication and radar detection, intercept, exploitation, geolocation, and disruption.[2] During and immediately after World War II, rapid advances in weapons, and especially aircraft and missiles, stimulated massive investment in EW-related technologies to detect adversaries and guide ships, planes, and weapons to their desired targets, as well as to protect friendly forces from detection and targeting by enemy EW efforts.[3] (See chapter on undersea cable developments by Kavanagh and Leconte in this volume.)

Over that past century or so, a ceaseless contest of EW innovation and adaptive countermeasures has continued across all major militaries, knowing that a failure to aggressively compete could lead to the destruction of an aircraft or a ship—even a navy or a nation. As a result, the Navy has explored new EW techniques and technologies, quickly developing countermeasures to an adversary's advances and then counter-countermeasures as needed.

⊢• IMPACT OF DIGITALIZATION ADDS COMPLEXIFICATION

With a long history of simultaneous advances happening in friendly and adversary capabilities, science and technology, and the operating environment, modern EW is becoming increasingly complex, powered by the meteoric rise of digital computers and artificial intelligence (AI). Digital information proved vastly superior with respect to mass storage, fast retrieval, rapid search and processing, and near-real-time transmission, plus the quality and quantity of communications services available through the EMS.

The Navy was quick to recognize the value of digital computers, and they are now integrated into naval platforms and weapons systems to process vast amounts of information rapidly and accurately in decision support systems, sensors systems, and weapons guidance systems.[4] (See discussion by Friedman in this volume.)

Due to the exponential increase in potential complexity, the maturation of AI in warfare will make EW and cyber warfare seem almost quaint. Especially in the last two years, AI has begun to offer a realistic promise of computers that can read, write, see, hear, speak, analyze, synthesize, make rational decisions, reason, and control other computers and physical objects. Daily revelations of new AI-related technologies are generating concepts and proposed capabilities that might revolutionize how we sense, understand, and act on future battlefields, all at the speed of wireless communications and digital computers—literally the speed of light. Like wireless communications, radar, and digital computers, AI-related invention, adoption, and evolution will be fully integrated in EW and cyber warfare and will be vigorously contested by our adversaries.

⊢• THE HIDDEN VULNERABILITY TO EW, CYBER, AND AI: LACK OF SKILLED OPERATORS

The Navy must be diligent to ensure it has invested in not just the acquisition of cutting-edge technologies, but also a cadre of operators who have the knowledge, technical skill, and readiness to use them in combat. In the twenty-first century, the United States, and especially the U.S. Navy, will need to wage EW and cyber warfare, as well as what former Defense Secretary Robert Work called algorithmic warfare.[5]

All wars—but especially future wars—from their outset, are a contest of rapid quality decision-making—command and control warfare 2.0. Exploiting and attacking an enemy's communications links, data in motion, data at rest, applications that process information, and how this information is presented to human decision-makers or to other systems while protecting our own—all will be foundational to any hope of victory. Whether at the tactical, operational, or strategic level, whether a single system, a system of systems, or the decision-making process itself, twenty-first-century warfighters must have the necessary knowledge and skills in algorithmic warfare, and they must know how the three disciplines of EW, cyber warfare, and AI can be used together as a form of combined algorithmic warfare arms to fight and win. Our adversaries, who hold the potential to be our future enemies in physical as well as cyber battle, know this as well. Winning or losing may very well depend on the side that can best dominate the tripartite EW, cyber, and AI "ether."

⊢• TWENTY-FIRST-CENTURY EW ESSENTIAL DETAILS

EW traditionally consists of three subdivisions: electronic protection, ensuring the secure and reliable use of the EMS for one's own purposes; electronic attack, disrupting, denying, interrupting, delaying, or deceiving the enemy; and electronic warfare support, detecting, classifying, and geolocating signals in the EMS.

These three subdivisions of EW are interdependent and mutually reinforcing with associated technologies, tactics, techniques, and procedures (TTPs) constantly and simultaneously evolving in response to change in three different areas—new friendly EMS-related technologies and TTPs, new enemy EMS-related technologies and TTPs, and new technologies and TTPs specifically for the EW community itself. Increasingly driving this equation are advances in commercial communications.

Future battlefield communications systems and networks will closely follow those of the commercial communications field, and the larger commercial communications innovation ecosystem continues to churn out a stream of new and astonishing inventions. Fully aware of the potential of these capabilities for military use, military acquisition program managers have been quick to adopt them. They have adapted long-standing policies and processes in ways that enabled the military to take advantage of the commercial products' dual-use capabilities, but these adaptations will need to continuously stay updated. Military forces, like the civilian sector, will continue to insist on the ability to transmit and receive information via high-quality, secure, reliable, and robust wireless networks. Both will expect users to be able to instantly contact any other user anywhere on the globe, to have access to immense amounts of "on-call" data and services via cloud-based storage and applications and to the enormous bandwidth needed for streaming video, video teleconferencing, and other, still unimagined, capabilities.

Furthermore, the commercial "Internet of Things" will beget an "Internet of Battlefield Things" as militaries follows the commercial sector trend of connecting not just people, but also all devices, to a wireless network.[6] That ubiquitous mesh of networks will support envisioned capabilities like the autonomous vehicles and vessels, digital twins, self-sensing and -reporting weapons, and the application of AI "at the edge" for all warfighting systems and functions.[7]

The exponentially increasing complexity of communications technology and its subsequent adoption by friendly and adversary militaries will create a tremendous challenge for the EW community. Understanding the foundational communications techniques and the technologies that power devices and networks has always been beyond most users, military or civilian. In the twenty-first century, it will be orders of magnitude more difficult.

To accommodate users who simply want their devices to "just work," the complexity will be intentionally abstracted away, to be managed by underlying control systems and computer algorithms. The overwhelming number of naive users of modern communication devices presents both challenges and opportunities when one considers that our adversaries face the same challenges. To protect friendly users and take advantage of the adversary's skills gaps, EW operators must commit to being true technical experts regarding understanding communications and other EMS-related technologies. These operators will very likely be the only ones who truly understand how a system works and who can develop the best TTPs and advanced technologies needed to protect friendly vulnerabilities and exploit and attack those of the adversary.

Twenty-first-century EW operators will be challenged to create exquisite effects on digital systems that mimic the advantages achieved in previous eras using analog EW systems against analog systems. Yesterday's analog barrage jamming will become tomorrow's mass issuing of false reports or false orders that look, feel, and sound exactly like the real thing. Radio frequency direction-finding will be replaced by a surreptitious forced self-reporting of a global positioning system or equivalent satellite-based location by, and to, an enemy system. Analog radio voice communications intercept will become the dual-routing or the hijacking of battlefield emails or chats in exploitation of the enemy's meshed networks.

⊢• TWENTY-FIRST-CENTURY CYBER WARFARE ESSENTIAL DETAILS

Cyber warfare, a term coming into common use around 2007, is reasonably defined as "the use of computer technology to attack personnel, facilities, or equipment with the intent of degrading, neutralizing, or destroying enemy combat capability, while protecting our own."[8] Naval information technology professionals have worked nonstop to patch military computer systems since the first computers put to sea simply to keep them working. It was decades after the introduction of digital computers into the fleet that the naval services finally developed a concept, a strategy, and the resources required to protect our digital systems when connected to networks. During this period of focus on defending computer systems and networks, a small and very secretive group also learned to exploit and attack our adversary's digital capabilities.

Today, our understanding of the capabilities and vulnerabilities of computer systems and networks has increased to a highly sophisticated level, and the Navy now has the tools, technologies, and TTPs it needs to protect its current computers and their associated networks. The secretive group that exploited and attacked others' computers has now become much less secretive, but much more critical to the mission. Like their EW counterparts, cyber warfare experts take actions that prevent an enemy from accessing, corrupting, or deleting data or modifying software applications in ways that lead to inaccurate results, disruptions in the timely flow of information across networks, or vulnerabilities elsewhere in the cyber domain, the EMS, or the physical domain. In its exploitative or offensive form, cyber warfare operators take actions in cyberspace that constitute or directly enable espionage, damage to virtual or physical assets, and degradation of the decision-making processes. Cyber warfare targets (to be protected, exploited, or attacked) consist of the data, applications, systems, and networks relied on by decision-makers or needed for operations.

The future of cyber warfare, like that of EW, will be increasingly driven by commercial technology maturation and innovation as well as the growing global community of operators highly educated in computer systems and networks and open to discovering new ways to exploit and attack them. Excellence in cyber warfare, whether practiced at the tactical, operational, or strategic level, is critical to a twenty-first-century military. Failing to protect one's own data, applications, and networks invites certain defeat. Protecting, exploiting, or attacking cyber targets requires a highly professional community that has deep understanding and technical expertise ranging from software applications to operating systems to physical connections between networks. While the complexity of the technologies and the breakneck pace of innovation certainly make this task daunting, not investing in robust and highly skilled cyber warfare specialists is tantamount to losing without fighting.

⊢• AI AND ALGORITHMIC WARFARE ESSENTIALS

While twenty-first-century EW and cyber warfare now offer steadily increasing advantages, the current revolution in warfighting in the ether comes from the software and physical applications of AI in what is now called algorithmic warfare. As AI technologies improve, their defensive, exploitative, and offensive elements must each be appreciated and applied both as independent capabilities as well as in combination with each other and with other kinetic and non-kinetic EW and cyber capabilities.[9] As algorithmic warfare matures, vulnerabilities and opportunities will become increasingly apparent. As one of "cyber's offspring" that is becoming critical to EW, AI can be considered a continuing evolution in EW and cyber warfare.[10]

Artificial intelligence begins with data, computational power, and a great deal of statistics built into models. The models are built with software and statistical techniques into "black boxes" that are iteratively "trained" to return a range of reasonable answers. Each is presented with training data and produces a result. These models are iteratively improved until the answer it provides is deemed a reasonable one, given the inputs. Over time, the system learns that certain stimuli should result in certain responses, such as recognizing the letter *A* in an image or finishing a sentence when presented with the first five words. At this point, the models are placed into service to augment or replace humans who previously performed this role.

Any prediction of what algorithmic warfare may look like in the twenty-first century is incredibly difficult as the technologies and techniques are still in their infancy and the integration of AI cannot be fully exploited before first resolving some never-before-considered legal and moral issues. AI's complexity not only challenges the skills of naval and national operators as we seek to integrate it for our use; it also offers adversaries and criminals opportunities to exploit or attack our AI systems. Like cyberwarfare or EW "attack surfaces" or "attack vectors," AI training data, trained models, environment of use, and testing regimes are highly vulnerable because how an AI system ranks outcomes or chooses the answers it does is often unclear even to highly skilled software engineers and data scientists who built it. Malicious actors have proved that by manipulating training data, models, or the operational data provided to trained models, they can cause AI-powered systems to provide wrong or nonsensical answers or no answers, or to break the system entirely.

While the future of algorithmic warfare is highly ambiguous, two things are certain. First, developing concepts, capabilities, and highly skilled operators will be an extremely complex undertaking. Second, we should consider the Russian radio operators at the Battle of Tsushima Strait and their admiral as a cautionary tale. We must not learn the utility of algorithmic warfare by allowing the enemy to fire effectively first.

⊢• CONCLUSION

One aspect of the future seems clear: computers will get smaller, faster, more sophisticated, and increasingly integrated through high-bandwidth wireless communications networks to connect people, things, information, and applications every minute of every day. These advances in computing power, data creation (especially high-quality data), and data transportability will drive even more impressive advances in AI, both the technologies themselves and their clever application to new use cases.

The militaries of the twenty-first century are equally predictable "writ large." Our militaries (including those of allies and partners), and those of our adversaries and enemies, will more quickly and more closely benefit from a constant stream of new technologies and techniques for battlefield use. Some future programs may resemble previous projects built purely for military use, such as the worldwide high-frequency radio detection system that provided geolocation of targets in the 1960s, the Bombe device at Bletchley

Park that broke Germany's Enigma code in World War II, or Project Maven that enabled drone imagery collection systems to characterize targets in the last decade.[11] Underlying the development and operation of these systems will be the extraordinary military members with the excellence needed in EW, cyber warfare, and algorithmic warfare. These experts will be critical to the future of the naval services and, therefore, the nation. To maintain a relevant modern Navy, concept and capability developers must untiringly prioritize addressing the challenges presented by the complexity and rapid pace of development of communications, the algorithmic trio of EW, cyber, and AI technologies. Naval warfighters must develop real expertise in all three in ways appropriate for their rank and role such that military forces can plan and conduct operations that deliver twenty-first-century battlefield effects. Fighting effectively will now require that we are fighting smart.

NOTES

1. National Security Agency, "Russian SIGINT and Electronic Warfare," *Cryptolog*, August 1976, 2.
2. J. B. Blish, "Notes on the Marconi Wireless Telegraph," U.S. Naval Institute *Proceedings* 25, no. 4 (October 1899), https://www.usni.org/magazines/proceedings/1899/october/notes-marconi-wireless-telegraph.
3. Vincent O'Hara and Leonard R. Heinz, *Innovating Victory: Naval Technology in Three Wars* (Annapolis, MD: Naval Institute Press, 2022).
4. David L. Boslaugh, *When Computers Went to Sea: The Digitalization of the United States Navy* (New York: John Wiley & Sons, 2003).
5. Sydney J. Freedberg, "'Algorithmic Warfare': DSD Work Unleashes AI on Intel Data," *Breaking Defense*, 28 April 2017, https://breakingdefense.com/2017/04/dsd-work-unleashes-ai-on-intel-data-algorithmic-warfare/. See Robert O. Work, "Foreword," in George Galdorisi and Sam J. Tangredi, *Algorithms of Armageddon: The Impact of Artificial Intelligence on Future Wars* (Annapolis, MD: Naval Institute Press, 2024), vii–x.
6. Neil Gershenfeld, Raffi Krikorian, and Danny Cohen, "The Internet of Things," *Scientific American* 291, no. 4 (2004): 76–81.
7. Matt Burgess, "What Is the Internet-of-Things? WIRED explains," *Wired*, 16 February 2018, https://www.wired.com/story/internet-of-things-what-is-explained-iot/.
8. Jayson M. Spade, *Information as Power: China's Cyber Power and America's National Security*, ed. Jeffrey L. Caton (Carlisle Barracks, PA: U.S. Army War College, 2012), 9.

9. Courtney Crosby, "Operationalizing Artificial Intelligence for Algorithmic Warfare," *Military Review* 100, no. 4 (2020): 42–51.

10. Chris C. Demchak, "What Corrodes Cyber, Infects Its Offspring: Unlearned Lessons for Emerging Technologies," *Cyber Defense Review* 7, no. 1 (Winter 2022): 153–60, https://cyberdefensereview.army.mil/Portals/6/Documents /2022_winter/16_Demchak_CDR_V7N1_WINTER_2022.pdf.

11. *Wullenweber* is the German World War II cover name for a circularly disposed antenna array that the United States adapted and utilized for radio direction-finding during the Cold War. Jim DeBrosse and Colin Burke, *The Secret in Building 26: The Untold Story of America's Ultra War against the U-Boat Enigma Codes* (New York: Random House, 2004). See also Penny Crofts and Honni Van Rijswijk, "Negotiating 'Evil': Google, Project Maven, and the Corporate Form," *Law, Technology, and Humans* 2, no. 1 (2020): 75–90, https://search.informit.org /doi/pdf/10.3316/informit.125958904331884.

18 Naval Kinetic Warfare and Cyber Roles

KENDRICK KUO and JON R. LINDSAY

The relationship between cyber operations and naval kinetic warfare is complicated. On the one hand, navies depend on information, so attacking information systems should degrade naval performance. On the other hand, naval warfare is fast and confusing, which should undermine cyber planning assumptions if they are even mildly out of date. The danger of naval cyber warfare is exceeded only by its difficulty in preparation and execution.

The sudden loss of navigation or fire control systems to enemy cyber operations would be a disaster for any commander at sea, to be sure. But a successful mission kill of enemy vessels at sea would also be a near-miraculous outcome for any attacking cyber component commander. While it is technically possible that cyber could be a game changer for naval combat, it is less operationally probable that cyber will change the game.

To understand why, it is necessary to appreciate both the similarities and the differences between the cyber and naval domains. One must compare these two operational domains to fully realize the advantages and disadvantages of using cyber operations for naval kinetic warfare, especially with respect to efficiency and deception issues. This chapter argues that cyber is better a complement to, than a displacement of, kinetic strikes.

⊢• SIMILARITIES WITHIN DOMAINS

The naval and cyber domains share notable characteristics. The first is that naval and cyber forces, each in their own way, help to improve strategic *efficiency*, which means doing more with less. They promise to economize limited resources and yield a relatively high return on investment. While warships are expensive, they enable a maritime power to spread influence around the globe. Because navies can rapidly go anywhere reachable by water, they are much cheaper than garrisoning the world.

Cyber operations offer similar efficiency advantages. Collecting intelligence through cyber operations can improve the efficiency of policy and targeting. Presumably, a covert operation like Stuxnet is more discreet and less risky than an airstrike. It is cheaper to steal intellectual property than to invent something from scratch.

A second similarity is that both domains prize *deception*, which means hiding what is present or showing what is not. Stealth and speed are important principles of naval warfare, which is fundamentally a problem of strategy and maneuver.[1] The difficulty of simply locating enemy vessels is a major theme in naval history. This puts a premium on intelligence collection as a means of penetrating deception, and on cryptography as a way of disguising communications. Antisubmarine warfare is, for example, above all a duel between hiders and finders. (See McGunnigle and Breuer, and Pugh in this volume.)

Cyber operations also depend on deception. To an extent, cyber operations are just a high-tech way to conduct espionage, subversion or sabotage, and counterintelligence. Offensive cyber operations rely on secret technical exploits of unguarded vulnerabilities to gain unauthorized access to networks. Hackers can also use social engineering to trick gullible users into revealing credentials. Defensive cyber operations similarly rely on network monitoring, honeypots (faked or sacrificed computer systems to draw out hackers), and other counterintelligence techniques to monitor and mislead intruders. Skilled intruders, therefore, must prioritize operational security to bypass defenses and remain hidden without compromising their valuable sources and methods. (See discussions by Poznansky and Demchak in this volume.) The offense-defense balance in cyberspace is an operational interaction between deception and counterdeception.[2]

Deception and efficiency go together. If an enemy can be tricked into helping, or at least not hurting, an operation or goal, it is possible to do more with less. If the defenders or attackers do not know where to concentrate their efforts, then they must be ready to defend anywhere. Alternately, if the enemy can be persuaded to concentrate somewhere else, then a smaller force can be used to get the job done with less resistance.

⊢• IMPROVING THE EFFICIENCY OF NAVAL WARFARE

Given these similarities, it is reasonable to expect that cyber operations and naval warfare should be complementary. (See also discussions in this volume by Tangredi, and Bebber and White.) Cyberspace should help to make a domain that prioritizes efficiency and deception more effective and deceptive. Navies can go anywhere in the ocean, but they can only move at flank speed (approximately 30 knots or 34.5 miles per hour). Cyber operations move at the speed of electrons transiting cable or satellite networks, and therefore could dramatically improve efficiency by immobilizing enemy ships or weapons systems long before they are in range of shipborne kinetic weapons.

Furthermore, in a direct support role for conventional naval forces, cyber operations might degrade the enemy's navigation tools, control of shipboard munitions, and the effectiveness of onboard systems, forcing ships to run aground or collide. Cyber operations can also cause shipboard munitions to fail at launch, launch prematurely, or even commit fratricide. At a broader level, cyber attacks can undermine naval platforms by disabling or damaging fire control and information systems, electrical supply, and environmental systems such as water and sewage management. In all these instances, the naval platforms are rendered "mission ineffective."

In an indirect role, cyber operations can facilitate non-cyber kinetic strikes. Cyber attacks can sow confusion in enemy ship systems or decision-making, both of which can then be exploited by physical engagements. An enemy is put in a disadvantaged position when a cyber operation opens a window of technical vulnerability, such as a timed malfunction of compromised critical equipment. Careful timing of such a "soft kill" is essential if it is to open a window of vulnerability for physical strikes to exploit. Cyber espionage can also reveal an enemy's operations and timing information—where naval assets will be at a given time or place—that a commander can leverage for surprise attack or use to concentrate a superior force.

Cyber kills, moreover, could help to economize on limited munitions in shipboard magazines. Ordnance stockpiles remain a concern for naval planners. In a major conflict, supplies will dwindle quickly. If cyber attacks can achieve mission kill of an enemy vessel, then they serve as a munition substitute.

Furthermore, unlike physical kinetic strikes, a cyber attack might preserve enemy platforms for capture or for negotiations. Navigation or fire control might need to be only temporarily deactivated or disrupted. This creates a window for friendly operations. But as the effects are reversible, the enemy only loses capability rather than platforms or lives. This could be politically advantageous, especially for de-escalating a conflict.

⊢• IMPROVING STANDARD DECEPTION IN NAVAL WARFARE

Many potential efficiency gains via cyber rely on deception. For example, enemy commanders may be surprised, and effectively ambushed, by malfunctions and mishaps. Cyber operations could also create unattributable friction that enemies, unaware of anything going wrong, blame on themselves. If the cyber domain is a domain of deception, then it should be especially useful for supporting the innate deception in naval maneuver warfare.[3]

Cyber operations, employed correctly, could also improve the performance of both hiders and finders to gain a relative advantage over the enemy. Cyber operations could help vessels remain hidden by blinding or spoofing enemy sensors or locating enemy vessels by spying on enemy command and control networks or implanting beacons by which to later locate enemy forces. A deceived commander may be convinced to commit her forces at the wrong time or place. When an adversary knows a cyber deception campaign is underway, such knowledge can lead the enemy to operate more cautiously or withhold forces out of fear of making a strategic misstep. In fact, the prominence of deception online may be enough to force an enemy to spend more resources and time on operational security.

Finally, blinding the enemy—compromising its intelligence, surveillance, and reconnaissance capabilities—undermines its defensive capacity, whether in terms of knowing where to maneuver for protection or its ability to effectively disrupt the kill chain. By improving deception and intelligence, cyber operations provide a decision advantage for friendly forces while degrading the efficiency of enemy decision-making.

The similarities between the cyber and naval domains—deception and efficiency—however, have tended to undermine credible signals of commitment (i.e., deterrence), and thereby increase strategic instability. The most credible signals are costly; only incredibly determined actors would make them. Efficiency means cost avoidance, and deception amounts to bluffing. If a bluff is shown to be a bluff in one key operation, the adversary is less likely to be deterred in the next situation unless the opponent demonstrates an even greater, more costly commitment. This is a problem for both domains.

To the extent that cyber operations enhance naval *warfare*, the greater level of efficiency and deception resulting from this combination will undermine naval *deterrence*. The same mobility intended for greater global influence also undermines the credibility of a commitment to fighting in any given place. Empirical studies show that countries that invest more in navies experience more militarized disputes.[4] Similarly, the secrecy that makes cyber options useful in intelligence and war also makes it difficult to credibly signal with them for deterrence.[5] An important nuance is that while the cyber domain itself is very unstable—there is pervasive cyber conflict every day—there is to date little evidence that cyber conflict escalates to other domains, suggesting there is something different about cyberspace.[6]

⊢• DIFFERENCES BETWEEN CYBERSPACE AND NAVIES

Despite their similarities, naval combat and cyber operations have quite different strategic characteristics. Navies deal with specialized, operational physical environments, whereas cyberspace is a man-made information infrastructure underpinning all military operations. Indeed, naval fleet battles are rare, intense, and high stakes, but cyber competition is common, pervasive, and individually less consequential. Command of the sea is critical for modern war, but most cyber operations produce ambiguous and indirect effects.

Warships are expensive, and fleet maneuver is hard to master. Losing the fleet can lose the war. By contrast, most cyber competition is better described as an "intelligence contest."[7] Hackers currently face negligible risk, but also inflict limited costs relative to war. Organizations and governments lose data all the time but continue to thrive.

Furthermore, naval combat is associated with pure anarchy where there are no overarching institutions with authority to settle interstate disputes. Cyber attacks are, conversely, associated with institutional networks and globalization sustained by a shared and persistent worldwide information infrastructure.

In sum, a fundamental mismatch exists between the political conditions for conflict in each domain. Naval war is a zero-sum contest *between* military organizations. But cyber conflict is a duel of deception and counterdeception *within* shared infrastructures linking institutions—more like an intelligence contest.

The more chaotic and disordered an environment, the harder it is to have accurate, up-to-date intelligence or to reliably communicate.[8] Equivalently, the more institutional constraints persist, the easier it is to collect and communicate. Physical war tends to go to extremes, but cyber conflict is more restrained because actors often want to preserve the potential for future exploitation and trade.[9] Cyber operations flourish in peacetime but have difficulty in the chaos of war's disruption of the institutionalized, relatively stable networks.

When these two quite different domains come together, will the cheap and easy features of the cyber domain amplify the volatility and stakes of the naval domain, or will the chaos and fluidity of naval kinetic warfare limit the relevance of non-kinetic cyber options? Or will the *more* exquisite cyber options become relevant for *less* intense forms of naval warfare?

⊢• THE DISADVANTAGES OF DIFFERENT DOMAINS

The answers to these questions remain unclear, but several downsides limit the potential impact of cyber operations on naval kinetic warfare.

Cyber operations are complex and require intensive coordination and long lead times, which reduce their effectiveness in the rapid decision cycles of modern warfare. Cyber attacks are inherently sensitive to changing context and being able to know and adapt in real time to the state of friendly, intervening, and target networks. Developing the right cyber tool involves esoteric engineering and timely and high-fidelity intelligence about suitable targets. Launching a cyber attack is the final act of a massive enterprise committing intensive investments. To reduce these operational disadvantages, navies must invest significant resources.

Finally, the enemy's behavior and investments matter. The enemy may not present an accessible digital target for cyber attack that is not fleeting or inconsequential. A powerful adversary invests in both peacetime and wartime countermeasures. A desirable target may therefore be invulnerable, or trained crews may patch an exploited vulnerability or quickly fix malfunctions. Cyber operations may not deliver the promised effects.

Given these possibilities, cyber dominance may not be possible, let alone confer asymmetric advantages. Navies that rely on cyber capabilities to wage kinetic warfare must grapple with inescapable dilemmas. The more networked a navy, the more dependent on cyber systems it is, the more susceptible it can be to attack. But if an enemy penetrates friendly computer networks, the enemy could be exposed to planted disinformation. Timing, windows of vulnerability in the enemy's network, and kinetic objectives may align only for a brief period, generating intense use-it-or-lose-it pressures. This time constraint creates incentives for all combatants for a preemptive cyber "first use" before an enemy discovers and patches security gaps or kinetic objectives become misaligned. The result is potential crisis instability.[10]

⊢• CONCLUSION: COMPLEMENTARY VERSUS ASYMMETRIC

Cyber operations will have future roles to play in naval kinetic warfare, but navies need to adapt to the dilemmas of cyber operations or risk counterproductive efforts.[11] If cyber complements rather than substitutes for kinetic strikes, then cyber operations properly understood could shift to naval or combined operations. To be sure, prudence dictates that navies continue exploring cyber in direct roles, but these might require greater resources and coordination than a physical attack, be more sensitive to contingencies, and risk inadvertently signaling a lack of resolve to go kinetic. Together, this analysis suggests that cyber, rather than being an asymmetric capability that levels the playing field for the weak, is an additional capability that strong and well-resourced militaries may be able to integrate into joint operations.

NOTES

1. Michael A. Palmer, *Command at Sea: Naval Command and Control since the Sixteenth Century* (Cambridge, MA: Harvard University Press, 2005).
2. Erik Gartzke and Jon R. Lindsay, "Weaving Tangled Webs: Offense, Defense, and Deception in Cyberspace," *Security Studies* 24, no. 2 (April–June 2015): 316–48.
3. Erik Gartzke and Jon R. Lindsay, "Windows on Submarines: The Dynamics of Deception in the Cyber and Maritime Domains," in *Issues in Maritime Cyber Security*, ed. Joseph DiRenzo III, Nicole K. Drumhiller, and Fred S. Roberts (Washington, DC: Westphalia Press, 2017), 417–32.
4. Erik Gartzke and Jon R. Lindsay, "The Influence of Seapower on Politics: Domain- and Platform-Specific Attributes of Material Capabilities," *Security Studies* 29, no. 4 (October–December 2020): 601–36. In the air domain, there is also evidence that domain- and platform-specific attributes can undermine military signaling. For example, see Abigail Post, "Flying to Fail: Costly Signals and Air Power in Crisis Bargaining," *Journal of Conflict Resolution* 63, no. 4 (April 2019): 869–95.
5. Erica D. Borghard and Shawn W. Lonergan, "The Logic of Coercion in Cyberspace," *Security Studies* 26, no. 3 (July–September 2017): 452–81.
6. Erica D. Lonergan and Shawn W. Lonergan, *Escalation Dynamics in Cyberspace: Bridging the Gap* (New York: Oxford University Press, 2023).
7. Robert Chesney and Max Smeets, eds., *Cyber Conflict as an Intelligence Contest* (Washington, DC: Georgetown University Press, 2023).
8. Jon R. Lindsay, *Information Technology and Military Power* (Ithaca, NY: Cornell University Press, 2020).
9. Jon R. Lindsay, "Restrained by Design: The Political Economy of Cybersecurity," *Digital Policy, Regulation, and Governance* 19, no. 6 (2017): 493–514.
10. Jason Healey and Robert Jervis, "The Escalation Inversion and Other Oddities of Situational Cyber Stability," *Texas National Security Review* 3, no. 4 (September 28, 2020).
11. Kendrick Kuo, "Dangerous Changes: When Military Innovation Harms Combat Effectiveness," *International Security* 47, no. 2 (Fall 2022): 48–87.

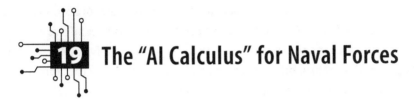

19 The "AI Calculus" for Naval Forces

JACK LONG and BRETT VAUGHAN

In 1956 the science and engineering of making intelligent machines didn't
have a catchy name. At this new field's now-legendary first conference, a
founding scholar, Herbert Simon, proposed "complex information processing." However, another founder—John McCarthy—proposed the name that
stuck: "artificial intelligence" (AI). Over the years, McCarthy's term has
become one of the most misunderstood in the world of information/cyber
technology and beyond, making it especially difficult to evaluate and assess
AI's true impact and potential.

AI is best described as a constellation of techniques that allow machines
to handle digital information—collecting, analyzing, presenting, or acting
on it to solve tasks that would otherwise seem to require human intelligence.
At its core, AI uses math to process vast amounts of data in ways that appear
intelligent to people. This large volume of math makes modern AI a profoundly
digital phenomenon driven by advances in computing and the growing availability of faster, more powerful systems.

For example, one of the earliest forms of military AI was the Cold War–
era "Semi-Automatic Ground Environment" (SAGE) system of enormous

computers and huge displays. Compared to other systems in use at the time, SAGE was incredibly complex. It processed data from many radar sites to produce a unified airspace image meant to alert the United States of a Soviet attack and direct the North American Aerospace Defense Command's response.[1] While there is as yet no definitive way to measure the relative intelligence of any given AI system, a practical approach is to compare it to the complexity of the tasks it can handle. Today, the exponentially growing power of AI can be seen in the increasing complexity of the tasks it can solve.

It is now clear that AI will be widely used in war by naval forces.[2] But making full use of its potential requires addressing some hard realities. Importantly, while the potential of AI may be huge, resources are not. It is not a magic elixir that can fix every problem.[3] Across the world, AI is having significant transformative effects on public and private enterprises, large and small. But the successes are not random—they are the result of the deliberative application of AI to the specific issues where it can have the greatest impact. U.S. naval forces will only realize the significant gains that can come from leveraging AI by the intelligent and deliberate pairing of the correct AI tools and methods to the corresponding naval operations. (See chapter by Dombrowski on a similar cyber and resources argument.)

The analysis of how to pair a problem with an AI tool/capability is the "AI calculus." It brings with it four imperatives: doing the calculus correctly, minding the metrics, investing in solid foundations, and fielding to scale in real environments, throughout ensuring a solid, secure data infrastructure and AI-competent workforce for the naval forces.

⊢• THE AI CALCULUS: MATCHING TOOLS AND TASKS

As the tools in the AI toolbox expand in both number and capability, those responsible for AI development and deployment must consider which tools are best suited to address their needs. Given AI's rapid encroachment recently into high-visibility use cases, many who are now expected to work with the technology do not understand the fundamentals of how AI works or where best to use it. Yet there are hundreds if not thousands of naval use cases where AI can support and advance better or faster decision-making.[4] For example, almost any operational or corporate decision within the Navy has the potential to be improved with AI-based decision aids.

The most compelling near-term tasks are those that play to machine strengths—that is, decisions where the involved volume of data and speed exceeds human capabilities. For example, in considering operational use cases, these tools often fall into the orient and decide phases of John Boyd's observe, orient, decide, and act loop.[5] Those tasks exist across the range of naval operations from maneuver and operations to intelligence, command and control, logistics, and force protection. An assessment of AI applicability to the tasks captured by the massive and comprehensive "Naval Task List" shows that a good portion of them are ripe for the application of AI.[6] Furthermore, Navy vessels have power, storage, and space, making them very capable platforms for hosting key portions of the AI "stack" (the connected systems needed to employ AI). These capabilities allow for the distributed deployment of AI at what is called the "edge"—that is, the vessels themselves.[7]

AI also has significant potential for increasing autonomy in air- or seaborne robotic systems already under development for use by all services (as noted in the chapter by Panter and Falcone in this volume). As AI becomes more accurate and portable, its host systems will add decisions performed internally to the machines that enhance environmental awareness, navigation, mission execution, automatic observation of ethical guidelines, and unprecedented human-machine teaming. The potential uses range widely from shipyards and headquarters to and throughout operational deployments—as has recently been demonstrated in reality by Task Force 59's experimentation in the Arabian Gulf region.[8]

Whatever the uses envisioned, the need for solid AI awareness and understanding will only grow in importance for the sea services in the future. A robust AI operations pipeline that links the development, testing, deployment, and monitoring of models in an iterative fashion will be needed to both deploy the technology to the right scale for operations and rapidly improve capability.

Carnegie Mellon University scholars coined the term "AI stack" in 2016 to describe how AI is implemented.[9] It is analogous to the open systems interconnection model that governs modern computer networking, and in reality, all AI depends on its cyber infrastructure to work properly and stay secure.[10] The AI stack describes the interweaving of interdependent elements such as data, computers, algorithms, and transport networks that are required to deploy and scale modern AI. It differs from its cyber underpinning (its "parent," according to Demchak in this volume), especially in its emphasis on the quality of the data that trains the models that later produce outputs with new data. Understanding this delineation of the stack helps naval forces decide what is needed to integrate AI into their operations. Modern software development has shifted in this direction, and AI deployment needs to leverage this model to be effective.

⊢• MINDING AI'S METRICS

It has proven difficult to quantitatively assess the productivity gains of cyber's digitization of work across society. The "productivity paradox" says that the more cyber is embedded, the more one seeks to do, so the less one can compare the previous era with the digitized one.[11] It is equally difficult to calculate the gains from wider integration of cyber's offspring from AI to quantum throughout the naval forces or the society writ large.

However, neither the United States and its allies nor their military services can wait until a consensus on such metrics emerges. Until then, the most useful approach is an overarching, relative comparison with the pacing peer competitor, China, and it is not looking that positive. One chapter author has asserted that "China now has the advantage in three of the 'four horsemen of AI' conflict (scale, foreknowledge/resilience, and strategic coherence), leaving only a fourth (speed in innovation and sharing) to the consolidated democratic civil societies."[12] Barring the sudden emergence of, and consensus on, exquisite alternative metrics any time soon, the naval services will also need to take into account how their integration of AI contributes to the wider society in the comparison of these four forces, a calculus that, in turn, affects their own deployments and mission success probabilities.

Importantly, the four horsemen are interdependent—to tame them, the sea services will have to pay attention to all four concurrently. Mastering them requires awareness, attention, and investment on a scale that matches the U.S. Navy's mastery of nuclear power. For AI, this starts with the foundations: data, computing power, and competency. These fundamentals have driven industry's rise over the past decade. If the naval services want to match this, they must also master the fundamentals.

⊢• INVESTING IN SOLID FOUNDATIONS

Fielding a technology without a clear use case or concept of operations is a recipe for suboptimal performance. This is as true for AI as for other technologies. And while AI is a wide-ranging enabler, effective application is dependent on tailored development, deployment, and monitoring in the intended application space. Naval forces are fortunate in that many of their current operational concepts—distributed maritime operations, expeditionary advanced base operations, logistics operations in contested environments, and joint operational art—can benefit from the application of AI tools that will enhance their operational outcomes.[13]

Deploying AI-enabled solutions in a distributed and contested environment will require new concepts of employment—ones that enable AI functionality beyond what is found in civilian use cases. Carnegie Mellon's "AI fusion" is one such concept.[14] This provides for the effective balancing of both centralized and distributed AI and ensures seamless use from enterprise to edge. This fits well with the need of naval forces to operate against an adversary actively trying to degrade the ability to communicate and function jointly as planned. What is missing today is a concerted effort by the sea services to actively integrate the AI fusion concept across existing naval operational concepts in order to generate operationally relevant, AI-enabled capabilities, concepts, and the relevant tactics, techniques, and procedures.

The current difficulty is that the sea services are on a linear trajectory to incrementally increase capabilities over time. By slowly and parsimoniously funding the integration of advanced AI tools, they are ceding key digital transformation advantages to adversaries and forgoing exponential increases in capability and productivity that can be achieved by appropriately updated organizations.[15] (See chapters by Bebber and White, Brutzman and Kline, and Ross and Warner in this volume.) Adherence to the fundamentals will ensure success not only in AI, but also across the range of emergent and disruptive digital technologies such as robotics, nano- and biotechnology, additive manufacturing, and others.

At this writing, generative AI is taking the world by storm. It is a form of AI in which the model not only provides answers to the questions it was trained to answer, but also demonstrates capability on tasks for which it was not explicitly trained, making unexpected statistically derived discoveries seemingly on its own. Bursting into wide public view in early 2023, generative AI is showing how the continuing growth in computing power, data, and algorithm development is leading to ever more powerful AI that can be applied to solve increasingly complex tasks. None of those three trends show any sign of slowing down soon.

This explosive development serves to reinforce the growing gap between the Navy's current investments and what it needs to invest in at foundation levels in AI to be successful. Though China has an advantage given its civil-military fusion model, the United States at this writing maintains the most advanced technology industry in the world.[16] But that is of no use to the sea services without relevant internal acceptance of the commercial or university advances and strong partnerships with AI developers in order to incorporate those innovations in the naval services. Nothing short of a "moonshot mindset" will drive the levels of investment and attention required to remedy this lagging condition.[17]

⊢• FIELDING TO SCALE FOR NAVAL USES

Given the ample opportunity for AI exploitation within the relevant naval operational concepts, the sea services need to aggressively explore where AI can have the highest impact. This requires both a top-down and bottom-up approach to enabling and exploiting these high-impact use cases. From the top will come resources and identification of critical gaps requiring filling. And from the bottom will come a wide range of use cases visible only to those whose day-to-day experience brings them into contact with the problems that advancing AI is now able to solve. By creating the organizational structure to marry these two viewpoints and pairing it with robust experimentation and use case analysis, the sea services will position themselves to have the greatest success in harnessing AI to meet operational needs. This pairing will also drive the required growth in trust in AI that can often be a silent impediment to its adoption.

Success with AI, however, will not come without a robust, near-term commitment of resources—that is, funding. While many describe the current epoch as an AI arms race, the Navy has yet to show indicators of shifting resources to invest to match those of our major adversaries.[18] Nor has there been a significant partnership with the private sector whose investment in AI has outpaced that of the U.S. government by more than an order of magnitude.[19] Absent this investment and commitment to work hand in glove with leading private sector entities, the sea services are destined to be laggards in AI capability. If challenged by an adversary that has invested in the means to harness AI at scale, the Navy will find itself on the wrong end of a modern war.[20]

⊢• FOUR IMPERATIVES FOR SUCCESS AT AI

If the military services of consolidated democracies do not get serious about accelerating AI deployment, they run the risk of ceding any operational advantage conveyed by advanced AI applications. AI is having an increasing effect on warfare today and a growing impact on sea operations, much like cyber has for the past three decades or more (see Demchak in this volume). The current inflection point represents a window of opportunity that cannot be missed. The four imperatives are critical if the sea services are to gain strategic purchase of AI as a critical enabler.

- *Do the calculus*: Begin with the intelligent pairing of the most appropriate type of AI for the given challenge while assessing the maturity of implementing AI for that use case.
- *Mind the metrics*: Use speed, scale, coherence, and resilience as barometers of success/progress.
- *Invest in the foundations*: Impactful AI capabilities rest on a solid base of data, computing power, and organizational competency; success rates increase when all three are present. Deficiencies in any of the three can result in marginal performance or mission failure.
- *Field to scale*: The lab is not the field. The quickest way to scale is focusing on practical applications and lessons learned in the field.

⊢• RICKOVER'S TIME HAS COME . . . AGAIN

There is one additional recommendation that the authors feel is necessary for successful AI adoption at scale by the sea services—call it the "Rickover

Option." Nearly a decade ago, there were calls for an AI Manhattan Project—or in the context of the U.S. Navy, an Adm. Hyman Rickover for AI. With large language models having burst onto the scene, and AI spreading into nearly every facet of life, a stronger case can be made that AI will have a more transformative effect on the U.S. Navy than nuclear power. But for the Navy to master nuclear power, it took a wholesale transformation of that field, including new personnel and acquisition systems, dedicated resources, and a determined, dedicated flag officer in the form of Admiral Rickover to drive and oversee the needed change. If the Navy is serious about harnessing the power of AI in the coming years, it should consider what changes are required to ensure that it has the people, processes, and culture to truly make the most of this new technology.

NOTES

1. Benj Edwards, "The Never-Before-Told Story of the World's First Computer Art (It's a Sexy Dame)," *The Atlantic*, 24 January 2013, https://www.theatlantic.com/technology/archive/2013/01/the-never-before-told-story-of-the-worlds-first-computer-art-its-a-sexy-dame/267439/.
2. For discussions from multiple perspectives on AI's use for naval forces in war, see Sam J. Tangredi and George Galdorisi, eds., *AI at War: How Big Data, Artificial Intelligence, and Machine Learning Are Changing Naval Warfare* (Annapolis, MD: Naval Institute Press, 2021).
3. Nina Kollars, "Battlefield Innovation on Patrol: Designing AI for the Warfighter," in Tangredi and Galdorisi, 118.
4. A wide range of cases from command and control to integrated fires are described throughout Tangredi and Galdorisi.
5. See discussion of AI and the OODA loop in George Galdorisi and Sam J. Tangredi, *Algorithms of Armageddon: The Impact of Artificial Intelligence on Future Warfare* (Annapolis, MD: Naval Institute Press, 2024), 76–77, 100–101.
6. Michael Schwille et al., *Handbook for Tactical Operations in the Information Environment: Online Appendices* (Santa Monica, CA: RAND, 2012), https://www.rand.org/content/dam/rand/pubs/tools/TLA700/TLA732-1/RAND_TLA732-1.appendixes.pdf.
7. Andrew W. Moore, Martial Hebert, and Shane Shaneman, "The AI Stack: A Blueprint for Developing and Deploying Artificial Intelligence" (conference paper), *Proceedings of SPIE Ground/Air Multisensor Interoperability, Integration, and Networking for Persistent ISR IX*, vol. 10635,

May 2018. Abstract available at https://www.ri.cmu.edu/publications /the-ai-stack-a-blueprint-for-developing-and-deploying-artificial-intelligence/.

8. Peter Ong, "U.S. Navy's New Task Force 59 Teams Manned with Unmanned Systems for CENTCOM's Middle East," *Naval News*, 9 September 2012, https:// www.navalnews.com/naval-news/2021/09/u-s-navys-new-task-force-59-teams -manned-with-unmanned-systems-for-centcoms-middle-east/.

9. "AI Fusion: Enabling Distributed Artificial Intelligence to Enhance Multi-Domain Operations & Real-Time Situational Awareness," Carnegie Mellon University, n.d., https://www.cs.cmu.edu/~ai-fusion/overview.

10. "What Is the OSI Model," *Cloudflare*, https://www.cloudflare.com/learning /ddos/glossary/open-systems-interconnection-model-osi/.

11. E. Brynjolfsson and L. M. Hitt, "Beyond the Productivity Paradox," *Communications of the ACM* 41, no. 8 (August 1998): 49–55.

12. Chris C. Demchak, "The Four Horsemen of Artificial Intelligence Conflict: Scale, Speed, Foreknowledge, and Strategic Coherence," in *Artificial Intelligence, Russia, China, and the Global Order*, ed. Nicholas D. Wright (Maxwell AFB, AL: Air University Press, 2019), 106–14, https://www.airuniversity.af.edu/Portals/10 /AUPress/Books/B_0161_WRIGHT_ARTIFICIAL_INTELLIGENCE_CHINA _RUSSIA_AND_THE_GLOBAL_ORDER.PDF.

13. On distributed maritime operations, see Edward Lundquist, "Distributed Maritime Operations Is the Navy's Operational Approach to Winning the High-end Fight at Sea," *Seapower*, 2 February 2021, https://seapowermagazine .org/dmo-is-navys-operational-approach-to-winning-the-high-end-fight-at -sea/. On EABO, see "Expeditionary Advanced Base Operations (EABO)," U.S. Marine Corps, 2 August 2021, https://www.marines.mil/News/News-Display Article/2708120/expeditionary-advanced-base-operations-eabo/. On LOCE, see "Littoral Operations in a Contested Environment (LOCE)," U.S. Marine Corps, 2 August 2021, https://www.marines.mil/News/News-Display/Article/2708135 /littoral-operations-in-a-contested-environment-loce/. On joint operational art, see Patrick C. Sweeney, *Operational Art Primer* (course instruction paper), U.S. Naval War College, 16 July 2010, https://www.moore.army.mil/mssp/PDF /nwc_sweeney_op_art_primer_16jul2010.pdf.

14. "AI Fusion."

15. Salim Ismail, Michael S. Malone, and Yuri van Geest, *Exponential Organizations: Why New Organizations Are Ten Times Better, Faster, and Cheaper than Yours (and What to Do about It)* (New York: Diversion Books, 2014).

16. Elsa B. Kania and Lorand Laskai, "Myths and Realities of China's Military-Civil Fusion Strategy," Center for a New American Security, 28 January 2021, https://www.cnas.org/publications/reports/myths-and-realities-of-chinas -military-civil-fusion-strategy.

17. Fei-Fei Li and John Etchemendy, "Why the U.S. Needs a Moonshot Mentality for AI—Led by the Public Sector," *Wall Street Journal*, 9 December 2023, https://www.wsj.com/tech/ai/artificial-intelligence-united-states-future-76c0082e.

18. See discussion on the AI arms race and lack of its recognition in the United States in Tangredi and Galdorisi, 46–67.

19. Tangredi and Galdorisi, 180–81, 188–89.

20. Michèle A. Flournoy, "AI Is Already at War," *Foreign Affairs* 102, no. 6 (November/December 2023): 56–69, https://www.foreignaffairs.com/united-states/ai-already-war-flournoy.

20 Cyber Threats to Unmanned and Autonomous Vessels

JOHNATHAN FALCONE and JONATHAN PANTER

I n late October 2022 seven small, unmanned surface vessels operated by the Ukrainian military slipped into the port of Sevastopol to attack the Russian Black Sea Fleet. Dramatic footage of this operation, filmed from one of the "sea drones," circulated widely on the internet—prompting extensive commentary about the future of warfare.[1] And indeed, the attack reflected one of the principal promises of unmanned maritime systems: the ability to conduct missions in dangerous or denied environments, at reduced cost and risk to personnel. But the popular hype about these emerging technologies also obscures a critical reality: unmanned and autonomous vessels face severe, and inherent, cyber security vulnerabilities in a harsh, unforgiving, very wet, and increasingly climate-turbulent environment surveilled by adversaries.

The purpose of this chapter is to illuminate the broad contours of this problem for planners at the operational level of war.[2] Two major paradoxes have emerged here. The more physically robust unmanned vessels may not be cyber-secure because of the remoteness involved in deployments. Making unmanned vessels more lethal individually can make the fleet itself less lethal.

The physical, organizational, and operational realities behind these paradoxes are the topics of this chapter.

⊢• REMOTE CONTROL

First, even simple unmanned vessels often depend on (or retain the capacity for) human support.[3] Since the Ukrainian vessels were canoe-sized craft on a one-way mission, they could readily have been designed for fully autonomous operation using existing technology. But these particular vessels still had communications gear, suggesting they retained the capability for command guidance.[4]

There are many reasons for such control, from equipment troubleshooting to ethical and legal constraints. But control requires remote communications, which can be intercepted, surveilled, and manipulated.[5] Second, efforts to reduce the need for remote communications by employing greater autonomy introduce another cybersecurity problem. As discussed in detail by Hilger in this volume, the control systems hardware and software required for autonomous operations are vulnerable to malicious compromise, both in development and during operations—especially when, as with Ukraine's sea drones, the technology comes from the civilian commercial market.[6]

⊢• AUTONOMY AND CYBER SECURITY

Autonomy is "the ability of a machine to execute a task or tasks without human input, using interactions of computer programming with the environment."[7] More concretely, hardware (such as cameras, sensors, and microchips) and software (the code driving machine action) combine to interact with the physical world to achieve a defined objective. Autonomous systems exist on a spectrum from partial to full autonomy (see figure 20-1). Even as the underlying technologies mature, the development of fully autonomous platforms or weapons systems is likely to be approached with caution for several reasons.

First, autonomy and its enabling technologies face a "trust problem"—many people do not reflexively trust computer programs to operate flawlessly.[8] Second, legal and ethical concerns can preclude full autonomy even when it is technically feasible. Third, there are practical reasons for constraining autonomy, such as preserving the capability for retargeting.[9] As a result, many

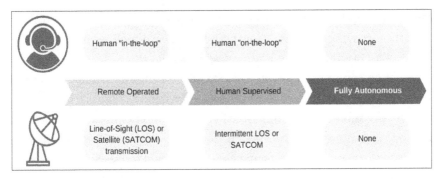

FIGURE 20-1. Graduated Autonomy Scale *Source: Created by the authors*

autonomous systems employ *graduated autonomy*: modes of operation that leave humans "in the loop" (with their permission required for some actions) or "on the loop" (in a supervisory role).[10]

Cyber security, in this context, is ensuring access to cyberspace to execute tasks—either autonomously or under the control of humans—and to move seamlessly between these two forms of control. It includes the ability of these systems to securely record, send, receive, and retrieve electronic data as necessary for operations. Finally, it includes ensuring systems can tolerate faults or abnormalities—even those originating from their own internal components— and operate in a predefined, degraded state if attacked.

⊢• UNMANNED VESSELS AND EXTERNAL COMMUNICATIONS

Due to the physical challenges of operations in the marine environment— which will not change even with improved sensors or software—all but the simplest unmanned vessels are likely to require extensive off-ship connectivity. Ships and submarines, with or without personnel on board, must have a means of propulsion, a power source, and auxiliary engineering systems, alongside other equipment that depends on a vessel's mission. Such systems must be robust to marine environmental conditions (such as wind, waves, and corrosion from seawater) in addition to physical stresses (like friction between parts) that machinery in any environment faces.

The more onboard systems a vessel has, the more likely it is to suffer equipment breakdown (referred to as "equipment casualty"). For instance, a large vessel may require more torque—therefore requiring a larger propulsion plant, with more moving parts, and more need for onboard cooling—than a smaller vessel does. In addition, the longer a vessel operates at sea, the more likely it is to suffer an equipment casualty—due to adverse environmental conditions, routine component degradation, or battle damage.

On both manned and unmanned vessels, equipment redundancies can postpone system-wide failure. But on unmanned vessels, sailors are not available to perform preventative maintenance or conduct immediate local repairs. Accordingly, unmanned vessels will require external (off-ship) communications, either on-demand or real-time, to report impairments to their readiness or to receive remote troubleshooting.[11] If unmanned vessels delay off-ship reporting for small casualties in order to reduce these communications, the casualties can worsen or trigger cascading effects, ultimately making off-ship reporting necessary regardless.

⊢• AUTONOMY AND THE "ATTACK SURFACE"

On-demand communications with human controllers can present a cyber attack vector or an electromagnetic targeting challenge.[12] Increasing the autonomy of unmanned vessels diminishes these threats by reducing the vessels' reliance on off-ship communications. But doing so is not a panacea.

First, instituting increased autonomy cannot solve the communications problem for every class of unmanned vessel. Unmanned systems carrying kinetic payloads (at least in the U.S. Navy context) will likely employ graduated autonomy due to the trust, legal, and ethical concerns identified earlier.[13] To keep humans in (or on) the loop, on-demand communications between human commanders and kinetic payload–carrying vessels will remain critical.

Second, greater autonomy requires a high level of fault tolerance, or a greater quantity of successful interactions between vessel hardware, code, and the environment. This complexity provides a would-be attacker with a larger attack surface, potentially granting more opportunities for exploitation or deception.[14] These attacks need not be transmitted through communications pathways, but can be embedded any time prior to operations, from initial system development to periodic maintenance.

Many enabling capabilities required for military vessel autonomy—such as software for engineering control systems, navigation, or contact management—are similar to those required for civilian applications.[15] Since the commercial market for ships is substantial, navies will likely make use of commercial off-the-shelf solutions and open architecture in vessel design and construction. Variation in the cyber security standards of military and civilian supply chains presents a potential cyber threat vector.

⊢• OVERVIEW: VULNERABILITIES IN NAVAL AUTONOMY

A cyber-resilient fleet must reduce the probability of malfunction from adversarial attacks and from self-inflicted or engineering-based cyber incidents. Autonomous vessels can be understood as part of a larger system consisting of two branches: the unmanned vessel at sea, and humans in (or on) the loop, whether stationed on board crewed ships or on land. This control structure means cyber vulnerabilities can be present in the interactions between the vessel and its handlers or maintainers, at the vessels' control station, and within the lifelines of the vessel itself (see figure 20-2).

Traditionally, cyber risk has been associated with external connectivity. However, the pervasive nature of onboard cyber vulnerabilities suggests that

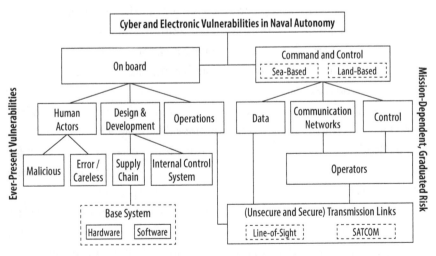

FIGURE 20-2. Simplified Unmanned Maritime System Vulnerability Tree *Source: Created by the authors*

autonomous operations (those conducted without external connectivity) remain vulnerable to cyber incidents. Autonomous operations must therefore be evaluated in an "assumed compromised" environment. Critically, however, the attacks discussed in the following sections may not be within the capability of all potential adversaries, since some require significant dedicated resources and technical intelligence collection.

⊢• ONBOARD VULNERABILITIES

The cyber resilience of an unmanned platform depends as much on engineering control as it does on secure communications and external control. In fact, unmanned systems are susceptible to cyber-based threats whether external network connections are active or intermittent, or even if they occurred only once. In other words, autonomous systems are vulnerable from initial development until the system is destroyed. Two such intra-vessel threats worth recognizing include supply chain–based vulnerabilities and internal network and control system reliability.

Advanced semiconductor production and integration represent the primary hardware supply chain threat. At the time of their production, these intermediate goods may be used for a range of applications. For example, graphics processing units—critical parts for autonomous technologies—were originally developed for image and video rendering. Their parallel processing technology enables high-performance computing, and programming flexibility supports their use in gaming, content creation, and machine learning algorithms. An undocumented or undesirable functionality retained in these chips can introduce an attack vector.

Moreover, at present, most advanced chips are fabricated outside of the United States.[16] The start-ups and corporations that integrate chips into vessels and payloads, and the military's own acquisition specialists, cannot test for every potential vulnerability, although the U.S. government does dedicate significant resources and oversight capability to the problem.[17]

Turning to the software supply chain, potential vulnerabilities exist because both vessels and payloads are developed using publicly available architecture in order to promote innovation and acquisition implementation.[18] Additionally, private companies building unmanned systems often utilize open-source code and libraries for everything from basic programming functions to complex system tasks. And since software bills of materials are generally not mandated by intermediate activities and end users, vulnerabilities in basic functions that impact operational systems may go unnoticed.

Vulnerabilities in these "building blocks" can allow remote code execution and system infiltration.[19] At the same time, there are advantages to open-source software as well, including its greater transparency to communities that can scan for vulnerabilities. The broader point is that there are security trade-offs with either option.

Electrical/mechanical processes such as steering, thrust, electrical power, and cooling are managed by operational technology networks and software-driven control systems. Representing an underappreciated attack vector in autonomous systems, the control systems critical to vessel functions can be targeted through network, supply-chain attacks, or control system–unique attack vectors such as insecure process sensors.[20]

Attackers may, for example, attempt to manipulate field device sensor data via wireless networks or modem connections to impact the operation of equipment.[21] Such attacks may aim to disrupt or modify installed transducers or software that processes the sensor data. Alternatively, they may disrupt data about the vessel's operability, so that personnel remotely monitoring the vessel delay, or prematurely activate, casualty response protocols.[22] Other methods of control system compromise include manipulating control update rates (causing system lagging) or triggering instabilities not accounted for by the system's designers.[23]

Finally, not all control system cyber vulnerabilities result from malicious activity. Since there are no technicians on board unmanned systems to perform local troubleshooting, self-inflicted errors are magnified. For example, actions taken to resolve cyber vulnerabilities in information technology (IT) systems (installing an update or "patch") may require the IT system to complete a greater number of authentications or other verification processes. Because, in many cases, operational technology system performance relies on the efficient functioning of the IT system, the increased demand on IT system resources (caused by a patch that requires more processes to run) may impact the data rate speed within the operational technology and control system. This is, effectively, a denial-of-service attack on one's own system. An overemphasis on preventing IT network attacks can therefore lead to various equipment malfunctions or complete shutdown, if not mitigated by system design or concepts of operations that limit the deployment of patches during missions.

⊢• COMMAND AND CONTROL VULNERABILITIES

Across the autonomy spectrum, unmanned vessels will require off-ship connectivity. Vessels will rely on data to operate autonomously and on multinodal networks to communicate with friendly forces and securely transmit information with its shore- or land-based command. The extent of cyber risk arising from these requirements depends on the mission assigned to an asset.[24]

Both in peacetime and during hostilities, unmanned vessels must operate safely in the vicinity of other vessels and otherwise account for their environment. Safe navigation and contact management require fusion of organically gathered and processed data (from cameras, radar, and other sensors) and inorganic data received from satellites, nearby vessels, or automatic identification system transponders. Many unmanned systems will also rely on global positioning system data for precise position, navigation, and timing. Reliance on satellites for weather and oceanic forecasting data also presents a vulnerability, as commercial and government-operated satellites are vulnerable to cyber intrusion.[25]

Using the autonomy to continuous human command spectrum in figure 20-1, the further a vessel is to the left, the more it will rely on military satellite communication if it is not configured for line-of-sight control by a local manned "mother ship." Space systems are comprised of three segments—user (the vessel itself), ground, and space—each of which presents a potential attack surface. If the adversary can deny the satellite in space or the ground station, then the vessel may be less effective. Reduced access to satellite-provided data, or diminished confidence in its validity, would reduce autonomous on-station time or increase the need for assured communication and control links with alternative data providers.[26]

Reliable and stable communications networks are critical to employing unmanned vessels within the U.S. Navy's distributed maritime operations concept.[27] Depending on the information a vessel requires, these networks may be secured or unsecured. For instance, an unsecured network may be appropriate for environmental data collection, as interception or even slight manipulation of this data might be deemed an "acceptable" risk in some circumstances.

For more sensitive network contributions, however—such as adversarial submarine force disposition or environmental data whose interception could betray an upcoming amphibious operation—encrypted communications will be necessary. Encrypted communications require replacing or destroying cryptographic keys periodically, and although some updates can be pushed "over the air," keys can fail to load, requiring in-person troubleshooting. Whether communications networks are unsecured (and susceptible to eaves-dropping, data tampering, spoofing, and denial-of-service vulnerabilities) or secured (and susceptible to authentication and denial-of-service vulner-abilities), unmanned vessels face inherent challenges to achieving assured communications within an information-sharing network.

Depending on a system's level of autonomy, command's trust in its reli-ability, and the legal and ethical implications of fully autonomous operations, manned operational centers will also need to exert positive control over uncrewed vessels. This includes the ability to monitor health and status updates from unmanned vessels. Control will rely upon available, authenticated, and authorized signal transmissions. Unsecured transmissions between the control station and vessel, of course, are subject to eavesdropping. Given secured signals, adversaries—rather than attempting to decrypt messages—can engage in denial-of-service or replay attacks. In a denial-of-service attack, an adversary would flood the vessel with authentication requests, denying receipt of command signals. In a replay attack, an adversary would identify and then resend a message to the originator, creating the impression that the control channel has been compromised.

⊢• ASSESSING CYBER EFFECTS AT THE OPERATIONAL LEVEL OF WAR

Given the likely variation among future unmanned vessels, both within and across navies, it will be impossible to defend against all potential cyber threats at all times. An attacker may target a vessel or sub-system based on the greatest *ease* of entry, or on the basis of the greatest anticipated *effect* (even if it means a more difficult attack). Effects can be analyzed at the tactical or operational levels of war, with the former degrading an individual platform's operability or a kill chain where that platform plays a critical role.

At the operational level of war, unmanned and autonomous vessels will not be employed in equal proportion across warfare areas. A cyber exploit that manifests across multiple unmanned vessels in a specific class, perhaps due to common architecture, would therefore compromise some warfare areas more than others.[28] Taking an "effects-based approach" to cyber defense, therefore, requires continuously assessing the extent to which each theater of operations, and each warfare area within it, depends on unmanned assets. Since unmanned assets are not yet deployed at scale, this requires some forecasting.

Unmanned vessels are most suited to applications where the gain from reducing risk to personnel outweighs the benefit of having humans on scene to solve complex problems, evaluate ambiguous data, or make ethical decisions. Such applications include intelligence, surveillance, and reconnaissance (surface and subsurface), minesweeping and minelaying, and electronic warfare. Less suitable applications include certain types of surface warfare and anti-submarine warfare.[29] Further complicating the picture, unmanned and autonomous assets are unlikely to be employed in equal proportion across every geographic theater of operation; nor is every adversary equally capable of delivering cyber effects.

⊢• CONCLUSION: PARADOXES OF CYBER DEFENSE FOR UNMANNED VESSELS

While the discussion in this chapter is necessarily brief, we conclude that planners must assume that unmanned vessels are cyber-vulnerable by default. In brief, communications result in cyber vulnerability; and attempts to "solve" communications needs using various forms of graduated autonomy result in other cyber vulnerabilities. In addition, credible cyber security will require not only addressing the vulnerabilities of individual platforms, but also ensuring that when a cyber attack is initiated, it cannot compromise an operation or warfare area as a whole. These guiding principles are enduring and not limited to the current state of the technology. In fact, further maturation of the technology may introduce new cyber security trade-offs.

First, making unmanned vessels more physically robust may not make them more cyber secure. Raising casualty control to the level of manned ships would require a higher frequency of off-ship communications, or more electronic and mechanical redundancies. On the one hand, multiple redundancies could make the system more fault-tolerant, raising the cost and effort required to achieve a successful compromise. On the other hand, added communications and redundancies both increase the cyber attack surface.

Second, making unmanned vessels more lethal may make the fleet less lethal. For unmanned platforms carrying kinetic payloads, ethics and legality pose a constraint on reducing reliance on communications, potentially making these platforms more cyber-vulnerable than non-kinetic unmanned assets. In addition, unmanned shooters will be governed by different failure protocols (e.g., fail-safe) in the event of cyber compromise or degradation. In other words, the "shooters" could be knocked out before the non-shooters: a challenge to a future fleet's lethality.

Given a constrained budget environment, efforts to recognize cost savings may incentivize the Navy to wholesale shift entire mission sets—especially intelligence, surveillance, and reconnaissance, minesweeping, and anti-submarine warfare—from manned to unmanned vessels. Planners should proceed with caution. The disparate cyber security characteristics of manned and unmanned vessels suggest that replacing one class of vessels with the other will very foreseeably affect survivability and lethality, but in ways that are as yet unknown.

NOTES

1. Lara Jakes, "Sea Drone Attack on Russian Fleet Puts Focus on Expanded Ukrainian Arms," *New York Times*, 21 October 2022, https://www.nytimes.com/2022/10/31/us/politics/russia-ukraine-ships-drones.html; Kyle Mizokami, "In a Historic First, Ukraine Attacked a Russian Fleet with Autonomous Robo-Ships," *Popular Mechanics*, 4 November 2022, https://www.popularmechanics.com/military/navy-ships/a41835387/ukraine-attacks-russian-fleet-with-robo-ships/.

2. This challenge is particularly important in light of the 2023 "Replicator Initiative" by the U.S. deputy secretary of defense, a call for thousands upon thousands of drones as a key tool against the People's Liberation Army. See Patrick Tucker, "'Hellscape': DOD Launches Massive Drone Swarm Program to Counter China," *Defense*

One, 28 August 2023, https://www.defenseone.com/technology/2023/08/hellscape-dod-launches-massive-drone-swarm-program-counter-china/389797/; Noah Robertson, "Replicator Drone Program Needs No New Money, Hicks Says," *Defense News*, 6 September 2023, https://www.defensenews.com/pentagon/2023/09/06/replicator-drone-program-does-not-require-new-money-hicks-says/.

3. While the U.S. military uses the term "unmanned" and occasionally "uncrewed," the civilian scientific and engineering fields generally refer to them as "robotics." For this chapter's focus on a lack of a crew, however, "unmanned" is an appropriate term.

4. In September 2022, a Ukrainian unmanned surface vehicle washed ashore in Sevastopol with what appeared to be a Starlink terminal on its stern. Vehicles similar to this were used in the Sevastopol attack. "How Elon Musk's Satellites Have Saved Ukraine and Changed Warfare," *The Economist*, 5 January 2023, https://www.economist.com/briefing/2023/01/05/how-elon-musks-satellites-have-saved-ukraine-and-changed-warfare.

5. Several weeks after the Sevastopol attack, for instance, Ukraine hacked and diverted an Iranian-made drone deployed by Russia. Ian Talley, "Ukrainian Analysis Identifies Western Supply Chain behind Iran's Drones," *Wall Street Journal*, 16 November 2022, https://www.wsj.com/articles/ukrainian-analysis-identifies-western-supply-chain-behind-irans-drones-11668575332.

6. H. I. Sutton, "Suspected Ukrainian Explosive Sea Drone Made from Recreational Watercraft Parts," *USNI News*, 11 October 2022, https://news.usni.org/2022/10/11/suspected-ukrainian-explosive-sea-drone-made-from-jet-ski-parts.

7. Vincent Boulanin et al., *Artificial Intelligence, Strategic Stability, and Nuclear Risk* (Solna, Sweden: Stockholm International Peace Research Institute, 2020), https://www.sipri.org/publications/2020/other-publications/artificial-intelligence-strategic-stability-and-nuclear-risk.

8. Sam J. Tangredi and George Galdorisi, "Introduction," in *AI at War*, eds. Sam J. Tangredi and George Galdorisi (Annapolis, MD: Naval Institute Press, 2021), 13. See also Michael C. Horowitz, "The Promise and Peril of Military Applications of AI," *Bulletin of the Atomic Scientists*, 23 April 2018, https://thebulletin.org/2018/04/the-promise-and-peril-of-military-applications-of-artificial-intelligence/.

9. Paul Scharre, *Army of None: Autonomous Weapons and the Future of War* (New York: W. W. Norton and Company, 2018), 54–55.

10. John Dowdy and Chandru Krishnamurthy, "Defense in the 21st Century: How Artificial Intelligence Might Change the Character of Conflict," in *Technology and National Security: Maintaining America's Edge*, eds. Leah Bitounis and Jonathon Price (Washington, DC: Aspen Institute, 2019), 87–90, https://www.aspeninstitute.org/wp-content/uploads/2019/02/2018-Tech-and-National-Security-FINAL.pdf.

11. For a more extensive discussion, as well as the drawbacks of failure to report casualties, see Jonathan Panter and Johnathan Falcone, "Feedback Loops and Fundamental Flaws in Autonomous Warships," *War on the Rocks*, 24 June 2022, https://warontherocks.com/2022/06/feedback-loops-and-fundamental-flaws -in-autonomous-warships/.

12. As an example, the Ukrainian drones mentioned earlier in this chapter were later revealed to require a ground-based control and data-processing center: Government of Ukraine, "Naval Drones," *United24: The Initiative of the President of Ukraine*, n.d., accessed 8 January 2023, https://u24.gov.ua/navaldrones.

13. Kelley M. Sayler, *Defense Primer: U.S. Policy on Lethal Autonomous Weapon Systems*, IF11150 (Washington, DC: Congressional Research Service, 15 May 2023), https://crsreports.congress.gov/product/pdf/IF/IF11150. Given the speed of modern naval warfare, however, added layers of control impose substantial tactical limitations. See Bradley Martin et al., *Advancing Autonomous Systems: An Analysis of Current and Future Technology for Unmanned Maritime Vehicles*, RR-2751 (Santa Monica, CA: RAND Corporation, 2019), 51–52, https://www.rand .org/pubs/research_reports/RR2751.

14. Scharre, 156–58.

15. This is not to say that *all* technologies will be commercially sourced. Indeed, many military-specific applications have no commercial analog, presenting a hurdle to unmanned vessel development. See Martin et al., 14–19.

16. Taiwan produces over 90 percent of advanced chips, in spite of recent efforts by China, the United States, and others to domestically produce these goods. The challenge lies in disparate production lines that includes chemicals, chip design software, and manufacturing tools and machines. See Chris Miller, *Chip War: The Fight for the World's Most Critical Technology* (New York: Scribner, 2022).

17. For instance, the Defense Microelectronics Activity (https://www.dmea.osd. mil/TrustedIC.aspx), the DoD Executive Agent for Anti-Tamper, Trusted Suppliers and Trusted Foundry programs (https://www.definedbusiness.com /supply_chain_security/casestudies/Trusted_Suppliers_Capabilities.pdf), and the Government-Industry Data Exchange Program (https://www.gidep.org/).

18. Unmanned maritime autonomy architecture is the Navy Program Execu-tive Office, Unmanned and Small Combatants, initiative to promote the development of common, modular, and scalable software for unmanned maritime vehicles that is independent of a particular autonomy implementa-tion through the use of standard interfaces; https://www.auvsi.org/unmanned -maritime-autonomy-architecture.

19. Two examples of exploited software vulnerabilities include the log4j vulnerability and SolarWinds hack. In each case, malicious code was delivered to systems and networks via a legitimate code process.

20. According to the Government Accountability Office, "Many legacy industrial control systems were not designed with cyber security protections because they were not intended to be connected to networks, such as the internet." As a result, many cyber security practices focus solely on securing information technology, rather than both information technology *and* operational technology, systems. See *Critical Infrastructure Protection: Actions Needed to Address Significant Cybersecurity Risks Facing the Electric Grid*, GAO-19–332 (Washington, DC: Government Accountability Office, 2019), https://www.gao .gov/products/gao-19–332.

21. Joe Weiss, "IEEE Paper on Process Sensor Monitoring—What You Need to Know about Process Sensor Cyber Security," *Unfettered Blog*, 2 November 2022, https://www.controlglobal.com/blogs/unfettered/blog/21437429/ieee-paper -on-process-sensor-monitoring-what-you-need-to-know-about-process-sensor -cyber-security.

22. Stuxnet is an example of malware (software-based) that specifically targets industrial control systems. The most infamous implementation of Stuxnet impacted Iranian nuclear facilities. Paul K. Kerr, John Rollins, and Catherine A. Theohary, *The Stuxnet Computer Worm: Harbinger of an Emerging Warfare Capability*, CRS 41524 (Washington, DC: Congressional Research Service, 9 December 2010), https://nsarchive2.gwu.edu/NSAEBB/NSAEBB424/docs/Cyber -040.pdf. A demonstration at the 2004 KEMA Control Systems Cyber Security Conference showed that attackers can hide this type of attack and spoof the watchfloor to indicate that all conditions are normal, or they can change what the watchfloor observes, triggering an unnecessary casualty response.

23. Joe Weiss, "Control System Device Insecurity Is Addressed by the Presidential Executive Order but Is Being Ignored at Your Own Peril," *Unfettered Blog*, 27 May 2020, https://www.controlglobal.com/home/blog/11296501 /information-technology.

24. Three concepts—data, communications, and control—are often used interchangeably. In an effort to reduce ambiguity, our discussion uses the terms in the following way: "data" refers to one-way, inbound information required for autonomous operation; "communications" refers to multi-path information sharing between the uncrewed vessel and a multi-node network; and "control" refers to up to two-way transmissions between a platform and its shore- or land-based command.

25. National Oceanographic and Atmospheric Agency satellites, for instance, were compromised on at least one known occasion in 2014. Mary Pat Flaherty, Jason Samenow, and Lisa Rein, "Chinese Hack U.S. Weather Systems, Satellite Network," *Washington Post*, 12 November 2014, https://www.washingtonpost

.com/local/chinese-hack-us-weather-systems-satellite-network/2014/11/12 /bef1206a-68e9–11e4-b053–65cea7903f2e_story.html.

26. Current military satellite communications are dependent on geostationary orbit satellites, but at the time of writing, the U.S. Department of Defense is investing in proliferated low–Earth orbit architectures to improve the resilience of space-based assets. Future integration of unmanned systems with such architectures, like the Space Development Agency's Transport Layer, SpaceX's Star Shield, or Amazon Kuiper, may reduce the vulnerabilities we identify here.

27. U.S. Department of the Navy, *Unmanned Campaign Framework*, 16 March 2021, https://www.navy.mil/Portals/1/Strategic/20210315%20Unmanned%20 Campaign_Final_LowRes.pdf?ver=LtCZ-BPlWki6vCBTdgtDMA%3D%3D.

28. The problem is potentially compounded by modular-mission platforms that share a common hull.

29. The reasons for these use-case limitations are beyond the scope of this chapter. See Scott Savitz et al., *U.S. Navy Employment Options for Unmanned Surface Vehicles (USVs)* (Santa Monica, CA: RAND Corporation, 2013), https://www. rand.org/pubs/research_reports/RR384.html. The Ukraine example offered in the chapter introduction is an outlier case for surface warfare. The Ukrainian drones were expendable assets deployed against fixed, in-port targets whose hostile identification was known in advance.

21 Undersea Operations and Cyber Warfare

JOHN McGUNNIGLE and PABLO BREUER

The undersea domain is a critical environment for military operations as well as for global trade, communication, scientific research, and, increasingly, for cyber operations and security. Cyber threats can severely disrupt the necessary services provided by the seabed and the water column—the two components of the undersea domain. Threats include physical damage, interference, and offensive cyber operations targeting undersea cables and other infrastructure on the bottom, and manned or unmanned vehicles and sensors floating above.

Governments and commercial organizations operating underwater systems must take steps to protect their systems and economies against these threats within both aspects of this domain. Hostile nation-states, criminal organizations, and other actors can pursue offensive cyber operations (OCO) at will to mimic, stimulate, or enhance the physical or accidental threats of nature and seafaring human activity, making defensive cyber operations (DCO) all the more important. Furthermore, with the rise of military-critical capabilities and assets in the undersea domain, effective policies and procedures cementing defensive cyber operations response actions (DCO-RA) are essential to respond quickly and effectively to offensive cyber actions by adversaries affecting the undersea domain. This chapter argues that the undersea domain's cyber security is key to naval superiority in sea control and in national defense for the coming era.

⊢• IMPORTANCE OF THE UNDERSEA DOMAIN

The strategic value of the ocean is a key factor in shaping the balance of power between nations. It supports a massive and much unexplored variety of essential economic and sustainability resources. (See related discussions by deWitte and Lehto in this volume.) Its underwater environment is increasingly home for critical military, transportation, communication, and scientific research operations. Most global trade is carried out by sea, which is the most cost-effective means of transporting goods, playing a critical role in the global economy.

The underwater domain is a key part of the global commons, and ensuring that it is used peacefully and responsibly is critical for the well-being of all nations. (See discussion by Tangredi on global commons in this volume.) According to the United Nations Conference on Trade and Development, over 80 percent of global trade by volume and more than 70 percent of global trade by value are transported by sea. Hence, military control undersea by democracies is important for maintaining the security and stability of the global community. An authoritarian nation dominating the undersea domain can enforce its own interests on natural resources access and trade routes and use that control for strategic advantages in military, trade, or political conflicts. Hence, the undersea domain cannot be left undefended.

Military control undersea is a means by which nations can project their naval power and support forward military operations at great distances for good or ill purposes. In times of conflict, the control and protection of sea lines of communication can determine the outcome of the war. German U-boat campaigns against Allied sea lines of communication in both World War I and II were to prevent essential military equipment and personnel from crossing the Atlantic and to deny foodstuffs, fuel, and materials for besieged Great Britain and, later, the Soviet Union. Tremendous effort and assets enhanced by groundbreaking code-breaking and signals interception—forerunners to cyber warfare operations—were needed to defeat these undersea warfare campaigns. (See Friedman in this volume.) In the Pacific, unrestricted undersea warfare by U.S. and Allied submarines ensured overseas resource-dependent Imperial Japanese manufacturing could not replace wartime military losses, fatally crippling the Imperial Japanese forces.

⊢• UNDERSEA WARFARE OPERATIONS

Undersea warfare plays a critical role in naval operations and as an important aspect of military strategy and capabilities. The oceans cover more than 70 percent of the Earth's surface, and roughly 95 percent of international data and voice communication is transmitted via undersea cables. A wide range of military activities takes place beneath the surface of the ocean including—but not limited to—activities by submarines and other underwater vehicles and systems intended to enhance a nation's military capability, sustain its economy, provide diplomatic influence, and collect relevant and timely information.

Submarines are obviously key components of undersea warfare capabilities due to the wide variety of missions they can perform. Relying in part on the properties of sea water, they are extremely stealthy and can operate undetected for long periods of time.[1] They can be equipped with a variety of weapons, such as torpedoes and missiles, to attack targets off or on shore. For example, ballistic missile-equipped submarines remain the most survivable leg of the U.S. strategic deterrence triad. They gather intelligence by using sensors to detect and track other vessels or undersea systems, and can be used to lay mines or other underwater explosive devices to defend against enemy naval attacks. Throughout the Cold War (1945–91), this intelligence gathering mission—even into Soviet ports—ensured accurate information on Soviet capabilities and thus played a pivotal role in long-term strategic stability.

Capabilities emplaced on the sea floor, such as the famed U.S. sound surveillance system, are also aspects of undersea warfare, as are deep submergence vehicles and autonomous underwater systems used in support of naval operations. (See discussion of the sound surveillance system by Kavanagh and Leconte in this volume.) Other nations operate or are developing similar systems.

├• DEFINING THE UNDERSEA DOMAIN: WATER COLUMN AND SEABED

├─∘ The Water Column

The ocean water column refers to the vertical profile of the ocean, which is divided into several distinct layers. These layers are determined by factors such as temperature, salinity, and depth, and each layer has its own unique properties and characteristics. Militaries (not just navies) use the ocean water column for a variety of purposes, including submarine operations, surveillance, and communication.

Submarines and unmanned underwater vehicles are the most obvious and important military capabilities in the ocean water column. Other military capabilities in the ocean water column, however, include underwater sensors and other monitoring systems used for surveillance and communication that are not exclusively tied to the seabed systems. Systems such as air-dropped sonobuoys and submarine-launched mine countermeasures submersibles can be deployed at different depths and may be connected to land-based or satellite networks for communication.

├─∘ The Seabed

Seabed warfare is a less well-recognized but equally important aspect of naval warfare to not only protect a country's interests and assets at sea, but also deny the use of the undersea domain to an enemy. Laid on the seabed in well-mapped pathways, undersea cables carry the bulk of the world's communications and critical data. These cables are also used for other purposes, including scientific research and the transmission of electricity. While generally considered to be physically reliable, they need to be properly maintained and defended, especially against deliberate physical or cyber sabotage by hostile nations. Naval operations seabed warfare now includes cables and other undersea systems defense along with more well-known missions involving mines or other underwater explosive devices, the placement of sensors or other underwater monitoring equipment, and the use of underwater vehicles on or near the seabed.

DEFINING AND DESCRIBING UNDERSEA-RELATED CYBER OPERATIONS

Although used daily with respect to U.S. military operations, cyber is not defined anywhere in U.S. military doctrine. Even the unclassified version of the U.S. Department of Defense's Joint Publication 3–12, *Cyberspace Operations*, does not define the term. In this discussion, we define "cyber operations" as operations that contain two or more of the following five pillars of information described by older unclassified versions of Joint Publication 3–13, *Information Operations*: computer network operations, psychological operations, operational security, military deception, and electronic warfare.

OCO by an individual or organization can target the operation of undersea infrastructures and systems. They can be carried out by nation-states, criminal organizations, or other actors.

Offensive Cyber Operations on the Seabed

Undersea cables are not immune to disruption in peacetime as well as wartime by OCO by criminal or military activities.[2] Deliberate attacks can be masked as accidents. Numerous incidents have been recorded, including, for example Atlantic cable cuts in 2022 that were attributed to suspicious activities by Russian fishing vessels.[3]

Interference with undersea cables rather than cuts can also occur. For example, some naval vessels have the capability to tap into or disrupt undersea cables for intelligence-gathering or other purposes. In addition, the use of certain types of sonar or other underwater equipment external to undersea cables can also potentially interfere with their operation.

OCO can also be executed on the underwater fiber-optic cables that carry most of the world's internet, phone, and other types of communication. (See Kavanagh and Leconte in this volume.) These attacks can potentially degrade, disrupt, deny, delay, detour, or compromise the data transmitted via the cables. There are several different ways that undersea cables could be vulnerable to cyber attacks. Hackers could gain access to the data transmitted via the cables by intercepting it as it is transmitted through the water. This "man-in-the-middle" attack could potentially be done by deploying specialized underwater equipment near the cables.[4] Another possibility is that attackers could physically access the cables themselves and either disrupt the data transmission or attach malicious hardware to the cables to gain access to the data. This access could be gained on the seabed or at cable landings on shore.

A final example of OCO undersea could be a submarine-launched cyber attack on an offshore oil rig whose foundations and operations rest on the seabed. The submarine could be used to launch a malicious code that could shut down communication networks, disrupt operations, or gain access to sensitive data.

⊢—○ Offensive Cyber Operations in the Water Column

Executed in various forms, OCO in the water column are aimed at manned and unmanned vessels and sensors as opposed to seabed-based targets. They involve gaining access to computer networks and systems to compromise the integrity or functionality of the wider system. Some ways that OCO on a system operating in the water column could be carried out include

1. Targeting the control systems and operational technology of a submarine or unmanned underwater vehicle: an attacker could attempt to gain access to the submarine's control systems and manipulate them to cause the submarine to behave in an unintended or dangerous manner.[5] (See the discussion of attacks on operational technology by Hilger in this volume.)

2. Disrupting communications: an attacker could try to disrupt the ability of a submarine, unmanned underwater vehicle, or undersea sensor system to communicate with other systems or vessels or with shore-based command and control centers. This could be done by jamming radio signals or by hacking into the communication systems and planting malicious software at a node associated with the underwater domain.

3. Gathering intelligence: an attacker could try to gather sensitive information about operations or capabilities by hacking into its computer systems and extracting data or traditional electronic intelligence.

4. Disabling weapons systems: an attacker could try to disable or manipulate the submarine's weapons systems, such as its torpedoes, mines, or
missiles, to render them ineffective. It is important to keep in mind
that any sensor connected to the network is a possible avenue for
injecting a malicious payload. As marine vessels (to include submarines) do not usually segregate operational networks, it is possible that
a properly engineered malicious signal received by sonar could be used
to affect navigation, fire control, or other mission-critical systems.

For example, in January 2021, Turla—a Russian cyber espionage group also
known as Venomous Bear and linked to Russian Federal Security Service
signals intelligence—was discovered to have been using a malicious backdoor
to gain access to sensitive information on a submarine communications
network.[6] The backdoor was found to have been deployed on multiple undersea
cables, allowing the hackers to gain access to data passing between ships and
shore-based networks.

The attack was initially discovered by security researchers at Symantec,
who believe the hackers were able to gain access to the submarine networks
after compromising computers associated with them. The group is believed
to have been targeting military, government, and research institutions in
Europe and the Middle East, including activities of U.S. Central Command.[7]

Considerable challenges to defending against cyber espionage in the
undersea domain exist. Adversaries do not always need exquisite sources
of intelligence. There is a wealth of open-source intelligence available on
undersea assets, and by using a variety of sources and methods, it is possible
to gain a good understanding of these assets and their capabilities. Open-
source intelligence, information that is publicly available and can be obtained
and used, is a significant enabler for an adversary's OCO. These sources of
open-source intelligence on undersea assets include news articles and other
media, government websites and documents, academic papers and research,
trade shows and conferences, social media and online forums. Specialized
open-source intelligence tools such as those of the company Shodan, for
example, are advertised as continuously scanning the internet for vulnerable operational technology devices.[8] (Many commercial competitors focus
exclusively on information technology.)

⊢• DEFENSIVE CYBER OPERATIONS IN THE UNDERSEA DOMAIN

Defensive cyberspace operations refer to the defensive measures taken by an organization or government agency to detect, analyze, and respond to cyber threats and attacks on their systems and networks. These actions can include implementing security controls, monitoring for suspicious activity, and launching incident response and recovery efforts. Programs such as information control and technical controls such as cable intrusion protection systems are two such examples of DCO.

The goal of DCO is to prevent or mitigate the impact of an adversary's or criminal's OCO and protect the organization's sensitive information and assets. These actions are typically carried out by a dedicated cyber security team or incident response team within the organization.

An example of DCO undersea is using mobile underwater sensor systems to detect, identify, and report malicious activity in the ocean environment. These systems use acoustic and optical sensors to detect, classify, and track submarines, ships, and other vessels, as well as monitor and detect unusual activity in the ocean environment. The data collected by these systems are then analyzed and used to detect malicious activity and take defensive actions to protect the undersea environment.

For example, in 2021 the U.S. Navy deployed a new cyber defense system on its submarines.[9] The system provides a secure, encrypted network connection to the submarine's command center, allowing for remote monitoring and control of the submarine's systems. This system also allows for remote updates to the submarine's software, allowing the Navy to quickly patch any security vulnerabilities. The system is designed to prevent malicious actors from gaining access to the submarine's systems, which could potentially be used to disrupt its operations.

⊢○ Defensive Cyber Operations Response Actions in the Undersea Domain

DCO-RA refer to the defensive measures taken by an organization or government agency to detect, analyze, and respond to cyber threats and attacks on their systems and networks. DCO-RA also include deliberate actions taken outside of the defended networks to protected and defend Department of Defense cyberspace capabilities. These capabilities are perhaps better understood as the cyberspace equivalent of "defensive counter-fires." DCO-RA actions in the water column could include all offensive cyberspace operations that are conducted in response to adversary OCO and that are intended to defend our own capabilities. These actions can also include implementing security controls, monitoring for suspicious activity, and launching incident response and recovery efforts.

The goal of DCO-RA is to prevent or mitigate the impact of OCO and protect the organization's sensitive information and assets. These actions are typically carried out by a dedicated cyber security team or incident response team within the organization. In the undersea domain, DCO-RA may involve deploying underwater sensors to detect malicious activity, implementing strong security protocols and systems, and regularly monitoring and updating the security of the systems.

⊢• CONCLUSION: A CONTINUUM OF OPERATIONS

To summarize, military capabilities in the undersea domain, including OCO, DCO, and DCO-RA, are essential for maintaining naval superiority, protecting natural resources and trade routes, and ensuring the security and stability of the global community.

None of these cyber operations are conducted individually. Instead, they are mutually supporting and collectively necessary. Like the seabed, the water column, the surface, and the air and space above, actions in one layer inevitably lead to effects in all the others. From perspectives on land, submarine and seabed operations may seem part of a silent service, but control of cyberspace requires mastery of a continuum that includes the cybered element of undersea warfare.

_____

NOTES

1. Since the 1980s there have been numerous claims that emerging technologies—such as blue-green lasers—will make the ocean transparent. All attempts have failed. See, for example, Norman Friedman, "Finding Submerged Submarines—with Lasers," U.S. Naval Institute *Proceedings* 119, no. 3 (March 1993): 132.

2. Colin Wall and Pierre Morcos, "Invisible and Vital: Undersea Cables and Transatlantic Security," Center for Strategic and International Studies,

11 June 2021, https://www.csis.org/analysis/invisible-and-vital-undersea-cables-and-transatlantic-security.

3. Lizbeth Kirk, "Mysterious Atlantic Cable Cuts Linked to Russian Fishing Vessels," *EUObserver*, 26 October 2022, https://euobserver.com/nordics/156342.

4. National Cyber Security Alliance, "Eight Myths about Hacking Fiber Networks (and Two Key Solutions)," https://staysafeonline.org/cybersecurity-for-business/eight-myths-hacking-fiber-networks-two-key-solutions/; David Griffiths, "The Global Internet Is Powered by Vast Undersea Cables. But They're Vulnerable," CNN, 26 July 2019, https://www.cnn.com/2019/07/25/asia/internet-undersea-cables-intl-hnk/index.html.

5. Dave Majumdar, "NAVSEA: Submarine Control Systems Are at Risk for Cyber Attack," *USNI News*, 8 December 2014, https://news.usni.org/2014/10/22/navsea-submarines-control-systems-risk-cyber-attack.

6. "Russian Cyber Espionage Group Uses Malicious Backdoor to Target Submarine Cables," Symantec Enterprise Blogs/Threat Intelligence, 21 January 2021, https://www.symantec.com/blogs/threat-intelligence/turla-malicious-backdoor-submarine-cables. This posting has been subsequently removed, but mention of the involved threat appears in U.S. Office of the Director of National Intelligence, *2001 Annual Threat Assessment of the U.S. Intelligence Community*, 9 April 2021, 10.

7. "Turla: A Closer Look at the Russian Cyber Espionage Group," Symantec Enterprise Blogs/Threat Intelligence, 14 December 2020.

8. "Search Engine for the Internet of Everything," Shodan corporate website, https://www.shodan.io/.

9. U.S. Navy, "Navy Deploys New Cyber Defense System to Submarines," 2021, https://www.navy.mil/submit/display.asp?story_id=113362 2, and https://www.navy.mil/documents/Submarine_Cyber_Defense_System.pdf (accessed 20 March 2023 but subsequently removed).

22 Naval and Cyber Dependence on Space and Satellites

GURPARTAP "G. P." SANDHOO

Since the 1950s, all elements of national security at every level of warfare have dramatically increased their dependence on space. Most commercial/civilian digital data is transmitted through undersea and terrestrial fiber-optic cables (as described by Kavanagh and Leconte in this volume). The data supporting modern military operations that is transmitted over long distances relies on satellites, as revealed by Ukraine's resort to commercial satellite internet retransmissions for command and control when land-based cyber infrastructures for communications have been either physically destroyed or denied through cyber attacks.[1] The extent of the space dependency of U.S. military operations goes far beyond that. In the past two decades, the U.S. military involvement in the space domain has evolved dramatically to include its weaponization as a warfighting domain as exemplified by the reformulation of the U.S. Space Command, the declaration of space as an operational domain by the North Atlantic Treaty Organization, and the creation of the U.S. Space Force.

The U.S. Navy lags in space. Despite requiring considerable (and currently scarce) financial resources, the Navy must be able to execute offensive and defensive operations against enemy ships, submarines, and missile-carrying aircraft at sea in a deeply cybered and space-dependent world. To do otherwise endangers the Navy's success in cyber and kinetic warfare against large, technically competent adversaries (technological near-peers) such as the People's Republic of China in future cyber and kinetic conflicts.

⊢• NAVAL ADOPTION AND DEEP RELIANCE ON SPACE

As the most expeditionary and widely dispersed force critically dependent on satellites and space-based systems for communications, precise navigation, and understanding of the operational environments, U.S. naval forces were early adopters of space-based capabilities. One of the earliest space-derived services, the U.S. Naval Observatory, has cataloged the stars since the mid-nineteenth century to help navigation in maritime, civil, and military terrestrial operations for fleet operations ranging over vast distances.[2]

This naval space reliance deepened with the development of surface warfare tactics and doctrine in the early 1900s, which required coordinated maneuvers at sea by ships beyond the line of sight. With the expansion into undersea warfare, the ability to "see"—detect, identify, and track or target maritime naval or commercial surface vessels at long range and undersea—led to technologies such as sonar. The integration of aviation into naval operations from the 1910s onward made technologies such as radar, invented in the 1930s, crucial to detecting enemy air forces in World War II.

The evolution of distributed naval operations from surface maneuvers to a three-domain warfare combination of undersea, surface, and air domains made naval warfare dramatically more complex and technologically dependent. In 1944 following the capture of German V2 rockets, Navy experimentation in space science and spacecraft technologies began on the effects of upper atmosphere solar and cosmic radiation on naval communications and helped to find usable radio channels. Between 1946 and 1952, the Naval Research Laboratory averaged more than ten experiments per year to altitudes of fifty to one hundred miles, resulting in the rapid development of new technologies.[3]

Furthermore, enhanced requirements for synchronized maneuvering, operations, and effects, along with continuous knowledge of the dynamic operational environment,[4] led to the development from the 1960s to the 1990s

of space-enabled technologies such as long-range over-the-horizon communications; global positioning, navigation, and timing (PNT); environmental
monitoring; signals and electronic signature detection; and missile warning.
(See discussion by Friedman in this volume.)

Around the same time, researchers began experimenting with methods of
capturing radar signals originating in the Soviet Union and Eastern Europe
that could—under certain atmospheric conditions—be detected at great
distances. This effort led to the study of the effects of the ionosphere on certain
frequencies, which laid the foundation for space-based signals intelligence
(SIGINT) or electronic intelligence.[5] Critical to all these space-based capabilities was the advancing evolution of networks and computers.

⊢• MARITIME DOMAIN EMBRACES SPACE AND CYBER

As the complexity of the maritime domain awareness challenge grew over
the last century, so did the need for space domain awareness and cyber competencies to ensure advanced and real-time information useful for combat
operations. Changes in atmospheric and metrological conditions can rapidly

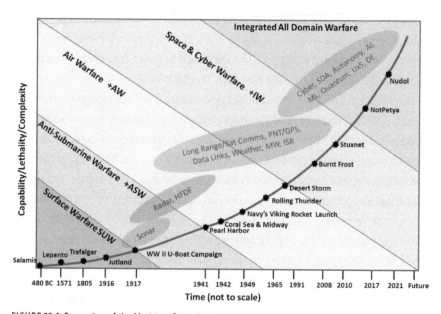

FIGURE 22-1. Expansion of the Maritime Domain *Source: Created by the author*

and significantly impact expeditionary naval forces operating where the full picture, including the physical and electromagnetic environment and especially the location of the enemy, is incomplete. Figure 22-1 provides an illustrated timeline of this continuing increase in the complexity and the operational-technological integration of navies across warfighting domains.

In the U.S. Navy, rising reliance on space services requires better networks and computers—that is, the evolution of cyberspace. Thus, the three-layer warfighting maritime domain (subsurface, surface, air) has expanded to include the space domain, and then cyberspace.[6]

⊢• FULL-SPECTRUM DEPENDENCE ON SPACE

Today the Navy and Marine Corps are more dependent on space-based capabilities than ever before. In addition to communications and navigation, space-based assets also provide maritime domain awareness with continuous, up-to-date information on naval air, land, and sea targets through weather forecasting; intelligence, surveillance, and reconnaissance (ISR); missile warning; position, navigation, and timing; satellite communications; and space domain awareness. These capabilities are categorized in table 22-1 and individually described in the following sections. The extensive community of organizations, systems, processes, and technologies providing these capabilities will soon be consolidated within the U.S. Space Force in accordance with the National Defense Authorization Act of Fiscal Year 2023.

TABLE 22-1. Critical Space-Based Enablers for Naval Warfare

Environmental Monitoring	Monitoring of terrestrial, maritime, and space weather
Intelligence, Surveillance, Reconnaissance	Understanding the battlespace
Missile Warning	Ensuring timely notification of missile activity
Position, Navigation, and Timing	Enabling precision maneuver and encrypted comms
Space-Based Communications	Ensuring voice and data connectivity while on the move
Space Domain Awareness	Understanding space assets that can observe operations

⊢• ENVIRONMENTAL MONITORING

The Naval Meteorology and Oceanography Command uses data from the Defense Meteorological Satellite Program, the WINDSAT sensor, the National Oceanic and Atmospheric Administration, and the National Aeronautics and Space Administration to provide critical environmental knowledge to naval forces deployed worldwide, including surface warfare, anti-submarine warfare, naval special warfare, mine warfare, air warfare, and information warfare.[7] The Navy's early environmental sensing programs were some of the first satellite payloads. A prime advantage of environmental satellites is their ability to gather data in remote or hostile areas where little or no data is available via surface reporting stations.

⊢• INTELLIGENCE, SURVEILLANCE, AND RECONNAISSANCE

ISR systems detect, locate, and process electronic emissions from potential military threats or criminal activities, sharing data in digital formats for tactical and technical intelligence, strategic warning, and mission planning. They also help identify potential threats in the electromagnetic spectrum, electronic warfare, and cyber domains.[8]

Synchronization and integration of ISR sensors is crucial for the digitized processing, exploitation, and dissemination of imagery and signals data and information. The primary agency responsible for designing, building, launching, and maintaining America's intelligence satellites is the National Reconnaissance Office. The two primary intelligence products from these space-based platforms—geospatial intelligence (GEOINT) and SIGINT— are disseminated to naval forces by the National Security Agency and the National Geospatial-Intelligence Agency, respectively, via the combatant commands.[9]

GEOINT has two primary modes of collection active and passive.[10] Active GEOINT uses traditional radar and synthetic aperture radar satellite payloads to provide an all-weather day/night capability with extremely high resolution. However, it is also vulnerable to jamming because the satellites actively emit radiation with high power requirements. Passive GEOINT collects imagery in the visible and infrared ranges of the electromagnetic spectrum with payloads that use radiation being emitted or reflected to identify objects of interest. Visible imagery provides the highest resolution but is weather- and time-dependent, with the ability to only collect during the day and in clear weather conditions. Infrared imagery provides night imagery in multiple spectral bands but has a lower resolution.

SIGINT is a much broader category of intelligence that encompasses several large subcategories, all of which rely on cyber mechanisms to function. These include communications intelligence, the collection and analysis of foreign communications; electronic intelligence, the collection and analysis of electronic emissions from systems such as radars, ships, airplanes, and missiles; and foreign instrumentation signals intelligence, the collection and analysis of signals emitted from weapons under development and testing. The National Security Agency is responsible for the SIGINT analysis and dissemination process, while the National Reconnaissance Office operates the space-based systems that collect and disseminate the SIGINT data.[11]

Maritime domain awareness is a mature naval application of SIGINT, which refers to the effective understanding of any vessels or objects in the maritime domain that could impact security, safety, economy, or the environment. Characterizing the signal is the first step in this complex process. In determining the type of signal and its origin, descriptors such as frequency, strength, and emission characteristics are used to identify the signal in question. SIGINT collection assets of the U.S. Navy have progressed from the use of high-frequency direction finders, coastal surveillance radars, and experimental space payloads with basic descriptors, to providing key strategic and later tactical intelligence for shipboard weapons systems, all of which depend on cyber-physical systems for their transmission and analysis.

⊢• MISSILE WARNING

Missile warning is derived from a system of space- and ground-based sensors crucial for timely detection of adversary use of ballistic missiles.[12] It is divided into two categories: strategic and theater warning. Strategic warning prioritizes accuracy above all else to prevent strategic mistakes and relies on a dual phenomenology consisting of ground radar and space-based infrared sensors. In contrast, theater warning prioritizes the speed of reporting, allowing personnel to seek shelter and cue ballistic missile defense assets to respond.[13]

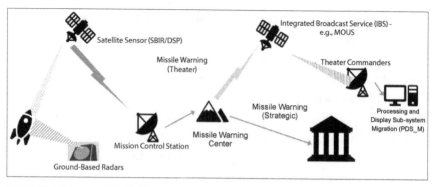

FIGURE 22-2. Anatomy of Missile Warning *Source: Created by author, based on the text of U.S. Navy Space Handbook*

The legacy but still primary missile warning system, the overhead persistent infrared system, is being replaced by space-based infrared systems and the Space Development Agency's sensor layer. The Defense Support Program satellites operated by the U.S. Space Force use sensors to detect the intense infrared heat emissions from missile or spacecraft launches and nuclear explosions. These satellites are in geostationary orbit and provide worldwide coverage of infrared sensors to detect heat from missiles or boosters. This process is depicted in figure 22-2.

Nuclear detection is a core part of the global positioning system (GPS) satellite system.[14] Nuclear detection is divided into two main components: the ground segment and the space segment, which consists of nuclear detonation detection sensors on GPS and Defense Support Program satellites.[15] Satellite systems are also critical to deeply computerized nuclear command, control, and communications.[16]

⊢• POSITION, NAVIGATION, AND TIMING

Position, navigation, and timing (PNT) are critical space-based capabilities for accurate, all-weather, worldwide navigation. Precise time is essential for synchronizing operations, including cryptographic systems for secure communication and the delivery of kinetic and non-kinetic effects.

The GPS developed by the United States is the most commonly used PNT system to provide precise, worldwide, day and night, all-weather navigation.[17]

The two foundations of GPS were developed by the U.S. Navy. In 1958 the Navy funded the Johns Hopkins University/Applied Physics Laboratory to develop Transit, an experimental satellite radio navigation program using the doppler shifts from satellite transmissions for distance measurements and reverse triangulation to pinpoint positions on the ground from the signals received.[18] Space-based Transit offered excellent positioning reliability and was subsequently adopted to support the Navy's submarine fleet. In 1971 the U.S. Naval Research Laboratory's TIMATION (Time and Navigation) program demonstrated that placing an accurate clock on the spacecraft, along with a passive ranging technique, provides the basis for a new and revolutionary navigation system with three-dimensional coverage (longitude, latitude, and altitude) throughout the world.[19]

The result—GPS—currently consists of twenty-four satellites in six orbital planes inclined fifty-five degrees to Earth's equatorial plane, providing around-the-clock global coverage. Three satellites are required to solve for a three-dimensional position solution (latitude, longitude, and height), and a fourth satellite is required to solve for the user's clock offset from GPS time.[20] The system includes ground monitoring stations to provide corrections and feedback.[21] Necessarily, the system is critically dependent on cyber-physical devices for transmission.

⊢• SATELLITE COMMUNICATIONS

Most naval communications are digitally transmitted through space-based assets. The communications are primarily divided into wide-band, narrow-band, and protected communications for strategic command and control.[22] Main satellite communications (SATCOM) systems used by the Navy and Marine Corps include[23]

- Military Strategic and Tactical Relay, a constellation of military communications satellites in geosynchronous orbit providing secure and jam-resistant worldwide communications[24]
- Advanced Extremely High-Frequency system, providing global, survivable/protected global communications for strategic and tactical command[25]

- Ultra-High Frequency Follow-On system, a U.S. Department of Defense (DoD) program sponsored and operated by the U.S. Navy to provide communications for airborne, ship, submarine, and ground forces[26]
- Enhanced Polar System, the next-generation SATCOM system to replace the current Interim Polar System and serve as a polar adjunct to the Advanced Extremely High-Frequency system[27]
- Wideband Global SATCOM system, enhancing DoD communication services currently provided by the Defense Satellite Communications System satellites and Global Broadcast System operating at an ultra-high frequency[28]
- Mobile User Objective System, secure ultra-high-frequency SATCOM for mobile forces[29]
- Global Broadcast Service, a one-way broadcast capability for timely delivery of unclassified and classified video, large quantities of unclassified or classified digital data, or other theater information transfer.[30]

⊢• SPACE DOMAIN AWARENESS

Space domain awareness (SDA), formerly known as space situational awareness, describes knowledge and understanding of the space environment through deeply digitized information on objects in space and their potential impacts on space operations. The concept of SDA has been recognized for satellite tracking by the U.S. government since 1958. The U.S. Navy was the first service to develop a system for detecting and tracking space objects not emitting electromagnetic energy. In the 1960s the newly established Advanced Research Projects Agency tasked the Navy with developing an operational U.S. space surveillance system to detect, identify, and track Earth-orbiting satellites. Following successful demonstrations, the system, designated WS-434, consisted of three transmitters and six receiver sites oriented to the 33.5-degree north latitude that all lower-orbiting objects must pass through at least once per day. Responsibility for the system, often referred to as the "space fence," was transferred to the U.S. Air Force in 2004 and was renamed the Air Force Surveillance System.[31] The Space Fence was transferred to the U.S. Space Force on 27 March 2020, when it was operationally accepted.[32]

In 2019 the terminology was changed from space situational awareness to space domain awareness to indicate the increased importance of the space domain. The Combined Force Space Component Command of U.S. Space Command is responsible for providing a digitized common operational picture for space operations.[33]

Three primary elements composing SDA are

- spaceflight safety and knowledge of orbiting objects and debris
- space control (detection), insight into an adversary's employment of space systems to include detection, characterization, attribution, and threat warning to facilitate maneuver or initiation of space protection capabilities
- space control (targeting), targeting of adversary space capabilities, and offensive space control.

The existence of uncontrolled "space junk" in orbit is an ongoing area of research since objects smaller than five to ten centimeters in diameter cannot currently be tracked with existing systems and sensors.[34] Additionally, with more space systems being placed in orbits beyond geosynchronous regimes and lunar orbits, SDA has expanded to include the ability to track space objects from low Earth orbit to cis-lunar space (which includes the Moon's orbital space).

⊢• CYBERSPACE SUSTAINS SPACE SYSTEMS

The use of space systems massively expands the size of the cyber domain beyond terrestrial wireless and fiber optic transmission. Commercial undersea cables cannot adequately transmit digital data critical for time-sensitive military operations. The use of Starlink in the war in Ukraine is one example of critical internet connectivity for military applications via commercial space-based platforms. Much, though not all, operational military communications must travel by DoD/government-controlled satellite networks and cyber-physical systems to ensure constant availability.

Transferring digital data for the command and control of modern electronic weapons systems and military/maritime operations interweaves the cyber domain, the space domain, the electromagnetic spectrum, and the systems' architectures from weapons systems engineering into mutual interdependence. The destruction or neutralization of a particular satellite system does not eliminate cybered communication, but it can limit its reach and effectiveness. Without connectivity, there is no cyberspace, and space is silent.

⊢• FROM LEADER TO LAGGARD

As with every emerging technology—and within every element of military competition—being the pioneer does not mean one remains the frontrunner. The diffusion of commercial technical information and the theft of military-related technology or intellectual property allows "fast followers" to overtake and surpass the previous technology leader. Like the evolution of cyberspace and emerging technologies (such as artificial intelligence, machine learning, edge computing, etc.), American dominance in space is continually eroding as potential opponents with lower economic costs copy or extract U.S. capabilities. Furthermore, the Navy's de facto decision to "divest from space" in the 1990s due to the post–Cold War budget drawdowns has made it a laggard in space capabilities.

This approach is no longer valid today, as these capabilities are more necessary than ever in the current era of Great Systems Conflict. The ability to conduct over-the-horizon targeting using organic assets is crucial for the U.S. Navy to succeed in competition with peer or near-peer adversaries. Legacy communications systems designed for worldwide coverage with a minimal number of satellites located in geostationary orbits provide limited coverage in high latitudes and polar regions.

Large investments are now being made in proliferated–low Earth orbit (P-LEO) architectures, and they could potentially address the current naval challenges, particularly in U.S. Indo-Pacific Command. Within the use of the electromagnetic spectrum, each space or cyber advance requires a matching maritime or terrestrial advance. For example, current ship antennas cannot track low Earth orbit satellites for communication. Naval forces struggle to keep up with the technology required for the integration of commercial systems as championed by U.S. Space Force when comparing the thirty- to fifty-year lifespan of ships to the two- to five-year technology refresh rate of the space systems under development.

To ensure operationally "resilient communications," satellites must have multiple means of communication, be unpredictable in maneuver, and possess a diversity of orbits, platforms, frequencies, and waveforms—none of which commercial satellites generally provide. Thus, the resilience of the "hybrid space architectures" concept developed in recent years to include commercial capabilities, such as fees for service to host payloads on commercial satellites, is a step in the right direction but adds uncertainty.[35] Commercial imagery and signals intelligence providers are now regularly used by DoD and the intelligence community to monitor routine and significant events.[36] However, commercial satellites are also susceptible to being suddenly unavailable by commercial owners' decisions or adversary hacking since the encryption and security of commercial systems are not on par with national security–focused space systems.[37]

Cyber-secure space-based systems under DoD control are critical for the increasingly short timelines for detecting, tracking, and identifying evolving threats (e.g., hypersonic missiles).[38] As artificial intelligence and machine learning technologies continue to mature, low-latency mission tasking and command and control will be critical in providing the dispersed fleet with defensive capabilities at the speed of the fight.

As in cyber, the Navy is now lagging in space—which endangers its success against large technically competent adversaries (technological near-peers) such as the People's Republic of China. The U.S. Navy must be able to execute offensive and defensive operations at operationally relevant timelines against enemy ships, submarines, hypersonic weapons, and missile-carrying aircraft at sea in a deeply cybered and space-dependent world. The Space Development Agency's Proliferated Warfighter Space Architecture offers significant benefits to U.S. naval operations, including enhanced communications, improved position, navigation, and timing services, missile detection and tracking, and rapid data transfer, increasing warfighters' lethality, maneuverability, and survivability. The Proliferated Warfighter Space Architecture is making a substantial investment, and it aims to provide cost-effective, proliferated space-based capabilities that enhance overall military effectiveness, including naval operations.[39] However, those capabilities will still require the expenditure of additional financial resources to equip the naval platforms funded by the Department of the Navy, funds that are currently in short supply.

NOTES

1. T. Michael Sheetz, "Elon Musk's SpaceX Sent Thousands of Starlink Satellite Internet Dishes to Ukraine, Company President Says," CNBC, March 22, 2022.
2. See https://www.cnmoc.usff.navy.mil/Our-Commands/United-States -Naval-Observatory/Frequently-Asked-Questions-about-the-USNO /Command-History-of-the-US-Naval-Observatory/.
3. Gary A. Federici et al., *From the Sea to the Stars: A Chronicle of the U.S. Navy's Space and Space-Related Activities, 1944–2009*, rev. ed. (Applied Research Laboratory, Pennsylvania State University, 2010).
4. Peter Jakab, "Eugene Ely and the Birth of Naval Aviation," National Air and Space Museum, 18 January 2011.
5. Daniel Parry, "Grab 1, First Operational Intelligence Satellite," U.S. Naval Research Laboratory, 22 June 2020.
6. Lesley Seebeck, "Why the Fifth Domain Is Different," *The Strategist*, 5 September 2019.
7. NOAA National Environmental Satellite, Data, and Information Service, "Our Satellites: Currently Flying," https://www.nesdis.noaa.gov/our-satellites /currently-flying; NOAA Office of Satellite and Product Operations, "Defense Meteorological Satellite Program"; U.S. Department of the Navy, COMNAVMETOCCOMINST 3140.1M, *U.S. Navy Meteorological and Oceanographic Support Manual*, 15 August 2011.
8. Joint Publication 3-14, *Space Operations* (U.S. Department of Defense, 26 October 2020, Incorporating Change 1), I-2, II-10.
9. U.S. Department of the Air Force, *AU-18 Space Primer* (Air University Press, September 2009), 143–44.
10. Jerry J. Sellers, *Understanding Space: An Introduction to Astronautics*, 4th ed. (McGraw-Hill, 2015).
11. U.S. National Security Agency/Central Security Service, "Signals Intelligence (SIGINT) Overview," n.d.
12. U.S. Department of Defense, "Ballistic Missile Defense System BMDS," in *MDA Ballistic Missile Defense System Handbook*, 26 October 2012.
13. U.S. Department of Defense, Inspector General, *Evaluation of the Integrated Tactical Warning/Attack Assessment Ground-Based Radars*, Report No. DODIG-2016–133, 9 March 2018.

14. U.S. Department of Defense, Inspector General, *Evaluation of the Space-Based Segment of the U.S. Nuclear Detonation Detection System*. Report No. DODIG-2018–160, 28 September 2018.
15. U.S. Department of the Air Force, PE 0305913F: *NUDET Detection System (Space)*, February 2012.
16. Suzanne Claeys et al., "NC3: Challenges Facing the Future System," *CSIS Briefs*, 9 July 32020.
17. "Performance Standards and Specifications," GPS.gov.
18. Robert J. Danchik and L. Lee Pryor, "The Navy Navigation Satellite System (Transit)," *Johns Hopkins APL Technical Digest* 11, no. 1/2 (1990): 97–101.
19. T. Thompson, "Historical Development of the Transit Satellite Navigation Program," paper AAS 07–334, *Proceedings of the AAS/AIAA Astrodynamics Specialists Conference* (San Diego, CA, 2007), 1307–30.
20. Federal Aviation Administration, "Satellite Navigation—GPS—How It Works."
21. "Control Segment," GPS.gov.
22. Joint Publication 3–14, *Space Operations*.
23. *AU-18 Space Primer*, Appendix D.
24. "Milstar Satellite Communications System," U.S. Space Force Space Operations Command.
25. "Advanced Extremely High Frequency System," U.S. Space Force Space Operations Command.
26. Franklin Diederich, "The Ultra-High-Frequency Follow-On (UFO) Program," Space Programs and Technologies Conference and Exhibit, 21–23 September 1993.
27. U.S. Department of Defense, MILSATCOM Systems Directorate, *Selected Acquisition Report (SAR) Enhanced Polar System (EPS)*, RCS: DD-A&T (Q&A)823–121.
28. "Wideband Global SATCOM Satellite," U.S. Space Force.
29. "Mobile User Objective System," *Military+Aerospace Electronics*, 23 February 2016.
30. "Global Broadcast Service," U.S. Space Force.
31. Gary A. Federici et al., *From the Sea to the Stars: A Chronicle of the U.S. Navy's Space and Space-Related Activities, 1944–2009*, rev. ed., 35–36.
32. See https://www.spaceforce.mil/News/Article/2129325/ussf-announces-initial-operational-capability-and-operational-acceptance-of-spa/.
33. "Combined Force Space Component Command," U.S. Space Force Space Operations Command.
34. Marshall H. Kaplan and Gurpartap Sandhoo, "The Challenges of Space Traffic Management," *Space News*, 18 February 2022.
35. John Parker, "Why a 'Hybrid' Space Architecture Makes Sense for Economic and National Security," *Space News*, 14 August 2022.

36. Sandra Irwin, "BlackSky, Maxar, Planet Win 10-year NRO Contracts for Satellite Imagery," *Space News*, 25 May 2022.
37. Frank Bajak, "Musk Deputy's Words on Starlink 'Weaponization' Vex Ukraine," *AP News*, February 9, 2023.
38. Kelly Sayler, *Hypersonic Weapons: Background and Issues for Congress*, CRS R45811 (Congressional Research Service, 13 February 2023).
39. See https://www.sda.mil/.

23 Cyberbiosecurity and the U.S. Navy

FRANK L. SMITH III

The intersection of cyber security and biosecurity is increasingly broad and consequential. The neologism "cyberbiosecurity" represents important challenges and opportunities for national security and human security alike. The implications for naval forces warrant special attention. In part, this is because these implications are not self-evident; in part, attention is warranted because the U.S. Navy is not predisposed to address the challenges and opportunities involved.

Cyberbiosecurity involves threats to cyberspace inspired by biology and, conversely, threats to biology—including human health—enabled by networked information technology. While biological systems can threaten digital systems, most cyberbiosecurity threats emanate from cyberspace and threaten biology.

Cyber-enabled synthetic biology for biological warfare and bioterrorism is one such threat. However, it is not necessarily the most likely, despite the dread that biological weapons can inspire. Cyber-fueled disinformation about health is more common. So too are cyber exploits of biomedical data and cyber attacks against biomedical infrastructure, all of which can reduce the health of naval personnel and the resilience of their fleets. If the Navy is to help mitigate these threats and play an effective role in cyberbiosecurity in the years ahead, it must address cultural biases and bureaucratic barriers.

├─• SECURITY IN VIVO AND IN SILICO

As the term suggests, cyberbiosecurity is about the intersection or inter-relationship between cyber security and biosecurity.[1] The objects that it refers to—including materials, information, and processes—can be biological in nature and relate to digital systems or vice versa. The same is true for the value of those objects, as well as the source of threats to them and protection for them.[2] This is a lot. How it all relates to naval operations may not be obvious.

One way to understand the broad interface between biology and cyberspace is in terms of five related but distinct kinds of threats: 1) bio-inspired cyber exploits, 2) cyber-enabled synthesis of biological weapons, 3) cyber-fueled disinformation about health, 4) cyber-exploited biomedical data, and 5) cyber attacks against biomedical infrastructure. Each is relevant to the Navy.

├─• FROM BIOLOGY TO CYBER

In contrast to land, sea, air, and outer space, the cyber domain is a human creation. Most threats to cyberspace involve human factors, all of which relate in one way or another to our biology as living organisms. While true, this formulation of threat is nevertheless too broad to analytically distinguish cyberbiosecurity from cyber security. Instead, it is more useful to consider more specific ways that biological systems threaten cyberspace.

From the early days of cyberspace, biological systems have inspired—directly and indirectly—both harmful and helpful applications of networked information technology. Just as the phrase "cyberspace" was famously coined by William Gibson in his 1982 novel *Burning Chrome*, the phrase "computer worm" was coined by John Brunner in his 1975 novel, *The Shockwave Rider*.[3] In 1984 Fred Cohen explicitly drew on "the biological analogy" of infection for his original formulation of the term computer "viruses."[4] We now take this terminology for granted.

Similarly, when the Defense Advanced Research Projects Agency (DARPA) established the first computer emergency response team in the aftermath of the Morris Worm in 1988, it claimed to model this team on the public health organizations that respond to biological viruses.[5] Even artificial intelligence (AI), which can be considered an offspring or cousin of cyberspace, has been inspired by biology.[6] For instance, "neural networks" have been loosely modeled on the neurons in living nervous systems ever since AI first emerged in the 1950s. Neuromorphic computing is also inspired by biological brains.

Beyond inspiration, more direct threats to cyberspace may one day come from biology through technologies such as biological computers, genetic data storage, and digital data collection from sensors based on living systems. For example, it is theoretically possible to encode malware into DNA as an attack vector to hack the computers used to sequence genetic data.[7] In addition, one can imagine naval applications of biocomputing and biosensors in salt water and other maritime environments that are hostile to electronics.

The practical significance of these novel threats and opportunities remains to be seen. For now, the human brain remains our most potent biological device—organ—for data processing and storage. Note that before the transistor was invented in 1947, the very term "computers" referred to women who used their brainpower to perform complex cryptographic and ballistic calculations during World War II.[8]

⊢• CYBER-ENABLED SYNTHESIS OF BIOLOGICAL WEAPONS

Most cyberbiosecurity threats are applications of digital technology that threaten biological systems, particularly human health and well-being. Perhaps the most dreadful threats are accidents or attacks that involve the synthesis or genetic engineering of pathogens enabled by cyberspace. In October 2023, President Joseph Biden issued an executive order on AI that highlights the "intersection of AI and synthetic biology," particularly the risk of these technologies being applied to develop or use biological weapons.[9]

To be clear, synthetic biology and genetic engineering are not required for biological weapons. Naturally occurring pathogens can be deadly on their own. During the Cold War, large-scale military testing demonstrated that these pathogens could be used to attack naval targets. In the United States, Project SHAD (Shipboard Hazard and Defense) simulated biological attacks on thousands of—often unknowing—sailors and marines using live agents such as tularemia and Staphylococcal enterotoxin B.[10] Naturally spread pathogens can affect naval operations as well. This threat was clearly demonstrated by the COVID-19 pandemic and contagion aboard the aircraft carriers USS *Theodore Roosevelt* and FS *Charles de Gaulle*, among other warships.[11]

Nor is cyberspace necessary for genetic engineering, as evidenced by thousands of years of plant and animal husbandry and domestication. Still, modern genetic engineering and synthetic biology depend on computer networks. Bioinformatics is computationally intensive. For instance, gene editing with clustered regularly interspaced short palindromic repeats (CRISPR) relies on cyberspace to identify potential targets for mutation and analyze the results. Machine learning and generative AI are also used to design CRISPR components and predict their effects.

Whether via CRISPR or other methods, a growing fear is that cyber-enabled genetic engineering will produce more deadly diseases (e.g., gain of function research that increases transmissibility or virulence).[12] These diseases could then spread by accident or design. China, Russia, and North Korea are suspected of having biological weapons programs or conducting dual-use research of concern that could be used to build such weapons.[13] Granted, biological weapons were outlawed by the 1972 Biological Weapons Convention. Their use is also considered taboo. However, the strength of these legal and normative prohibitions is debatable (e.g., the Soviet Union built a massive biological weapons program after it signed the arms control treaty that banned them).

Bioterrorism is another possibility.[14] Before the doomsday cult Aum Shinrikyo killed more than a dozen people with sarin gas in 1995, it tried and failed to use botulism and anthrax to attack targets around Tokyo—including the U.S. naval bases at Yokohama and Yokosuka.[15] Biological weapons are cheaper and easier to acquire than nuclear weapons. Much of the information required to build them is readily available on the internet. However, they are still not easy to develop and use. The question remains whether non-state actors will invest the added effort to genetically engineer pathogens when the barriers to violence with guns and conventional explosives are much lower.

Biosafety accidents would appear the more common threat. With the assistance of cyberspace, countless government, academic, and industry laboratories conduct research that involves genetic engineering. Only a small fraction of these labs conduct dual-use research of concern, which includes gain of function research with pathogenic organisms that could escape bio-containment. Yet "normal" accidents happen. The risks to public health are nontrivial. Military servicemembers are not immune to these risks, and Navy labs are not immune to human error.

⊢• CYBER-FUELED HEALTH DISINFORMATION

To date, the most common cyberbiosecurity threat—common to the point of being endemic—is deceptive information about health and healthcare that is spread through cyberspace. Of course, health is not entirely unique in this regard. Cyberspace is awash with conspiracy theories. These include conspiracies about the Navy, with allegations ranging from the teleportation of the destroyer USS *Eldridge* to alien sightings by naval aviators.[16]

Whatever the topic, social media is a powerful tool for spreading information at speed and scale. Health has proven to be a prominent topic for misinformation and disinformation online. Infectious diseases are particularly salient, as illustrated by false and misleading stories surrounding outbreaks of Ebola, Zika, and coronavirus. In several instances, conspiracy theories about the COVID-19 pandemic spread from the dark corners of the internet to mainstream politics. Along with domestic sources, foreign influence operations by China and Russia feed into this information environment, including false accusations to tarnish the reputation of the United States and fellow democracies.[17]

This threat is not new, but cyberspace can make it worse. In the 1980s "active measures" by the Soviet Union successfully spread disinformation that blamed the Pentagon for HIV/AIDS.[18] In the 2000s the U.S. Naval Medical Research Unit was effectively driven out of Indonesia over controversies and conspiracy theories about H5N1 influenza.[19] Controversy surrounding COVID-19 on the USS *Theodore Roosevelt* in 2020—and its potential spread to Guam—further illustrates that the Navy is vulnerable to this kind of threat.[20] The same can be said about opposition to vaccination in the naval special warfare community, among other examples.

Sailors, marines, and their families are people. Their perceptions are influenced by cyberspace. In addition to sowing fear, uncertainty, and doubt among the wider public, the spread of misinformation and disinformation about health and healthcare can fuel distrust in the military chain of command and undermine good order and discipline.

⊢• CYBER-EXPLOITED BIOMEDICAL DATA

Fake news is not the only cyberbiosecurity threat that involves the misuse of information online. Cyber exploits of biomedical data are another challenge. Chinese and Russian intelligence services have used hacking to steal vaccine research.[21] In other instances, the confidentiality of otherwise private, proprietary, or sensitive health information has been lost through data breaches, intellectual property theft, and bad advertising. The integrity of important datasets is also at risk.

Here again, the Navy is not immune. Military medical records have been breached, with unauthorized access and disclosure of information about thousands of patients exposed by the Department of Veteran Affairs and, in at least one instance, millions of medical records stolen from a defense contractor.[22] In addition, promotional data released in 2017 by a fitness tracker company revealed the locations of sensitive military sites around the world, along with patrol routes and other patterns of life that threaten operational security.[23] (Subsequently, smart watches with fitness tracking and internet connectivity have been banned from sensitive military installations.)

These examples are part of a larger potential problem. Vast amounts of biomedical, biometric, and genomic data are being amassed by governments, academia, and industry. Intended applications range from healthcare and law enforcement to agriculture and AI. Yet even when the initial intent is benign, this data can be stolen, misused, and manipulated. If genomic databases are manipulated, for example, then diagnostics and drug discovery could suffer.[24] The integrity of epidemiological data—including information collected by the Department of Defense Global Emerging Infections Surveillance program—is another potential target, especially given the geopolitics of blame for outbreaks such as COVID-19 and pandemic influenza.

One threat actor of concern is the People's Republic of China, due in part to its penchant for intellectual property theft and interest in biotechnology.[25] Using AI and other cyber tools, it is possible that China could exploit the data

it acquires to gain economic and military advantages. The Chinese government's use of biometric facial recognition to surveil and suppress people in
Xinjiang and elsewhere adds to this concern.[26]

That said, stolen data is probably harder for China to exploit than is often
assumed. As Kathleen Vogel and Sonia Ben Ouagrham-Gromley argue,
"There are major challenges in trying to use biomedical big data for any kind
of applied purpose."[27] The data is heterogenous. So too are the different ways
that it gets collected, processed, and stored—all of which make biomedical
data difficult to understand, let alone repurpose in different social contexts.
Greater scrutiny is warranted to assess this kind of threat to the Navy and
U.S. national security more broadly.

⊢• CYBER ATTACKS AGAINST BIOMEDICAL INFRASTRUCTURE

Critical infrastructures, such as the electrical grid and transportation, have
long been targets of concern for cyber security. Not only do we depend on
these systems, but they also involve hardware and machines through which
attacks in cyberspace could translate into physical damage. The healthcare
sector, including public health, is critical infrastructure for the Navy and
general population. Unfortunately, much of this infrastructure depends on
vulnerable information and operational technologies. Biomanufacturing and
networked medical devices have cyber vulnerabilities as well.

Ransomware is a prime example. Along with costing the healthcare sector
billions of dollars per year, this sort of cyber attack against the availability of
information systems has crippled hospitals and killed patients as a result.[28]
Ransomware—and destructive malware that masquerades as it—has put
healthcare at risk even when hospitals are not the intended target. Along
with paralyzing the shipping giant Maersk, for instance, the 2017 Russian
cyber attack called NotPetya crippled the pharmaceutical giant Merck. One
consequence was a vaccine shortage.[29] The biomanufacturing sector has
been targeted as well.[30] Whether cyber crime or sabotage, these attacks could
threaten healthcare for sailors, marines, and their dependents; they could also
threaten supply chains that the Navy depends upon.

Medical devices are another potential target. Former Vice President Dick
Cheney famously had the Wi-Fi connection to his pacemaker disabled for

fear of hacking.[31] Arguably, prosthetic limbs that DARPA helped develop for military amputees are hackable as well.[32] As the Navy pursues other brain-computer interfaces, the potential attack surface will expand.

⊢• NETWORKS, ORGANISMS, AND ORGANIZATIONS

Of course, threats are only part of the cyberbiosecurity equation. There are countless opportunities to increase security at the interface of cyber and bio. For instance, some of the same dual-use technology that could fuel biological warfare and bioterrorism can also be used—as often intended—to improve drugs and other medical countermeasures to combat infectious disease.

Unfortunately, the Navy is not well positioned to take advantage of these opportunities and manage cyberbiosecurity risks to the fleet. Historically, neither cyber security nor biosecurity have been mainstream interests or core competencies for the U.S. Department of Defense in general and the Navy in particular. (See related discussions on Navy-specific cyber security shortcomings by Dombrowski, Bebber and White, Brutzman and Kline, Cleary, and Ross and Warner in this volume.) As a result, the combination of cyber and bio is unlikely to fare well in military and naval thinking.

Why not? In part, most cyberbiosecurity threats are non-kinetic. They are not bullets or bombs that cause penetrating or blunt force trauma. They do not explode (e.g., as discussed in the chapter by Kuo and Lindsay). Consequently, the timing and mechanisms of damage they cause differ from the projectile weapons and explosives that the armed services prefer to think about.[33] The Navy's service culture also tends to focus more on weapons platforms—ships, submarines, aircraft—and less on sailors and other people who are at the greatest risk from cyberbiosecurity threats.[34]

In addition, improving cyberbiosecurity involves cooperation with other government agencies, as well as with academia and industry (as discussed in chapters by Jones, deWitte and Lehto, and Demchak). Cooperation is difficult for large bureaucracies. The Navy is not alone in this regard. But the impetus to cooperate is low when the issues involved are not the kinds of kinetic problems that the organization is predisposed culturally and historically to solve. Similarly, cooperation on cyberbiosecurity involves sharing information and coordinating action with nontraditional partners. It is difficult enough for the Navy, Army, Air Force, and Space Force to work together as a joint force (not to mention working with allied and partner militaries). It is harder still for the Navy to also work with the Department of Health and Human Services, for example, as well as with big pharma and social media companies at home and abroad.

Cyberbiosecurity challenges and opportunities need the Navy's attention and action now. They will continue to do so in the future. Overcoming the obstacles of service culture and bureaucratic politics requires understanding the relationships at work along this interface before adversaries exploit them to harm our naval forces onshore or at sea.

NOTES

1. Jean Peccoud et al., "Cyberbiosecurity: From Naive Trust to Risk Awareness," *Trends in Biotechnology* 36, no. 1 (2018): 4–7, https://doi.org/10.1016/j.tibtech .2017.10.012; Lauren C. Richardson et al., "Cyberbiosecurity: A Call for Cooperation in a New Threat Landscape," *Frontiers in Bioengineering and Biotechnology* 7 (June 2019), https://www.frontiersin.org/articles/10.3389/fbioe.2019.00099; Siguna Mueller, "Facing the 2020 Pandemic: What Does Cyberbiosecurity Want Us to Know to Safeguard the Future?" *Biosafety and Health* 3, no. 1 (February 2021): 11–21, https://www.sciencedirect.com/science/article/pii/S2590053620301129; Thom Dixon, "The Grey Zone of Cyber-Biological Security," *International Affairs* 97, no. 3 (May 2021): 685–702, https://doi.org/10.1093/ia/iiab041.
2. Barry Buzan, Ole Wæver, and Jaap de Wilde, *Security: A New Framework for Analysis* (Boulder: Lynne Rienner Publishers, 2022).
3. John F. Shoch and Jon A. Hupp, "The 'Worm' Programs—Early Experience with a Distributed Computation," *Communications of the ACM* 25, no. 3 (March 1982): 172–80, https://doi.org/10.1145/358453.358455.
4. Fred Cohen, "Computer Viruses: Theory and Experiments," 1984, https://web .eecs.umich.edu/~aprakash/eecs588/handouts/cohen-viruses.html.
5. Defense Advanced Research Projects Agency, "DARPA Establishes Computer Emergency Response Team," 13 December 1988, https://mirror.apps.cam.ac.uk /pub/doc/cert/CERT_Press_Release_8812. Despite roughly analogous threats and response requirements, however, there are striking differences in how these fields are organized. Frank L. Smith III, "Malware and Disease: Lessons from Cyber Intelligence for Public Health Surveillance," *Health Security* 14, no. 5 (2016): 305–14, https://doi.org/10.1089/hs.2015.0077. Also see appendix D1, "Surveillance, Research, Prevention Efforts in the Area of Infectious Diseases:

Applicability of CDC Experience to a National Center for Information Systems Security," in Defense Science Board, *Report of the Defense Science Board Task Force on Information Warfare-Defense* (Washington, DC: Office of the Under Secretary of Defense for Acquisition and Technology, 1996).

6. Chris C. Demchak, "What Corrodes Cyber, Infects Its Offspring: Unlearned Lessons for Emerging Technologies," *Cyber Defense Review* 7, no. 1 (Winter 2022): 153–60, https://cyberdefensereview.army.mil/Portals/6/Documents/2022 _winter/16_Demchak_CDR_V7N1_WINTER_2022.pdf?ver=tktgiDLOrUt3Q dsoKdej1g%3D%3D.

7. Ed Yong, "These Scientists Took Over a Computer by Encoding Malware in DNA," *The Atlantic*, 10 August 2017, https://www.theatlantic.com/science/archive/2017/08 /these-scientists-took-over-a-computer-by-encoding-malware-in-dna/536361/.

8. Jennifer S. Light, "When Computers Were Women," *Technology and Culture* 40, no. 3 (July 1999): 455–83, http://www.jstor.org/stable/25147356.

9. The White House, Executive Order on the Safe, Secure, and Trustworthy Development and Use of Artificial Intelligence, 30 October 2023, https://www.whitehouse .gov/briefing-room/presidential-actions/2023/10/30/executive-order-on-the- safe-secure-and-trustworthy-development-and-use-of-artificial-intelligence/.

10. Institute of Medicine, *Long-Term Health Effects of Participation in Project SHAD (Shipboard Hazard and Defense)* (Washington, DC: The National Academies Press, 2007).

11. For example, Bradley Martin and Trupti Brahmbhatt, *Readiness Implications of Coronavirus Infections on U.S. Navy Ships* (Santa Monica, CA: RAND Corporation, 2021), https://www.rand.org/pubs/research_reports/RRA468–1.html.

12. Among others, see Rami Puzis et al., "Increased Cyber-Biosecurity for DNA Synthesis," *Nature Biotechnology* 38, no. 12 (2020): 1379–81.

13. U.S. Department of Defense, *Strategy for Countering Weapons of Mass Destruction 2023*, 4–5, https://media.defense.gov/2023/Sep/28/2003310413/-1/-1/1/2023_STRAT EGY_FOR_COUNTERING_WEAPONS_OF_MASS_DESTRUCTION.PDF.

14. U.S. Department of Justice, *AMERITHRAX Investigative Summary*, 19 February 2010, https://www.justice.gov/archive/amerithrax/docs/amx-investigative -summary.pdf.

15. Fortunately, the cult used nonvirulent or contaminated strains that did not kill anyone. See Richard Danzig et al., *Aum Shinrikyo: Insights into How Terrorists Develop Biological and Chemical Weapons* (Washington, DC: Center for a New American Security, 2011).

16. "Philadelphia Experiment," Naval History and Heritage Command, 8 September 1996, https://www.history.navy.mil/research/library/online-reading-room /title-list-alphabetically/p/philadelphia-experiment.html.

17. Among others, see Miriam Matthews, Katya Migacheva, and Ryan Andrew Brown, *Superspreaders of Malign and Subversive Information on COVID-19: Russian and Chinese Efforts Targeting the United States* (Santa Monica, CA: RAND Corporation, 2021), https://www.rand.org/pubs/research_reports/RRA112–11 .html; Jennifer Hunt, "Countering Cyber-Enabled Disinformation: Implications for National Security," *Australian Journal of Defence and Strategic Studies* 3, no. 1 (July 2021): 83–88, https://doi.org/10.51174/AJDSS.0301/MLTD3707.

18. Douglas Selvage, "Operation 'Denver': The East German Ministry of State Security and the KGB's AIDS Disinformation Campaign, 1985–1986 (Part 1)," *Journal of Cold War Studies* 21, no. 4 (Fall 2019): 71–123, https://doi.org/10.1162 /jcws_a_00907.

19. Frank L. Smith III, "Advancing Science Diplomacy: Indonesia and the U.S. Naval Medical Research Unit," *Social Studies of Science* 44, no. 6 (December 2014): 825–47, https://doi.org/10.1177/0306312714535864.

20. David Welna, "Guam Locals Unhappy with Housing U.S. Sailors from Coronavirus-Hit Aircraft Carrier," NPR, 2 April 2020, https://www.npr.org /sections/coronavirus-live-updates/2020/04/02/826262256/guam-locals- unhappy-with-housing-u-s-sailors-from-coronavirus-hit-aircraft-carrier. It is possible that military information and influence operations also undermined COVID-19 vaccination efforts in the Indo-Pacific. Chris Bing and Joel Schectman, "Pentagon Ran Secret Anti-Vax Campaign to Undermine China during Pandemic," Reuters, 14 June 2024, https://www.reuters.com/investigates/special -report/usa-covid-propaganda/?utm_medium=Social&utm_source=twitter.

21. National Cyber Security Centre, "Advisory: APT29 Targets COVID-19 Vaccine Development," 16 July 2020, https://www.ncsc.gov.uk/files/Advisory-APT29- targets-COVID-19-vaccine-development.pdf. Also, U.S. Department of Justice, "Two Chinese Hackers Working with the Ministry of State Security Charged with Global Computer Intrusion Campaign Targeting Intellectual Property and Confidential Business Information, Including COVID-19 Research," 21 July 2020, https://www.justice.gov/opa/pr/two-chinese-hackers-working-ministry -state-security-charged-global-computer-intrusion.

22. See Leo Shane III, "Attack on VA Computer Systems Exposed Personal Information of about 46,000 Veterans," *Military Times*, 14 September 2020, https:// www.militarytimes.com/news/2020/09/14/attack-on-va-computer-systems -exposed-personal-information-of-about-46000-veterans/; Christopher Maag, "Data Breach Hits 5 Million Troops," *Military.com*, 4 October 2011, https://www .military.com/money/personal-finance/banking-and-savings/data-breach-hits- 5-million-troops.html.

23. Jeremy Hsu, "The Strava Heat Map and the End of Secrets," *Wired*, 29 January 2018, https://www.wired.com/story/strava-heat-map-military-bases-fitness -trackers-privacy/.

24. Boris A. Vinatzer et al., "Cyberbiosecurity Challenges of Pathogen Genome Databases," *Frontiers in Bioengineering and Biotechnology* 7 (2019): 106, https:// doi.org/10.3389/fbioe.2019.00106.

25. Of course, theft is not the only data source for China, nor is it necessarily the most significant. By consuming services such as social media and genetic tests, Americans have freely sold large amounts of biomedical and biometric data to Chinese companies on their own accord.

26. See discussion in George Galdorisi and Sam J. Tangredi, *Algorithms of Armageddon: The Impact of Artificial Intelligence on Future Wars* (Annapolis, MD: Naval Institute Press, 2024), 46–49, 53–54, 56–59.

27. Kathleen M. Vogel and Sonia Ben Ouagrham-Gormley, "China's Biomedical Data Hacking Threat: Applying Big Data Isn't as Easy as It Seems," *Texas National Security Review* 5, no. 3 (Summer 2022): 83–98, https://tnsr.org/2022/04 /chinas-biomedical-data-hacking-threat-applying-big-data-isnt-as-easy-as-it -seems/#_ftn3.

28. Paul Bischoff, "Since 2016, Ransomware Attacks on Healthcare Organizations Have Cost the US Economy $77.5BN in Downtime Alone," *Comparitech*, 23 October 2023, https://www.comparitech.com/blog/information-security /ransomware-attacks-hospitals-data/; Hannah Neprash, Claire McGlave, and Sayeh Nikpay, "We Tried to Quantify How Harmful Hospital Ransomware Attacks Are for Patients. Here's What We Found," *STAT*, 17 November 2023, https://www.statnews.com/2023/11/17/hospital-ransomware-attack-patient -deaths-study/#:~:text=From%202016%20to%202021%2C%20we,types%20 of%20health%20insurance%20coverage; National Audit Office, "Investigation: WannaCry Cyber Attack and the NHS," 25 April 2018, https://www.nao.org uk/wp-content/uploads/2017/10/Investigation-WannaCry-cyber-attack-and -the-NHS.pdf.

29. Donovan Guttieres, Shannon Stewart, Jacqueline Wolfrum, and Stacy L. Springs, "Cyberbiosecurity in Advanced Manufacturing Models," *Frontiers in Bioengineering and Biotechnology* 7 (September 2019), https://www.frontiersin.org /articles/10.3389/fbioe.2019.00210/full.

30. Lily Newman, "Devious 'Tardigrade' Malware Hits Biomanufacturing Facilities," *Wired*, 22 November 2021, https://www.wired.com/story/tardigrade -malware-biomanufacturing/.

31. "Dick Cheney Feared Assassination via Medical Device Hacking: 'I Was Aware of the Danger,'" ABC News, 19 October 2013, https://abcnews.go.com/US /vice-president-dick-cheney-feared-pacemaker-hacking/story?id=20621434.

32. Julia Alexander, "The Prosthetic DEKA Arm Is Hackable and a Legal Mess," VICE, 3 June 2014, https://www.vice.com/en/article/ezvvvz/the-deka-arm-is -hackable-and-that-might-open-up-a-legal-can-of-worms.

33. Frank L. Smith III, *American Biodefense: How Dangerous Ideas about Biological Weapons Shape National Security* (Ithaca: Cornell University Press, 2014).

34. See Carl H. Builder, *The Masks of War: American Military Styles in Strategy and Analysis* (Baltimore: Johns Hopkins University Press, 1989). Also, S. Rebecca Zimmerman et al., *Movement and Maneuver: Culture and the Competition for Influence among the U.S. Military Services* (Santa Monica, CA: RAND Corporation, 2019), https://www.rand.org/pubs/research_reports/RR2270.html.

SECTION 4

FUTURES

24 Secure, Survive, Strike

Cyber Strategy and the U.S. Navy

PETER DOMBROWSKI

Offensive-minded and *forward-deployed* define the strategy, culture, and self-identity of the U.S. Navy. However, for reasons ranging from aligning authorities, to the nature of current experiences, to the allocation of resources, these strike-oriented principles may not be effective as guides for naval *defense* and *resilience* in the coming era of intense cybered conflict.

STRATEGIES AND CYBER

All service strategic visions are subordinate to broad national-level strategic frameworks found in the National Security Strategy and the National Defense Strategy and in specific issue-area and regional strategic documents issued by Office of the Secretary of Defense (OSD). U.S. Navy "strategic visions"— including the most recent strategy, *Advantage at Sea* (2020)—must fit within the frameworks of those overarching documents.[1]

Service subordination to higher level strategies is even more pronounced in cybered conflict because cyber operations can have effects beyond the operational control of military units and are national, not solely Department of Defense (DOD), responsibilities.[2] Furthermore, OSD explicitly shapes the individual services' approach through a series of cyber security and cyber conflict documents starting with the 2011 *DOD Strategy for Operating in Cyberspace*.[3]

Consequentially, as the Navy prioritizes resources, manpower, and institutional focus on cyber forces versus its other roles and missions, it must make clear—for internal and external audiences—the limits to the role of cyber in naval strategy. In addition, Russia's war against Ukraine has revealed dimensions of cybered conflict affecting how the U.S. Navy understands and articulates its role in cyber operations in its strategic visions.

⊢• BRIEF REVIEW OF NAVY CYBER STRATEGY

The U.S. Navy was an early entrant to assessing how cyber operations would impact military strategy, operations, and tactics. Some have argued that the Navy's culture and traditional concern with commerce protection are why it is particularly suited to operate in the cyber domain.[4] Others maintain that "rather than a 'global commons,' cyberspace functions as a mosaic of adjoining, and sometimes overlapping territorial seas."[5] All these concepts are particularly familiar to maritime forces. Indeed, more than a decade ago, Chris Demchak and I argued that "the Navy may be uniquely qualified to adapt to cybered conflict" but that only trial by fire would tell.[6]

To understand the evolution of the U.S. Navy's relationship to cyberspace in recent years, it is useful to review the results of the period following the reestablishment of the Tenth Fleet and the overarching Fleet Cyber Command in order.[7] (The roots of Navy cyber operations are also discussed in the chapters by Friedman, Bebber and White, and Pugh in this volume.)

The official Tenth Fleet account maintains that the command was formed in response to the White House *Cyberspace Policy Review* of May 2009, which stated that "America's failure to protect cyberspace is one of the most urgent national security problems facing the new administration."[8] Then–Secretary of Defense Robert Gates required all services to provide the new Cyber Command with a component cyber command and support. In return and like its fellow military services and other government agencies, the Navy responded with both alterations in strategic thinking and institutional adjustments.

The growth of the Tenth Fleet and the Fleet Cyber Command is intimately tied to the progress of the Navy's strategic engagement with cyberspace. Tenth Fleet was originally a shore-based World War II command dedicated to applying scientific and mathematical techniques to coordinate the hunting and killing of German U-boats in the "war of the Atlantic." The commander of the modern Tenth Fleet is dual-hatted. As commander, Tenth Fleet, the admiral is responsible for the overall naval information warfare mission—which includes multiple means of electronic warfare. As commander, Fleet Cyber Command, the admiral is responsible for the cyber operations within Tenth Fleet's overall information warfare mission.

Since the reestablishment of Tenth Fleet in 2010, Fleet Cyber Command has employed more than fourteen thousand cyber professionals and fields forty cyber mission force teams in sixteen locations outside the contiguous United States "to deliver offensive and defensive cyber effects." Defensive responsibilities include "Navy's cyber forces [that] operate and defend the Navy's expansive, global network—including the sensor grid, communications systems, modem defenses and more than 750,000 user accounts—afloat and ashore."[9]

In 2015 the three sea services issued a revised version of the 2007 strategic vision statement, *A Cooperative Strategy for 21st-Century Seapower*, subtitled *Forward, Engaged, Ready*. In many ways, this document—the immediate predecessor of *Advantage at Sea*—was the most comprehensive statement on maritime cyber operation and strategy to be issued to date. First, *A Cooperative Strategy for 21st-Century Seapower* clearly recognized the dangers posed by cyber conflict: "New challenges in cyberspace and the electromagnetic spectrum mean we can no longer presume to hold the information 'high ground.' Opponents seek to deny, disrupt, disable, or cause physical damage to our forces and infrastructure with advanced networked information systems. The exploitation of space, cyberspace, and the electromagnetic spectrum threatens our global [command and control]. Naval forces must have the resilience to operate under the most hostile cyber and electromagnetic conditions."[10]

Second, it also pledged all-domain access for the Navy and the joint force including within the cyber domain and against growing adversary capabilities:

"Cyberspace operations, including both defensive and offensive measures, which preserve the ability to utilize friendly cyberspace capabilities; protect data, networks, net-centric capabilities, and other designated systems; and project power by the application of force in or through cyberspace."[11]

The updated *Cooperative Strategy for 21st-Century Seapower* also committed to providing the means to defend the fleet in the face of adversary cyber operations: "Extend our cyber security and resiliency by addressing the acquisition and modernization of our platforms, systems, and information technology networks; by instituting quality assurance programs to protect critical warfighting capabilities; and by establishing common technical standards, certifications, and authorities to sustain the readiness of our cyber programs and systems."[12]

However, the 2020 *Advantage at Sea*, the follow-on and last major strategic vision statement by the U.S. Navy and the other sea services, was relatively silent on the role of cyber in maritime security.[13] Nevertheless, it did stress two points: potential adversaries—especially China and Russia—have developed robust cyber capabilities that may threaten U.S. interests, and the three sea services should take an integrated approach to all warfighting domains, including cyber.[14] It notes: "Naval Service cyber teams provide U.S. forces the ability to detect and defend against attacks on American and allied networks. Exposing our competitors' malign cyber activities—whether against military or civilian networks—allows network vulnerabilities to be closed, raises the reputational costs, and lowers the effectiveness of future cyber aggression."[15]

Aside from the general proposition that top-end strategy documents are rarely very specific, another reason for the relative silence of *Advantage at Sea* on cyber operations is that the Navy itself soon published a focused strategy for cyberspace, the *Department of the Navy Cyberspace Superiority Vision*.[16] Additional inferences can be derived from the ongoing operations of the Tenth Fleet, the Navy Cyber Command. The *Navy Cyberspace Superiority Vision* aligns the Navy view with emerging joint doctrine. Joint Publication 3–12, *Cyberspace Operations*, defines cyberspace superiority as "the degree of dominance in cyberspace by one force that permits the secure, reliable conduct of operations by that force and its related land, air, maritime, and space forces at a given time and place without prohibitive interference."[17]

Like other service documents, these recent Navy strategic visions for the maritime domain and the cyber sphere are subordinate to national and OSD guidance. Notably, the previous decade has seen a significant shift in national strategy with the release of the 2018 Department of Defense Cyber Strategy. National policy became an effort "to defend forward to disrupt malicious cyber activity at its source, including activity that falls below the level of armed conflict."[18] Further, American cyber forces are expected to campaign continuously "to intercept and halt cyber threats, degrade the capabilities and networks of adversaries."

This new guidance of forward defense and persistent engagement shifts "DOD and [U.S. Cyber Command]'s posture in cyberspace from reactive to proactive." In fact, U.S. Cyber Command makes a direct analogy to the roles and functions of the Navy:

Just as the U.S. Navy keeps the peace by sailing the seas, or the U.S. Air Force secures air space by patrolling the skies, [U.S. Cyber Command] actively seeks out threats in cyberspace and eliminates them to defend the United States and its allies. However, just as a navy goes underway from a port or an airplane takes off from a runway, and thus are legitimate targets during times of conflict—persistent engagement involves targeting adversary cyber capabilities and their underlying infrastructure. This approach prevents adversary nations and non-state actors from launching disruptive and destructive cyber attacks in the first place.[19]

⊢• REAL-WORLD CYBERED CONFLICT WITH THE RUSSIA-UKRAINE WAR

Until 2014, visions of cybered conflict in future wars were either hypothetical or extrapolated from previous limited conflicts and campaigns. Today, the Russia-Ukraine conflict has passed through three phases of cybered conflict: peacetime competition, crisis, and war. Moreover, the nature of the war has evolved from hybrid to irregular to frozen to a "hot" high-technology war involving many of the most destructive weapons available today as well as some degree of cyber warfare.

Although a full account of highly classified and secretive cyber operations available for evaluation remains to be seen, the U.S. Navy's cyber involvement in Ukraine has been publicly revealed only for the pre-crisis phase. As members of U.S. Cyber Command's national mission teams, Navy and Marine Corps experts played a significant role in defending Ukrainian networks from "malicious cyber activity" during the run-up to the 24 February 2022 invasion by Russia. The "hunt forward" team was intended to bolster Ukrainian network resilience through "intelligence-informed" defensive operations enabled by the Volodymyr Zelenskyy government providing American "cyber warriors" with necessary systems access.[20] That said, the Navy's direct role (as opposed to individual contributions) in cyber conflict appears minimal except in supporting the Ukrainian Navy and any North Atlantic Treaty Organization or European Union maritime activities in the Black Sea. Here, the U.S. Navy does have the ability to support the development of resilient systems, including defensive capabilities, and the ability to reconstitute cyber and other naval capacities in the event of Russian aggression or exploitation by non-state proxies of Russia.

Nonetheless, with the prospect of conflict with the People's Republic of China apparently rising, the Navy must be prepared for intense, wide-ranging, and extended cybered conflict. Little comfort should be taken from the alleged lesser role of cyber operations in the Russia-Ukraine war.

├─• FUTURE OF NAVY CYBER STRATEGY: EXPECTATIONS AND RECOMMENDATIONS

Given the recent experiences on the joint and maritime levels, the evolution of the Navy's cyber vision will not be static, and the Navy's roles and missions in future conflict will include the service's cyber capabilities as deployed in the numbered fleets or in Tenth Fleet. Recently, some congressional leaders have been critical of the Navy's cyber efforts, with similar dissatisfaction expressed by former Chief of Naval Operations Adm. Michael Gilday.[21] Future changes in the Navy's strategic cyber vision will certainly have to be pursued carefully while still synchronized with national-level policies. Coordinating closely with OSD, the joint force and the wider intelligence community will remain critical to avoid duplication and operational contradictions with the various cyber forces used by other services, commands, and agencies of the United States.

More specifically, the U.S. Navy should focus its limited cyber forces and budgets on investing specifically in defensive measures and resilience. In many of the most challenging strategic scenarios facing the United States, the naval forces will be the proverbial "sharp point of the spear" to provide sustained kinetic fires in the combat theater to support national objectives. If any potential adversary can use cyber attacks to disrupt and diminish naval operations in theater, it will severely impact the joint force overall: "It is unclear whether even the most highly digitized/cybered systems can themselves survive on the modern battlefield in a conflict between technological near peers in which cyberspace and the electromagnetic spectrum is contested."[22]

Yet, Navy units are not currently suited to conducting offensive cyber operations. Offensive cyber operations should be the focus of naval forces only within the wider context of national strategy and, to a limited extent, applied to tactical operations in support of naval presence and naval power projection.

The Navy's cyber strategy—whether appearing in a stand-alone document for the Tenth Fleet, or in a vision statement about maritime and naval strategy as a whole—should recognize that the U.S. Navy requires additional legal authorities, tactical and operational capacities, and command and control arrangements—not to mention considerably greater amounts of dedicated resources and seriously creative strategic rethinking—to conduct offensive cyber operations in highly contested global hotspots. Future naval strategic documents, whether single-service or maritime tri-service (such as *A Cooperative Strategy for 21st-Century Seapower* and *Advantage at Sea*), should acknowledge these realities rather than attempting to poach on authorities and capabilities best left to other agencies. While Admiral Gilday recognized this discrepancy in 2022 and called for service-retained cyber forces and capabilities in the form of tactical cyber units, the Navy has yet to establish one.[23]

The critical issue is exactly how the Navy will allocate the resources devoted to defense, resiliency, and "strike." In my view, the two former objectives— defense and resilience—should have precedence over the last, "strike." The good news is the most recent Navy cyber vision document begins with a focus on "sustained investment in dynamic cyber security defenses to protect our systems from attacks."[24] The better news is that the most recent Navy cyber strategy document argues that "resiliency is key to success, and we envision a [Department of the Navy] that can 'fight hurt.'"[25]

However, it remains the essence of Navy culture to operate offensively and forward. Although too much can be read into the language of strategy documents—especially between the Department of the Navy and the Office of the Secretary of the Navy—there are signs that the traditional Navy emphasis on the offensive and "away games" will remain. [26] The U.S. Navy pledges that "it is not enough to statically defend our systems, installations, and networks. We must dynamically project power in and through cyberspace as part of integrated deterrence." [27] The Secretary of the Navy has stated that the service must "make cyber security a top priority, *increasing our lethality* [emphasis added], improving readiness, and sustaining resilience in cyberspace." [28]

The reality is that the actual allocation of naval resources to cyber capabilities—whether greater or less—will speak more strongly as organizational ground truth than mere words inserted in doctrine and steeped in cultural preferences.

NOTES

1. U.S. Department of the Navy, *Advantage at Sea: Prevailing with Integrated All-Domain Naval Power*, December 2020. For an assessment of impediments to the success of this strategic vision, see Sam J. Tangredi, "Disadvantages Ashore: Constraints on Achieving Integrated All-Domain Naval Power," *Naval War College Review* 76, no. 3 (Summer 2023): 36–76. The term "strategic vision" is used instead of *strategy* (as in the *Maritime Strategy*) because "from the perspective of the Joint Staff, the Services man, train, and equip, but do not create strategy," which is the exclusive purview of the combatant commanders. See Sam J. Tangredi, "Running Silent and Algorithmic: The U.S. Navy Strategic Vision in 2019," *Naval War College Review* 72, no. 2 (Spring 2019): 129–65.

2. Chris C. Demchak, *Wars of Disruption and Resilience: Cybered Conflict, Power, and National Security*, Studies in Security and International Affairs (Athens: University of Georgia Press, 2011), especially chapter 1.

3. See Cheryl Pellerin, "DoD Releases Its First Strategy for Operating in Cyberspace," American Forces Press Service, 15 July 2011, https://www.army.mil/article/61720/dod_releases_first_strategy_for_operating_in_cyberspace.

4. W. Alexander Vacca, "Military Culture and Cyber Security," *Survival* 53, no. 6 (December 2011–January 2012): 170.

5. Sam J. Tangredi, "From Global Commons to Territorial Seas: A Naval Analogy for the Nationalization of Cyberspace," *Military Cyber Affairs* 3, no. 1 (2018): 4.

6. Tangredi, "From Global Commons," 9.

7. Nancy Norton, "The U.S. Navy's Evolving Cyber/Cyber security Story," *The Cyber Defense Review* 1, no. 1 (Spring 2016): 21–26. See also Peter Dombrowski

and Chris Demchak, "Cyber War, Cybered Conflict, and the Maritime Domain," *Naval War College Review* 67, no. 2 (Spring 2014): 90–92.

8. U.S. Tenth Fleet, "United States TENTH Fleet from Anti-submarine Warfare to Cyberspace," https://www.fcc.navy.mil/ABOUT-US/US-TENTH-FLEET-HISTORY/.

9. U.S. Department of Defense, "Posture Statement of Vice Admiral Ross Myers, Commander, United States Fleet Cyber Command before the 117th Congress Senate Armed Services Committee Subcommittee for Cyber Security, April 5, 2022," https://www.armed-services.senate.gov/imo/media/doc/VADM%20Myers%20Statement%20Cyber%20Hearing%20Statement.pdf.

10. U.S. Department of the Navy, *A Cooperative Strategy for 21st-Century Seapower: Forward, Engaged, Ready*, March 2015, https://apps.dtic.mil/sti/pdfs/ADA615292.pdf, 8.

11. *A Cooperative Strategy for 21st-Century Seapower*, 21.

12. *A Cooperative Strategy for 21st-Century Seapower*, 33.

13. Between *A Cooperative Strategy for 21st-Century Seapower* and *Advantage at Sea*, the Navy released two statements that might be understood as commentaries or updates to underlying Navy and national strategic documents: *Design for Maintaining Maritime Superiority 1.0* (January 2016) and *Design for Maintaining Maritime Superiority 2.0* (December 2018). Neither document broke much new ground or employed the term "cyber," but both reemphasized and elaborated on "increasingly influential force is the rise of the global information system" (*Design 1.0*, 2).

14. *Advantage at Sea*, 3–4, 7.

15. *Advantage at Sea*, 12.

16. U.S. Department of the Navy, *Department of the Navy Cyberspace Superiority Vision*, October 2022, https://media.defense.gov/2022/Oct/19/2003098777/-1/1/0/DEPARTMENT%20OF%20THE%20NAVY%20CYBERSPACE%20SUPERIORITY%20VISION.PDF.

17. *Department of the Navy Cyberspace Superiority Vision*.

18. For an overview of the 2018 strategy, see Nina Kollars and Jacquelyn Schneider, "Defending Forward: The 2018 Cyber Strategy Is Here," *War on the Rocks*, 20 September 2018, https://warontherocks.com/2018/09/defending-forward-the-2018-cyber-strategy-is-here/.

19. U.S. Cyber Command Public Affairs Office, "CYBER 101—Defend Forward and Persistent Engagement," 25 October 2022, https://www.cybercom.mil/Media/News/Article/3198878/cyber-101-defend-forward-and-persistent-engagement/.

20. U.S. Cyber National Mission Force Public Affairs, "Before the Invasion: Hunt Forward Operations in Ukraine," U.S. Cyber Command, 28 November 2022.

21. Tyson B. Meadors, "Cyber Warfare Is a Navy Mission: The Navy Needs Its Own Specialized Cyber Force to Fulfill Its Traditional Mission of Protecting the Nation's Maritime-Based Economy," U.S. Naval Institute *Proceedings* 148, no. 9 (September 2022): 435.

22. Sam J. Tangredi, "Four Questions Indicating Unlearned Lessons Concerning Future Military Digital Systems and Fleet Design," *Cyber Defense Review* (Winter 2022): 175–76.

23. Derek Bernsen, "The Navy Needs a Cyber Course Correction," U.S. Naval Institute *Proceedings* 148, no. 8 (August 2022), https://www.usni.org/magazines/proceedings/2022/august/navy-needs-cyber-course-correction.

24. Department of the Navy, *Cyberspace Superiority Vision*, October 2022.

25. *Cyberspace Superiority Vision*.

26. Montgomery McFate, "Being There: U.S. Navy Organizational Culture and the Forward Presence Debate," *Defense & Security Analysis* 36, no. 1 (2020): 42–64.

27. McFate.

28. Carlos del Toro, "One Navy-Marine Corps Team: Strategic Guidance from the Secretary of the Navy," October 2021, 4.

25 Fleet Resilience in Cybered Conflict

ROSS A. MYERS and MICHAEL WARNER

Every conflict today holds a cyber dimension, even in the maritime domain. Modern naval operations rely on digital networks that link functions aboard ships, between ships, and to command and support functions ashore. That means the resilience of those networks and the personnel who operate them has become "commander's business," from the fleet to the individual ship level.

Naval doctrine is only now catching up with this reality. Indeed, fleet resilience would seem to be a doctrinally unfamiliar term. For instance, the Joint Staff's *DoD Dictionary of Military and Associated Terms* (November 2021 edition) defines a fleet as "an organization of ships, aircraft, Marine Corps forces, and shore-based fleet activities under a commander who may exercise operational, as well as administrative, control."[1] That same dictionary, however, offers no definition of "resilience." Perhaps the closest synonym listed in the dictionary is "sustainment," which appears to be a matter of provisioning and human relations (entailing "logistics and personnel services required to maintain and prolong operations until successful mission accomplishment").[2]

This oversight lies in scholarship as well as in doctrine. Historians love debating the mechanical aspects of sea power (guns, hulls, propulsion, aircraft, etc.). It is essential, however, to also inquire into the technology that *guides* the ships so they can act in concert with each other and with other instruments of national power. It is vital to understand how they are sustained—not only supplied and manned—but maintained fit for service and combat-effective at the individual, unit, and force levels.[3]

Sustaining effective command at sea is not a mere mechanical, logistical, or personnel matter. Mission success in operations designed to maintain maritime superiority requires a toughness (resilience) in the maritime force that is an order of magnitude greater than the traditional command of ships and sailors. (See discussion of systemic resilience by Demchak in this volume.) It requires resilience in four elements of force projection: the platforms (primarily ships and aircraft), their weapons, the operational systems that enable them, and the sailors and their leaders. Each of these four elements requires a digitally networked or "cyber" resilience.

⊢• "THE MODERN NAVAL PARADIGM"

Strategic naval power began with the age of exploration, specifically with Western notions of sea control relying on celestial navigation. Portugal, Spain, Holland, and England were able to visualize whole oceans as arenas for the application of force. Guided by astronomical tables, fine instruments, and increasingly accurate charts—in short, by applied data—these national powers learned how control of key shipping lanes could shape global events. The colonial age that followed rested on naval power. European influence, however, was originally confined to coastal regions. Not until the Industrial Revolution could the European powers extend their colonies far inland.

Recognizing this strategic reality, the Anglo-American powers have held on to strategic superiority in the maritime domain since the 1700s. From the start of the industrial age, they led in applying data for tactical and operational control. Radio control in battle, aided by cryptology, fostered Anglo-American maritime dominance and preeminence in global communications and intelligence in the twentieth century.

Of course, this dominance did not go unchallenged. The most serious challenges came from submarines in World War I and then from guided aerial systems in World War II: first Japanese carrier bombers, and then German and Japanese missiles (the latter being human-guided). The missile threat would grow in the Cold War. Yet the Anglo-American powers, in concert, beat back four major challenges to their control of the seas—in 1918 (German U-boats), twice in 1945 (German U-boats and the Imperial Japanese Fleet), and in 1989 (the Soviet Navy in the Cold War). That dominance—what we call the "modern naval paradigm"—has helped keep order in what has been labeled the Long Peace (1945–2022), the most prosperous era the world has ever known.[4]

The paradigm depends on many factors: good ships, deadly weapons, reliable communications, actionable intelligence, aggressive commanders, and stout sailors. Also, it rests on the ability to collect and move data, first within the warships themselves, and then across ships operating as formations and fleets. All of these elements must be resilient to keep ships on station, to win battles, and to recover from damage and disruption with crews ready to serve.

⊢• RESILIENCE OF PLATFORMS

With some exceptions (i.e., aircraft carrier flight decks), today's warships are thin-skinned, lacking the armor that once protected battleships, the primary naval weapons for roughly half a century. Thus, naval combatants today are more vulnerable to guided missiles and the fires they ignite. Witness the sinking of the Russian cruiser *Moskva* in April 2022. Struck by Ukrainian missiles, the *Moskva* was apparently devastated by resulting magazine ignitions and electrical fires and soon sank under tow.[5]

The U.S. Navy is well aware of such vulnerabilities. Hence, its fleet carriers are not only the world's largest warships but arguably the toughest and most combat power–capable as well, at least in a physical sense. Naval websites feature spectacular photos of the successful shock test of the new carrier USS *Gerald Ford* in 2021, showing the enormous eruption of seawater produced by twenty tons of explosives detonating near the carrier's hull.[6] This most powerful carrier ever is designed for resilience, particularly for operational efficiency and stamina.

Considered from a cyber angle, the USS *Gerald Ford* also exemplifies forward-leaning design. She was built to rely on networked digital systems; gone are the days when computers were retrofitted into odd spaces in combatant's hulls, which then had to be cut open to install software upgrades.[7] Her reactors produce more power, and her internal networks and systems will keep her on station and combat-effective if working as designed. That caveat, however, is key to resilience.

Indeed, the USS *Gerald Ford*'s own family of highly digitized systems could become a vulnerability, as congressional overseers have worried.[8] The physical or cyber disruption of electrical power, connectivity, or data integrity might prove more disruptive to her operational capability than they would to earlier, less digitally dependent *Nimitz*-class carriers. (On inadvertent combinatorial vulnerabilities, see Falcone and Panter in this volume.) Her systems are, in theory, easier to upgrade, but the same cannot be said of many of the "legacy" platforms sailing with her, whether in the U.S. or allied navies.[9]

War is hard on ships, whether or not they sustain battle damage. Once damaged, they must be repaired as soon as possible. Here is a growing challenge for navies that have cut back on specialist sailors (especially engineers) while adding ever more complex equipment to their ships.[10] If no one physically aboard can repair engines or other gear at sea, the ship must find a port for maintenance. Even there, the needed work might not be done quickly, since experts who know how to effect a specialized repair might be on the other side of the country—or in a different country altogether. All these considerations factor into the resilience of platforms.

⊢• RESILIENCE OF WEAPONS

Resilience of weapons is less intuitive. Are they useful against many targets and from many platforms? For example, U.S. naval aviators trained to use all flight decks in 1942; Japanese aviators learned to operate only from their home carrier, meaning their squadrons could not be swapped across ships without retraining. This made a difference to planners after the Battle of Coral Sea, when the Americans lost a carrier (USS *Lexington* [CV 2]) and saw another (USS *Yorktown* [CV 5]) damaged, with heavy losses to their air wings. While both Japanese fleet carriers at the Coral Sea battle (IJN *Shokaku* and *Zuikaku*) survived—the latter unscathed by American bombs and torpedoes—their air wings were similarly mauled and took months to reconstitute. The result was that the physically intact *Zuikaku* sat out the Battle of Midway four weeks later, while the hastily repaired *Yorktown* fought with a fresh air wing (from the idled USS *Saratoga*).[11] Midway was thus a fight between four Japanese carriers versus three American. Had the resilience of the two naval forces been reversed, five Japanese carriers would have battled two American carriers at Midway, with strategically ominous results for the United States.[12]

Other questions about weapons systems and munitions abound. How many does one have on hand? How reliable are they? Argentina's brave pilots hit many more Royal Navy ships than they sank off the Falklands in 1982, partly because old fuses detonated fewer than half of their bombs.[13] Modern war rapidly uses up expensive ordnance; how fast can such munitions be replenished and the weapons that launch them be repaired?

The cyber analogy to weapons resilience is obvious. How effective are the digital payloads to be used to penetrate or disrupt enemy systems? How detectable are such tools by ubiquitous personal security products (e.g., antivirus suites)? How readily can they be modified, upgraded, and/or restocked with improved versions? Are their operators trained to be versatile in their employment? All of these questions and more concern naval cyber warriors on both sides of the offense-defense divide. The "capabilities development" support to improve and replenish these cyber tools, moreover, must be ready to work fast and well, and that itself requires sustained leadership attention and investment.[14]

⊢ RESILIENCE OF SYSTEMS

Our next category is, for want of a better term, "systems" resilience. The functions (hardware, organizations, procedures, installations, support, etc.) that enable ships and forces to act in concert, particularly communications, surveillance, and intelligence, must work not only together but also in ways that provide timely and actionable information to commanders and crews. For instance, during World War I, wireless telegraphy and signals intelligence—rather than episodic, draining North Sea patrols—enabled the Grand Fleet to bottle up the kaiser's dreadnoughts and enforce the allied blockade of the Central Powers.[15]

This command, control, communications, intelligence, surveillance, and reconnaissance (C3ISR) aspect of fleet resilience transitioned to digital networks beginning in the 1960s and has since become heavily reliant on the internet. For Western navies, C3ISR is the most thoroughly cybered element of them all and, consequently, has perhaps the most significant cybersecurity vulnerabilities.

These "systems" functions consume two inputs above all: bandwidth and data. If amateurs once debated tactics while naval professionals talked logistics, today's professionals talk bandwidth. It determines the amount of data that can be transferred at any moment. Ships (and aircraft), by definition, operate without high-capacity landlines, and their network connections depend on fixed or mobile transmitters, the latter often on satellites. Bandwidth is thus a precious commodity, and any disruption is a serious concern.

The sourcing, utility, and accuracy of the data moving along that bandwidth entail a whole separate set of considerations for fleet resilience. Data is the new fuel oil for fleet operations. Whereas naval battles in World War II frequently revolved around the combatants' respective propulsion and aviation fuel levels, the data available to commanders and targeteers is shaping modern naval campaigns. This insight underlies the Navy's current concept of distributed maritime operations and will be crucial to its success, or lack thereof.[16] Acquiring more and better data and denying one's own to the enemy have become prime considerations not only for planners but also for skippers. The fleet that does this better over the long haul will have a greater strategic impact.

⊢• RESILIENCE OF PERSONNEL

Finally, we reach personnel resilience, the character and applied proficiency of the sailors and their leaders. Are they trained, are they brave, and are they tough? The loss of the *Moskva* last year may be attributed to an unready crew, unable or perhaps unwilling to save their ship in a crisis. The saving of the USS *Stark* (FFG 31) in 1987 makes a good counterpoint example; the frigate survived hits by two Iraqi-launched Exocet missiles through heroic damage control.[17] The crew of the USS *Cole* (DDG 67) performed similarly well after a terrorist bomb crippled the destroyer in 2000; she is still in service today thanks in large part to "excellent damage control."[18]

But we must shun complacency. In 2020 the amphibious assault ship USS *Bonhomme Richard* burned pierside in San Diego. Damage control mistakes meant the total loss of a capital ship that should have rendered useful service for decades longer.[19]

The cyber aspect of this resilience feels less obvious but still significant. Cyber attacks on resilience reach further than traditional attacks—even into the home life of sailors. Are the sailors focused, or are they feeling vulnerable in both work and private life? Is the latter because an opponent is threatening them via social media? Or is an adversary "doxing" their families back home by sharing personal details or private documents online to harm or shame them? Or are foes manipulating their credit scores or even online bank accounts? The possibilities for such actions to distract naval personnel seem limitless in an era of ubiquitous online access. A good example is again the war in Ukraine, in which cyber warfare and social media are used on both sides with enormous impact.

⊢• THE CYBERED FUTURE CONFLICT AND RESILIENCE

Future research in the field of naval cyber might profitably address two types of questions. First, practitioners and policymakers will want to know "What next?" for all four of the above categories of fleet resilience. They will naturally demand evidence to support recommendations, especially those for revising long-standing policies or committing additional resources in a time of stiff competition for budgets and manpower. What does the record of recent conflicts tell us about the survivability of platforms, and how can they be made easier to hide, and better able to withstand attacks? With regard to weapons, which of them work best under which conditions, and how can we stockpile them in quantities that suffice for various purposes and contingencies but do not detract from other fields of national defense?

Naval systems must all be modernized in order to keep up with potential opponents' technological advancements, and commanders would wish it done all at once—but obviously, this is not possible. So how, when, and where shall we prioritize what to patch in order to eliminate the worst vulnerabilities while gaining the most collateral benefits?[20] Second, planners and leaders will want to know how to ensure a consistent, predictable influx of talented and motivated sailors, officers, and support personnel. How can this be accomplished, short of throwing funds at the problem in ways that waste taxpayer dollars and try congressional patience?

Scholars will have a different set of questions to guide research and debate. Some might be answered in part by additional declassification and release of records, especially on the historical evolution of the Navy and its capabilities since the Cold War. However, that is likely to take decades, and in the meantime, scholars should seek to offer preliminary answers to the questions above (especially where they can provide a long-term perspectivew on the issues) and should also ponder some of the larger contextual issues. The very purpose for sustaining naval might should top that list. What is, for instance, the place of maritime power in globalized international relations between nuclear armed rivals?

The young Samuel Huntington—later to be a preeminent scholar—contemplated just this issue in 1954, asking what the U.S. Navy would do in a Cold War in which it had no other navies to fight.[21] He answered his own question by arguing that the Navy's mission had shifted from sea control to power projection—to serving strategy by placing the instruments of national power into far forward regions much closer to adversaries. Huntington's answer in 1954 might or might not be the correct answer for the 2020s and remains worthy of contemplation and debate. It is fair to ask: what is the next shift?

In conclusion, the modern naval paradigm now confronts fleet resilience challenges that are new or at least intensified. The challenge will be not just to refit, repair, and reconstitute, but to do so at speed. Interoperability and adaptability will be key; the navy that can keep platforms on station, with effective suites of weapons and systems—and sailors trained and determined to employ them—will be the navy that wins.

Navies can master this enduring paradigm only if they ensure their own mastery of the four elements of resilience—and do so in the face of uncertainty of the actions of other navies. True resilience brings with it a psychological element that can—and must—act as a deterrent to any challenger. Even in a deeply cybered world, naval power, like deterrence, lies in the minds of the admirals, the sailors they command, and the policymakers who steer and sustain the navies.

NOTES

1. *DOD Dictionary of Military and Associated Terms* (as of November 2021), 84, https://irp.fas.org/doddir/dod/dictionary.pdf.
2. *DOD Dictionary*, 206.
3. Trevor Prouty, "Forward Battle Damage Repair Keeps Ships in the Fight," U.S. Naval Institute *Proceedings* 148, no. 1 (January 2022): 18–23, https://www.usni.org/magazines/proceedings/2022/january/forward-battle-damage-repair-keeps-ships-fight.
4. John Lewis Gaddis, *The Long Peace: Inquiries into the History of the Cold War* (New York: Oxford University Press, 1989).
5. "Sunken Russian Warship *Moskva*: What Do We Know?" *BBC News*, 18 April 2022, https://www.bbc.com/news/world-europe-61103927.
6. Sam LaGrone, "VIDEO: Explosive USS *Gerald R. Ford* Shock Trial Registered as 3.9 Magnitude Earthquake," *USNI News*, 19 June 2021, https://news.usni.org/2021/06/19/video-explosive-uss-gerald-r-ford-shock-trial-registered-as-3-9-magnitude-earthquake.
7. David B. Larter, "The Future of the U.S. Surface Fleet: One Combat System to Rule Them All," *Defense News*, 14 January 2019, https://www.defensenews.com/naval/2019/01/14/the-future-of-the-us-surface-fleet-one-combat-system-to-rule-them-all/.
8. Nicholas H. Guertin, Director, Operational Test and Evaluation, U.S. Department of Defense, *FY2021 Annual Report*, January 2022, 142–45, https://www.dote.osd.mil/Portals/97/pub/reports/FY2021/other/2021_DOTEAnnualReport.pdf?ver=YVOVPcF7Z5drzl8IGPSqJw%3d%3d.
9. Sydney J. Freedberg, "Navy Needs Plan to Update Old Ships' Weapons: Hill Staff," *Breaking Defense*, 22 June 2018, https://breakingdefense.com/2018/06/navy-needs-plan-to-update-old-ships-weapons-hill-staff/.
10. Mohit Kaushik, "How Maintenance Work Is Done Onboard a Ship?" *Marine Insight*, 10 August 2021, https://www.marineinsight.com/guidelines/how-maintenance-work-is-done-onboard-a-ship/
11. John B. Lundstrom, *The First Team: Pacific Naval Air Combat from Pearl Harbor to Midway* (Annapolis, MD: Naval Institute Press, 1984), 317, 457.
12. Jonathan B. Parshall, "What Was Nimitz Thinking?" *Naval War College Review* 75, no. 2 (Spring 2022): 92–122, https://digital-commons.usnwc.edu/nwc-review/vol75/iss2/8/.
13. George C. Wilson, "A Falklands Break for British," *Washington Post*, 31 July 1982, https://www.washingtonpost.com/archive/politics/1982/07/31/a-falklands-break-for-british/c1900c59-cfb2-401a-82a7-06766002fb98/.

14. J. D. Work of National Defense University recently offered perhaps the only public discussion of these matters. See his "Offensive Cyber Operations and Future Littoral Operating Concepts," *Military Cyber Affairs* 5, no. 1 (May 2022): 20–22, https://digitalcommons.usf.edu/cgi/viewcontent.cgi?article=1084&context=mca https://digitalcommons.usf.edu/cgi/viewcontent.cgi?article=1084&context=mca.

15. See Christopher Andrew, *Her Majesty's Secret Service: The Making of the British Intelligence Community* (New York: Viking, 1986), 99; Winston Churchill, *The World Crisis: 1911–1918* (New York: Free Press, 1959 [1931]), 335.

16. Chief of Naval Operations, *Navigation Plan 2022*, 8, https://media.defense.gov/2022/Jul/26/2003042389/-1/-1/1/NAVIGATION%20PLAN%202022_SIGNED.PDF.

17. Chairman of the Joint Chiefs of Staff to the Secretary of Defense, *Formal Investigation into the Circumstances Surrounding the Attack on the USS* Stark *(FFG 31) on 17 May 1987*, 3 September 1987, https://www.jag.navy.mil/library/investigations/USS%20STARK%20BASIC.pdf.

18. Captain [redacted], USN, to Commander, United States Naval Forces Central Command, *Command Investigation into the Actions of USS Cole (DDG 67) in Preparing for and Undertaking a Brief Stop for Fuel at Bandar at Tawahi (Aden Harbor) Aden, Yemen on or about 12 October 2000*, 27 November 2000, 18, https://www.history.navy.mil/content/dam/nhhc/browse-by-topic/ships/uss-cole/pdf/INVESTRPT.pdf.

19. Vice Chief of Naval Operations, *Command Investigation into the Facts and Circumstances Surrounding the Fire Onboard USS* Bonhomme Richard *(LHD 6) on or about 12 July 2020*, 15 September 2021, https://www.secnav.navy.mil/foia/readingroom/HotTopics/BHR%20and%20MFR%20Investigations/For%20Release%20BHR%20Command%20Investigation%20(20%20Oct%2021).pdf.

20. To address this, during his tenure as Chief of Naval Operations (2019–2023), Adm. Michael Gilday initiated an effort called Performance to Plan (P2P) to achieve this prioritization. This effort is continuing. See "Performance to Plan: An Engine to Get Real Get Better," U.S. Navy Official Website, n.d. (accessed 1 November 2023), https://p2p.navy.mil/.

21. Samuel P. Huntington, "National Policy and the Transoceanic Navy," *U.S. Naval Institute Proceedings* 80, no. 5 (May 1954): 483–93.

26 From Panic to Pragmatism

Naval Supply Chain Cyber Vulnerabilities in Peace and War

JASON VOGT and NINA KOLLARS

The maritime supply chain and its cyber vulnerabilities receive considerable public interest only when a major disruption occurs. Usually, headlines and commercial panic follow. Today, whether it is the 2021 blockage of Suez Canal traffic by the grounded massive container ship *Ever Given*, the 2020 COVID-19 interference with world trade flows, or the 2023 ransomware attack on the Japanese port of Nagoya, the attention comes with rising concerns about maritime cyber weaknesses.[1] Each major disruption is treated as if it were a surprise. Even if the event does not involve an issue of national security, the panic and wild speculation can dominate the news and political discussion in the United States and its allies for weeks. For example, the 2021 grounded *Ever Given* was not carrying U.S. or North Atlantic Treaty Organization military equipment, key supplies critical for allied military operations, or even fuel bound for a U.S. or allied naval base.[2] Rather, the wind moved the massive ship off its course, causing global delays of goods delivery and imposing considerable costs in time and hard currency for businesses.[3] The notably volatile press response to a critical issue does indeed help to shed light on the problem of potentially brittle supply chains governed across countries and seas, managed across international organizations with overlapping mandates, and implemented across corporations big and small alike. (See Jones, and Wells and Klimburg in this volume.) For those weeks, the public once again became aware that the world, including governments and militaries, is supplied by sea.

However, after the panic of each event dies down, the maritime domain remains fragmented in management and maintained "on the cheap." Instead of broadly induced panics, what is needed is a more careful public identification of which critical components necessitate what type of policy solutions. Weaknesses in the global maritime supply chain need to be addressed with a "nested framework" for pragmatism, not panic—especially with regard to cyber, navies, and naval systems. Applying that framework indicates that, while cyber threats on wartime logistics may pose a critical challenge to naval operations, they are also more difficult to carry out than cyber attacks in peacetime against overall maritime supply chains.

⊢• NESTED FRAMEWORK FOR PRAGMATIC APPROACHES

No navy can afford to protect everything in their supply chains against a cyber attack. Adversaries' offensive cyber strategies can present endless combinations of attacks across three seascapes—maritime transportation, navies at peace, or navies at war—with varying costs and incentives of each cyber attack.

Targeting commercial maritime supply chains provides the largest cyber attack surface and can be applied more flexibly in a wider number of contingencies. However, lengthy or large supply chains involving competitive production encourage some often-obscure systemic redundancies that lessen the overall impact of cyber attacks. Peacetime cyber attacks on naval supply chains where defenses are not on alert can potentially provide an adversary with the most consequential access. But the usefulness of this method to degrade an opponent's fighting capacity is less certain if ship maintenance and due diligence are observed and the adversary does not know precisely when war will occur. A successful attack on a shipbuilding supply chain could have some implications for production timelines, but it is unlikely to impact a current fight. In an ongoing wartime conflict, cyber attacks on naval logistics supply chains may have near-term operational effects, but conducting a direct kinetic attack on logistics infrastructure and the supplies themselves may be more effective.

Understanding the risk within the maritime supply chain and generating pragmatic solutions require an examination based on a nested framework. The overarching problem is that cyber vulnerabilities pose widely consequential dangers across global maritime supply chains, both commercial and naval. The next and narrower set of cyber vulnerabilities are those specifically found in the U.S. Navy's global logistics infrastructure. Overlaid on these concentric circles is the distinction between the vulnerabilities faced by navies in their peacetime missions versus their wartime responsibilities. Successful wartime cyber attacks on logistics may have the most direct impact on naval operations; they will also be harder to carry out than peacetime cyber attacks because those likely to be targeted will be on higher alert.

⊢• RISK AND RESILIENCE OVERVIEW OF COMMERCIAL MARITIME SUPPLY CHAINS

Riven with cheaply maintained and loosely governed systems that rely on public infrastructures such as ports highly susceptible to criminal and state-sponsored cyber attacks, the maritime domain is cyber-insecure. From the legacy hardware and software security systems already at risk in ports, to the influence operations that can easily target small populations of critical mariners and crane operators, the seascape of potential things that are vulnerable is overwhelming.[4] (See discussion by Jones in this volume.)

But vulnerability is not the same thing as high risk if the context differs. Calculating risk requires thinking about the probabilities in the objectives and motives of specific threat actors and the operational criticality of threatened supplies. A car left unlocked in a parking garage where carjacking is rampant is more at risk than one unlocked in a locked private garage in a remote location. Choices need to be made and certain degrees of risk accepted. In principle, what is needed in a cyber risk assessment of the maritime supply chain is a comprehensive study of its dependencies to create a practical model of what constitutes critical unrecoverable damage, what is an acceptable loss, and what needs to be addressed with policy measures and public (governmental) security controls. Cyber defenses for the maritime supply chain cannot defend every aspect of the chain or any aspect all the time. To attempt so would be prohibitively expensive and be likely to fail.

Ultimately, the maritime shipping industry's view of cyber supply chain risk is about the money, especially if interruptions of the maritime shipping industry could cost billions of dollars in disrupted goods delivery. Even if a dominant shipping company that provides services to other shipping firms suffers a digital outage like Maersk did with the 2017 NotPetya attack, that does not mean its competitors are similarly financially affected. Shipping has become historically cheap, with competing firms striving to keep costs down. Recovering from minor cyber attacks is more affordable than any effort toward absolute security. As a result, individual shippers are incentivized to avoid spending resources on cyber security beyond immediate needs, particularly if they have not experienced a major, debilitating cyber attack.

And they may be justified in that so far because the maritime system as a whole has proven more resilient than its individual parts. By dint of their heterogeneous and organically grown nature, large, long-running, multiparty complex systems serendipitously can possess hidden redundancies providing unexpected resilience. To date, this relatively inadvertent robustness also means no one participant feels obligated to protect the otherwise functioning overall system, only their own particular slice. The result is, as noted, a highly cyber vulnerable but differentially at risk global maritime system. It is not even clear whether attempts to unify or institutionalize this system into a smoother fabric to make it effectively cyber-protected as a whole—such as the now-defunct Maersk TradeLENS program—could have adverse effects on this apparently organic resilience. (See Jones in this volume.)

↦ NAVY'S SUPPLY CHAIN RISK IN PEACE

The risks to individual maritime firms, however, do not always constitute concerns for national security. As scary as the NotPetya disruption was for the maritime shipping industry's bottom line, the actual threat to the U.S. Navy supply chain in peacetime differs and is a narrower sphere of possibilities. The spillover from large financial damages and a more limited supply of Ikea furniture to national security damages and a limited supply of critical weapons system parts is not automatic. Additionally, cyber security concerns for the U.S. Navy supply chain in a time of peace are different than in a time of war.

In a time of peace, the U.S. Navy's concerns about the supply chain are "enterprise" concerns, more about building and maintaining a fleet than operating it. The Navy enterprise's demands upon global supply chains—while vast and heavily bottlenecked—are extremely varied given the often bespoke, very specific, and largely domestically fulfilled nature of the U.S. defense industrial base. The unique parts essential to enable a modern navy to operate with a full suite of sensors and communications are not necessarily closely linked to the broader maritime supply chain.

Nonetheless, the Navy supply chain's cyber security risks rest largely on the potential for degraded or compromised electronics and other components or parts that may be implanted maliciously by an adversary to deny effective use in combat. Compromised electronics could harbor mechanisms that could both spy on, or deny, operations by naval assets in a period of conflict. Since warships are essentially floating computers, the challenge of ensuring that the most critical components of the ship—propulsion, communication, navigation, and fires—are cyber-secure will occur in one of two places: in the shipyards where they are built, or at the piers when they are maintained or updated. (See Hilger in this volume.) Those two places present key moments when the wider maritime supply chain touches the ships, and when the most care can be taken to mitigate the risk of implants and compromise.[5]

Preparation and due diligence research are the most important solutions to the cyber security threat to naval systems during building and maintenance. During design and development of critical components for ships, due diligence in supply chain risk management (SCRM) is already required for Department of Defense (DOD) acquisitions personnel. Additionally, the DOD chief information officer—assigned in accordance with DOD Instruction 500.90 to maintain the Risk Management Framework Knowledge Service—issued a guidance (*Cybersecurity for Acquisition Decision Authorities and Program Managers*) for best practices to ensure that SCRM processes are in keeping with current standards.[6]

The difficult issue for cyber security in the Navy shipbuilding supply chain, therefore, is not the absence of standards, but capacity of acquisition managers to do the work of assessment and review. Maturity of SCRM practices and in the broader understanding the electronics supply chain feeding critical naval systems would have the greatest effect in reducing cyber risks, but the Navy has a labor shortage. Since the average build time for a surface warship or submarine is three to five years (assuming the platform is a continuation of an existing ship class), ensuring a sufficient trained workforce appears to be a key bottleneck, more so than delays in access to raw materials or key components.[7]

⊢• NAVY'S SUPPLY CHAIN RISK IN WAR

In a time of directly contested logistics and kinetic conflict, the Navy's most pressing maritime supply chain vulnerabilities are operational—particularly the flow of supplies and repair parts to the Fleet. The primary cyber security threats shift from the shipyard to the theater of operations, threatening combat supply and maintenance. Currently, the wartime supply and maintenance systems rely on a series of *unclassified* data networks and software systems. Like the general maritime supply chain, the larger the number of operating units and the further the Fleet is from safe locations, the more the supply chain becomes a complex and distributed multiagency affair subject to enemy attack. Under these conditions it is difficult, perhaps impossible, to protect the entirety of this network, but there may be critical components—such as the Navy's logistics systems—that are worth the majority of cyber security investment.

Although a subset of the larger DOD defense logistics enterprise, the U.S. Navy supply chain focuses on the building, sustaining, and repairing of surface and subsurface combat vessels, and supporting aircraft. While the Navy can replenish some basic supplies like food and water from contracted local sources globally, sustaining its combat systems depends on unique supply chains that connect the Navy's logistical elements with specialized venders who can provide sensitive munitions, repair parts, and often bespoke maintenance services.[8]

Automated information systems are key to managing this complex global logistical system. Supply chain managers measure and anticipate the demand from the Fleet through these systems and forward it to the defense industrial base, while simultaneously tracking where needed items and services are in the logistical enterprise. Repair parts are a special class of supply. Broken systems must first be identified by crews and repair request communicated to the naval logistics enterprise, before the system can respond with a maintenance solution, which often requiring a ship to move to a port with specialized facilities where space is at premium. Understanding which ships are available from a maintenance perspective and where needed supplies are located, also known as in-transit visibility, is critical for operational commanders making decisions about how to employ their forces.

Over the past thirty years, the Navy has managed its logistics operations through a patchwork of legacy information systems separated by commodity and echelon. For example, completely separate logistics systems manage its food, fuel, and ammunition, as well as maintenance for ships and aircraft. Some parts of the existing information technology architecture were developed in the 1990s and have not kept pace with the modern information technology performance and security standards.[9]

From a cyber security perspective, the primary threat to these systems is that malicious cyber actors will identify a backdoor into these systems, similar to what Russian intelligence services achieved in the 2021 SolarWinds compromise, allowing unfettered access to the entire system whether in peacetime or war.[10] Once inside a supply chain management system, potential adversaries would have the ability to monitor the maintenance conditions of various naval platforms, as well as where specific items are being shipped, potentially giving them broad insight into the fleet's operations and readiness. In wartime, they may also be able to manipulate data within the system, canceling orders or rerouting supplies, causing confusion and crucial delays in high-tempo combat operations. Finally, they could also crash the systems or deny legitimate users access to them. The time-consuming loss of, or attempt to recover, massive amounts of critical data could shape the course of the war.

Currently the Navy is investing in new supply and maintenance management systems to help consolidate the Navy logistics enterprise, enhancing overall supply chain performance but also improving the network's cyber security. These new systems must adhere to guidelines set forth in DOD's 2019 Digital Modernization Strategy, which calls for all new DOD systems to shift to a cloud-based architecture to create a common cyber security environment able to rapidly adapt to threats at scale across the entire network. These newer systems are meant to give naval commanders increased confidence that their logistics data is secure, reliable, and recoverable.

⊢• KEY TAKEAWAY CONCERNING THE U.S. NAVY SUPPLY CHAIN

With no indisputable solutions to ensuring operational and tactical cyber security in a kinetic engagement, a comprehensive assessment of risk as to what assets are critical under varying conditions and with what alternate expected costs will have to suffice. Recognition of the distinctions between systemic maritime and naval, and between peacetime and wartime, cyber threat vectors—and the use of the cyber risk nested framework suggested here—should improve operational assessments of both systemic risk and the required levels of critical investment.

NOTES

1. Jacob Benjamin, "OT Cybersecurity Breach Disrupts Operations at the Port of Nagoya, Japan," *Dragos*, 11 July 2023, https://www.dragos.com/blog/ot-cybersecurity-breach-disrupts-operations-at-the-port-of-nagoya-japan/.
2. Anna Cooban, "Ikea Furniture Is Still Stuck on the *Ever Given* alongside $550,000 Worth of Wearable Blankets, 2 Months after the Ship Was Freed from the Suez Canal," *Business Insider*, 16 June 2021, https://www.businessinsider.com/ever-given-suez-canal-stuck-product-still-onboard-ikea-shipping-2021-6.
3. Chris C. Demchak and Michael L. Thomas, "Can't Sail away from Cyber Attacks: 'Sea-Hacking' from Land," *War on the Rocks*, 15 October 2021, https://warontherocks.com/2021/10/cant-sail-away-from-cyber-attacks-sea-hacking-from-land/.
4. Joseph Kramek, *The Critical Infrastructure Gap: U.S. Port Facilities and Cyber Vulnerabilities* (Washington, DC: Center for 21st Century Security and Intelligence at Brookings, 2013), https://www.brookings.edu/wp-content/uploads/2016/06/03-cyber-port-security-kramek.pdf.
5. Cristina T. Chaplain, *Weapon Systems Cybersecurity: DoD Just Beginning to Grapple with Scale of Vulnerabilities*, GAO-19–128 (Washington, DC: Government Accountability Office, 9 October 2018), https://www.gao.gov/assets/gao-19–128.pdf.
6. U.S. Department of Defense, DOD Instruction 5000.90, "Cybersecurity for Acquisition Decision Authorities and Program Managers," 31 December 2020, 5, https://www.esd.whs.mil/Portals/54/Documents/DD/issuances/dodi/500090p.

PDF; U.S. Department of Defense, Chief Information Officer, *Cyber-Supply Chain Due Diligence Researcher's Guide: DCIO/CS Risk Assessment & Operational Integration* (Washington, DC: Institute for Defense Analysis, 2022), https://www.denix.osd.mil/ict-scrm/denix-files/sites/81/2022/07/Supply-Chain-Due-Diligence-Researchers-Guide.pdf.

7. Sam LaGrone, "Submarine Supply Chain Largest Barrier to Improving Virginia Attack Sub Schedule, Says Boykin," *USNI News*, 8 May 2023, https://news.usni.org/2023/05/08/submarine-supply-chain-largest-barrier-to-improving-virginia-attack-sub-schedule-says-boykin.

8. Jared Serbu, "New Navy Approach to Supply Chain Elevates Data-Driven Decisions to C-Suite," *Federal News Network*, 23 August 2021, https://federalnews-network.com/on-dod/2021/08/new-navy-approach-to-supply-chain-elevates-data-driven-decisions-to-c-suite/.

9. Bradley Wilson et al., *Naval Aviation Maintenance System: Analysis of Alternatives*, RR 2974.1 (Santa Monica, CA: RAND, 2020).

10. Vijay A. D'Souza, "SolarWinds Cyberattack Demands Significant Federal and Private-Sector Response (infographic)," U.S. Government Accountability Office, 22 April 2021, https://www.gao.gov/blog/solarwinds-cyberattack-demands-significant-federal-and-private-sector-response-infographic.

 **27** Fleet Design for the Cyber Future

JOHN ARQUILLA

During the past two hundred years in naval affairs, the impact of advancing industrial technologies upon the design of fleets was profound, often transformational. Sail gave way to steam propulsion, solid shot to exploding shells, wooden vessels to ironclads, and battleships to aircraft carriers. The submarine emerged to challenge the supremacy of surface vessels, even in the face of the latter's eventual marriage to airpower—so much so that, as military historian John Keegan argued, in the wake of the South Atlantic War in 1982, "the surface ship . . . cannot defend itself at all against the nuclear-powered submarine." This observation led him to conclude that "command of the sea in the future unquestionably lies beneath rather than upon the surface."[1]

⊢• PURPOSE VERSUS APPLIED TACTICS: MAHAN AND TIRPITZ

What guided the radical redesigns of sea power during these years? For Alfred Thayer Mahan in the late 1800s, *purpose* was the driving force behind fleet design. He believed the most fundamental goal of a navy, in peace and war, was the protection of the seagoing commerce upon which the prosperity of the world depended. That goal entailed a sharp focus on the "wide common, over which men may pass in all directions."[2] For purposes of warfighting, although Mahan derived his insights from the age of sail, he was prescient about the future of navies. He enjoined them to seek "powers to injure an enemy from a great distance, to maneuver for an unlimited length of time without wearing out the men, to devote the greater part of the crew to offensive weapons."[3]

In his most influential books and other studies, Mahan went on at length about the importance of strategy and doctrine but had little to say about how the long-range striking power and unlimited maneuver capabilities were related to fleet design. His contemporary (and great admirer), Alfred von Tirpitz, had the task of building an almost entirely new fleet for imperial Germany in the same era. He took design to heart and did his best at "translating in shipbuilding our conception of warfare." He went on at greater length about the need to couple design tightly with notions of battle. As he summed up the matter: "Naval shipbuilding is applied tactics."[4]

But Tirpitz focused more on the linkage between tactics and fleet design than he did on bringing a broader "conception of warfare" into the process.[5] In the event, he built a battle fleet that significantly outperformed the Royal Navy at the Battle of Jutland in 1916, yet this tactical victory could not alter the strategic naval balance. Only the submarine, at the time almost completely undetectable when submerged, could have shifted the scales. However, Tirpitz chose to design a fleet heavy on surface warships and far too light on submarines, and he lost the war at sea.

⊢• BROADER DESIGN QUESTIONS

Thus, there are broader design queries that fleet-builders must consider, beyond the direct matter of what types of vessels and weapons will ultimately be engaging the enemy: What should the mix or composition of naval forces and armaments look like overall? Should fleet design reflect a "big bet" on just one type of vessel, with supporting ships and other craft all subordinate to it? Or is there a need for broad preparation to hedge against the different types of naval missions and, to use Tirpitz's term, "conceptions of warfare"? Addressing these questions must undoubtedly form a central focus of the discourse on designing the future fleet.

To inform that discourse and the debates that will arise, it will be important to think about how technology may affect the future face of naval battle and how to embed tactics in naval design. But it will be just as critical to have a vision of the future guiding the mix or composition of vessels, aircraft, and armaments to develop well before armed conflict erupts once again. DuPont Corporation director K. K. Casey observed when testifying before the Nye-Vandenberg Committee five years prior to the Japanese attack on Pearl Harbor in December 1941, "Wars frequently begin ten years before the shooting starts."[6]

What, then, is the current technological state of play, and what do the latest trends suggest as to the future courses of development in naval affairs that should bear upon fleet design? And how will all this affect the overall conception of war at, and from, the sea? The answers to these questions are central to the process of designing the future of sea power.

⊢• INFORMATION AND LETHALITY

The response to the first query is that the key advances in cyber have given navies potential for sharing situational awareness and coordinating action to a degree never before envisioned. (See discussion by Friedman in this volume.) More than just cyberspace, cyber is a realm that encompasses overall notions of information flows and their management by means of control through feedback.

The former Chief of Naval Operations, Adm. John Richardson, grasped this concept well. His *Design for Maintaining Maritime Superiority, 2.0* depicts a "networked Navy" able, via swift information flows, to fight in decentralized unison, putting more units in action more often.[7] In this vision, Admiral Richardson sought to actualize "Metcalfe's law," which holds that the power of a network is the square of the number of interconnected nodes.[8] Dense, ubiquitous connectivity, resilient due to multiple redundancies, would not only be the foundation of the information systems design of the future fleet. It should also enable doctrinal innovation as well, perhaps along the lines of the "distributed lethality" idea that emerged as a concept in the mid-2010s.[9]

As to this lethality itself, the inherent information content of naval weaponry today reflects Mahan's point about having "powers to injure an enemy from a great distance," but not necessarily his injunction to devote most naval resources—material and human—to the offense. Indeed, the guidance package of many naval weapons has become so improved that the age-old link between range and accuracy has been decoupled. Naval warfare—other domains as well—can no longer be seen simply in terms of hurling mass and energy at the foe. Lethality is now heavily influenced by the added cyber variable of the information content of weapons. Those who would deny a fleet access to certain seas or littorals (think China) will also have cybered weapons with huge information content to use in defense and offense against the fleet and naval forces of other democratic nations. (See discussions by Ross and Warner, Demchak, and Kania in this volume.) Such systems also move swiftly and convey defensive advantages in denying the approaching fleet its aims, perhaps at hypersonic speeds.

Navies faced a similar problem in World War II when shore-based attack aircraft began to operate against fleets. The *Luftwaffe* inflicted severe damage on the Royal Navy during the campaign for Norway in 1940. But, as Bernard Brodie pointed out just a few years later, a future attacking fleet would still be able to approach a hostile coast from different directions to overcome enemy air defense by using its information advantage in selecting where to strike. A defender would always have to guard against the offense's multiple possible points of attack.[10]

⊢• EXPEDITIONARY WARFARE IN THE CYBER AGE

The foregoing implies a need for fleet designers to think in terms of how the traditional mission of landing expeditionary forces upon a hostile shore can be accomplished in the cyber age. Clearly, there will be a critical need to achieve an information advantage over the enemy with regard to the time and place of landing. In an age of ubiquitous sensors of wide variety, from undersea to orbit, preventing the foe from acquiring knowledge of the impending action via suppression of the opposing sensor arrays and their links to higher levels of command will prove daunting. The use of missiles and attack aircraft from the sea on the chosen landing point might simply tip off the enemy.

Thus, cultivating a capability for launching calibrated cyber attacks on enemy sensors and information systems very close to, perhaps even right at, the time of a landing may prove an essential part of future amphibious warfare. "Land-sea operations," to use Brodie's term, have always been an essential mission of navies and cannot be neglected in the future, even in the face of skillful opponents with smart weapons and sensors.[11] While offensive cyber capabilities will prove important to their future viability, it probably makes good sense to consider doctrinal adjustments as well. (See discussions by Brutzman and Kline, Cleary, and Dombrowski in this volume.)

For example, the model provided by the Allied amphibious invasions in North Africa and Europe during World War II and the Navy-Marine island-hopping campaign in the Pacific may be too large-scale. Such a pattern of landings today would be too big, too easy to detect, and too easily targeted and met with lethal response. Even successful disruptive cyber attacks might not prove enough to obscure such a landing. All of this means that, like any thorough design process, the future navy should take a systems-level approach to the amphibious mission.

If the increasingly smart weaponry of the cyber age is going to turn large forces into easy targets, perhaps a different concept of operations should be considered. That is, beyond the pure technological components of the design, a doctrinal element should be addressed as well. An interesting possibility might be glimpsed in the approach used by the Japanese in the Malayan campaign during World War II (December 1941–February 1942), which relied heavily on "infiltration and exploitation" by small, mobile forces.[12] In a little over two months, Japanese combat teams, often moving and landing by motorized barges, outdueled a force more than three times their size and compelled the largest surrender of troops (eighty thousand) in the history of the British Empire at the seemingly impregnable fortress of Singapore. The idea of conducting future amphibious operations consisting of many small units of action, striking simultaneously at a range of spots, might be just the solution for a cybered age, providing fresh energy for a naval mission whose obsolescence has been repeatedly—and wrongly—predicted time and again, from Gallipoli to Normandy, to Inchon and beyond.

⊢ COMPOSITION OF THE FLEET

There remains the matter of considering the implications of the cyber age for the broader composition of the fleet. Should carrier strike groups remain a central focus of sea power? What of submarines, including their role as part of the nuclear triad? Should a big bet be made on one type of major vessel and its supports? Can a "broad preparation" design do better?

Such questions should be pondered in the process of designing, or rather redesigning, the fleet for twenty-first-century operations. Such a fleet faces fresh technological challenges posed by cyber matters ranging from interconnectivity and networking to sensor ubiquity, and on to the information content of weapons. What should be done when the information content is so extensive in a weapon or platform that it may operate autonomously? As discussed in chapters by Falcone and Panter, Tangredi, and Pugh, this latter point also calls for close assessment in the design process.

With regard to naval airpower, these cyber challenges may mean designing future squadrons comprised of a mix of human-piloted planes, drones, and fully autonomous aircraft flying from carrier decks. Planes without pilots on board can be designed in a way that goes far beyond the tolerance of the human body, and robot aircraft maneuvers will outpace even what a human drone pilot can do. And in 2020 artificial intelligence (AI) took on an expert human pilot in simulated F-16 dogfights, winning all five encounters—what one report called "a landmark win for artificial intelligence in warfare."[13]

Robots, perhaps very tiny ones, may also prove essential to the defense of surface ships that come under multidirectional attack from swarms of kamikaze drones and hypersonic missiles. Indeed, it may become clear that only a counter-swarm can defeat a swarm. And having swarm tactics emerge in the naval doctrines of potential adversaries is not limited to the Russians and Chinese. The Iranians, for example, are pursuing swarming—what they call *esba* or "saturation" tactics—and they have become essential in their Great Prophet exercises: "While Iran's naval forces are dwarfed by the U.S. Navy, its commanders practice so-called 'swarm tactics' aimed at overwhelming the U.S. carriers that pass through the strait on their way in and out of the Persian Gulf."[14] Clearly, there is an important place for defensive AI swarms in the design of the future fleet.

As for aircraft carriers themselves, there remains the open question as to how long they will or should remain the capital ship of the U.S. Navy. Alternative ideas about how to distribute naval airpower widely—by having a variety of smaller carrier platforms—have been considered.[15] But this is an issue in which doctrinal aspects of design will likely prove useful and open up interesting alternatives.

For example, over the near term, advances in smart, swift naval weaponry will continue to emerge in rapid succession. However, changes in the composition and mix of ship types will move much more slowly. Thus, it might prove prudent to protect the large carriers by having them operate at a significant distance from the immediate vicinity of zones of armed conflict. This solution would be very much akin to the concept of operations employed by British Admiral Sandy Woodward in the South Atlantic War (1982), during which he kept his carriers well east of the Falklands, but still in range to wage, and ultimately win, the war in the air there.[16] This sort of precautionary approach could work well in, say, protecting Taiwan from a Chinese invasion. It would also allow implementation of the networked operations that Admiral Richardson envisioned, and those that Adm. Thomas Rowden developed in his conception of distributed lethality.

⊢• DOCTRINAL ADJUSTMENTS

During this period when doctrinal adjustment maintains existing capabilities and relies on the increased information content of weaponry to enhance the ability to—as Mahan describes—"injure an enemy from a great distance," it would be possible for the Navy to build toward a fleet comprised of "many and small" units of action—all networked to optimize their capacities. The same approach could be taken to developing a new paradigm for the future of expeditionary/amphibious operations as well.

Against the above courses of action, potential adversaries will have only "raider warfare" to fall back upon—at least in the near term. But this can be a dire threat in itself. Long-standing in Russian naval doctrine, their submarines today could still surge out to attack the highly vulnerable oil supertankers and more, to potentially devastating effect. As German Admiral Edward Wegener noted in his classic study of Soviet-era naval power, the key for the Russians would be to strike hard right from the outset. As Wegener described in the 1970s, "Shortly after the beginning of a war . . . the presence of all their available submarines at sea might bear fruit."[17]

Indeed, this threat should reinforce the importance of anti-submarine warfare capability as a prominent consideration in the future design of the fleet. It will not be enough to rely upon even the excellent capabilities of the suite of sensors that exist today under the rubric of "undersea surveillance"—the descendants of the pioneering sound surveillance system and the towed-array sensor system.[18]

The fleet will need to be able to detect, track, and strike swiftly at surging enemy submarines before they can inflict grievous damage. Dealing with this threat may entail the development and use of fully autonomous undersea craft and weapons that can deploy from surface vessels, aircraft, or submarines.

Another aspect of the submarine threat, the possibility of attacks aimed at disrupting the undersea cable networks, across which over 95 percent of international communications (some of them military) flow, should be anticipated in visions of future fleet design. (See discussion by Kavanagh and Leconte in this volume.) As Nicole Starosielski, a leading scholar of this system, has concluded, the undersea network is "precarious rather than resilient."[19]

Russian submarines, and the "research vessel" *Yantar*, have long shown interest in locating and patrolling near the cable lines, as have similar Chinese vessels more recently.[20] This is an additional threat from submarines—basically a dagger at the throat of global cyber connectivity—that should galvanize innovative thinking about the design of the fleet in its role as guardian of what, as noted above, Mahan called the "wide common, over which men may pass in all directions."[21]

↦ CODA: SAGE GUIDANCE FROM THE NAVY'S LATTER-DAY MAHAN, WAYNE HUGHES

In any design process, but especially one aimed at the crucially important realm of future military and security affairs in a cyber age replete with ever smarter, often autonomous weapons and systems, it is imperative to understand the state of play technologically. As this chapter has argued, this understanding extends to the matters of how cyber connectivity allows fleet networking and to tactical implications of the emergence and diffusion of weapons whose information content has grown immensely.

As in so many areas of naval affairs, the work of the late Wayne Hughes has much to say that speaks to the key factors that will shape the future of sea power in a cyber age. In the third edition of his classic *Fleet Tactics,* in which he was joined by Rear Adm. Robert Girrier, there are some profound insights that should help immeasurably as we contemplate the design of the future fleet. Four of the relevant trends that they glimpsed:

- The breadth and intricacy of sensor and communications networks and meshing technologies are growing at a very rapid pace.
- Weapon range and lethality have expanded the size of the no-man's land between fighting fleets. Small combatants, some unmanned, must occupy the intervening surface, and the importance of aerial and undersea vehicles has been promoted.
- Growth in weapon range and lethality has led to an increase in land-sea interactions. Naval battles increasingly include forces based ashore.
- There is a trend toward spreading forces out, while using command and control to concentrate firepower from dispersed formations and dispositions.[22]

These insights speak eloquently to the crucial importance of connectivity, how cyber, in its control-through-feedback manifestation, is radically improving the accuracy of weapons at ever greater ranges, and to the doctrinal implications of the tremendous spreading out of naval battlespaces.

The challenge of designing the future fleet for a cyber age is daunting. But we have enough good guidance to view what lies ahead with hope, even optimism.

NOTES

1. Both quotes from John Keegan, *The Price of Admiralty: The Evolution of Naval Warfare* (New York: Viking, 1989), 272.
2. Alfred Thayer Mahan, *The Influence of Sea Power upon History, 1660–1783* (Boston: Little, Brown, and Company, 1894), 25.
3. Mahan, 4.
4. Grand Admiral von Tirpitz, *My Memoirs,* vol. 1 (New York: Dodd, Mead and Company, 1919), 174, 177.
5. Von Tirpitz. See discussion on Tirpitz in John Arquilla, "A Study in Technology Strategy: The Curious Case of Alfred von Tirpitz," *Comparative Strategy* 36, no. 2 (2012): 143–52.

6. Creel's testimony is described in John Edward Wiltz, "The Nye Committee Revisited," *The Historian* 23, no. 2 (1961): 211–33.

7. Office of the Chief of Naval Operations, *Design for Maintaining Maritime Superiority, 2.0* (December 2018), https://media.defense.gov/2020/May/18/2002301999/-1/-1/1/DESIGN_2.0.PDF.

8. See Bob Metcalfe, "Metcalfe's Law after 40 Years of Ethernet," *Computer* 46, no. 12 (December 2013): 26–31, https://doi.org/10.1109/MC.2013.374.

9. On this doctrine, see Vice Admiral Thomas Rowden, "Distributed Lethality," U.S. Naval Institute *Proceedings* 141, no. 1 (January 2015): 18–23.

10. Bernard Brodie, *A Layman's Guide to Naval Strategy* (Princeton: Princeton University Press, 1944), especially 153–55.

11. Brodie, 148–50.

12. On this concept, see Allan Millett, "Assault from the Sea: The Development of Amphibious Warfare between the Wars," in *Military Innovation in the Interwar Period*, ed. Williamson Murray and Allan Millett (Cambridge: Cambridge University Press, 1998), 89. For a detailed account of the campaign, see James Leasor, *Singapore: The Battle that Changed the World* (Garden City, NY: Doubleday & Company, Inc., 1968).

13. Kyle Mizokami, "AI vs. Human Fighter Pilot: Here's Who Won the Epic Dogfight," *Popular Mechanics*, 25 August 2020, https://www.popularmechanics.com/military/aviation/a33765952/ai-vs-human-fighter-pilot-simulated-dogfight-results/.

14. See two articles in the *Associated Press* by Jon Gambrell: "Amid U.S. Tension, Iran Builds Fake Aircraft Carrier to Attack," 10 June 2020, https://www.ksat.com/news/2020/06/09/amid-us-tension-iran-builds-fake-aircraft-carrier-to-attack/; and "Iran Missiles Target Fake Carrier, U.S. Bases on Alert," 29 July 2020, https://apnews.com/article/strait-of-hormuz-dubai-ap-top-news-iran-united-arab-emirates-b931ea8d6751c953233665202a59e5e1.

15. Wayne Hughes, "Restore a Distributable Naval Air Force," U.S. Naval Institute *Proceedings* 145, no. 4 (April 2019): 24–27.

16. See Admiral Woodward's thoughtful account of this war, *One Hundred Days: The Memoirs of the Falklands Battle Group Commander* (New York: Harper, 1992, rev. ed. 2012). See also Jeffrey Ethell and Alfred Price, *Air War South Atlantic* (New York: Scribner, 1984).

17. Edward Wegener, *The Soviet Naval Offensive* (Annapolis, MD: Naval Institute Press, 1975), 69.

18. On the heyday of the sound surveillance system, see Edward Whitman, "SOSUS: The Secret Weapon of Undersea Surveillance," *Undersea Warfare* 7, no. 2 (Winter 2005), https://www.public.navy.mil/subfor/underseawarfaremagazine/Issues/Archives/issue_25/sosus.htm.

19. Nicole Starosielski, *The Undersea Network* (London: Duke University Press, 2015), 10.

20. See, for example, David Sanger and Eric Schmitt, "Russian Ships Near Data Cables Are Too Close for U.S. Comfort," *New York Times*, 26 October 2015, https://www.nytimes.com/2015/10/26/world/europe/russian-presence-near -undersea-cables-concerns-us.html. See also Brendan Cole and John Feng, "Chinese Ship Suspected of Undersea Cable Sabotage Detained in 'NATO Lake,'" *Newsweek*, 20 November 2024.

21. Mahan, 25.

22. From Captain Wayne P. Hughes Jr., USN (Ret.), and Rear Admiral Robert P. Girrier, USN (Ret.), *Fleet Tactics and Naval Operations*, 3rd ed. (Annapolis, MD: Naval Institute Press, 2018), 211. The bulleted points are all direct quotes from their text.

28 Network-Optional Warfare and Data-Centric Security

DON BRUTZMAN and JEFF KLINE

Despite common current practice, naval forces do not have to engage in constant, centralized communication. Deployed naval vessels have demonstrated independence of action in stealthy, coordinated operations for hundreds of years.

However, since the 1990s, the U.S. fleet has been designed with the assumption that constant digital connectivity can and must be maintained by warships in order to conduct successful combat operations. In part, this assumption is the result of practical adoption of the concept of network-centric warfare (NCW) during an era in which digital technology proliferated and competent enemies shrank.[1] The NCW approach to combat has proven highly successful—when the United States and allies have faced less technologically capable opponents who were not able to effectively attack the allied digital nodes necessary for command and control.

Unfortunately, the assumption that connectivity can be maintained when facing near-peer opponents is a premise that can easily result in defeat. Such threats to connectivity are demonstrated continuously in the ongoing conflict within the cyber domain. Like naval operations against a technologically capable opponent, connectivity in cyberspace is always under threat and therefore provides a useful analogy for understanding how to fight in an "electromagnetic night."

⊢• DEVELOPMENT OF A NETWORK-OPTIONAL WARFARE CONCEPT

Perceived dependencies to maintain NCW connectivity—throughout the fleet, from fleet to shore commands, and within the joint force—continue to dominate planned fleet operational strategies and cyber activities. Corresponding vulnerabilities can be catastrophic for individual ships, battle groups, and fleet operations. The term "network-optional warfare" (NOW)—coined by the late Capt. Wayne P. Hughes Jr., USN—intentionally contrasts with fleet information architectures that are based solely on network-centric warfare. The goal of NOW is to mitigate the risk of these connectivity dependencies, because the limitations of continuous communications are simply becoming too great a vulnerability in the face of emerging threats from modern-day opponents in harsh, unforgiving environments.[2]

From this perspective, stealth is a fundamental game changer for sustained forward presence and reduced operational vulnerability to attack. NOW capabilities to reduce fleet vulnerabilities include emissions control (EMCON), optical signaling, concise messaging, data-centric security, and semantic coherence. NOW can also be the anchor for a comprehensive data strategy for autonomous systems and their ethical control by human warfighters. Each of these areas of endeavor applies information science principles to achieve deliberate, stealthy, and minimalist tactical communications.

Impressive advances in robotics have been made in tandem with the development of cyberspace. NOW approaches are necessary for hybrid human and robotic naval forces to overcome vulnerabilities from conducting constant communications, which can result in lack of stealth and dependence on continuous data exchange. Agile "radio silence" EMCON and judicious use of low probability of intercept communications can restore naval covertness and tactical surprise. (See related discussion by Pugh in this volume.) Data-centric security makes deployed naval robots and remote sensors more secure.

⊢• INEVITABILITY OF FIGHTING IN ELECTROMAGNETIC NIGHT

To understand the need for NOW, one must grasp that high-technology warfighting will be dominated by periods of "electromagnetic night" in which the digital transfer of information will be significantly disrupted. In fact, such a period might last for an entire war. It does not necessarily mean that all connectivity is lost with no data communicated, but it does mean that data transfer will be limited. NOW is an approach for operating naval forces under conditions of limited communications and limited data exchange.

NOW is particularly needed as the U.S. Navy and allies move toward developing an increasing range of robotic systems that need command and control by humans. It is the policy of the United States that lethal force can only be applied under direct human control.[3] (See related chapter by Higson and Passerello in this volume.) Under conditions of limited or no communications, it is not reasonable to think that hundreds or thousands of robotic systems can operate under direct networked control with humans in every loop. Different approaches to network security, information assurance, and operational control are necessary for effective integration of human-supervised semi-autonomous robotic systems into naval operations.

This electromagnetic night has been studied in a series of Naval Postgraduate School campaign analyses, capstone projects, and war games conducted by mid-grade officers since 2005. This research has identified several major warfighting impacts related to the trends of greater ranges and speeds of missiles, and in use of uncrewed systems in maritime warfare. The confluence of these two trends enables long-range scouting with multiple sensors in all domains (from outer space to the sea floor), but also increases the vulnerability of large naval formations to attack beyond their response range. Communications transmissions increase platform detectability, resulting in significant vulnerabilities.

Unfortunately these disadvantages are not always prominently considered in concepts like the U.S. Navy's distributed maritime operations and the U.S. Marine Corps' expeditionary advanced base operations, which offer alternatives to traditional carrier-centric task force and amphibious group warfighting operations. When leveraging new technologies, alternative naval force designs can replace a portion of the large-ship platform-centric fleet with systems of human-robot platforms in the air, on the sea, and ashore.[4] (See also chapters by Cleary and Tangredi in this volume.) Such systems might deploy as local reconnaissance strike networks to deny sea access in littoral regions.[5] They might be designed to act independently by providing their own scouting, targeting, command and control, and strike capabilities when long-range communications are not available. If carefully employed, new concepts for force design remove the total dependence on a theater-wide network to provide warfighting capabilities inside contested regions.[6] In other words, hybrid human-robot systems can operate stealthily using NOW.

Two factors make NOW critically important. The first is an adversary's ability to focus both kinetic and non-kinetic weapons against a wide area network while denying local regions remote access to space systems communications. The second is an adversary's ability to locate and target ships and expeditionary units that actively radiate radar or transmit electronic signals. These factors place large networks at risk and may even inspire individual units in that network to *not* contribute to the network's information. Instead, local unit commanders must attempt to operate in total restricted emissions control in order to remain untargeted.

These factors exist for the adversary as well. As a result, future naval battles may be decided by who best fights in this electromagnetic night, where all active electromagnetic transmissions are minimized for survival and both sides employ advanced passive sensors, visual and physical deception and decoys, masking techniques, and off-axis active uncrewed sensors. This dynamic provides motivation to develop technologies (or rediscover proven methods) for covert line-of-sight communications, especially those that enable littoral forces to provide their own targeting and strike. These combined technologies, methods, tactics, and future fleet designs form the foundation for developing the concept of NOW as a complementary alternative to network-centric warfare.

⊢• NAVAL COMMUNICATION AND NOW

While developing robotic systems, the U.S. Navy must recognize that deployment of uncrewed systems and remote sensors across the world's oceans is not likely to enjoy secure network connections everywhere. Operators need to be able to launch robotic systems in communications-contested environments with confidence that they can operate as intended, without needing constant communications that reveal critical information about friendly forces.

Communications networks for the ocean environment vary significantly from land-based communications systems, and tactical employment of communications channels afloat is inherently complex. Communications throughput varies with distance, time of day effects, and both daily and seasonal weather effects, as well as whether they are submerged, near-surface, atmospheric without high-power ground stations, or vertical to high-altitude or orbital craft. Transmission ranges may be far shorter or far longer than desired. Meanwhile passively receiving networked communications from sources ashore and aloft is often far simpler and less detectable than sending messages to recipients. Avoiding unnecessary network transmissions is the heart of EMCON policies and removes most long-range detection vulnerabilities. Mission durations and message delays of minutes, hours, days, weeks, and sometimes even months may be acceptable if necessary. Deliberate planning as to when messages deserve to be sent is important and embedded in NOW design principles. In any case, always-on centralized communications cannot provide sustainable wide network coordination when Mother Nature and opponents can each thwart communications. (See the environmental challenges in chapter by Falcone and Panter in this volume.) Decentralized and undetected operations are less prone to opponent denial.

In earlier days of limited communications, independent command authority was a core characteristic of naval warfighting. This is still the norm in the submarine force, where outbound communications are rare. Passive reception of data communications is always allowed since data capture does not reveal a passive listening platform's presence. Active transmission of data communications by submarines is rare, with total EMCON the norm to maintain stealth. Under these circumstances, mission capabilities nevertheless remain potent. Deployed units are not dependent on constant communications that can be disrupted by adversaries and largely remain in control of their own operations.

A Naval Postgraduate School thesis investigated the broad feasibility of total radio-frequency (RF) EMCON for expeditionary advanced base operations.[7]

Key aspects of signaling and messaging were considered for coordinated operations in order to identify gaps and dependencies. Careful analysis revealed no major obstacles to successful operations under RF EMCON conditions, consistent with a NOW approach. Supporting forces to amphibious operations must also observe RF EMCON, since an expeditionary landing force following RF EMCON cannot remain covert if supporting ships are not.

Optical communications are also suitable for many tasks in NOW. Laser signaling requires extremely precise two-way tracking and directional pointing between end points, while optical light signaling does not. Significant differences between EMCON policies for each service also need to be coordinated in advance for NOW; otherwise, joint forces cannot achieve consistent levels of covertness.

The application of NOW principles to operational units requires a considerable degree of data security for the data that is available, particularly in the operation of robotic systems. Data-transmission links to robots operating at extended ranges are rare and limited, since they make forces afloat more vulnerable. Decoupling secure data from networks can help.

⊢• DATA-CENTRIC SECURITY WITHIN NOW

The implications of a data-centric approach are broad as increasingly capable robots and mobile sensors complement human-driven forces. In essence, *artificial intelligence (AI) turns data into information for humans.* However sophisticated, AI software does not replace human responsibility. Conversely, *repeatable AI requires repeatable data.* If real-world data cannot be consistently recorded and shared for comparison and analysis, sustained improvement is not possible.

Data-centric security offers a different set of network options for future naval communications. The initial insight is that relevant information collected and processed by a robot can be immediately encrypted without needing onboard decryption capabilities. Such data can be stored for long durations or passed over arbitrary (possibly nonsecure) networks without fear of compromise, since decryption is only possible for the originating ship's force personnel. Practical approaches exist today that leverage existing policies, infrastructure, and control by already-qualified personnel, using common access cards or similar security tokens. This is especially important as fleet force design undergoes the major refactoring needed to shift many tasks and roles from human-driven platforms toward human-supervised autonomous systems.

Data compression using a coherently defined signal book, applied compatibly with identity-based authentication and limited decryption of encrypted data, enables efficient messaging. Strong protections for tactical data, across network-centric and network-optional operations, benefit remote command authority and operational freedom of action. Utilizing the understanding of all trusted personnel within an already-existing security infrastructure can make data communications with any robotic system as trusted as any secure email. Because this approach is simple to achieve and costly to thwart, data-centric security provides an asymmetric advantage. Such repeatable capabilities are possible today and are likely necessary for sustained secure operations by naval robots and mobile sensors.

⊢• DATA-CENTRIC FOCUS INTEGRATES TECHNICAL STRENGTHS

While most communications efforts are concerned with channels and network protocols, what needs to be exchanged during operations is the shared information of timely, relevant interest. Taking a data-centric focus involves data models, compression, and concise messaging prior to adding security wrappers.

For example, much work has shown that carefully specified data models enable strict validation of data. Data models define formal structures for information, enabling common processing by diverse software platforms. Data models define a controlled vocabulary of terms with specific data types (string, integer, floating-point array, etc.) that can be immediately checked for correctness by a wide variety of tools. Data models also define the *meaning* of each term—the semantics of each information item. Valid data syntax is essential—handling garbles or incorrect representations requires significant additional source code and can cause unexpected, unrecoverable problems. Valid data syntax means that interoperability is possible for collectors, processors, analysis tools, and archival reuse—that is, data of interest can be shared.

Beyond good data models, incorporating NOW requires data compression and efficient messaging.[8] Compression is an essential capability for recorded data because afloat networks are typically bandwidth-constrained and require precious, potentially contested resources. Potential benefits include

- greater throughput in limited-bandwidth channels
- smaller size to reduce transmission exposure
- greater capacity for power-constrained uncrewed systems, leading to longer endurance.

Unfortunately, most naval data is not compressed efficiently, treating all data as plain-text strings that have little redundancy for compressibility—for example, equivalent "0" and "0.0" and "+0.00000" strings are handled differently and inefficiently. Numeric compression is far more efficient, and tokenized strings matching a controlled vocabulary are even further compressible. With a structured data model applied, recorded data can be carefully compressed.

Of further interest for use by robots and uncrewed systems is that decompression performance is far more efficient because decompressed results go straight into memory, rather than requiring a second pass of computationally expensive string parsing to extract numeric data. Given that reduced computational cost results in reduced energy expenditure, significant operational duration improvements for remote systems appear possible.

Another path is through the use of asymmetric encryption and authentication, adapting the existing defense infrastructure for key distribution and identity-verification procedures to also support robotic systems. When pursuing asymmetric data security despite network weaknesses, robotic systems can be treated differently. For example, mobile robots and remote sensors are each simultaneously "data in motion" from an external perspective, and "data at rest" from an internal perspective. For example, a robot "data mule" sent from ship to shore effectively transports data without any network protocol. Common sensing/scouting roles collect sensitive information that holds interest to other external entities, but not necessarily the robot itself. This implies that a robot sensor can first collect, then process and classify, then encrypt data "at birth" for secure storage. Again, there is no need for the remote system to decrypt previous data. Data-centric security reduces vulnerability of tactical information to capture and exploitation.

⊢• THE FUTURE FIGHT

Fighting in the electromagnetic night must be expected. It is possible to build the "fires" network from bottom-up, not network centric–out. Data-centric security for robots allows ships to adopt a partitioned cellular warfare concept for sea—network-enabled and network-optional, not network-dependent. Figure 28-1 illustrates such points by updating a classic naval scouting mission.

In "network-centric" warfare, the network becomes a capital ship and target of adversary action. Such a single-point-failure vulnerability is unacceptable

---

Scenario: Robot scouts are patrolling the outer perimeter of a ship's operating area, over the horizon, without direct communications. Each robot is instructed to use passive long-range sensors for maximum covertness.

- One robot scout detects an opponent platform, confirms classification, then tracks and follows the opponent.
- Current rules of engagement prioritize maintaining contact and preserving stealth unless hostile actions are detected.
- Robot senses opponent preparations for weapons launch, confirming hostile intent.
- Alert message sent to overhead asset using low-bandwidth optical data bits, with receipt confirmation not possible for the given communications channel.
- Robot returns to planned rendezvous area with parent ship, but no receiving platform found for relaying the message further.
- Robot instead heads toward shore; once nearby, penetrates hostile cellphone or Wi-Fi network, then resends the crucial contact report. Data is signed, compressed, encrypted.
- Shore facility receives time-critical message over open internet; in turn uses broadcast for relaying encrypted (or decrypted) data to original ship (which is still at covert location)
- Robot splashes/crashes and self-destructs, accomplishing mission using data-centric security without compromising human forces.
- Data-centric security data store on robot remains unexploitable even if onboard computer is compromised.

FIGURE 28-1. Tactical Use Case: Robot Scout Communications Resilience

and unnecessary. Who fights best in the electromagnetic night? Removing network dependence or, better yet, giving warfighters new options for when to use the network is powerful. Data-centric security for NOW can enable robots and sensor systems to operate in a complementary manner that strengthens current naval cyber warfare practices.

NOTES

1. Network-centric warfare is originally described in Arthur K. Cebrowski and John H. Garstka, "Network-Centric Warfare—Its Origin and Future," U.S. Naval Institute *Proceedings* 124, no. 1 (January 1998): 28–35, https://www.usni.org/magazines/proceedings/1998/january/network-centric-warfare-its-origin-and-future.

2. The network-optional warfare website includes numerous research products. Donald P. Brutzman, Network-Optional Warfare (NOW) website, Naval Postgraduate School, https://nps.edu/web/now.

3. Kathleen H. Hicks, "Autonomy in Weapon Systems," Department of Defense Directive 3009.09, 25 January 2023, https://www.esd.whs.mil/portals/54/documents/dd/issuances/dodd/300009p.pdf.

4. The concept of a bimodal fleet, one with both traditional multi-mission ships and smaller, numerous platforms to operate in high-risk environments was proposed by Wayne Hughes in 2007. Since then, this design concept has matured from numerous analyses reflected in a series of journal publications. See Wayne P. Hughes Jr., "A Bimodal Force for the National Maritime Strategy," *Naval War College Review* 60, no. 2 (Spring 2007): 29–48, https://digital-commons.usnwc.edu/nwc-review/vol60/iss2/5; James Wirtz, Jeffrey Kline, Phillip Pournelle, and Mie Augier, "The Maritime Strategic Imperative," *The RUSI Journal* 166, no. 3 (2021): 34–44; Jeffrey Kline, James A. Russell, and James J. Wirtz, "The U.S. Navy's Generational Challenge," *Survival: Global Politics and Strategy* 64, no. 4 (August-September 2022), https://www.tandfonline.com/doi/full/10.1080/00396338.2022.2103264; and James Wirtz, "Unmanned Ships and the Future of Deterrence," U.S. Naval Institute *Proceedings* 147, no. 7 (July 2021), https://www.usni.org/magazines/proceedings/2021/july/unmanned-ships-and-future-deterrence.

5. Alexander Bordetsky, Stephen Benson, and Wayne P. Hughes Jr., "Hiding Comms in Plain Sight: Mesh Networking Effects Can Conceal C2 Efforts in Congested Littoral Environments," *Signals Magazine* (June 2016): 42–44.

6. Jeffrey E. Kline, "Impacts of the Robotics Age on Naval Force Design, Effectiveness, and Acquisition," *Naval War College Review* 70, no. 3 (Summer 2017): 63–78, https://digital-commons.usnwc.edu/nwc-review/vol70/iss3/5/.

7. Matthew J. Simard, "Muted Messaging: Achieving Total Radio Frequency (RF) Emissions Control (EMCON) for Expeditionary Operations in a Contested Battlespace," master's thesis, Naval Postgraduate School, June 2023.

8. Steven Debich, Bruce Hill, Scot Miller, and Don Brutzman, "Being Efficient with Bandwidth," U.S. Naval Institute *Proceedings* 140, no. 7 (July 2014): 76–78, https://www.usni.org/magazines/proceedings/2014/july/professional-notes.

29 Off-Net Cyber

Navigating the Next Naval Revolution

CHRIS CLEARY

The next fight against a future adversary will be like no other prior conflict. The use of non-kinetic effects and defense against those effects prior to and during kinetic exchanges will be the deciding factor in who prevails.

The Navy and Marine Corps have provided sustained forward presence and expeditionary capabilities for centuries. In addition to the naval cyber forces already provided to U.S. Cyber Command, the Department of the Navy should expand its role in expeditionary cyberspace operations that require execution at physical proximity to adversary networks. (See discussion by Bebber and White in this volume.) In this way, the naval services can leverage their foundational competency of providing forward presence to apply it to joint cyberspace operations. For cyber warfare to become a core competency, it must be woven into our most enduring missions—not merely exist alongside them.

If we compare today's ongoing "cyber revolution" to the nuclear revolution, it is still 1950. The tools of cyber warfare, the balance between attacker and defender, the respective roles of the military services, and the theoretical frameworks beneath it all remain in flux. The most recent addition to the mix, generative artificial intelligence, promises to upend even those few delicate concepts of operation the U.S. military has developed in the first two decades of the twenty-first century.[1]

Large questions remain under debate, especially for the Navy. First, is cyber a warfighting domain? Second, does the Navy have a unique strategic role in cyberspace compared to the other services? Third, if it does, what principles should guide the Navy's conduct in this domain at the operational level of war? This chapter addresses those questions in order. The first part suggests how the Navy should understand cyber as inherent to its posture and strategic outlook. Building off this foundation, the second part introduces "off-net cyber": a principle to guide the Navy's preparation for, and conduct of, offensive cyber warfare. The final section offers recommendations to make off-net cyber a reality.

⊢• IS CYBER A WARFIGHTING DOMAIN?

Answering "yes" to this question was not always a foregone conclusion. The current model, wherein cyber capabilities are provided to each of the combatant commands via the services, rather than organic to them, has inhibited the development of a Navy-specific approach to this domain.[2] The consequences of cyber operations, however, can be just as impactful as traditional military actions, with potential effects on economic stability, national security, and even civilian well-being. Traditional military domains—land, sea, air, and space—have now extended into the vast and intricate realm of cyberspace.

Cyber warfare involves the use of digital tools and technologies to compromise, disrupt, or destroy information systems, networks, and infrastructure found in, and critical to, those traditional military domains. This form of the fight can range from sophisticated nation-state attacks targeting critical infrastructure to subversive activities conducted by non-state actors. In contemporary conflicts, the battles fought in this digital domain can prove as crucial as those in physical spaces.

Yes, cyber is unequivocally a warfighting domain, marking a paradigm shift in the nature of warfare. Governments worldwide recognize the significance of cyber capabilities and invest heavily in developing offensive and defensive strategies. (See elaborating strategic cybered conflict discussions in this volume by Dombrowski and Friedman, respectively.) Cyber operations can be used independently or as force multipliers with traditional military actions. As such, the integration of cyber capabilities into military doctrines underscores the acknowledgment that cyberspace is a warfighting domain where strategic objectives are pursued and defended.

⊢• WHAT IS THE NAVY'S UNIQUE STRATEGIC ROLE?

Integrating cyber warfare as a "core competency" alongside aviation, surface, and undersea warfare within the Navy signifies the acknowledgment of the changing landscape of conflicts. Modern warfare demands a blend of kinetic and non-kinetic effects, where cyber capabilities play a pivotal role (as argued by multiple authors in this volume including Bebber and White, and Kuo and Lindsay). By treating cyber as a core competency, the Navy aligns itself strategically with the evolving nature of warfare.

The Navy's historical expertise in sustained forward presence and expeditionary capabilities becomes an asset available for the cybered fight. Cyber forces can extend the Navy's reach by engaging from forward locations in expeditionary cyberspace operations, leveraging physical proximity to adversary networks. This reflects the Navy's traditional and uniquely strategic outlook.

Furthermore, cyber's inclusion as a core competency enhances the Navy's ability to project power and defend in cyberspace itself. This, in turn, contributes to the overall deterrence posture, dissuading potential adversaries through a holistic approach, creating a truly comprehensive defense strategy (a "collective systemic resilience" as argued by Demchak in this volume). The seamless integration of cyber with traditional naval warfare domains better positions the service to use and then adapt to future threats that are even more deeply digitized, such as robotics and autonomous weapons.[3]

⊢• NAVAL CYBER PRINCIPLE FOR OPERATIONAL LEVEL OF WAR: DEVELOP OFF-NET CYBER

In future conflicts among peers and near-peers, network disruptions are inevitable. A forward positioned Navy fully integrating cyber will have strategically invested in "off-net" cyber capabilities to ensure operational resilience. The key to off-net cyber is the organic generation of access and effects within naval platforms able to successfully conduct cyber operations even in denied, degraded, intermittent, and limited environments.[4]

This proactive principle for the operational level of war ensures the investment in naval forces' capabilities to agilely manipulate the cyber environment through the electromagnetic spectrum even when traditional network connectivity is compromised or unavailable (as discussed by Brutzman and Kline in this volume). Moreover, these investments position the Navy to overcome challenges associated with disrupted communications and networks coming from more traditional environmental or military sources. Adept off-net cyber ensures sustained operational connectivity among local units as well.

⊢ A THEORY OF THE FIGHT: OPERATING "ON THE EDGE" WITH OFF-NET CYBER

There is much the U.S. Navy can do to shape the use of cyber for a maritime conflict, but it must first appreciate how cyber warfare differs in a contested sea environment compared to a land environment. The Navy has a particular strategic outlook whose orientation resonates well with concepts of maneuver in cyberspace. Warfare in all domains is characterized by a forward "edge"—defined here as the limits of a force's ability to achieve its intended aims—whether those aims are delivering fires, demonstrating national resolve, conducting military operations other than war, or others.[5] In naval warfare, this edge has progressively expanded with technological progress since the age of sail. Previously, for instance—before the availability of resupply at sea—the Navy's strategic and operational edges were determined by the availability of friendly ports of call for sailors' sustenance, or by the amount of food a ship could carry on board, or by the crew's ability to follow rationing. Tactical edges, too, existed: in the age of naval gunfire, there were limits on how far a ship could lob a shell.

Technological innovation has continued to expand these edges, although more so in the realm of tactics and operations than strategic reach. (See discussion by Sandhoo in this volume.) Steam, for example, provided previously unimaginable speed and liberated ships from the winds (although it introduced a new operational edge, the availability of coaling stations). Another example, the ship-launched cruise missile, permitted ships to engage targets over the horizon. Strategic reach, on the other hand, has traditionally been expansive—the Navy can reach most nations (and all other navies) via the sea—and then limited thenceforth by an asset's maximum endurance on station, the quality of its weapons, the proficiency of its crew, and other factors.

For a brief period in the 1990s, with the advent of networks and the internet, the outer edges—or strategic and operational bounds of U.S. sea power—appeared greater than ever before.[6] Forces in theater could be supplied with instant communications, and with information from the entire battle force, via internet technology. Meanwhile, inorganic cyber forces, operating from the homeland and supporting the deployed fleet, could extend the fleet's range nearly limitlessly—potentially delivering cyber attacks on any target with an internet connection far inland.

This largely uncontested era was short-lived. The adversary caught up; the internet became a double-edged sword. The Navy soon realized that future naval operations would be defined by contested communications and networks. The "edge" was once again constrained. There would be no guarantee that the inorganic data an individual unit, or a strike group, had come to rely upon would be forthcoming, nor that command and control and other functions, especially those beyond line of sight—from the homeland or maritime operational centers in theater—would be available when needed.

But this "denied, degraded, intermittent, and limited" warfighting environment of the future, in a way, is not far removed from how the Navy has always fought. The maritime domain shares much in common with the cyber domain. (See discussion by Tangredi in this volume.) Today's world, for instance, is fully connected, even "hyper-connected" across people, organizations, nations, and technology. One can hardly go anywhere without a mobile device or terrestrial infrastructure built to support a mobile device. Cyberspace operators know this; for the most sophisticated ones, the whole planet is their "edge" of operations. Those operating in cyberspace can reach anyone but can be reached by anyone in return.

So, too, are ships and submarines at sea always operating on the edge. They can, and have been expected to, fight anywhere. Concepts like rear-area, forward line of own troops, forward edge of the battle area, and bastion are equally porous at sea as they are at the edge in cyberspace. Long before computers and the internet existed, the Navy's efficacy depended on its ability to sustain without logistical support, deliver effects without information from back home, and stand ready to meet the enemy at any moment (even en route to the perceived "front"). The seas have been the source of international connectivity, civilian and military, for millennia; a force that operated in this fluid medium had access to nearly anyone and could itself be accessed by its enemies.

The Navy now faces a world in which the expanded edge it expected from cyberspace suddenly became a risk and a constraint, but it can reach to its own history for the solution. The key was, and is now, about maintaining the edge by means that are organic to the force: building resilience in an environment assumed to have no strategic connection. (See discussion of resilience by Ross and Warner in this volume.) The emphasis must be preserving operational connectivity—that between local units in-theater—and restoring it to basic functionality if disrupted. Failing that, the emphasis must be on finding ways to deliver cyber effects even in the absence of any external connectivity at all.

Enter off-net cyber as integrated component of Navy maneuver and fires fighting at the edge in the twenty-first century. Off-net cyber operations occur at the intersection of military maneuver forces and operations, absent the requirement for remote access (i.e., on-net operations). Given the expected denied, degraded, intermittent, and limited operations environment naval forces anticipate in present and future conflicts, naval forces will need to generate access and effects organically from within naval platforms and combat systems. The ultimate objective of off-net cyber is to enable further-on conventional movement and maneuver, as well as remote cyber operations (whether exploit or attack). This includes, critically, efforts to manipulate the cyber environment via the electromagnetic spectrum when network connectivity is unavailable or denied. Ships can remain on station, where they need to be to achieve effects.

Despite the appearance that cyber reaches everywhere on the globe, physical presence remains at the heart of the very purpose of navies, and indeed that of ground and air forces as well.[7] If the Navy's objective is, for instance, maritime domain awareness, it is certainly possible to collect, collate, analyze, and create a common operational picture on shore, but the data must come from somewhere: the sensors of ships physically on-station. Off-net cyber is a means of ensuring that, assuming the disruption of strategic communications, the Navy retains the ability to execute modern warfare: that it retains the "edge" provided by all previous advances in naval technology, from computerized monitoring of hull, mechanical, and electrical systems, to global positioning system–dependent land-attack missiles.

Importantly, off-net cyber is not the ability to fight without a network. It is the ability to air-gap one's network and fight even though it may be compromised from when it was online previously (due to remote code execution). The naval force can fight hurt, but with the network (versus fight hurt without the network, as suggested by Brutzman and Kline in this volume). It can deliver kinetic fires by maintaining some operability in the naval force's positioning, navigation, and timing, targeting, local intranets, and so on. With off-net cyber, the force can deliver "cyber fires" by having personnel organic to the ship/submarine who know how to exploit undersea cables, board and reverse-engineer adversary unmanned capabilities/buoys/captured assets, jam communications, or intermittently get online to deliver cyber fires or pass requests for supporting cyber fires to national-/fleet-level authorities or local friendly forces.

In an environment likely to be cluttered with small adversarial unmanned assets intended to complicate our targeting problem, the need is for personnel on board the forward forces with the expertise to tell us which of those to target (based on, say, known command and control parameters of the adversary's uncrewed vessels fleet) to maximize operational gain from each round we expend.

The ultimate objective is a perspective shift: any naval asset operating in the maritime domain—for the reasons described above—is a cyberspace fires platform at the edge. All platforms, aviation, surface, and subsurface, must come ready to check on station (secure), generate targets and fires (strike), and fight hurt (survive).

Investing in off-net cyber for naval forces is an acceptance of what already is and what is coming. The globe is fully connected if not hyper-connected across people, organizations, nations, and technology. The Navy and its operations in the maritime domain have more in common with cyberspace than anyone or anything. There is no living off the land (sustainment/logistics) at sea;

concepts like rear-area, forward line of own troops/forward edge of the battle area, and bastion are as porous at sea as they are at the edge in cyberspace.

Consequently, by definition, everywhere a naval platform or expeditionary maneuver element is operating, they are operating at the edge, and they need to be able to conduct off-net operations in order to survive and succeed.

NOTES

1. Department of the Navy officials thus far see generative artificial intelligence as a security risk. See Department of the Navy Chief Information Officer, *DON Guidance on the Use of Generative Artificial Intelligence and Large Language Models*, 6 September 2023, https://www.doncio.navy.mil/ContentView.aspx?id=16442; Kirsten Errik, "Navy Discourages Military Generative AI, LLM Usage," *Federal News Network*, 10 October 2023, https://federalnewsnetwork.com/artificial-intelligence/2023/10/navy-discourages-military-generative-ai-llm-usage/.

2. Tyson B. Meadors, "Cyber Warfare Is a Navy Mission," U.S. Naval Institute *Proceedings* 148, no. 9 (September 2022): 68–73, https://www.usni.org/magazines/proceedings/2022/september/cyber-warfare-navy-mission.

3. See discussion on autonomous weapons in George Galdorisi and Sam J. Tangredi, *Algorithms of Armageddon: The Impact of Artificial Intelligence* (Annapolis, MD: Naval Institute Press, 2024), 74–82.

4. An excellent study of critical communication links that emerge in environments of denied, degraded, intermittent or limited communication is Mark E. Nissen and Shelley P. Gallup, *Art and Science of JADC2 Conceptualization from a Navy Perspective*, NPS-22-N184-A (Monterey, CA: Naval Postgraduate School, December 2022).

5. Cheryl Pellerin, "DoD Extends Technological, Operational Edge into the Future," *DoD News Features*, 14 December 2015, https://www.defense.gov/News/News-Stories/Article/Article/634115/dod-extends-technological-operational-edge-into-the-future/.

6. See discussion in Sam J. Tangredi, "Beyond the Sea and Jointness," in *The U.S. Naval Institute on Naval Strategy*, ed. Thomas J. Cutler (Annapolis, MD: Naval Institute Press, 2015), 141–50.

7. See Sam J. Tangredi, "The Fall and Rise of Naval Forward Presence," U.S. Naval Institute *Proceedings* 126, no. 5 (May 2000): 28–32, https://www.usni.org/magazines/proceedings/2000/may/fall-and-rise-naval-forward-presence.

30 New Theory of Navies

Maritime, Air, Space, and Cyber

SAM J. TANGREDI

I n 2018 the U.S. Department of Defense finally concluded that the U.S. Cyber Command was a navy. In that year, the *Department of Defense Cyber Strategy* shifted the focus of U.S. Cyber Command from land-centric concepts of warfare to the operational concepts of *defend forward* and *persistent engagement*. Both concepts mirror the U.S. naval missions of forward deployment and naval presence—which, since the 1980s, have usually been combined under the term *forward presence*.

This is not mere similarity or happenstance. Cyberspace is a fluid medium more similar to an ocean than to a fixed plot of land. Computers may sit in particular locations, but digital signals flow. For military forces to operate effectively in oceans requires the adoption of concepts derived from naval operations as long conducted by the U.S. Navy and Marine Corps. Basic strategic principles applicable to naval warfare differ greatly from those appropriate for land combat. The tenets of Alfred Thayer Mahan and Julian Corbett rule in cyberspace, not those of Carl von Clausewitz and Baron de Jomini.

⊢• WHAT IS A NAVY?

Navies are those military forces that operate in the fluid mediums—domains, if it is necessary to use that politically loaded Department of Defense term—that humans use for commerce, communications, and transportation, but cannot or do not normally inhabit.[1] These include oceans, air, space, and cyber. Due to length and scope limitations, this chapter will only discuss ocean-going and cyber forces in detail.

At the most basic level, navies and armies are fundamentally different instruments of power.[2] The evolutions of their employment in war and peace are unique in themselves. The primary purpose of an army is to defeat an enemy's military forces, conquer its territory, and garrison its state in preparation for the postwar denouement.

The purpose of navies (which also include major components of air forces and space and cyber forces) is to access (and, in wartime, control) the global commons and deliver access to the enemy's territory for land forces to wage a decisive campaign. Navies also provide kinetic and non-kinetic fires against the opposing armed forces, fires that can reach into the enemy's territory or external territory under the enemy's control.

It is possible for navies to "win" a war without the resort to land forces, but that is circumstantial and depends on the enemy's objectives, calculation of risks and outcomes, and willingness to accept (at least temporarily) a "defeat." Navies are not wet armies.

For the United States, its navies consist of the U.S. Navy, U.S. Marine Corps (in amphibious and littoral expeditionary operations), long-range aviation elements of the U.S. Air Force, U.S. Space Force, and U.S. cyber forces.

⊢• COMMONS, CYBERSPACE, AND GLOBAL POWER

In modern international law, the large environmental mediums that humans use for communications and transportation to support commerce, but that are not inhabitable or normally inhabited, are considered global "commons." They are open to use by those nations or groups that have the capabilities and determination to reach and use them. The perimeters of these commons are often under the legal or de facto control of a nation-state—such as twelve-mile territorial seas or sovereign airspace over land. However, the commons themselves are not.

In some cases, the particular activities conducted within these commons may be governed (or even restricted) by agreements among actors who would otherwise fight over those resources. (See the chapter by Wells and Klimburg.) Such agreements include environmental protection (primarily pollution control), restrictions on overfishing, maritime traffic separation lanes, conservation of natural resources, and other exploitative activities. Nevertheless, these agreements are often violated by the more aggressive users, such as by the People's Republic of China in the South China Sea.

The early internet promoters intended cyberspace to be a worldwide, free, open, democratizing commons. However, the originally border-free cyberspace has gradually acquired its own "territorial seas." These emerge in every nation that demands sovereign control of cyberspace within their territorial borders. China and Russia, for example, have long asserted that their national cyberspace is sovereign territory to be controlled by their own rules. Since 2016 and a United Nations–brokered international consensus, most major nations have acknowledged national cyber sovereignty. Whether or not such national jurisdictions are defensible in the face of hackers and democracy activists remains a question. Nevertheless, territorial seas pose a significant challenge to the cyber forces of the United States and its allies in terms of the global navigation of cyberspace.

Throughout history, those nations with well-gated and -defended territorial seas have been able to maximize their own use of the maritime commons. In some cases, state-sponsored marauders—as well as naval forces—had the ability to sail outward unimpeded into global oceans, but to also run to these safe havens after their exploits or battles. This continues in part today; witness Somali pirates.

Similarly, states protecting their national cyberspace as such a sea ensure their cyber forces—military, commercial, or criminal—can access the open worldwide cyberspace while their regime restricts the global access to their domestic digital societies and blocks possible retaliation for bad behaviors (as argued by Demchak in this volume).[3] One state that has achieved exceptional domestic cyber isolation—North Korea, the most successful totalitarian regime in history—does so by forgoing all access but military and state-sponsored exchanges. For years under international sanctions—in essence, commercial blockade (another naval concept)—the Kim Jong Un regime nonetheless accesses international cyber networks for espionage and revenue-seeking cyber attacks, which partially substitute for lost economic returns.[4]

Yet, territorial seas can be penetrated and controlled by dominant navies. In principle, naval forward presence provides military access to regions where its forces are not based, including, if required, the ability to enter defended territorial seas. It is the placement of ready forces within a region of crises without infringing on the sovereignty of, requiring permission from, or deriving basic sustainment through, any other state. By having such forces effectively loitering in place, whether in oceans, space, or cyberspace, the United States is better positioned to move additional forces into the region, domain, or medium, minimizing barriers that can be put in the way of long-distance transport of distantly located surge forces.[5] Regimental or battalion-sized units require amphibious or prepositioned shipping—what was frequently referred to as a "sea base" during the 1990s and early 2000s—in order to bring their equipment into the theater.[6] Forward-deployed naval forces protect the viability and usefulness of a sea base.

"Defending forward" is equivalent to being forward-deployed within the cyberspace commons, enabling cyber actions to be "surged" into operation with timely intelligence and still viable network access. Maintaining penetration of the enemy network despite reconfigurations, updates, or other defense measures would have already been achieved. Fighting from a far distance or from a standing position presents natural disadvantages to a military force by slowing its ability to engage rapidly—the conceptual equivalent of being inert. Similarly, a purely defensive, distant posture in cyberspace where the natural laws of physics control electrons also cedes initiative to the enemy.

↦ FORWARD PRESENCE, DEFEND FORWARD, AND PERSISTENT ENGAGEMENT

Forward presence is a naval term that seeks to describe the ability—and regular practice—of combat-ready naval forces to be routinely positioned in potential regions of crises during times of peace or non-hostilities. Forward presence implies the continual presence of combat-ready forces to areas where the United States does not have fixed land bases, often just offshore of inherently hostile states that might not otherwise be deterred from precipitous actions against neighbors. It has been argued that the U.S. Navy's long-term ability to access and dominate, if necessary, the global ocean commons is a major reason that the United States has been considered the sole remaining military superpower since the 1990s.[7] During the 1990s and even before, forward presence was considered one of four major strategic missions of the Navy and Marine Corps in times of peace.[8]

The concept of forward presence holds strong strategic logic for adoption by a global power. It is a proactive posture designed to prevent enemies, crises, and conflicts from approaching the shores, skies, and land territory of the homeland or that of allies. The underlying premise is that waiting for an enemy to attack on U.S. soil—or allowing a crisis to directly affect the economic well-being or lives of Americans or U.S. allies and partners—prior to taking action is a disastrous posture.

Waiting for hostile forces to conduct major cyber attacks on American infrastructure and interests and crouching in an exclusively cyber defense posture are similarly disastrous. As noted in an assessment of U.S. Cyber Command's (USCYBERCOM's) first ten years: "Evidence began mounting after 2013 . . . that defensive deterrence strategies were ineffective against the vast majority of cyber aggression, which was taking place below the threshold of armed attack."[9] Additionally, the difference between the other common fluid mediums—that cyberspace is a human-made domain with many diversified avenues of attack—means that there are too many complex connections, poorly coded programs, neglectful owners/operators, and vulnerable networks to provide absolute security for every vulnerable network without being proactive against organized malicious actors. Loitering forward to detect and respond to emerging threats is not optional for defense of this commons any more than it is for a global sea power.

Defend forward, therefore, is defined by USCYBERCOM as "disrupt[ing] malicious cyber activity at its source, including activity that falls below the level of armed conflict."[10] Similar to (maritime) naval forward presence, these operations are carried out in time of "peace" or pre-hostilities along the spectrum of cybered conflict stretching from peace to war. And similar to (maritime) naval forces, a defend forward posture allows for the rapid, on-scene response to a crisis by knowledgeable human-machine teams: "This means if a device, a network, an organization, or adversary nation is identified as a threat to U.S. networks and institutions, or is actively attacking them in or through cyberspace—it can expect the United States to impose costs in response."[11] Such language indicates that USCYBERCOM could conduct its own cyber attack against a threat or to stop cyber attacks on any U.S. network, regardless of the ownership of the network, if it is in the U.S. interest. Persistent engagement is defined by USCYBERCOM as an "operational framework" in which "cyber operators constantly work to intercept and halt cyber threats, degrade the capabilities and networks of adversaries, and continuously strengthen the cybersecurity of the Department of Defense."[12] There is no police force within cyberspace. In principle, modern professional policing is best done by "a cop on the beat" present in the neighborhood or rapidly available to respond to crises. In a global common open to criminals, civilians, and adversaries alike, that monitor and defuse function must be carried out by forward-deployed forces on the scene. Effective suppression of emerging cyber threats to U.S. citizens and allies across the global cyber commons requires a persistent engagement approach in order "to protect and serve."[13]

⊢• DEFENDING A COMMONS REQUIRES COOPERATION

Given the enormity of the oceans and the actions of adversaries, naval forward deployment often requires allies, and cyberspace is no different. The nature of maritime naval operations and the maritime environment itself facilitates cooperation of the navies of like-minded nations.[14] For example, since the establishment of the North Atlantic Treaty Organization (NATO), close cooperation between allied navies has become increasingly efficient. Indeed, the former Soviet navy had clandestine access to the common NATO naval signaling codebook in the Cold War, on occasion even joining combined NATO naval exercises.[15] Arguably, allied naval cooperation was easier to achieve than cooperation between NATO's armies, since they shared a common operational signal code.

At the end of the 1990s and the height of the post–Cold War globalization—"America's unipolar moment"—Chief of Naval Operations Adm. Michael Mullen, USN, conceived of a "1,000-ship navy" that would consist of an interoperative fleet (including coast guards) of allies and partners led by the U.S.

Navy.[16] Although the concept was dropped due to the increasing hostility of Russia and China, it illustrated the potential breadth of acceptance of naval cooperation to maximize the value of existing resources.

As a navy, cyber forces could benefit from similar acceptance and arrangements on cyber defense among allies, particularly in NATO and the European Union (as argued by Tiirmaa-Klar in this volume). Indeed, there is already a considerable degree of cooperation across these two unique institutions, but more is needed. Democratic states facing an international system dominated by several cyber-competent, large-scale autocracies are much like navies where the adversary can easily decode their communications and plans. They cannot survive or defend their access to the global commons without close cooperation in collective cyber defense of their democratic cybered commons.[17] Operating as cooperative navies, cyber forces have the potential to unify cyber defense of the democratic community—including commercial firms—in ways that avoid issues of sovereignty, such as basing agreements, legal status of forces, and personnel infrastructure.

⊢• CONSTRUCTING A THEORY OF NAVIES FOR A CYBERED WORLD

The term "theory" is used very loosely in everyday speech. It is often used to mean "abstract thought" or "speculation." However, in a formal or scientific sense, a theory is an "analysis of a set of facts in their relations to one another," leading to a hypothesis for testing and eventually "a plausible or scientifically accepted general principle."[18] Theories explain outcomes not by prediction but by logical inspection of contributing axioms. Given the preceding analysis of how cyberspace and navies correspond as naval forces, the following set of axioms—statements that are established, generally accepted, or self-evidently true—is offered as the rudiments of a new theory of "navies" operating in fluid but not necessarily liquid mediums.

- Axiom 1. Military forces that operate in the fluid mediums that humans use for commerce, communications, and transportation, but cannot or do not normally inhabit, are "navies."
  - Corollary: These "navies" include forces on, under, and above oceans, in space, and in cyberspace.

- Axiom 2. "Navies" necessarily rely on historically evolved naval strategic principles of (1) forward deployment of forces and (2) naval "presence" as a function of having to defend borders and trade across otherwise uninhabitable environments.
  - Corollary: These naval principles apply to cyberspace operations in both military and civilian homeland defense organizations.
  - Corollary: These naval principles are reflected in the cyberspace operational concepts of "defend forward" and "persistent engagement."
- Axiom 3. Navies generally operate in peacetime in a manner similar to their operations in war, functioning as "geoeconomic" trade-enhancing instruments as well as "geopolitical," episodically destructive elements of national statecraft and survival.[19]
  - Corollary: As a navy, military cyber forces operate under peacetime conditions in manners similar to naval defense of trade and combat operations, albeit with more frequency in the latter.
- Axiom 4. Navies by themselves are rarely the forces decisive to the outcome of the conflict determined on land, but they are the prerequisites for access by land forces across the relevant commons and supporting subsequent operations.
  - Corollary: Access to and control of oceans may not be absolutely necessary for every conflict or trade dispute involving other navies, but access in cyberspace is a prerequisite for almost every form of modern cybered combat.
- Axiom 5. "Navies" and armies are not functionally equivalent due to the differing nature of the mediums of operation.
  - Corollary: Despite current requirements to enforce "jointness" in operations, navies and armies continue to demonstrate substantial incompatibilities in planning, posture preferences, effectiveness measures, and resource requirements.
  - Corollary: Cyber operations, tools, tempo, and functions are "naval" in their operational differences with land forces, and operating cyber forces as land armies inhibits their effectiveness in peace and war.

At the end of the day, operating cyber forces as a navy is essential to their successful contributions from peace through war. Viewing all forces operating in fluid environments—naval, air, space, and cyber forces—as navies allows for considerable benefits that may determine the longer-term survival of consolidated democracies. These include more common operating principles, more allied acceptance of cooperative behaviors, and more operational experience in peacetime to support critical innovations in wartime. National and allied survival in the forthcoming Great Systems Conflict era is likely to depend on how these forces are viewed, organized, trained, operated, and resourced starting now.

To provide for American and allied security and prosperity in the current era of potential great systems conflict, the U.S. Department of Defense and allied services must accept this naval hypothesis as an enduring principle. Waiting to validate it in war—as the United States and allies have sometimes done in the slower, analog past—will be much too late.

NOTES

1. For a preliminary discussion of this logic, albeit in the context of globalization, see Sam J. Tangredi, "Beyond the Sea and Jointness," U.S. Naval Institute *Proceedings* 127, no. 9 (September 2001): 60–63, https://www.usni.org/magazines proceedings/2001/september/beyond-sea-and-jointness, also republished in Thomas J. Cutler, ed., *The U.S. Naval Institute on Naval Strategy* (Annapolis, MD: Naval Institute Press, 2015), 141–50.

2. Tangredi.

3. On the People's Republic of China "great firewall," see Elizabeth C. Economy, "The Great Firewall of China: Xi Jinping's Internet Shutdown," *The Guardian*, 29 June 2018, https://www.theguardian.com/news/2018/jun/29/the-great -firewall-of-china-xi-jinpings-internet-shutdown; Yaqui Wang, "In China, the 'Great Firewall' Is Changing a Generation," *Politico*, 1 September 2020, https://www.politico.com/news/magazine/2020/09/01/china-great-firewall -generation-405385. On Russian experiments in cutting Internet access, see "Russia Disconnects from the Internet in Tests as It Bolsters Security—RBC Daily," *Reuters*, 22 July 2021, https://www.reuters.com/technology/russia -disconnected-global-internet-tests-rbc-daily-2021-07–22/; Timmy Broderick, "Russia Is Trying to Leave the Internet and Build Its Own," *Scientific American*, 12 July 2023, https://www.scientificamerican.com/article/russia-is-trying-to

-leave-the-internet-and-build-its-own/https://www.scientificamerican.com
/article/russia-is-trying-to-leave-the-internet-and-build-its-own/.

4. Cynthia Brumfield, "North Korea's State Hacking Program Is Varied, Fluid, and Nimble," *CSO*, 30 October 2023, https://www.csoonline.com/article/657312/north-koreas-state-hacking-program-is-varied-fluid-and-nimble.html.

5. Barry R. Posen, "Command of the Commons: The Military Foundation of U.S. Hegemony," *International Security* 28, no. 1 (Autumn 2003): 5–46.

6. See Sam J. Tangredi, "Sea Basing—Concept, Issues, and Recommendations," *Naval War College Review* 64, no. 4 (Autumn 2011), https://digital-commons.usnwc.edu/nwc-review/vol64/iss4/5.

7. Posen.

8. On forward presence as a strategic concept, see Cdr. Sam J. Tangredi, USN, and Cdr. Randall G. Bowdish, USN, "Core of Naval Operations: Strategic and Operational Concepts of the United States Navy," *The Submarine Review*, January 1999, 14–15.

9. Emily O. Goldman, "The Cyber Paradigm Shift," in *Ten Years In: Implementing Strategic Approaches to Cyberspace*, ed. Jacquelyn G. Schneider, Emily O. Goldman, and Michael Warner, Newport Paper 45 (Newport, RI: Naval War College Press, 2020), 34, https://digital-commons.usnwc.edu/usnws-newport-papers/45/.

10. U.S. Cyber Command, "CYBER 101—Defend Forward and Persistent Engagement," 25 October 2022, https://www.cybercom.mil/Media/News/Article/3198878/cyber-101-defend-forward-and-persistent-engagement/.

11. U.S. Cyber Command.

12. U.S. Cyber Command.

13. Motto of the San Diego Police Department—and undoubtedly others.

14. Various forms of naval cooperation are discussed in the essays in Sam J. Tangredi, ed., *The U.S. Naval Institute on Naval Cooperation* (Annapolis, MD: Naval Institute Press, 2015).

15. There were apocryphal incidents in which Soviet warships brazenly joined NATO naval formations and conducted their maneuvers in accordance with the tactical orders of the NATO group commander. See *The Reminiscences of Vice Admiral Gerald E. Miller, U.S. Navy (Retired)* vol. II, USNI Oral History Program (Annapolis, MD: U.S. Naval Institute, 1984), 686–90.

16. Bryan G. McGrath, "1,000-Ship Navy and Maritime Strategy," U.S. Naval Institute *Proceedings* 133, no. 1 (January 2007), https://www.usni.org/magazines/proceedings/2007/january/1000-ship-navy-and-maritime-strategy.

17. See, for example, Chris C. Demchak, "Cyber Competition to Cybered Conflict," in Schneider, Goldman, and Warner, eds., *Ten Years In.*

18. Definitions are from *Webster's Ninth New Collegiate Dictionary* (Springfield, MA: Merriam-Webster, 1985), 1223.
19. Colloquially, the gun is loaded, cocked, and ready, but—in principle—the actual shot at an enemy is conducted only in war. The gunner necessarily trains, exercises, improves, and, staying "within sight of the potential opponent," hopefully deters hostile actions.

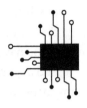

Conclusion

Alternative Future of Cybered Warfare and Navies: A Conclusion?

CHRIS C. DEMCHAK and SAM J. TANGREDI

"The Navy lacks an 'agreed to' strategic, operational, and tactical view of what it believes war in the maritime domain will look like over the next five to ten years, when advanced capabilities brought on by accelerating technologies such as hypersonic weapons, artificial intelligence, autonomous systems, quantum computing, and free space optics complicate an already challenging environment."[1]

Is this a fair assessment?

The chapters of this volume identify the many issues involving cybered warfare in the maritime world. While many of these issues are being examined by members of the sea services and maritime industries, they remain difficult to address since they require additional resources and organizational changes. In identifying the wide range of issues, many of the chapter authors make recommendations as to how maritime infrastructure can be protected, what steps maritime industries can take to protect themselves, what offensive actions will be required, and how the sea services can be best postured to conduct defensive and offensive cybered warfare.

However, these recommendations are in a sense "aspirational"—a word often defined as meaning "a strong desire to achieve something high and great." Until they are put into policy or adopted as practices, they remain but desires. It is our intent to make a contribution to formulating the ideas that might eventually form the "agreed-to" strategic, operational, and tactical views of the naval services, the combined sea services, and those that direct, manage, and operate the maritime transportation system on which the global economy depends.

To a very real extent, we are all already on the front lines of cybered conflict. The reality is that our use of cyberspace has massively magnified existing and new vulnerabilities and risks. As discussed in the chapter by Demchak, cyberspace—a human-created, now nearly universal substrate to all societies—was built on the cheap with naivete and hubris, and without security in mind. It was viewed as universally benign and meant to be the great (open and low-cost) unifying economic and social tool that would further the democratization and globalization of humanity. And it was left to spread into every societal function without any civic or security guardrails.

Clearly, throwing open, insecure cybered connections out all over the world in poorly coded products was the wrong approach. Today, endemic to the maritime environment as much as to the terrestrial are cyber vandalism, cyber crime, cyber espionage, state-sponsored cyber coercion and theft, and what can be called cyber terrorism, as identified by DeWitte and Lehto. At the same time, the growing divide of the world between democratic allies and authoritarian nations ensures that cyber will routinely be used as a weapon—not only within cyberspace itself, but directly into every other domain.

That is why we use the term "cybered warfare" as well as "cyber warfare." This is perhaps the most complicated factor: navies, maritime industries, and everything else are dependent on digital information traveling through cyberspace in order to function effectively. We cannot sail away from cyberspace: hence, the calls for resilience and unity among the democratic states in dealing with the threats and perhaps utilizing opportunities to control our cyber destinies—in war as in peace.

⊢• THE DIFFICULT FUTURE OF CYBER AND ITS OFFSPRING

To broaden an analysis of the above epigraph, it seems clear that the emerging technologies mentioned—all of which have already emerged to some degree—have dependencies on digital communication links, most of which dwell in cyberspace (and often via seabed cables). As one of the editors (Demchak) often remarks, these technologies are, in effect, "cyber's offspring."

Hypersonic weapons cannot be effectively controlled without wireless communications traveling through the ether that is the realm of electromagnetic warfare. The greatest use of artificial intelligence (AI) thus far has been internetted. Even autonomous systems, as Falcone and Panter note in their chapter, have deep cyber vulnerabilities in the operating technologies. These are vulnerabilities, as described by Hilger, in every modern ship. As noted by Pugh, Sandhoo, and Bebber and White, respectively, quantum computing, electronic warfare, and free space optics are of no value without transmitted data. So, what is the future of cyber warfare from a naval perspective?

Nearly all the chapter authors have been associated with the study of cybered conflict for a decade or more. Yet few have attempted to describe a vision of what succeeding generations might encounter.

Perhaps this omission is because there are so many current threats and unresolved issues that it exhausts our minds to visualize cyberspace beyond the present decade. There is so much to fix now in order to ensure our national security on land, at sea, and in air and space that it is hard to realistically visualize the future cyber. Even the national cyber security community's first "blockbuster" book, the 2010 *Cyber War* by Richard Clarke and Robert Knake, largely dealt with scenarios created by then-current—and still-current—cyber vulnerabilities.

Others have added their vision in many ways, some as embedded introductory stories to start a serious treatise and others as key memes in their entire novel. Unfortunately, many give in to describing fantasies that will continue to violate the laws of physics. For example, since we do not really know what constitutes "consciousness," how can anything describe future singularity? It makes for good movies, but bad science.

The difficulty is that all these authors with their transitional backgrounds—those whose lifespan includes current digital transformations—cannot easily envision what cyber warfare will be when young sailors, soldiers, marines, airmen, and guardians interpret threats and act. At best, current generations can only provide outlines of what is possible in what is called "software-defined warfare"[2] and what the best tools are to enact those visions or innovate into other outcomes. This situation is made worse by several characteristics of the seemingly enduring cybered military environment.

⊢• ESTABLISHED CHARACTERISTICS OF THOUGHT

At their base, militaries are aspirational organizations in modern democracies. They train against a future that may or may not occur. Their trade journals and magazines are filled with "parables." If servicemembers write and publish to suggest improvements—which is what the chapter authors of this book are also doing—the intent is that others should aspire to do what the authors are recommending. What one can infer relatively reliably, however, is that the authors' service or organization is not doing this right now—in effect, there is no agreed-to approach. Nonetheless, they compose these articles almost with an ingrained belief in serendipity—that by writing these aspirations down and publishing them, something good will come.

This cultural predilection has an enormous effect when a service or a military organization is attempting to upgrade to new technologies. Local units experiment, and when successes occur or ideas for how they might occur emerge, local authors want others to avoid the time and burden they spent to find those solutions. Journal after journal is filled with these positively written aspirational solutions meant to help the overarching enterprise.

Unfortunately, cyber is not a particularly aspirationally friendly technology, especially for navies. It was promoted to, and imposed on, a military that did not already have a function and a vision that captured how cyber would help it achieve its aspirations faster, more accurately, or less tediously. In the 1980s and then the 1990s, computers originally flourished in the back offices where one found typewriters, supply clerks, and intelligence analysts, not the heroes of frontline combat.

As a result, cyber has had difficulty displacing the fundamental vision of how war is fought by any particular service despite whatever digitization-promoting language senior officers may have used. Over time, it has slowly ingratiated itself across aeronautics, forward-leading ground troops, and the command centers of naval vessels, not to mention, of course, communications hubs. But it has not significantly changed the aspirational vision of war that each of the services would like to be able to fight successfully.

Worthy of note is that AI will not have as much difficulty in absorption because it is the offspring of cyber. It will, and already has begun to, slide into all the spaces cyber has carved out in backroom administration, information developments and sharing, and a host of embedded digitized technologies. Its speed, data capture, and performance possibilities are much more likely to directly begin to affect the course of conflict, unlike its underlying cyber parent. Still, one only succeeds where the other already has bulldozed its way inside.

Furthermore, in terms of how wartime versus peacetime operations differ, naval services are the least aspirational—and most concrete in approach—when compared to the ground and air services. Neither the ground nor the air forces largely perform in peace as they would in wartime. Ground services can be used on a routine basis in natural disasters, but they are not in those circumstances doing what their visions of war tell them they will do. It is a similar story for air services. However, other than firing their weapons systems off large vessels, the day-to-day routine of deployed naval services is more or less what they would be doing in times of war.

This constant, consistent pattern of operation reinforces a very concrete vision of what is to be done if the fleet's vessels are deployed in peace, crisis, or war. And that vision is today not explicitly deeply digitized. It therefore becomes exceptionally difficult for otherwise time- pressed officers and senior enlisted to envision how much better at X or Y function their lives would be with some cyber application. They can visualize what war and their role in it would be like, but that vision is not particularly heavily or accurately digitized.

⊢ YET, PERHAPS A GLIMPSE

With both our main concern—defining cyber warfare from a naval and maritime point of view—and the concern expressed by the opening epigraph, this conclusion attempts to offer an alternative future of war vision as a compilation—an aspirational vision, if you will—built from the expertise in this volume. With that being said, it is useful to construct a vision of cyber warfare with navies from the varied chapters of this volume in order to cement the contribution of this generation of authors. It is an exercise in what one can know today and can reasonably envision for the near- and midterm. It is meant to help fill the gap.

⊢—◦ Envisioning Future War

In this cybered future, technological developments have exponentially advanced, and the scale of their spread has increased the hubris and coercion campaigns of the globe's major authoritarian states. Diplomatic peace and stability efforts have failed (see Wells and Klimburg), and the world finds itself on the brink of a new kind of war where homelands are crippled by cyber and space warfare (see Sandhoo, Ross and Warner, and Demchak), and combat is dominated by AI-guided machines employed at maximum available scale and, by necessity, maximum disconnected autonomy (see Cleary, Arquilla, Brutzman and Kline, and Tangredi).

Tools of conflict have expanded far beyond the terrestrial and well into the digital and extraterrestrial in a multi-domain war that challenges the post–Cold War foundations of international security and warfare (see Demchak, Poznansky). This hypothetical conflict, set in an era where digital infrastructure has become as critical as physical territory, would redefine the nature of military engagement across sea, cyberspace, and space (see Cleary, Dombrowski, Sandhoo, and Tangredi).

⊢—◦ War Begins

The conflict begins with a series of destructive cyber attacks on defending democratic allies' critical infrastructures with returned cyber fires at the aggressor combatant states. The long years of opposing states secretly inserting and maintaining malicious, crippling software inside the national systems of other states now offer adversaries the abilities to attack not only into, but across, defending states (see Kania, Work). Soon all states and their allies are dragged into the conflict (see Tiirmaa-Klaar, Kim).

Leaders find the poorly financed resilience of their home sociotechnical-economic system severely challenged, losing vast portions of their domestic and international abilities to communicate, mobilize, perform emergency responses, keep supply chains functioning, and maintain societal order. Internal power grids fail erratically, digital networks go dark with no warning, and food and goods deliveries are stalled, suspiciously missing, or unexpectedly returned to ports.

With major critical infrastructures struggling to keep functioning, civil or commercial organizations are unable to alert and transport conventional forces to deployment centers. Syncing operations with allies for force multipliers is disorderly or disrupted. Societal internal order begins to require soldiers on the streets to tamp down panic and social media–fueled chaos. Reservists called into service have enormous difficulty arriving at assembly stations or ships on time, or never receive the call, further crippling any timely, conventional mobilization.

Combatant states and nations involved as collateral damage find themselves blind, deaf, and isolated with unreliable or cut undersea cables, unresponsive cyber-/debris-destroyed satellites, broken land distribution systems, frozen coastal transport, and other gaps from years of underfunded defense organizations (see Kavanagh and Leconte, deWitte and Lehto, Sandhoo, Hilger, Koch). Resorting to legacy unconnected systems is proving limited and dangerous as all forms of air, rail, and port transportation and deliveries become mostly inoperative.

Naval assets already at sea or able to launch rapidly are quickly redeployed to locate missing commercial vessels, repair critical cables, defend overseas bases and allies, and provide eyes, ears, and fighting power, but they have difficulty responding to homeland instructions. One by one, whole fleets seem to wink out of communications, no longer tracked by or communicating through satellites. Some report incoming fire before going silent.

In one after another emergency landing by overseas flights seeking the nearest airport after losing all satellite guidance and communications, pilots report seeing plumes of smoke dotting the oceans along their flight path. In a world heavily reliant on digital technology for both civilian life and military operations, these attacks create chaotic opening salvos of a new kind of war—one that spans the globe and specifically disrupts the ocean-spanning connectivity critical to the lifeblood of the major combatant nations and their allies.

⊢─○ Rise of Cybered/AI Warfare

In the absence of their pivotal transportation and communication systems, the warring states turn to their most advanced assets that are either forward-deployed or launchable: autonomous forms of AI-guided naval machines and cyber warfare. To restart and defend the passage and deliveries of maritime shipping, repair and barricade undersea cables, and replace or substitute for missing satellites, nations will seek to use whatever they already have in inventory in autonomous vessels, submarines, and drones, as well as autonomous prepositioned cyber weapons in adversary systems.

After most, if not all, of the conventional forces are rendered dysfunctional, these self-guided tools are likely to be the primary means of engaging the enemy, able to operate independently of compromised networks and make tactical decisions forward, at distance from shore, and in real time (see Cleary, Tangredi, Brutzman and Kline). Much, however, will depend on how much and how resiliently aggressors, defenders, or their respective allies have invested in these capabilities well in advance of this conflict (see Dombrowski, Warner and Ross, Vogt and Kollars, Tiirmaa-Klaar, Kim, Arquilla, Falcone and Panter, Demchak, Long and Vaughan).

⊢─○ Blue Theater of War

When the first few days of smoke, sinking, and chaotic static ends, the ongoing battle zones will be unlike any seen before. The vast expanses of the world's oceans become automated multilayered checkerboards, dotted with robotic combatants hunting each other in silence (McGunnigle and Breuer). Surface and subsurface drones skim the waves or the top layers of the water column, executing reconnaissance missions and launching surprise attacks on enemy vessels and returning to stealthy submersible motherships, now less trackable due to loss of satellite imagery.

Below them, autonomous fleets of small and large submarines lurk in the depths, using deception, nearly silent propulsion, and quantum-enhanced, AI-guided sonar to track and destroy targets with smart torpedoes and other weapons. Littering the ocean floor's crevices and valleys are the corpses of the destroyed robotic fighters, gathering particularly along the commercial vessel and cable corridors of the sea where the battles are likely to be heaviest. These autonomous vessels, submarines, and drones patrol the oceans, executing complex maneuvers and engaging in battles with precision beyond human capabilities.

With the loss of existing commercial communications, some of these robotic drones, subs, or vessels act part-time as in situ analysts and/or as transceivers self-organized into ad hoc AI-defined ephemeral communications networks to report battle and other maritime data back to the home command's remaining networks to the extent possible. These actions may be pretrained, or they may be spontaneously and organically learned by the swarms in situ. The absence of human crew may eliminate the risk of major losses of life in immediate combat, but the quiet technical autonomy of destruction massively increases the psychological warfare and strategic tension of defending society under these circumstances.

Commercial maritime organizations accustomed to the automatic availability of modern cybered systems are now forced to operate mostly in silence, blind, and dependent on cyber/AI robotic fleets for national as well as their own survival. Over time, some of the remaining functional vessels encounter, or are found by, some of these autonomous entities acting as self-organized transceivers and are able to communicate locations and status through circuitous ad hoc networks back to headquarters. Reports are sketchy and incomplete. Some vessels are limping home. Some submarine skippers are simply staying down low, unable to trust the autonomous fleets passing over their heads, hoping to find a safe place to try to communicate. Some are gone, hunted by autonomous vessels by the enemy or by blue force autonomous systems by mistake.

⊢○ Cyber Front Lines

Parallel to the deceptive, distant, and critical physical confrontations at sea, a relentless digital war also rages despite being disjointed by the national gaps in electrical power, software reliability, and international connectivity. Campaigns designed around expectations of international sources of feedback are stalled by the silence, driven to older forms of relay communications internally but especially with external partners.

Both sides deployed AI algorithms buried in malicious cyber programs before the war to lay the groundwork to trigger sabotage of the other's unmanned systems. Cyber warriors across all nations focus on any options they can access, particularly interested in turning enemy machines into autonomous Trojan horses or rendering them inoperative. Deception becomes critical in order to hijack and employ for other purposes whatever command or control mechanisms adversaries have constructed to support their fight in the dark night of this digitized war, especially the ocean-spanning spontaneous AI-guided linked robotic systems.

As the war grinds on and "innovations of necessity" roughly re-create the communications linkages of the prewar societies, nothing digitized can be trusted without question. Even more AI is deployed across the cybered infra-structures as detectors of intruders, fake software, and information manipula-tions. Distinctions between front lines at sea and home front blur as cyber operatives become creative and their campaigns become more AI-driven and autonomous. Cyber warriors at home become critical comrades in the survival of the robotic fleets (see Bebber and White, Pugh, Kuo and Lindsay, Falcone and Panter). Cyber operatives and AI algorithms work tirelessly to use the ephemeral access opportunities and breach the enemy's cyber defenses to take control of their autonomous systems or disable them entirely and win back the seas and space. This cyber front is as critical as the physical one, with the power to turn the tide of battle by seizing control of the enemy's unmanned assets.

⊢○ The Absorption of Near Space

As the conflict erupts, it inevitably reaches into space where satellites and orbital platforms are primary initial targets (see Sandhoo). The combatants deploy AI-guided space drones and autonomous satellites equipped with offensive and defensive systems. These machines are tasked with disrupting enemy communications, navigation, and surveillance capabilities, as well as protecting their own space-based assets.

Orbital skirmishes involve a mix of direct attacks on satellites, cyber warfare hijacking or disabling of space-based systems and their supporting mesh networks, and the deployment of kinetic anti-satellite weapons. The debris generated from these encounters is weaponized to pose the equivalent of mine fields, preventing the safe orbits of other satellites from both combatants and uninvolved states alike and fragmenting or destroying communications globally.

The result is dense, tense global competition in demands for the minimal remaining communications links from the operational satellites of uninvolved nations, rendering communications with remaining and intact military or commercial vessels at sea nearly unusable.

⊢○ Cybered Warfare's Impact on Society

However this war ends—if it ever formally does—it ushers in a new era of military strategy, where the emphasis shifts from human valor and sacrifice to technological superiority, immutable power of scale, ubiquitous deception, and systemic cyber resilience. This multi-domain conflict, spanning sea, cyberspace, and space, signifies a monumental shift in the nature of warfare. The reliance on AI and autonomous systems raises critical questions about the ethics of warfare, the role of human decision-making, and the risks of escalation in a world where machines can act faster than humans can react.

The war demonstrates the vulnerability of modern societies to attacks on their technological infrastructure, underscoring the need for resilience and defense by design. As the dust settles, the combatant states, and the international community at large, are left to grapple with the implications of this new era of warfare. The combatant states, having witnessed the double-edged sword of advanced AI in warfare, double down on a new arms race—not for nuclear weapons, but for the most advanced and secure autonomous combat systems and cyber defense capabilities.

This naval war, fought with barely hundreds of sailors at sea, nonetheless ripples through all the involved states' homelands and kills or cripples hundreds of millions from the loss of infrastructure including healthcare, livelihoods, and futures. It reshapes the realities of war back to being whole-of-society system-versus-system struggles regardless of the distance to any putative front line.

⊢• BACK TO REALITY

Whether or not it would make a good movie, nothing in the above scenario defies the laws of science. All could be seen as an eventual consequence of the realities of a shoddy, insecure cyberspace substrate today. By default, it is designed in a way to give bad actors access to any location reachable by some form of network. That is what future generations have been bequeathed.

The real solution would be to change the code, practices, and incentives for security that drive the internet, information technology in general, and the development of new technologies to more secure outcomes by default. Realistically, the chance of that happening in any near term is nil. Major corporations will need to lose exceptional amounts of money and market share to cybercrime and attacks by hostile state actors that cause continuing infrastructure disruption. Then, sensing more profits to be made from just programming poorly in a rush, patching, and whack-a-mole defending, software, hardware, and telecommunications companies—and their customers—will listen. Until then, cyberspace will remain the extremely vulnerable societal (including maritime) substrate that underpins the entire system.

Decades ago, the Department of Defense (DOD) attempted to create its own more secure computer language—Ada. The U.S. Navy was in the forefront of this effort. In fact, in 1991 DOD required all its software to be compiled in Ada. That mandate lasted only six years; in 1997 DOD (re)adopted the much cheaper use of commercial off-the-shelf software, with all its built-in vulnerabilities.

Perhaps that vulnerability is an advantage for our military and intelligence units in penetrating the networks of potential enemies. Obviously, U.S. Cyber Command exploits every advantage that weak codes bring. But to use two accurate clichés: The enemy gets a vote, and the good guys don't always win. For naval and other military forces operating high-technology weapons at sea or in the field or air, a non-resilient, commercially oriented cyberspace ensures ships, weapons, people, and communications are all vulnerable.

The cybered war is going to be fought at sea in ships and aircraft—whether uncrewed or not—possibly with little or no connectivity with higher headquarters or U.S. Cyber Command itself. This expectation is why the naval/ sea services need to retain and develop more robust cyber capabilities and expert personnel.

In a cybered future war like the one we have outlined, cybered war will be an all-hands conflict, and if the sea services do not retain, grow, and reward their cadres of cyberwarriors, it is unlikely to go well. Fort Meade, headquarters of U.S. Cyber Command and the National Security Agency, is *not* going to be the front line. As noted in the chapters by Kania and Work, the potential enemies are already strongly, dangerously "voting" with their scale and undeterrable strategic coherence (China) and with their criminals and ruthless persistent opportunism (Russia).

Given the scale of the potential autocratic opposition, the democratic states need to more strongly band together—such as in the recommended Cyber Operational Resilience Alliance to create scale of their own. Creating interoperability creates its own vulnerabilities, but they would be smaller than those that currently exist.[3] This interoperability can begin in the fluid and adaptable environment of the maritime transportation system on which practically all international trade relies. As a first step, the combined democracies could more effectively protect their maritime infrastructure. Of course, like all options, this requires resourcing and, unfortunately—to use one of our previous examples—Chinese container cranes are cheaper.

Ultimately, the naval/sea services (and maritime industries) cannot simply sail away from the vulnerabilities of cyberspace. No matter the options chosen—and whether or not the future cybered war takes the form we suggested—they are going to have to fight defensively and offensively in, through, and enabled by, cyberspace. Tactical cyber strikes will have to be used alongside kinetic strikes. Defenses and offensive capabilities will have to be on the edge of the forward maritime forces.

That is the reality we have sought to convey in this volume.

NOTES

1. T. J. White, Danelle Barrett, and Jake Bebber, "The Navy Is Not Ready for the Information War of 2026," U.S. Naval Institute *Proceedings* 150, no. 2 (February 2024): 22–29, https://www.usni.org/magazines/proceedings/2024/february/navy-not-ready-information-war-2026.
2. S. R. Soare et al., "Software-Defined Defence: Algorithms at War," International Institute for Strategic Studies, 2023.
3. C. C. Demchak, "We Need a NATO/EU for Cyber Defense," *Defense One* online, 14 March 2019, https://www.defenseone.com/ideas/2019/03/we-need-nato-eu-cyber-defense/155779/.

ABOUT THE CONTRIBUTORS

EDITORS

CHRIS C. DEMCHAK, PHD, is the Grace Hopper Chair of Cyber Security and the senior cyber scholar, Cyber and Innovation Policy Institute, U.S. Naval War College, and holds degrees in engineering, economics, and comparative complex organization systems/political science. Her publications/current research are on cyberspace as a global, insecure, conflict-prone "substrate"; applying a socio-technical-economic systems approach to comparative institutional evolution with emerging technologies; "cyber's offspring" in adversaries' cyber/artificial intelligence/machine learning campaigns; virtual wargaming for learning; and national/enterprise resilience against complex systems surprise. Works published or in progress include *Wars of Disruption and Resilience* (2011); *Great Systems Conflict: Rise of Cyber Westphalia and Collective Resilience*; *Organizing for Great Systems Conflict*; and *Sustaining a Digital Democracy.*

CAPT. SAM J. TANGREDI, USN (RET.), is the Leidos Chair of Future Warfare Studies and professor of national, naval, and maritime strategy at the U.S. Naval War College. In addition to command at sea, he served as strategic planner and director of strategic planning teams in the Pentagon. He has published seven books, over two hundred journal articles, and numerous reports and presentations for a wide range of government and academic organizations. He co-edited *AI at War: How Big Data, Artificial Intelligence, and Machine Learning Are Changing Naval Warfare* (Naval Institute Press, 2021). His book *Anti-Access Warfare: Countering A2/AD Strategies*—widely considered the definitive work on that subject—was re-released in paperback in 2023. His latest book (co-authored with George Galdorisi) is *Algorithms of Armageddon:*

The Impact of Artificial Intelligence on Future Wars (Naval Institute Press, 2024). A graduate of the U.S. Naval Academy class of 1978, he earned an MA from the Naval Postgraduate School and a PhD from the University of Southern California.

CONTRIBUTORS

JOHN ARQUILLA is distinguished professor emeritus at the U.S. Naval Postgraduate School. Best known for his ideas about cyber warfare and swarm tactics, he has also written or co-authored a dozen books and over one hundred articles across a range of topics in military and security affairs. His 1993 co-authored article "Cyber War Is Coming!" (*Comparative Strategy* and RAND report) was one of the very first public assessments of the potential for cyber warfare.

CDR. ROBERT "JAKE" BEBBER, USN, is a cryptologic warfare officer. His previous assignments include Navy Information Operations Command Maryland, U.S. Seventh Fleet staff, U.S. Cyber Command, Carrier Strike Group TWELVE, Information Warfare Training Command Corry Station, and U.S. Special Operations Command. His writings have appeared in U.S. Naval Institute *Proceedings, Orbis, Comparative Strategy, Journal of Information Warfare,* and elsewhere. He holds a PhD in public policy.

PABLO BREUER is a twenty-two-year veteran of the U.S. Navy. His tours included top-level positions at U.S. Special Operations Command Donovan Group, SOFWERX, the National Security Agency, U.S. Cyber Command, and U.S. Naval Forces Central Command. He is the co-founder of the Cognitive Security Collaborative and co-author of the DISARM (Disinformation Analysis and Response Measures) framework, the methodology used by the U.S. and EU governments and NATO to address misinformation and disinformation. He is a sought-after speaker in the fields of cyber security, mis- and disinformation, and protecting critical assets from attack.

DON BRUTZMAN is a U.S. Naval Academy graduate in the class of 1978, retired submarine officer, and computer scientist teaching at the Naval Postgraduate School. He received the Vice Adm. Charles B. Martell—David Bushnell Award from the National Defense Industrial Association Undersea Warfare Division in 2021. His research interests include underwater robotics, 3D computer graphics, good old-fashioned artificial intelligence (GOFAI), and large-scale virtual environments.

CHRIS CLEARY is vice president for global cyber practice for ManTech. Previously, he was the first congressionally mandated principal cyber advisor to the Secretary of the Navy and the Department of the Navy's first chief information security officer. He led the development and publishing of the department's 2023 *Cyberspace Superiority Vision* and subsequent 2024 *Cyber Strategy*. Cleary is a retired naval reserve officer who served sixteen of twenty-four years on active duty in a variety of leadership roles ashore and afloat. He is a 1996 graduate of the U.S. Naval Academy and 2012 graduate of the Naval War College.

PAULA DeWITTE is a professor of practice in computer science and engineering and an adjunct professor of law at Texas A&M University. Previously, she held positions in start-ups focusing on applying research and developing technology for complex industrial problems in Austin as well as in Houston. She holds a patent in drilling fluids optimization. She has a BS and an MS from Purdue University, where in 2015 she was honored as distinguished alumna in the mathematics department, school of science; a PhD in computer science from Texas A&M University; and a JD from St. Mary's University. Her most recent publications are three book chapters focusing on different aspects of maritime cybersecurity.

PETER DOMBROWSKI is the William Ruger Chair of National Security Economics and professor of strategy in the strategic and operational research department of the Center for Naval Warfare Studies at the U.S. Naval War College. His most recent books are *Across Type, Time, and Space: American Grand Strategy in Comparative Perspective* (2021), co-authored with Simon Reich, and *Security Studies in a New Era of Maritime Competition* (2023), co-edited with Jonathan D. Caverley. He received his BA from Williams College and an MA and a PhD from the University of Maryland.

LT. CDR. JOHNATHAN FALCONE, USN, serves as chief engineer on board a littoral combat ship. He is a graduate of the Princeton School of Public and International Affairs and Yale University. His writings have appeared in *Bulletin of the Atomic Scientists* and *War on the Rocks*, among others. In 2022 he was awarded the Alfred Thayer Mahan Literary Award by the Navy League of the United States.

NORMAN FRIEDMAN is an internationally known strategist and specialist in the history of weapons designs and development. He has written more than forty books on such topics as network-centric warfare, the maritime strategy, and ship and aircraft design, and hundreds of articles on naval and defense issues, and he has appeared on television programs on networks including PBS, the Discovery Channel, C-SPAN, and National Geographic. He worked for over a decade as a personal consultant to the Secretary of the Navy, beginning with Secretary John Lehman, as well as for the Secretary of the Navy's office of program appraisal, and the advanced studies group at the U.S. Naval War College. Friedman holds a BS and PhD in theoretical physics from Columbia University.

CAPT. DANIELLE M. HIGSON, JUDGE ADVOCATE GENERAL CORPS, USN, is a qualified information warfare officer, currently serving as a military professor of joint military operations at the U.S. Naval War College. During her career, she has served as the legal advisor at various levels of command at sea and ashore at joint, multinational, and interagency commands, and she gained significant expertise in cyber and intelligence law while providing operational legal advice at the National Security Agency, U.S. Cyber Command, and U.S. Fleet Cyber Command/U.S. Tenth Fleet. She earned a BA from Johns Hopkins University, an MA from the U.S. Naval War College, a JD from the University of Virginia School of Law, and an LLM in international and operational law from the U.S. Army Judge Advocate General Legal Center and School, with a focus on cyber law. Publications include "Applying the Law of Neutrality while Transiting the Seas of Cyberspace," *American University National Security Law Brief* 6, no. 2 (2016).

CDR. RYAN HILGER, USN, is an active-duty Navy engineering duty officer who has served on two submarines, in the Pentagon, and in acquisition program offices. He earned a master's degree in mechanical engineering from the Naval Postgraduate School and is a doctoral candidate in systems engineering at Colorado State University. He has been widely published in U.S. Naval Institute *Proceedings*, CIMSEC, and other outlets, and is a nonresident senior fellow at the Atlantic Council's Cyber Statecraft Initiative.

BRUCE D. JONES is a senior fellow with the Talbott Center on Security, Strategy, and Technology at the Brookings Institution. He is the author of the best-selling *To Rule the Waves: How Control of the Oceans Shapes the Fate of the Superpowers* (2021), which was selected for the Chief of Naval Operation's professional reading list. He is also the author of several books and essays on international order, U.S. grand strategy, and global governance. Prior to joining Brookings, he directed the New York University Center on International Cooperation, and served with the United Nations in the Middle East and at headquarters.

ELSA B. KANIA is a PhD candidate in Harvard University's department of government. She is also an adjunct senior fellow with the Technology and National Security Program at the Center for a New American Security. Her research focuses on China's military strategy, defense innovation, and emerging technologies, and she has published widely on those subjects. Her many reports include *AI Weapons in China's Military Innovation* (2020), and she has testified multiple times to the congressionally chartered U.S.-China Economic Security Review Commission. She serves as an officer in the U.S. Navy Reserve.

CAMINO KAVANAGH is a visiting senior fellow at the Department of War Studies, King's College London. Having spent the first decade of her career working in conflict and post-conflict settings, she now works on issues relevant to cyberspace and emerging technologies, global governance, international security, crisis, and conflict. Her most recent research is focused on governance and security of critical undersea infrastructure. She earned her PhD in 2015 from the Department of War Studies, King's College London. Recent publications include *Murky Waters: Subsea Communications Cables and Responsible State Behaviour* (2023).

SO JEONG KIM is a director of emerging security studies and a senior research fellow of the Institute for National Security Strategy (INSS) in Seoul and adjunct research fellow of the Center for Strategic and International Studies in the United States. Before joining INSS, she worked at the National Security Research Institute, South Korea's government-funded research institution, from 2004 to February 2022 as a team lead. She earned her doctorate degree in 2005 from the Graduate School of Cybersecurity of Korea University. She has authored or co-authored various articles, reports, and academic papers, including an evaluation of cyberattack severity and a proposal for a national response matrix.

ALEXANDER KLIMBURG is a nonresident senior associate at the Center for Strategic and International Studies and a scholar of cyber conflict. Previously, he was the head of the Center for Cybersecurity at the World Economic Forum and director of the Global Commission on the Stability of Cyberspace, as well as being affiliated with a number of think tanks including the Harvard Belfer Center and the Atlantic Council. He holds degrees from the London School of Economics, the School of Oriental and African Studies, and the University of Vienna. Since 2010 he has authored dozens of publications including *The Darkening Web: The War for Cyberspace* (2017).

JEFF KLINE is professor of practice in military operations analysis at the U.S. Naval Postgraduate School. A retired Navy captain, he served in many different class warships from missile-armed patrol hydrofoil to aircraft carriers and also on Navy staffs ranging from tactical destroyer squadrons to the Office of the Secretary of Defense. Jeff's graduate degrees are in operations research from the U.S. Naval Postgraduate School and in national security from the National War College. His most recent publication is *The U.S. Navy and the Rise of Great Power Competition: Looking beyond the Western Pacific* (2023), co-authored with James Wirtz and James Russell.

LT. CDR. BRYAN KOCH, USCG, currently serves as the Coast Guard/Department of Homeland Security liaison to the INDOPACOM Joint Intelligence Operations Center. He previously served as the commanding officer of 1790 Cyber Protection Team. His previous assignments include 1790 Cyber Protection Team, Coast Guard Detachment of the Cybersecurity and Infrastructure Security Agency, Coast Guard Cyber Command, Coast Guard Base Boston, and CGC *Vigilant* (WMEC 617). He holds an MS in information assurance and an MBA from Northeastern University and a BS in electrical engineering from the Coast Guard Academy His publications include *Detection and Mitigation of Malicious Modifications on the Minnowboard Turbot.*

NINA KOLLARS is associate professor in the Cyber and Innovation Policy Institute of the U.S. Naval War College. She is also the executive director of MarSec@ICSVillage, which is a maritime vulnerability playspace at the one of the world's largest and longest enduring hacking conferences, DefCon. She previously served in the Office of the Secretary of Defense as an advisor to the under secretary for defense of research and engineering. Kollars identifies as a hacker but has also earned a PhD in security studies from The Ohio State University and publishes in both academic and policy outlets on issues of cyber defense, military adaptation, and emerging technologies.

KENDRICK KUO is assistant professor in the strategic and operational research department at the U.S. Naval War College and a core faculty member in the Cyber and Innovation Policy Institute. Previously, he was a predoctoral fellow at Texas A&M University's Albritton Center for Grand Strategy and a Hans J. Morgenthau Fellow at the University of Notre Dame. Kuo holds a PhD in political science from the George Washington University.

RAYNALD LECONTE is chief executive officer of Cilandak Consulting, a business and management consulting company operating in Southeast Asia. Previously he spent over a decade as chief executive officer of Orange Marine, a company that operates six cable ships, successfully implementing transpacific and transatlantic cable projects, among others. He also served as chief financial officer for the wholesale division of Orange Marine from 2004 to 2007, and prior to this held positions in Orange, France Telecom, and French PTT. Raynald earned a master's in physics from Paris Orsay University in 1976 and attended the École Nationale Supérieure des Télécommunications in 1985. He is a frigate captain in the reserve of the French Navy.

COL. MARTTI LEHTO, FINNISH ARMY (RET.), works as a research director in the University of Jyväskylä. His research areas are cyber security and cyber warfare. He served for thirty years in the Finnish Air Force, and his last duty was as deputy chief of staff for logistics and armaments in Air Force Command. He is also an adjunct professor in the National Defence University in air and cyber warfare. He holds a PhD in military sciences.

JON LINDSAY is associate professor at the School of Cybersecurity and Privacy and the Sam Nunn School of International Affairs at the Georgia Institute of Technology. He holds a PhD in political science from the Massachusetts Institute of Technology and an MS in computer science from Stanford University. He is the author of *Information Technology and Military Power* (2020) and co-author of *Elements of Deterrence: Strategy, Technology, and Complexity in Global Politics* (2024). He has also served in the U.S. Navy with operational assignments in Europe, Latin America, and the Middle East.

JACK LONG is a U.S. Marine Corps reservist at the Office of Naval Research, where as an individual mobilization augmentee he served as a deputy to the Navy chief AI officer. In 2023 he was activated to full-time service as the chief AI officer upon the retirement of his predecessor. Upon finishing his PhD work at Johns Hopkins University in 2005, he joined the Marines. When previously on active duty, he made multiple deployments to support combat operations in the U.S. Central Command region. He also earned an MBA at the University of Oxford, worked for McKinsey & Company, and started his own consulting firm.

CAPT. JOHN McGUNNIGLE, USN (RET.), served as commanding officer of USS *New Hampshire* (SSN 778), and commander, Submarine Squadron FOUR. Among other assignments, he was special assistant for artificial intelligence and machine learning to commander, Submarine Force, where he co-founded and led a joint Department of Defense AI project, Project Harbinger. He earned a BS in computer science (with distinction) from the U.S. Naval Academy and an MA in operations research from the U.S. Naval Postgraduate School, and his publications have appeared in *PHALANX* and *Naval Research Logistics*. He is co-founder, president, and chief technical officer of Spear AI, a company focused on data and applied AI in the maritime domain.

THOMAS MORSE is a U.S. Marine Corps officer who has served in multiple cyber and intelligence roles over the course of his career, including as commander, Combat Mission Team 1. He is a veteran of Operation Enduring Freedom and Operation Iraqi Freedom and a graduate of the University of Virginia.

VICE ADM. ROSS A. MYERS, USN (RET.), is a career carrier naval aviator who commanded at all levels within the U.S. Navy and joint service including forward deployed naval forces, commander, Carrier Air Wing FIVE. Most recently he served as commander, U.S. Fleet Cyber Command/TENTH Fleet/Navy Space. Previously, he was vice deputy director for nuclear, homeland defense, and current operations, Joint Staff (J33); commander, Carrier Strike Group FIFTEEN; director of plans and policy (J5), chief of staff, and deputy commander at U.S. Cyber Command. He earned a BS from Kansas State University, an MBA from the University of Kansas, and an MS from the National War College.

JONATHAN PANTER is a PhD candidate in the department of political science at Columbia University. He previously served as a surface warfare officer in the U.S. Navy, deploying twice in support of Operation Inherent Resolve. His policy analysis has been featured in *Foreign Policy, War on the Rocks,* and *Bulletin of the Atomic Scientists,* among other publications. He holds an MPhil and MA in political science from Columbia and a BA in government from Cornell University.

CAPT. ROBERT J. PASSERELLO, JUDGE ADVOCATE GENERAL CORPS, USN (RET.), serves as national security counsel supporting the secretary of defense's directorate for global investment and economic security. Previously, he served as general counsel to Fleet Cyber Command/Tenth Fleet, deputy legal advisor to the National Security Council, in U.S. Central Command, and as a faculty member of the U.S. Naval War College, among many other operational assignments. He earned a JD in 1996 from Western New England University School of Law, an MA in 2003 from the U.S. Naval War College, and an MS in 2015 from National Defense University.

MICHAEL POZNANSKY is associate professor in the strategic and operational research department and a core faculty member in the Cyber and Innovation Policy Institute at the U.S. Naval War College. Poznansky was previously assistant professor in the Graduate School of Public and International Affairs at the University of Pittsburgh. He is the author of *In the Shadow of International Law: Secrecy and Regime Change in the Postwar World* (2020). He received his PhD in foreign affairs from the University of Virginia.

RANDY PUGH is the vice provost for warfare studies and the director of the Naval Warfare Studies Institute at the U.S. Naval Postgraduate School. He is a retired colonel, U.S. Marine Corps, commanded Second Radio Battalion and Marine Corps Intelligence Schools, and served in combat in Iraq, Afghanistan, and the Philippines. He earned degrees from the U.S. Naval Academy, the U.S. Naval Postgraduate School, the Marine Corps Command and Staff College, and the U.S. Naval War College.

CAPT. GURPARTAP "G. P." SANDHOO, USN (RET.), is a retired U.S. government senior executive. He was the deputy director at the Intelligence Advanced Research Project Agency and spent the majority of his career at the U.S. Naval Research Laboratory, including as head of the spacecraft engineering division. Additionally, he was the distinguished visiting professor in the Robert A. Heinlein endowed astronautics chair at the U.S. Naval Academy and holds five earned degrees, including a doctorate in aeronautics, astronautics, and propulsion.

FRANK L. SMITH III is professor and director of the Cyber and Innovation Policy Institute at the U.S. Naval War College. His interdisciplinary research and teaching examine the relationship between emerging technology and international security. Previous work includes his book, *American Biodefense: How Dangerous Ideas about Biological Weapons Shape National Security* (2014), as well as articles published in *Security Studies, Social Studies of Science, Security Dialogue, Health Security, Asian Security*, and *The Lancet*. He earned a PhD in political science and a BS in biological chemistry, both from the University of Chicago.

HELI TIIRMAA-KLAAR was until recently the director of the Digital Society Institute at the European School of Management and Technology in Berlin. She now devotes her time to aiding the defense of Ukraine. Previously she served as ambassador for cyber diplomacy and director general for the cyber diplomacy department at the Estonian Ministry of Foreign Affairs (2018–21) and as a head of cyber policy coordination at the European External Action Service. She has led the development of the Estonian cyber security strategy, co-led preparation for European cyber security strategies, and was assigned to the North Atlantic Treaty Organization international staff to prepare the organization's cyber defense policy. She was a Fulbright Scholar at the George Washington University and has published in several academic journals throughout her career.

BRETT VAUGHAN concluded a thirty-four-year career in defense, intelligence, science, and technology in 2023, culminating in his four-year tenure (2019–23) as the Office of Naval Research AI portfolio manager and the first Chief AI Officer of the U.S. Navy. He is now the chief executive officer of Raise the Colors LLC, an AI advisory, and also serves as an advisor on the boards of RAIN Defense + AI and KNEXUS inc.

JASON VOGT is an assistant professor in the strategic and operational research department of the Center for Naval Warfare Studies at the U.S. Naval War College. He is a cyber wargaming expert and has participated in the development of multiple wargames at the Naval War College. He previously worked for the Defense Intelligence Agency and served on active duty as an Army officer. He holds an MA in global security studies from Johns Hopkins University.

MICHAEL WARNER serves as command historian at U.S. Cyber Command and has written extensively on cyber and intelligence history, policy, and strategy. His latest book (co-authored with John Childress) is *The Use of Force for State Power: History and Future* (2020).

CAPT. LINTON WELLS II, USN (RET.), chairs the advisory group to the C5I Center at George Mason University and is a member of the university's National Security Institute. In fifty-one years of Department of Defense service (including twenty-six years as a surface warfare officer), he served as deputy under secretary of defense, principal deputy assistant secretary, acting assistant secretary of defense (networks and information integration), and Department of Defense chief information officer. He earned a BS in physics and oceanography from the U.S. Naval Academy in 1967, an MS in mathematical sciences (in operations research), and a PhD in international relations from Johns Hopkins University. Publications include *Japanese Cruisers of the Pacific War* with Eric Lacroix (Naval Institute Press, 1997), co-editor of *Innovative Learning: A Key to National Security* (2015), and numerous monographs and articles on national security issues.

VICE ADM. T. J. WHITE, USN (RET.), is a national security practitioner with over thirty years of experience as a strategist and cyber operations expert leading joint military formations and combined intelligence community organizations. Before retiring as a vice admiral, he commanded at all levels within the Navy and joint service, most recently as the commander, U.S. Fleet Cyber Command/United States TENTH Fleet/U.S. Navy Space Command, and previously as the commander, U.S. Cyber National Mission Force/U.S. Cyber Command. He is the former director of intelligence for U.S. Indo-Pacific Command and has served globally in various combat zones and conflict areas supporting competition dynamics. A 1989 CINCPACFLT Shiphandler of the Year, he misses his days driving a battleship.

J. D. WORK is a professor at the National Defense University College of Information and Cyberspace. His research focuses on cyber intelligence and decision advantage, operational art in offensive and counter-cyber campaigns, and strategy in conflict and competition. He has over twenty-five years' experience working in cyber intelligence and operations roles for the private sector and U.S. government. Dr. Work holds additional affiliations with the Saltzman Institute of War and Peace Studies at the School of International and Public Affairs at Columbia University, the Atlantic Council's Cyber Statecraft Initiative, and the Krulak Center for Innovation and Future Warfare at Marine Corps University.

286, 303–4, 327, 343–44, 353, 361, 363,
366–68, 373, 376, 380–81
  commercial satellite internet
  retransmissions for command
  and control, 270
  critical internet connectivity, 279
  Proliferated Warfighter Space
  Architecture, 281
  lagging cyber-secure space-based
  systems, 281
  position, navigation, and timing
  (PNT)l, 276
  resilience of the "hybrid space
  architectures, 281
  satellite communications
  (SATCOM), 277
  space domain awareness, 272–73, 279
  space junk, 279
socio-technical-economic systems (STES),
4,16–17, 376, 385
  substrate underlying all societies, 16,
  19, 372, 381–82, 385
software bills of materials (SBOMs), 251
Space Command, U.S., 270, 279
Space Force, U.S., 270, 273, 276–78, 280,
361
strategy, 7, 22, 80, 88, 100, 134, 155–61, 173,
183, 205–6, 222, 228, 243, 262, 301–7, 318,
331, 342, 354, 381, 385, 387–89, 395–97
submarines, 52, 69, 71, 110, 168, 182, 210,
247, 262, 267, 271, 281, 292, 313, 331,
335–37, 345, 356, 378, 389
substrate. See socio-technical-economic
systems (STES)
systemic elements, 4, 6, 8, 17–18, 31, 42, 47,
73, 86, 106, 143, 147–48, 156, 190–94,
205–6, 208, 223, 237, 270, 279, 312–13,
318, 326, 361, 367

Tallinn Manual II, 95–6
technology diffusion, 21

"theory of action", 17
"theory of navies", 360, 366, 367
trade, global, 1, 4, 26, 29, 33, 45, 87, 134, 170,
232, 260–61, 266–68, 321, 367, 374, 383

Ukraine, 45, 71, 88, 110, 167–73, 203,
209–10, 246, 270, 279, 302, 305–6, 317,
395
undersea cables, 4, 17, 65–68, 70, 72, 110,
260–66, 358, 377–78
undersea warfare, 108, 169, 262, 268, 271,
354. See also submarines
  Nord Stream gas pipeline, 169
  offensive cyber operations in the
  water column, 265
  open-source intelligences, 266
  seabed warfare, 263
  sound surveillance system, 262
  undersea hackers, 266
unmanned. See autonomous systems
United Nations:
  Convention on the Law of the Sea III
  (UNCLOS III), 82
  Group of Governmental Experts
  (GGE), 86
  High Seas Treaty (2023), 85
  Open-Ended Working Group, 86.
  See also international law

Vincennes (CG 49), 119

warfighting, 2, 7, 127, 133–35, 143–45,
204, 210, 221, 223, 270, 273, 304, 331,
343–45, 353–56. See also cyber warfare,
network-centric warfare, network-
optional warfare
  at the edge in cyberspace, 356, 359
whole-of-government, 7

zero days, 20
zero trust, 73, 161

The Naval Institute Press is the book-publishing arm of the U.S. Naval Institute, a private, nonprofit, membership society for sea service professionals and others who share an interest in naval and maritime affairs. Established in 1873 at the U.S. Naval Academy in Annapolis, Maryland, where its offices remain today, the Naval Institute has members worldwide.

Members of the Naval Institute support the education programs of the society and receive the influential monthly magazine *Proceedings* or the colorful bimonthly magazine *Naval History* and discounts on fine nautical prints and on ship and aircraft photos. They also have access to the transcripts of the Institute's Oral History Program and get discounted admission to any of the Institute-sponsored seminars offered around the country.

The Naval Institute's book-publishing program, begun in 1898 with basic guides to naval practices, has broadened its scope to include books of more general interest. Now the Naval Institute Press publishes about seventy titles each year, ranging from how-to books on boating and navigation to battle histories, biographies, ship and aircraft guides, and novels. Institute members receive significant discounts on the Press' more than eight hundred books in print.

Full-time students are eligible for special half-price membership rates. Life memberships are also available.

For more information about Naval Institute Press books that are currently available, visit www.usni.org/press/books. To learn about joining the U.S. Naval Institute, please write to:

Member Services
U.S. Naval Institute
291 Wood Road
Annapolis, MD 21402-5034
Telephone: (800) 233-8764
Fax: (410) 571-1703
Web address: www.usni.org

www.ingramcontent.com/pod-product-compliance
Lightning Source LLC
LaVergne TN
LVHW092011050326
832904LV00001B/13